Humanitarian Assistance in International Law

Humanitarian Assistance in International Law

MARINA SHARPE
Associate Professor of International Law, Royal Military College Saint-Jean, Canada

OXFORD
UNIVERSITY PRESS

OXFORD
UNIVERSITY PRESS

Great Clarendon Street, Oxford, OX2 6DP,
United Kingdom

Oxford University Press is a department of the University of Oxford.
It furthers the University's objective of excellence in research, scholarship,
and education by publishing worldwide. Oxford is a registered trade mark of
Oxford University Press in the UK and in certain other countries.

Published in the United States of America by Oxford University Press
546 Fifth Avenue, New York, NY 10036, United States of America.

British Library Cataloguing in Publication Data
Data available

Library of Congress Control Number: 2026944258

ISBN 9780198994701

DOI: 10.1093/9780198994695.001.0001

Printed and bound by
CPI Group (UK) Ltd., Croydon, CR0 4YY

FSC www.fsc.org
MIX
Paper | Supporting responsible forestry
FSC® C013604

The manufacturer's authorized representative in the EU for product safety is
Oxford University Press España S.A. of Parque Empresarial San Fernando de Henares,
Avenida de Castilla, 2 – 28830 Madrid (www.oup.es/en or product.safety@oup.com).
OUP España S.A. also acts as importer into Spain of products made by the manufacturer.

For Lila River Sharpe Sillery

Acknowledgements

This book would not exist without Merel Alstein's support for it; an Insight grant from the Social Sciences and Humanities Research Council of Canada; and the dedication of my research assistants Benjamin Bushell, Hye Joon Lee, Maxime Touchette, Natalie Plante, and Poonam Sandhu. To the five of you: I am grateful for your commitment to this project and look forward to supporting each of you as your careers flourish. I also acknowledge with thanks Chelsea Kay's work on the index and tables and the additional funding I received from the Canadian Defence Academy Research Program.

This book was enriched by the individuals who agreed to be interviewed for the article on which Chapter 2 is based: Aurelien Buffler, Edward Tsui, Hugo Slim, and Jan Eliasson. I am also grateful to Carla Ferstman, Emanuela-Chiara Gillard, Eve Massingham, James Hathaway, Lakmini Seneviratne, Livia Hadorn, and Tristan Ferraro for discussing parts of the book with me or providing written feedback. Their input was invaluable (and any errors are, of course, mine alone).

The idea for this book emerged when I was Senior Legal Officer with UNHCR's Representation to the African Union. I thank Cosmas Chanda and Leonard Zulu for the opportunity and the whole 'Project 2019' team. I will always be grateful for the early support I received from the Pierre Elliott Trudeau Foundation, which enabled me to embark on the path that led here.

Four institutions have provided exceptional support: the International Committee of the Red Cross, Oxford University Press, the *Faculté de droit* at the *Université de Sherbrooke,* and Royal Military College Saint-Jean. I participated in the ICRC's 15th Advanced Seminar in International Humanitarian Law for Academics and Policymakers and the 34th International Conference of the Red Cross and Red Crescent, both important opportunities for learning and informal exchange. I thank Bruno Demeyere (International Review of the Red Cross) and Elizabeth Rushing (Humanitarian Law & Policy Blog) for publishing early and abbreviated versions of Chapter 2, and Etienne Kuster for his work connecting the ICRC to academia. At OUP, my thanks go to Jack McNichol, Rebecca Lewis, Rizwaan Ahmad, Robert Cavooris, and the Newgen production team. *Université de Sherbrooke* provided exceptional support in my application for an Insight grant and in its ongoing administration of the award. I am particularly grateful to research advisor Safa Ben Saad. Finally, I am grateful to my colleagues at RMC Saint-Jean for their understanding and support as I devoted much time to this book over the past several years. I am especially grateful to Élisabeth Vallet and Rosemarie Hamel.

Above all, I am grateful for the support of my friends and family, especially William Sillery, Naomi Sharpe, and Lila Sillery. As I was completing the manuscript, my daughter Lila made a 'let her cook' sign for my office door—and did they ever let me. Lila, this book is dedicated to you, MPC.

Contents

PART IV. CONCLUSIONS

Table of Cases

EUROPEAN COURT OF HUMAN RIGHTS

INTERNATIONAL COURT OF JUSTICE

INTERNATIONAL CRIMINAL COURT

INTERNATIONAL CRIMINAL TRIBUNAL FOR RWANDA

INTERNATIONAL CRIMINAL TRIBUNAL FOR THE FORMER YUGOSLAVIA

SPECIAL COURT FOR SIERRA LEONE

Table of Treaties

REGIONAL TREATIES

Acronyms and Abbreviations

AP	Protocols Additional to the Geneva Conventions of 12 August 1949
ARIO	International Law Commission Articles on the Responsibility of International Organizations
ARSIWA	International Law Commission Articles on Responsibility of States for Internationally Wrongful Acts
ASEAN	Association of South-East Asian Nations
AU	African Union
CAR	Central African Republic
CDO	Civil defence organization
CERF	Central Emergency Response Fund
CESCR	Committee on Economic, Social and Cultural Rights
CIDA	Canadian International Development Agency
CIHL	Customary international humanitarian law
CMCS	Office for the Coordination of Humanitarian Affairs civil-military coordination service
DAC	Organisation for Economic Cooperation and Development, Development Assistance Committee
DfID	United Kingdom Department for International Development
DHA	Department of Humanitarian Affairs
DMZ	Demilitarized zone
DPKO	Department of Peacekeeping Operations
DPO	Department of Peace Operations
DRC	Democratic Republic of the Congo
DRR	Disaster risk reduction
ECOMIL	Economic Community of West African States Mission in Liberia
ECOSOC	Economic and Social Council
EEZ	Exclusive economic zone
ERC	United Nations Under-Secretary-General for Humanitarian Affairs and Emergency Relief Coordinator
EU	European Union
EUCPM	European Union Civil Protection Mechanism
FAO	Food and Agriculture Organization of the United Nations
FCCDA	Framework Convention on Civil Defence Assistance
GC	The Geneva Conventions of 12 August 1949
GHF	Gaza Humanitarian Foundation
HAP	Humanitarian Accountability Partnership
IAC	International armed conflict
IASC	Inter-Agency Standing Committee
ICC	International Criminal Court

ICCPR	International Covenant on Civil and Political Rights
ICDO	International Civil Defence Organization
ICESCR	International Covenant on Economic, Social and Cultural Rights
ICISS	International Commission on Intervention and State Sovereignty
ICJ	International Court of Justice
ICL	International criminal law
ICRC	International Committee of the Red Cross
ICTY	International Criminal Tribunal for the Former Yugoslavia
IDF	Israel Defense Forces
IDL	International disaster law
IDP	Internally displaced person
IDRL	International disaster response law
IFRC	International Federation of Red Cross and Red Crescent Societies
IHL	International humanitarian law
IHRL	International human rights law
IIHL	International Institute of Humanitarian Law
ILC	International Law Commission
IMO	International Maritime Organization
INSARAG	International Search and Rescue Advisory Group
IOM	International Organization for Migration
IPC	Integrated Food Security Phase Classification initiative
IPU	Inter-Parliamentary Union
IRL	International refugee law
IRU	International Relief Union
MCDA	Military and civil defence assets
MINUSCA	United Nations Multidimensional Integrated Stabilization Mission in Central African Republic
MINUSMA	United Nations Multidimensional Integrated Stabilization Mission in Mali
MINUSTAH	United Nations Stabilization Mission in Haiti
MONUSCO	United Nations Stabilization Mission in the Democratic Republic of the Congo
MSF	*Médecins sans Frontières*
MSS	Multinational Security Support Mission (Haiti)
NATO	North Atlantic Treaty Organization
NGO	Non-governmental organization
NIAC	Non-international armed conflict
OAG	Organized armed group
OCHA	Office for the Coordination of Humanitarian Affairs
ODA	Official development assistance
OECD	Organisation for Economic Cooperation and Development
OHCHR	Office of the United Nations High Commissioner for Human Rights
PIL	Public international law
PoW	Prisoner of war
R2P	Responsibility to protect
SAR	International Convention on Maritime Search and Rescue
SOLAS	Convention for the Safety of Life at Sea

SPM	Special political mission
TFEU	Treaty on the Functioning of the European Union
UAE	United Arab Emirates
UK	United Kingdom of Great Britain and Northern Ireland
UN	United Nations
UNAMI	United Nations Assistance Mission in Iraq
UNAMID	United Nations-African Union Mission in Darfur
UNAMIR II	United Nations Assistance Mission in Rwanda II
UNCCP	United Nations Conciliation Commission for Palestine
UNCLOS	United Nations Convention on the Law of the Sea
UNDAC	United Nations Disaster Assessment and Coordination
UNDP	United Nations Development Programme
UNDRO	United Nations Disaster Relief Organization
UNFPA	United Nations Population Fund
UNGA	United Nations General Assembly
UN-Habitat	United Nations Human Settlements Programme
UNHCR	Office of the United Nations High Commissioner for Refugees
UNICEF	United Nations Children's Fund
UNIFIL	United Nations Interim Force in Lebanon
UNISFA	United Nations Interim Security Force for Abyei
UNMISS	United Nations Mission in South Sudan
UNOSOM II	Second United Nations Operation in Somalia
UNPROFOR	United Nations Protection Force (former Yugoslavia)
UNRRA	United Nations Relief and Rehabilitation Administration
UNRWA	United Nations Relief and Works Agency for Palestine Refugees in the Near East
UNSC	United Nations Security Council
US	United States of America
USAID	United States Agency for International Development
VCLT	Vienna Convention on the Law of Treaties
WASH	Water, sanitation, and hygiene
WCO	World Customs Organization
WFP	World Food Programme
WGCAC	Working Group on Children and Armed Conflict
WHO	World Health Organization

PART I
INTRODUCTION

1
Humanitarian Assistance in International Law

1. Introduction

Politics and the rising frequency of armed conflict have,[1] over the past two decades or so, made the provision of humanitarian assistance—always vital for those in need of it—one of the most significant, and often contested, issues in international relations. This period has seen events such as the massive Indian Ocean tsunami; Myanmar's initial refusal to admit assistance following Cyclone Nargis; the Assad regime's denial of relief to opposition-held north-west Syria, prompting the United Nations (UN) Security Council to impose cross-border relief operations;[2] the abdication by European states of their rescue obligations in the Mediterranean, leading to mass drownings and compelling non-governmental organizations (NGOs) to fill the search-and-rescue gap;[3] Ethiopia's siege of its Tigray region; and, most recently, the impeding by conflict parties of assistance destined for civilians in desperate need in Gaza and Sudan, contributing to man-made famines in both places.[4] Some of these events have spurred legal developments[5] or advanced understanding of how international law governs humanitarian assistance.[6] Yet this is the first monograph to provide a comprehensive account of that legal framework across all contexts in which international humanitarian assistance is delivered: armed conflict, situations of violence below the threshold of armed conflict, peacetime disasters, mixed situations, and at sea.[7]

[1] Siri Aas Rustad, 'Conflict Trends: A Global Overview, 1946–2024' (*PRIO*, 2025) <https://www.prio.org/publications/14453> accessed 7 August 2025. It is often stated that the number of natural disasters is also increasing. However, Alimonti and Mariani's analysis of the period 1900 to 2022 found a linear upward trend between 1900 and around 1950, followed by rapid growth to 2000, and thereafter a decrease (Gianluca Alimonti and Luigi Mariani, 'Is the Number of Global Natural Disasters Increasing?' (2024) 23 Environmental Hazards 186).

[2] See Chapter 5, Section 4.4.2.

[3] See Chapter 4, Section 4.3.

[4] IPC, 'Sudan: Acute Food Insecurity Snapshot: October 2024–May 2025' (24 December 2024) <https://www.ipcinfo.org/fileadmin/user_upload/ipcinfo/docs/IPC_Sudan_Acute_Food_Insecurity_Oct2024_May2025_Snapshot.pdf> accessed 6 August 2025; IPC, 'Gaza Strip: Famine Confirmed in Gaza Governorate, Projected to Expand' (22 August 2025) <https://www.ipcinfo.org/fileadmin/user_upload/ipcinfo/docs/IPC_Gaza_Strip_Acute_Food_Insecurity_Malnutrition_July_Sept2025_Special_Snapshot.pdf> accessed 23 August 2025.

[5] See Chapter 4, Section 2.3.2.

[6] See Chapter 3, Section 4.2.

[7] There are monographs that examine specific situations (Matthias Vanhullebusch, *The Law of International Humanitarian Relief in Non-International Armed Conflicts* (Brill 2021) and Vijitha Veerakatty, *Arbitrary Withholding of Consent to Humanitarian Relief in Non-International Armed Conflict: Legal Regulations and Consequences* (Brill 2024)), that address most but not all contexts (Emilie

Humanitarian Assistance in International Law. Marina Sharpe, Oxford University Press. © Marina Sharpe 2026.
DOI: 10.1093/9780198994695.003.0002

The book proceeds from a core argument: existing international law on humanitarian assistance is largely adequate. Where gaps exist, notably in disasters and situations of violence not amounting to armed conflict, legal developments are already underway,[8] though they are stalled in respect of the latter.[9] The most significant problem relates—as in many areas of international law concerned with human dignity—to compliance by states, coupled with a lack of public awareness that humanitarian access to individuals in need is often a matter of legal obligation for the conflict party or state in control of them. In short, humanitarian assistance is governed not by goodwill, but by law; however, the law is often inadequately implemented and disseminated.

This shapes the book's structure, focus, and central objective. It is not organized by legal regime, which suggests fragmentation. It does not focus on inchoate rights, which implies that the law is inadequate, nor on how state sovereignty might operate to limit humanitarian assistance, because this concern is already built into the rules.[10] Rather, Part II is structured around the cross-cutting humanitarian principles and broad factual contexts in which humanitarian assistance is provided (armed conflict and peacetime), and Part III by type of humanitarian actor.[11] By covering all the contexts in which humanitarian assistance is delivered and all the major categories of actor who provide it, with a focus on state obligations in these contexts and to these actors, the book aims to bolster understanding of humanitarian assistance as a matter of international legal obligation. It also aims to be a resource for students, scholars, policymakers, and humanitarian personnel—who work not within legal regimes but in real-world environments, such as in wars, in disasters, or at sea.

This introductory chapter begins by explaining what is meant by humanitarian assistance and related terms (relief, humanity, impartiality, neutrality, independence, and humanitarian access). It then presents the book's structure and contents in more detail, followed by a section that delineates what the book excludes.

2. Humanitarian assistance

Humanitarian assistance cannot be understood in isolation from the broader notion of humanitarian action, of which it is a component part. Humanitarian action is the

Kuijt, *Humanitarian Assistance and State Sovereignty in International Law: Towards a Comprehensive Framework* (Intersentia 2015)), and that address humanitarian assistance as well as protection (Dug Cubie, *The International Legal Protection of Persons in Humanitarian Crises: Exploring the Acquis Humanitaire* (Hart 2017)).

[8] See Chapter 4, Section 2.3.2.

[9] See Chapter 4, Section 3.

[10] See *Case Concerning Military and Paramilitary Activities in and Against Nicaragua* (*Nicaragua v United States of America*) (Merits) [1986] ICJ Rep 14 (*Nicaragua*) para 242, where the Court notes that there 'can be no doubt that the provision of strictly humanitarian aid to persons or forces in another country, whatever their political affiliations or objectives, cannot be regarded as unlawful intervention, or as in any other way contrary to international law'. See also the discussions of affected state consent throughout (Chapter 3, Sections 4.3 and 6.1; Chapter 4, Section 2.3.2.1; and Chapter 5, Section 4.4.2). These explain that humanitarian assistance must be provided at the affected state's request or with its consent, which may not be withheld in violation of international law.

[11] An early monograph also used an actor-based structure: Peter MacAlister-Smith, *International Humanitarian Assistance: Disaster Relief Actions in International Law and Organization* (Springer 1985).

work 'of saving lives, alleviating suffering and maintaining human dignity in the face of man-made crises and natural disasters'.[12] In practice, humanitarian action consists of protection work and the provision of humanitarian assistance. Protection refers to all 'activities aimed at obtaining full respect for the rights of the individual in accordance with the letter and spirit of the relevant bodies of law (i.e. International Human Rights Law (IHRL), International Humanitarian Law (IHL), International Refugee Law (IRL))'.[13] Examples of protection include measures to prevent individuals from being exposed to sexual and gender-based violence and advocacy actions. Protection is beyond the scope of this book,[14] which of course focuses on the other dimension of humanitarian action: humanitarian assistance.

There is no single legally binding definition of humanitarian assistance. The term has been defined by a range of actors, including scholars,[15] learned societies,[16] humanitarian actors, and states. These definitions have much in common: they essentially conceptualize humanitarian assistance as basic goods and services provided to ensure the survival and dignity of individuals in a crisis situation. Essential goods and services include 'food, medicines, shelter and health care',[17] and drinking water, clothing, and fuel; humanitarian assistance may also include cash and vouchers.[18] Some definitions additionally specify that the goods and services must be provided in accordance with the humanitarian principles of humanity, impartiality, neutrality, and independence,[19] which are defined later in this section.

[12] United Kingdom Department for International Development, 'Saving Lives, Relieving Suffering, Protecting Dignity: DfID's Humanitarian Policy' (2006), cited in Jeff Crisp, 'Humanitarian Action and Coordination' in Thomas G Weiss and Sam Daws (eds), *The Oxford Handbook on the United Nations* (2nd edn, OUP 2018) 583.

[13] Inter-Agency Standing Committee (IASC), 'Policy: Protection in Humanitarian Action' (*IASC*, 2016) <https://interagencystandingcommittee.org/iasc-protection-priority-global-protection-cluster/iasc-policy-protection-humanitarian-action-2016> accessed 9 August 2025, 2. This IASC definition originates from a series of workshops and consultations convened by the International Committee of the Red Cross (ICRC) between 1996 and 2000 (Dug Cubie, 'Complementarity Between Human Security and Legal Frameworks for Humanitarian Action' in Gerd Oberleitner (ed), *Research Handbook on International Law and Human Security* (Edward Elgar 2022) 262).

[14] On the role of protection within humanitarian action, see Kate Mackintosh, 'Reclaiming Protection as a Humanitarian Goal: Fodder for the Faint-Hearted Aid-Worker' (2010) 1 Journal of International Humanitarian Legal Studies 382.

[15] See, for example, Walter Kälin, *Internal Displacement and the Law* (OUP 2023) 206–07.

[16] See, for example, Institute of International Law, Bruges session (2003) <https://www.idi-iil.org/app/uploads/2017/06/2003_bru_03_en.pdf> accessed 18 May 2023, art I, which provides that humanitarian assistance 'means all acts and activities for the provision of materials and services of an exclusively humanitarian character, indispensable for the survival and fulfilment of the essential needs of the victims of disasters'.

[17] UNGA, 'Strengthening of the Coordination of Humanitarian Emergency Assistance of the United Nations', Res 46/182 (19 December 1991) A/RES/46/182 (Res 46/182) Annex, para 6.

[18] Cash and voucher assistance can, in the right circumstances, afford 'recipients greater dignity and choice, which they tend to use to meet their needs in ways that are more targeted and appropriate than the provision of predetermined items or services'. Additionally, cash and vouchers can be less expensive to provide than in-kind assistance and may support local economic growth (David Fisher, 'A Glass Half Full: The International Law Commission's Draft Articles and the Operational Challenges of International Disaster Response' (2020) 1 Yearbook of International Disaster Law 93, 113).

[19] See, for example, UN Office for the Coordination of Humanitarian Affairs (OCHA), 'Oslo Guidelines on the Use of Foreign Military and Civil Defence Assets in Disaster Relief' (2007) <https://www.unocha.org/publications/report/world/oslo-guidelines-guidelines-use-foreign-military-and-civil-defence-assets-disaster-relief-revision-11-november-2007-enzh> accessed 28 May 2025, para 1, which provides that humanitarian assistance is 'aid to an affected population that seeks, as its primary purpose, to save lives

Missing from many definitions of humanitarian assistance is the notion of subsidiarity. The state has primary responsibility to meet the basic needs of individuals within state territory or subject to the state's power or effective control. This obligation emanates from sovereignty.[20] It also derives from IRL and IHRL,[21] specifically the rights to food, water, shelter, and health,[22] especially the 'minimum core' of these rights;[23] the rights to life and security of the person;[24] and the prohibition of torture and other cruel, inhuman, or degrading treatment or punishment.[25] A state's obligation to meet the needs of civilians within its territory or control during times of humanitarian emergency has been reaffirmed by the UN Security Council,[26] the General Assembly,[27]

and alleviate suffering of a crisis-affected population. Humanitarian assistance must be provided in accordance with the basic humanitarian principles of humanity, impartiality and neutrality'; ReliefWeb, 'Glossary of Humanitarian Terms' (2008) <https://reliefweb.int/report/world/reliefweb-glossary-humanitarian-terms-enko> accessed 7 August 2025, 29; Global Affairs Canada, 'Glossary of International Assistance Terms' <https://www.international.gc.ca/transparency-transparence/international-assistance-report-stat-rapport-aide-internationale/glossary-glossaire.aspx?lang = eng#h.> accessed 9 August 2025, which defines humanitarian assistance as 'assistance designed to save lives, alleviate suffering, and maintain and protect human dignity during emergencies and in their aftermath. Humanitarian assistance is delivered consistent with the principles of humanity, impartiality, neutrality, and independence'.

[20] While the ICRC describes the obligation as 'self-evident as it relates to territorial States and their own populations' (Nils Melzer, *International Humanitarian Law: A Comprehensive Introduction* (ICRC 2019) 250), it was spelled out by the International Commission on Intervention and State Sovereignty (ICISS), which developed the notion of 'sovereignty as responsibility' (ICISS, 'The Responsibility to Protect: Report of the International Commission on Intervention and State Sovereignty' (2001) <https://www.globalr2p.org/resources/the-responsibility-to-protect-report-of-the-international-commission-on-intervention-and-state-sovereignty-2001/> accessed 14 August 2025, para 2.15).

[21] The state also has relevant responsibilities under the law of the sea; see Chapter 4, Sections 4.1 and 4.2.

[22] International Covenant on Economic, Social and Cultural Rights (adopted 16 December 1966, entered into force 3 January 1976) 993 UNTS 3 (ICESCR) arts 11 and 12, read with: Committee on Economic, Social and Cultural Rights (CESCR), 'General Comment No. 4: The Right to Adequate Housing (Art. 11(1) of the Covenant)' (1991) E/1992/23; CESCR, 'General Comment No. 12: The Right to Adequate Food (Art. 11)' (12 May 1999) E/C.12/1999/5, paras 15, 17, 19, and 38; CESCR, 'General Comment No. 15: The Right to Water (Arts. 11 and 12 of the Covenant)' (20 January 2002) E/C.12/2002/11, para 25; CESCR, 'General Comment No. 14: The Right to the Highest Attainable Standard of Health (Art. 12)' (11 August 2000) E/C.12/2000/4, para 40; Convention on the Rights of the Child (adopted 20 November 1989, entered into force 2 September 1990) 1577 UNTS 3 (CRC) art 24.

[23] CESCR, 'General Comment No. 3: The Nature of States Parties' Obligations (Art. 2, Para. 1, of the Covenant)' (14 December 1990) E/1991/23, para 10.

[24] International Covenant on Civil and Political Rights (adopted 16 December 1966, entered into force 23 March 1976) 999 UNTS 171 (ICCPR) arts 6(1) and 9(1), read with Human Rights Committee, 'General Comment No. 6: Article 6 (Right to Life)' (30 April 1982) HR1/GEN/1/Rev.9, para 5.

[25] ICCPR (n 24) art 7; Convention against Torture and Other Cruel, Inhuman or Degrading Treatment or Punishment (adopted 10 December 1984, entered into force 26 June 1987) 1465 UNTS 85, arts 2 and 16; CRC (n 22) art 37(a); *Obligations of Israel in Relation to the Presence and Activities of the United Nations, Other International Organizations and Third States in and in Relation to the Occupied Palestinian Territory* (Advisory Opinion) 2025 <https://www.icj-cij.org/sites/default/files/case-related/196/196-20251022-adv-01-00-en.pdf> accessed 31 October 2025 (*Israel Obligations AO*) para 155.

[26] See, for example, UNSC Res 2417 (24 May 2018) S/RES/2417, preambular para 22; UNSC Res 2573 (27 April 2021) S/RES/2573, preambular para 18.

[27] UNGA Res 46/182 (19 December 1991) A/RES/46/182, Annex, para 4, which provides that each state 'has the responsibility first and foremost to take care of the victims of natural disasters and other emergencies occurring on its territory'. See also UNGA Res 43/131 (8 December 1988) A/RES/43/131, preambular para 2.

and in soft law.[28] The obligation as it relates to internally displaced persons (IDPs) is specified in the Guiding Principles on Internal Displacement,[29] and it is treaty-based in Africa.[30] Humanitarian assistance is subsidiary to this core obligation; it is provided when the state is unable or unwilling to meet or fully meet its primary responsibility. Subsidiarity should be reflected in definitions of humanitarian assistance because without it, assistance can be seen as relieving the state of its primary responsibility, whereas it does no such thing. Rather, when humanitarian assistance is needed, it is because the state has failed to fulfil its obligations.

A second issue, relevant to definitions that invoke the humanitarian principles (and addressed in detail in Chapter 2),[31] is that some recognized humanitarian actors operate according to a slightly different set of humanitarian principles than those listed above, but this does not necessarily undermine the humanitarian nature of the assistance they provide.

To reflect common understandings of the term while also addressing these two issues, humanitarian assistance is conceptualized here to mean essential goods and services provided in accordance with the principles of humanity, impartiality, neutrality, and independence—or a similar set of principles—to save lives, alleviate suffering, and uphold human dignity, when the state is unable or unwilling to fulfil its primary responsibility in this regard.

'Humanitarian assistance' and 'relief' are sometimes used interchangeably. However, in both armed conflict and peacetime, 'relief' is a term of art that refers specifically to humanitarian assistance provided in response to emergency situations.[32]

As the humanitarian principles are constitutive of humanitarian assistance as defined above, they are explained briefly here; they are addressed in detail in Chapter 2. Humanity is humanitarian action's *raison d'être*; it requires that human suffering be addressed wherever it is found. Impartiality is the fundamental principle guiding

[28] International Institute of Humanitarian Law, 'Guiding Principles on the Right to Humanitarian Assistance' (1993) 33 International Review of the Red Cross 519, principle 4, which provides that the 'primary responsibility to protect and assist the victims of emergencies is that of the authorities of the territory in which the emergency causing urgent humanitarian needs occurs'; OCHA, 'Guidelines on the Use of Military and Civil Defence Assets to Support United Nations Humanitarian Activities in Complex Emergencies' (revision 1, 2005) <https://www.unocha.org/publications/report/world/guidelines-use-military-and-civil-defence-assets-support-united-nations-humanitarian> accessed 9 June 2025, para 56; Principles and Good Practice of Humanitarian Donorship (2003, revised 2018) <https://www.ghdinitiative.org/ghd/gns/principles-good-practice-of-ghd/principles-good-practice-ghd.html> accessed 28 May 2025, para 5.

[29] ECOSOC, 'Report of the Representative of the Secretary-General, Mr Francis M Deng, Submitted Pursuant to Commission Resolution 1997/39, Addendum, Guiding Principles on Internal Displacement', E/CN.4/1998/53/Add.2 (11 February 1998) principle 3(1), which provides that '[n]ational authorities have the primary duty and responsibility to provide protection and humanitarian assistance to [... IDPs] within their jurisdiction', and principle 25(1), which provides that the 'primary duty and responsibility for providing humanitarian assistance to [... IDPs] lies with national authorities'.

[30] Convention for the Protection and Assistance of Internally Displaced Persons in Africa (adopted 23 October 2009, entered into force 6 December 2012) 49 ILM 86, art 5(1), which provides that 'States Parties shall bear the primary duty and responsibility for providing protection of and humanitarian assistance to [... IDPs] within their territory or jurisdiction'.

[31] See Chapter 2, Section 2.

[32] ICRC, 'ICRC Q&A and Lexicon on Humanitarian Access' (2014) 96 International Review of the Red Cross 359, 367. See Chapter 3, Section 1.3.

humanitarian action; it means that assistance should be allocated solely according to need and without discrimination. Neutrality and independence are means of ensuring humanity and impartiality; in other words, they are operational principles that facilitate humanitarian access.[33] Neutrality means that humanitarian actors should not take sides in hostilities or engage in political, racial, religious, or ideological controversies. Independence requires that humanitarian action be implemented autonomously from any political, economic, military, or other objectives held by any actor in the place where the action is undertaken.

It is also worth explaining the notion of 'humanitarian access', as the term is widely used but rarely defined. A recent (armed conflict-specific) United Kingdom publication is a notable exception. It defines humanitarian access as having two dimensions: 'the ability of humanitarian actors to conduct humanitarian relief operations as foreseen by IHL and in accordance with humanitarian principles' and 'the ability of civilians to access basic goods and services, including when provided as humanitarian assistance'.[34] The notion of humanitarian access used here is similar to the first of these dimensions: it is the ability of humanitarian actors to provide humanitarian assistance. For reasons of space, how international law might support individuals' efforts to access assistance is not addressed in this book.[35]

Additional terms that depend on or relate to a particular context (armed conflict or peacetime) are defined in Chapters 3 and 4.[36]

3. Structure

As mentioned at the outset, this book is divided into two main parts. Part II, comprised of Chapters 2 through 4, sets out the core legal framework. It begins in Chapter 2 with an examination of the history of the humanitarian principles of humanity, impartiality, neutrality, and independence and their legal character and normative content for each major category of humanitarian actor: the UN, non-state actors (the International Red Cross and Red Crescent Movement (the Movement) and NGOs), and states—categories the book revisits in Part III.

Part II then explores the international legal rules applicable to the provision of humanitarian assistance in both armed conflict and in peacetime. Chapter 3 covers armed conflict. It begins by drawing an important distinction between preventive assistance and emergency relief operations, to highlight the rules on the former following a period during which much attention has rightly focused on the latter. Emergency relief operations are then addressed in depth, including key practical modalities and arrangements, such as humanitarian corridors and protected zones; the applicable legal framework; how understanding of this framework has evolved in light

[33] Note, however, that impartiality must also be operationalized.

[34] UK Foreign, Commonwealth & Development Office and Ministry of Defence, 'Conflict, Hunger and International Humanitarian Law: A Practitioner's Legal Handbook' (2025) <https://www.gov.uk/government/publications/conflict-hunger-and-international-humanitarian-law-a-practitioners-legal-handbook> accessed 23 May 2025, 67.

[35] For analysis of this issue, see ibid, ch 7.

[36] See Chapter 3, Section 1.3 and Chapter 4, Section 2.

of access challenges in the early 2010s; and supplementary rules privileging certain types of assistance and relating to particular beneficiaries. There is also a section dedicated to the unlawful impeding of relief operations, including both strategic consent withheld in violation of international law—and whether this should be characterized as 'arbitrary' or 'unlawful'—and violation of the implementation obligation to allow and facilitate relief. This discussion of unlawful impeding also addresses the principal reason conflict parties invoke to limit humanitarian access—military necessity, both in general and in the context of siege warfare—and the consequences of unlawfully withheld strategic consent for the UN and states, on the one hand, and non-state humanitarian actors on the other. After outlining and contextualizing the law, Chapter 3 concludes by addressing individual accountability and international responsibility for violating it.

Chapter 4 considers the legal regulation of humanitarian assistance in peacetime, including disaster, mixed, and maritime contexts, and situations of violence not amounting to armed conflict. It begins by outlining the current patchwork state of international disaster response law (IDRL). Early efforts to bring coherence to this patchwork, especially regarding humanitarian access, consisted largely of arguments for an individual right to assistance in disasters. More recent systematization work—started by the International Federation of Red Cross and Red Crescent Societies (IFRC) and culminating with the adoption by the International Law Commission of Draft Articles on the Protection of Persons in the Event of Disasters—has centred on the affected state's duties in relation to offers of assistance. Chapter 4 tracks this evolution and explains the current status of IDRL: efforts by states to adopt a comprehensive IDRL treaty by 2027. The chapter then addresses the law in mixed situations and the practical reality in situations of violence not amounting to armed conflict, in which the extent of state obligations regarding humanitarian access relates to cooperation with the ICRC when it exercises its right of initiative. Finally, Chapter 4 addresses humanitarian assistance for maritime migrants under the law of the sea.

Part III, comprised of Chapters 5 through 7, examines the major categories of humanitarian actor listed earlier in this section. Chapter 5 on the UN addresses its historical role and its contemporary coordination and funding architecture; norm-generating actors and bodies (the Secretary-General, the Economic and Social Council, the General Assembly, and the Security Council); and key operational entities (UNHCR, UNICEF, WFP, UNRWA,[37] peacekeeping operations, and special political missions). Chapter 6 on non-state actors covers the Movement—which consists of the ICRC, IFRC, and National Red Cross and Red Crescent Societies—and NGOs. Chapter 7 addresses states as humanitarian actors, including both their role as donors and their direct civil defence and military involvement in the provision of humanitarian assistance in both armed conflict and in peacetime. Part IV, comprised of Chapter 8, concludes the book.

While the legal framework is for the most part laid out in Part II, aspects of the law that are inherently tied to one particular type of humanitarian actor or to humanitarian personnel are addressed in Part III. Thus, for each category of actor in Part

[37] These acronyms are defined in Chapter 5 and in the list of acronyms and abbreviations.

III, the book covers how international law facilitates (or not) its work, including the protection of operations and personnel—a critical issue as the risks faced by humanitarians are rising.[38] Chapter 6 devotes particular attention to how medical NGOs are protected in armed conflict by surveying the IHL regime on health care, which is less protective than commonly thought. Chapter 7 covers the IHL regime on third state civil defence assistance in armed conflict.

It should be clear from the foregoing that this is a broad monograph—one could write an entire book on topics that here constitute mere sections, and indeed other scholars have done so[39]—because that was the nature of the gap in the literature. However, the existence of this gap should not be taken to suggest that there is a paucity of scholarship on humanitarian assistance. There are many article-length works on specific aspects of it, as the bibliography attests. Many of these articles and chapters were written in the last decade, for reasons explained in Chapters 3 and 4.[40] This scholarship is footnoted throughout, to point readers to resources that will enable them to explore issues that this book does not, because of its breadth, address in depth.

Also to assist the reader, the book makes extensive use of chapter and section cross-references. The greatest challenge in writing a book about humanitarian assistance—a subject that has not been comprehensively systematized by an authoritative external source such as a treaty—was determining how to organize it. No single structure could be mutually exclusive and collectively exhaustive. For instance, the Gaza Humanitarian Foundation could have been addressed in Chapter 2, in the context of the humanitarian principles, but it is instead examined in Chapter 7 as an atypical instance of state humanitarian action. Humanitarian assistance provided in armed conflict by third state civil defence organizations could equally have been treated in Chapter 3 on armed conflict, but is likewise considered in Chapter 7, alongside other forms of state engagement in humanitarian assistance. The role of NGOs in maritime search and rescue could have been analysed in Chapter 6 on non-state humanitarian actors but is instead discussed in Chapter 4 on the peacetime legal framework. Cross-references guide readers to material that may be located outside the chapter they expect and also point them to relevant discussions elsewhere in the book.

4. Scope

There are several exclusions from this book. For reasons of space, the regional and sub-regional planes are largely not addressed. However, some regional and sub-regional instruments and organizations are mentioned where they are particularly relevant. Part III focuses on the most significant types of humanitarian actor—the UN, Movement components, NGOs, and states—and does not cover other categories of actor that may assist in crisis, such as affected community initiatives, diaspora

[38] UN Secretary-General, 'Protection of Civilians in Armed Conflict: Report of the Secretary-General' (15 May 2025) S/2025/271, para 35.
[39] See Vanhullebusch (n 7) and Veerakatty (n 7).
[40] See Chapter 3, Section 4.2 and Chapter 4, Section 2.3.

networks, and the private sector. These are excluded because they do not always act, or even aim to act, in accordance with humanitarian principles.

As the book is about international law, it does not cover the domestic regulation of humanitarian assistance as such; it does, however, address how international law facilitates the provision of humanitarian assistance, a matter of growing importance as it becomes more regulated at the domestic level.[41]

This book focuses squarely on international humanitarian assistance. Accordingly, the legal frameworks that regulate the treatment of specific groups that often require such assistance, notably IDPs and refugees, fall outside its scope—and have been analysed in depth elsewhere.[42] Additionally, a state's obligations to IDPs and refugees under these legal frameworks come within its primary responsibility (explained in Section 2 above), whereas humanitarian assistance is subsidiary to and thus distinct from this.

Narrower excluded issues are identified where relevant in the text.

Unless otherwise indicated, this book is current as of 1 August 2025.[43]

[41] Heike Spieker, 'The Legal Framework of Humanitarian Action' in Pat Gibbons and Hans-Joachim Heintze (eds), *The Humanitarian Challenge: 20 Years European Network on Humanitarian Action* (Springer 2015) 155–57; David Matyas, 'Humanitarians and their Law(s): An Expanded Inquiry' in Heike Krieger, Pablo Kalmanovitz, and Stavros-Evdokimos Pantazopoulos (eds), *Yearbook of International Humanitarian Law, Volume 26 (2023)* (TMC Asser Press 2025) 16–23.

[42] See, for example, Marina Sharpe, *The Regional Law of Refugee Protection in Africa* (OUP 2018); Guy Goodwin-Gill and Jane McAdam, *The Refugee in International Law* (4th edn, OUP 2021); James Hathaway, *The Rights of Refugees Under International Law* (2nd edn, CUP 2021); Bríd Ní Ghráinne, *Internally Displaced Persons and International Refugee Law* (OUP 2022); Kälin (n 15).

[43] The manuscript was updated to the extent possible in October 2025 to reflect the *Israel Obligations AO* (n 25) issued that month.

PART II
LEGAL FRAMEWORK

2
The Humanitarian Principles

1. Introduction

Humanitarian principles are doctrine that most humanitarian actors follow in planning and conducting humanitarian operations—whether during armed conflict or in peacetime—to centre their rationale and maximize access and impact. The 'most' in the preceding sentence reflects the fact that states do not always make strategic-level decisions in the humanitarian arena in line with the principles.[1] Humanity, impartiality, neutrality, and independence are typically viewed as 'the' humanitarian principles. Humanity requires that human suffering be addressed wherever it is found. Impartiality means that assistance should be allocated solely according to need and without discrimination. Neutrality and independence are operational means of ensuring humanity and impartiality. Neutrality means that humanitarian actors should not take sides in hostilities or engage in political, racial, religious, or ideological controversies. Independence, or operational independence, requires that humanitarian action remain autonomous from the political, economic, military, or other objectives of actors in the context where the action is implemented.[2]

Analyses of these principles often focus on their meanings[3] and/or the challenges of applying them in practice.[4] This chapter, by contrast, addresses more foundational questions: whether humanity, impartiality, neutrality, and independence can be accurately designated 'the' humanitarian principles; how these principles came to govern the whole humanitarian sector; the principles' legal character and normative content; and, more fundamentally, whether the principles should even be construed as having objective meanings. Inherent to these questions is an argument about the importance of analysing the humanitarian principles from the disciplinary perspectives of history

[1] See Chapter 7, Section 1.

[2] These principles are defined in more detail in Section 4.4.2 below.

[3] See, for example, David P Forsythe, 'On Contested Concepts: Humanitarianism, Human Rights, and the Notion of Neutrality' (2013) 12 Journal of Human Rights 59; Laura Hammond, 'Neutrality and Impartiality' in Roger Mac Ginty and Jenny H Peterson (eds), *The Routledge Companion to Humanitarian Action* (Routledge 2015); Hugo Slim, *Humanitarian Ethics: A Guide to the Morality of Aid in War and Disaster* (OUP 2015) chs 2–3; Larissa Fast, 'Unpacking the Principle of Humanity: Tensions and Implications' (2016) 97 International Review of the Red Cross 111.

[4] See, for example, Fiona Terry, 'The International Committee of the Red Cross in Afghanistan: Reasserting the Neutrality of Humanitarian Action' (2011) 881 International Review of the Red Cross 175; Stuart Gordon and Antonio Donini, 'Romancing Principles and Human Rights: Are Humanitarian Principles Salvageable?' (2016) 97 International Review of the Red Cross 77; Ed Schenkenberg van Mierop, 'Coming Clean on Neutrality and Independence: The Need to Assess the Application of Humanitarian Principles' (2016) 97 International Review of the Red Cross 295; Marc DuBois and Sean Healy, 'Imperfect Relief: Challenges to the Impartiality and Identity of Humanitarian Action' (2024) 106 International Review of the Red Cross 90.

Humanitarian Assistance in International Law. Marina Sharpe, Oxford University Press.
DOI: 10.1093/9780198994695.003.0004

and law. The principles are often covered ahistorically,[5] as if how they came to govern humanitarian assistance is unimportant because their value is evident.[6] Legal analysis is equally scant. The limited international law scholarship that exists relates mostly to the principles of neutrality and impartiality,[7] likely because the latter features in the Geneva Conventions (GCs),[8] their Additional Protocols (APs),[9] and the International Court of Justice's (ICJ) *Nicaragua* judgment,[10] while neutrality has an autonomous international humanitarian law (IHL) meaning. There is one piece addressing impartiality and neutrality as well as humanity.[11]

These gaps in the literature are significant. While it is widely known that the humanitarian principles are based on the first four Fundamental Principles of the International Red Cross and Red Crescent Movement (the Movement),[12] this is typically stated without substantiation or attribution.[13] Further, this common knowledge

[5] Joël Glasman, 'The Invention of Impartiality: The History of a Humanitarian Principle, from a Legal, Strategic and Algorithmic Perspective' (*Centre de Réflexion sur l'Action et les Savoirs Humanitaires*, 2020) <https://www.msf-crash.org/en/publications/invention-impartiality-history-humanitarian-principle-legal-strategic-and-algorithmic> accessed 8 February 2021. See also Eleanor Davey, 'Thinking Principles Through the Past' in Chatham House, 'Internal Coherence in the Efforts of Humanitarian Organizations to Operate in Accordance with Humanitarian Principles in Armed Conflict' (2022) <https://chathamhouse.soutron.net/Portal/Public/en-GB/RecordView/Index/191963> accessed 10 November 2022.

[6] An exception is Joël Glasman, *Humanitarianism and the Quantification of Human Needs: Minimal Humanity* (Routledge 2019), which covers the history of impartiality. For histories of humanitarianism more generally, see Michael Barnett, *Empire of Humanity: A History of Humanitarianism* (Cornell University Press 2011) and Bruno Cabanes, *The Great War and the Origins of Humanitarianism 1918–1924* (CUP 2014).

[7] Frits Kalshoven, 'Impartiality and Neutrality in Humanitarian Law and Practice' (1989) 29 International Review of the Red Cross 523; Marc Weller, 'The Relativity of Humanitarian Neutrality and Impartiality' (1997) 91 American Society of International Law Proceedings 441; Kubo Mačák, 'Principles of Neutrality and Impartiality of Humanitarian Action in the Aftermath of the 2011 Libyan Conflict' in Andrej Zwitter and others (eds), *Humanitarian Action: Global, Regional and Domestic Legal Responses* (CUP 2015); Kubo Mačák, 'A Matter of Principle(s): The Legal Effect of Impartiality and Neutrality on States as Humanitarian Actors' (2016) 97 International Review of the Red Cross 157.

[8] Geneva Convention for the Amelioration of the Condition of the Wounded and Sick in Armed Forces in the Field (adopted 12 August 1949, entered into force 21 October 1950) 75 UNTS 31 (GCI) arts 3(2) and 9; Geneva Convention for the Amelioration of the Condition of Wounded, Sick and Shipwrecked Members of Armed Forces at Sea (adopted 12 August 1949, entered into force 21 October 1950) 75 UNTS 85 (GCII) arts 3(2) and 9; Geneva Convention Relative to the Treatment of Prisoners of War (adopted 12 August 1949, entered into force 21 October 1950) 75 UNTS 135 (GCIII) arts 3(2) and 9; Geneva Convention Relative to the Protection of Civilian Persons in Time of War (12 August 1949) 75 UNTS 287 (GCIV) arts 3(2), 10, 59, and 61.

[9] Protocol Additional to the Geneva Conventions of 12 August 1949, and relating to the Protection of Victims of International Armed Conflicts (adopted 8 June 1977, entered into force 7 December 1978) 1125 UNTS 3 (API) arts 5(3), 5(4), 9(2)(c), 22(2)(b), 60(2), and 70(1); Protocol Additional to the Geneva Conventions of 12 August 1949, and relating to the Protection of Victims of Non-International Armed Conflicts (adopted 8 June 1977, entered into force 7 December 1978) 1125 UNTS 609 (APII) art 18(2).

[10] *Military and Paramilitary Activities in and against Nicaragua (Nicaragua v United States of America)* (Merits) [1986] ICJ Rep 14.

[11] Kate Mackintosh, 'The Principles of Humanitarian Action in International Humanitarian Law' (*ODI Humanitarian Policy Group*, 2000) <https://www.odi.org/sites/odi.org.uk/files/odi-assets/publications-opinion-files/305.pdf> accessed 12 June 2020.

[12] The Movement consists of the International Committee of the Red Cross (ICRC), the International Federation of Red Cross and Red Crescent Societies (IFRC) and all national Red Cross and Red Crescent societies. The Fundamental Principles are listed in Section 2. The Movement is addressed in Chapter 6, Section 2.

[13] Examples in this regard are provided in Section 3.

about the principles' origin seems to have precluded analysis of how the principles of one organization—albeit a critically important one in the humanitarian field—came to also apply to organizations in the sector's other major categories of actors: non-governmental organizations (NGOs) and the United Nations (UN).[14] Legal analysis is important to counter inaccurate claims about the principles being binding as a matter of international law,[15] particularly IHL, and having objective meanings. Drawing on historical research and legal analysis, which builds on the work of Mačák and Weller,[16] this chapter demonstrates that while the humanitarian principles do have common roots in the Fundamental Principles of the Red Cross Movement (Fundamental Principles), their legal character and normative content are inherently relative, depending on the source of the principle in question for the humanitarian actor concerned.

The chapter begins by determining, in Section 2, whether and on what basis certain principles constitute 'the' humanitarian principles. Section 3 then articulates the history of how the principles became relevant first to the Movement and subsequently diffused to humanitarian NGOs and the UN. Section 4 analyses the principles' legal character in general and in relation to each of the above-mentioned categories of humanitarian actors, plus states, demonstrating that whether the principles are legally binding for a given humanitarian actor depends on their source for that actor. Section 4 also analyses the principles' normative content, demonstrating that each principle does not—and, legally, cannot—have one fixed or objective meaning. While there are common understandings of the principles, legally, each principle's normative content flows from its source for the actor in question. Section 5 concludes.[17]

2. The notion of 'the' humanitarian principles

Humanity, impartiality, neutrality, and independence are usually identified as 'the' humanitarian principles. For example, they are identified as such by UN bodies such as the Office for the Coordination of Humanitarian Affairs (OCHA)[18] and the Office of the UN High Commissioner for Refugees (UNHCR);[19] by the African Union (AU)[20]

[14] States are also important humanitarian actors, and several have adopted humanitarian principles. However, it is not possible to analyse the history of how humanitarian principles came to govern states as a category because whether and how individual states have adopted humanitarian principles is specific to each state.

[15] Examples in this regard are cited in Section 4.

[16] Mačák 2016 (n 7); Weller (n 7).

[17] An early version of this chapter was previously published as: Marina Sharpe, 'It's All Relative: The Origins, Legal Character and Normative Content of the Humanitarian Principles' (2024) 106 International Review of the Red Cross 12.

[18] OCHA, 'OCHA on Message: Humanitarian Principles' (*OCHA*, July 2022) <https://www.unocha.org/sites/unocha/files/OOM_Humanitarian%20Principles_Eng.pdf> accessed 26 July 2022.

[19] UNHCR, *Emergency Handbook* (4th edn, UNHCR 2015) <https://emergency.unhcr.org/> accessed 23 February 2021.

[20] African Union Convention for the Protection and Assistance of Internally Displaced Persons in Africa (adopted 23 October 2009, entered into force 6 December 2012) 49 ILM 86 (Kampala Convention) art VI(3).

and European Union (EU);[21] in the Sphere Handbook;[22] and in academic literature.[23] However, these four are not the only humanitarian principles. Some non-state actors and initiatives use the four plus additional principles. For example, the Movement uses seven Fundamental Principles: humanity, impartiality, neutrality, independence, voluntary service, unity, and universality. The NGOs Oxfam and Save the Children each use impartiality and independence.[24] The Humanitarian Accountability Partnership (HAP) 'Standard Principles' are humanity, impartiality, neutrality, independence, participation and informed consent, duty of care, witness, redress, transparency, and complementarity.[25] The 1994 Code of Conduct for the International Red Cross and Red Crescent Movement and Non-Governmental Organizations in Disaster Relief[26] (the Code of Conduct) includes the principles of humanity, impartiality, and independence (framed hortatorily), a neutrality-like principle, and six additional principles:

1. The humanitarian imperative comes first [humanity].
2. Aid is given regardless of the race, creed or nationality of the recipients and without adverse distinction of any kind. Aid priorities are calculated on the basis of need alone [impartiality].
3. Aid will not be used to further a particular political or religious standpoint [cf neutrality].[27]
4. We shall endeavour not to act as instruments of government foreign policy [independence].
5. We shall respect culture and custom.
6. We shall attempt to build disaster response on local capacities.
7. Ways shall be found to involve programme beneficiaries in the management of relief aid.

[21] Joint Statement by the Council and the Representatives of the Governments of the Member States meeting within the Council, the European Parliament and the European Commission, 'The European Consensus on Humanitarian Aid' [2008] OJ C 25, 1, which notes that the 'EU is firmly committed to upholding and promoting the fundamental principles of humanity, neutrality, impartiality and independence' (para 10).

[22] Sphere, *The Sphere Handbook: Humanitarian Charter and Minimum Standards in Humanitarian Response* (Sphere Association 2018) <https://spherestandards.org/wp-content/uploads/Sphere-Handbook-2018-EN.pdf> (Sphere Handbook) accessed 30 June 2025. See Chapter 6, Section 3.2.

[23] See, for example, Elizabeth Ferris, *The Politics of Protection: The Limits of Humanitarian Action* (Brookings 2011) 11; Walter Kälin, *Internal Displacement and the Law* (OUP 2023) 216.

[24] Sharpe (n 17) 48.

[25] HAP, *The 2010 Standard in Accountability and Quality Management* (2nd edn, HAP 2010) <https://pseataskforce.org/uploads/tools/the2010hapstandardinaccountabilityandqualitymanagement_hapinternational_english.pdf> accessed 22 February 2021, 8–9.

[26] While the Code of Conduct's full title mentions only 'Disaster Relief', it applies equally in armed conflict, as evidenced by its initial statement of purpose: in 'the event of armed conflict, the present Code of Conduct will be interpreted and applied in conformity with international humanitarian law'. Perhaps the intent was for 'disaster' to be understood as inclusive of armed conflict, a usage that was not uncommon at the time.

[27] This principle is similar but not identical to neutrality, as the Code of Conduct goes on to specify that humanitarian actors can 'espouse particular political or religious opinions' (3). Neutrality, by contrast, is typically understood as precluding humanitarian actors from taking sides in hostilities or engaging in 'controversies of a political, racial, religious or ideological nature' (OCHA (n 18)). The Code of Conduct's departure from the typical understanding of neutrality is not surprising, as neutrality is the most controversial of the humanitarian principles and has been explicitly rejected by some NGOs, such as Oxfam and *Médecins Sans Frontières* (MSF).

8. Relief aid must strive to reduce future vulnerabilities to disaster as well as meeting basic needs.
9. We hold ourselves accountable to both those we seek to assist and those from whom we accept resources.
10. In our information, publicity and advertising activities, we shall recognise disaster victims as dignified humans, not hopeless objects.[28]

Prior to 2003, the UN used fewer than four principles. For example, the General Assembly recalled in 1990 that 'in the event of natural disasters and similar emergency situations, the principles of humanity, neutrality and impartiality must be given utmost consideration by all those involved in providing humanitarian assistance'.[29] The UN's current humanitarian architecture was created in 1991 by General Assembly resolution 46/182.[30] The resolution's substantive portion, an annex, begins with 'Guiding Principles'. The second principle provides that '[h]umanitarian assistance must be provided in accordance with the principles of humanity, neutrality and impartiality'; independence is not mentioned.[31] This tripartite formulation was subsequently reaffirmed by both the General Assembly[32] and the Security Council.[33] It is not that these entities deemed independence unimportant. Rather, there was no role, in an international organization comprised of member states, for a principle understood at the time to mean autonomy from states.[34]

In 2003, the General Assembly recognized that independence 'is also an important guiding principle for the provision of humanitarian assistance'.[35] Following this resolution, when they invoke the humanitarian principles, both the General Assembly and the Security Council list all four.[36] The International Law Commission (ILC), however, omitted independence from the relevant provision (draft article 6) of its 2016 Draft Articles on the Protection of Persons in the Event of Disasters (the Draft Articles).[37] The summary of the debate relating to draft article 6 notes that 'suggestions

[28] IFRC and ICRC, 'The Code of Conduct for the International Red Cross and Red Crescent Movement and Non-Governmental Organizations (NGOs) in Disaster Relief' (1994) <https://www.icrc.org/en/doc/assets/files/publications/icrc-002-1067.pdf> accessed 30 June 2025, 3–5.

[29] UNGA Res 45/100 (14 December 1990) A/RES/45/100 (Res 45/100) preambular para 14.

[30] UNGA 'Strengthening of the Coordination of Humanitarian Emergency Assistance of the United Nations', Res 46/182 (19 December 1991) A/RES/46/182 (Res 46/182). See Chapter 5, Section 2.2.

[31] Res 46/182 (n 30) Annex, para 2.

[32] See, for example, UNGA Res 51/194 (10 February 1997) A/RES/51/194, preambular para 12; UNGA Res 58/114 (17 December 2003) A/RES/58/114 (Res 58/114) preambular para 4.

[33] See, for example, UNSC Res 1296 (19 April 2000) S/RES/1296, para 11; UNSC Presidential Statement 7 (2000) S/PRST/2000/7, para 9.

[34] Interview with Edward Tsui (Chappaqua, New York, 29 June 2022).

[35] Res 58/114 (n 32) preambular para 5.

[36] See, for example, UNGA Res 60/124 (8 March 2006) A/RES/60/124, preambular para 4; UNGA Res 69/243 (11 February 2015) A/RES/69/243, preambular para 2; UNGA Res 72/132 (15 January 2018) A/RES/72/132, preambular para 2; UNGA Res 74/118 (20 January 2020) A/RES/74/118, preambular para 3; UNGA Res 76/167 (7 January 2022) A/RES/76/167, preambular para 5; UNSC Res 2228 (29 June 2015) S/RES/2228, para 17; UNSC Res 2274 (15 March 2016) S/RES/2274, preambular para 24; UNSC Res 2417 (24 May 2018) S/RES/2417, preambular para 19; UNSC Res 2504 (10 January 2020) S/RES/2504, para 6.

[37] ILC, 'Report of the International Law Commission on the Work of its 68th Session' (2 May–10 June 2016 and 4 July–12 August 2016) A/71/10 (ILC Report) para 48.

included adding a reference to the principle of independence'.[38] No explanation is provided as to why this suggestion was not retained, and the principle of independence is not mentioned in the ILC's commentary on draft article 6.[39]

At least three multilateral sources use some subset of the four principles plus non-discrimination as an additional stand-alone principle. This is somewhat unusual, because in conceptualizations where the humanitarian principles are humanity, impartiality, neutrality, and independence, non-discrimination is typically a dimension of impartiality.[40] Principle 24(1) of the UN's 1998 Guiding Principles on Internal Displacement provides that humanitarian assistance to internally displaced persons (IDPs) 'shall be carried out in accordance with the principles of humanity and impartiality and without discrimination'.[41] Draft article 6 notes that response 'to disasters shall take place in accordance with the principles of humanity, neutrality and impartiality, and on the basis of non-discrimination, while taking into account the needs of the particularly vulnerable'.[42] The Treaty on the Functioning of the European Union (TFEU) provides that '[h]umanitarian aid operations shall be conducted in compliance with the principles of international law and with the principles of impartiality, neutrality and non-discrimination'.[43] Non-discrimination was likely added to these three sources to mirror the relevant AP rules on emergency relief operations in armed conflict, which mention non-discrimination in terms of 'without any adverse distinction'.[44]

Academics also have varying conceptions of the humanitarian principles. Slim identifies thirty-three principles 'routinely used in the pursuit of humanitarian action'.[45] Mackintosh (writing before 2003) omits independence.[46] Kälin notes that two new humanitarian principles, 'do no harm' and 'accountability to affected persons', may be emerging.[47] Given these variations, the basis on which humanity, impartiality, neutrality, and independence are often identified as 'the' humanitarian principles is not immediately clear. Slim's classification of the thirty-three humanitarian principles he identifies is instructive in this regard. He articulates four categories of humanitarian principles: principles in law;[48] principles of action; principles of dignity,

[38] ILC, 'Report of the International Law Commission on the Work of its 62nd Session' (3 May–4 June and 5 July–6 August 2010) A/65/10, para 313.

[39] ILC Report (n 37) commentary to art 6.

[40] The other dimension is proportionality; see Section 4.4.2.

[41] ECOSOC, 'Report of the Representative of the Secretary-General, Mr Francis M Deng, Submitted Pursuant to Commission Resolution 1997/39, Addendum, Guiding Principles on Internal Displacement', E/CN.4/1998/53/Add.2 (11 February 1998).

[42] ILC Report (n 37).

[43] Consolidated versions of the Treaty on the European Union and the Treaty on the Functioning of the European Union [2016] OJ C202/1 (TFEU) art 214(2).

[44] API (n 9) art 70(1); APII (n 9) art 18(2); see Chapter 3, Section 4.

[45] Slim (n 3) 40.

[46] Mackintosh (n 11).

[47] Kälin (n 23) 223–24. For examples of the different humanitarian principles used or recognized by multilateral and joint initiatives, individual NGOs, the Movement, select states, and UN entities, see Sharpe (n 17) Annex 1.

[48] This list consists of state/non-state responsibility, proportion and restraint, distinction, humane treatment, protection, assistance, precaution, military necessity, humanitarian initiative, and asylum (Slim (n 3) 40).

participation, and stewardship; and principles of effectiveness.[49] Perhaps, then, what many describe as 'the' humanitarian principles are more accurately described using the alternative formulation 'principles of humanitarian action'. Indeed, Slim's 'principles of action' are humanity, impartiality, neutrality, and independence.[50]

Humanity, impartiality, neutrality, and independence might also be singled out because they are particularly important. When additional principles are mentioned, humanity, impartiality, neutrality, and independence are typically listed first, as in the examples above. Of the seven Fundamental Principles, Forsythe notes that 'only the first four really count',[51] while Barnett explains that humanity, impartiality, neutrality, and independence are 'most important'.[52]

Terming humanity, impartiality, neutrality, and independence 'the' humanitarian principles thus obscures the reality that some actors use more principles, while others employ fewer. To account for this, these four principles are here conceptualized and often termed—where not too grammatically cumbersome—the 'core humanitarian principles',[53] based on their particular importance and the fact that humanitarians often speak of the 'core four'.

It is also worth addressing the order in which the principles are listed. Humanity, neutrality, impartiality, and independence is typical in the UN. Independence at the end reflects its later adoption; the order of the first three principles reflects General Assembly resolution 46/182, though it is not clear why the resolution ordered them in that way. In the Movement, the order of neutrality and impartiality is reversed: humanity, impartiality, neutrality, and independence. This is intentional and meaningful. In his commentary on the Fundamental Principles, Pictet explains that they 'do not all have the same importance. They have a hierarchical order, indicated [. . .] by the sequence in which they are presented'.[54] Other actors tend to use either the UN or the Movement order. The Movement order is most logical, as it reflects the ethical nature of the first two principles (humanity and impartiality) and the fact that neutrality and independence are operational means of ensuring them.

3. History

There is little detailed scholarship on how the core humanitarian principles came to govern international humanitarian assistance. When the principles' history is addressed, it is in terms of vague links to the ICRC or the Movement more generally. For example, Weiss explains that the ICRC derived the core humanitarian principles 'after decades of experience about which principles were most effective in accessing war

49 Slim (n 3) 40.
50 ibid.
51 David P Forsythe, *The Humanitarians: The International Committee of the Red Cross* (CUP 2005) 161.
52 Barnett (n 6) 137.
53 cf the EU terminology of 'fundamental humanitarian principles' (n 21). Core is preferred because 'fundamental' has legal meaning in some contexts (e.g. 'fundamental rights' in EU law).
54 Jean Pictet, 'The Fundamental Principles of the Red Cross: Commentary' (*International Federation of Red Cross and Red Crescent Societies*, 1979) <https://www.icrc.org/en/doc/resources/documents/misc/fundamental-principles-commentary-010179.htm> accessed 2 July 2024, 8.

victims' and they 'subsequently became the mantra of all humanitarians'.[55] An OCHA note on the core humanitarian principles explains that they 'are derived from the Red Cross Movement's "fundamental" principles'.[56] In his history of humanitarianism, Barnett explains that in elaborating the Fundamental Principles, ICRC officials were fully 'aware that they were debating not only the principles of the ICRC but also humanitarianism writ large'.[57]

Such accounts do not illuminate how the core humanitarian principles came to govern humanitarian actors outside the Movement. Indeed, Glasman explains that principles

> are omnipresent in humanitarian discourse, but little interest is shown in their history. They are often regarded as being timeless: they are vaguely linked to the Red Cross, often without any further clarification, and it is almost always said that they are universal. Just like Athena being born from the forehead of her father, Zeus, humanitarian principles seem to have emerged 'ready made' from [ICRC founder] Henri Dunant's forehead. However, this magical vision of humanitarian principles is dangerous. It is based on realities that lack historical context and are therefore unarguable. In fact, these 'universal' principles are the result of very real conflicts. They reflect interests that can be situated and dated.[58]

There are distinct but connected histories of the principles in relation to NGOs, on the one hand, and the UN, on the other. These categories of actors are addressed in turn. The Movement is at the root of the humanitarian principles for both, so it is addressed first.

3.1. The International Red Cross and Red Crescent Movement

The history of the Fundamental Principles has been addressed by scholars of the Movement.[59] These Fundamental Principles were the genesis of the core humanitarian principles for both NGOs and the UN, so their history merits broader attention. In 1859, Swiss businessman Henri Dunant witnessed the bloody aftermath of the Battle of Solferino, part of the war to unify Italy. The extent of the carnage overwhelmed both sides' capacity to care for wounded soldiers. Dunant mobilized a local

[55] Thomas G Weiss, 'Humanitarian Action' in Jacob Katz Cogan, Ian Hurd, and Ian Johnstone (eds), *The Oxford Handbook of International Organizations* (OUP 2016) 305.

[56] OCHA (n 18).

[57] Barnett (n 6) 137.

[58] Glasman (n 5).

[59] See, for example, André Durand, '*Quelques remarques sur l'élaboration des principes de la Croix-Rouge chez Gustave Moynier*' in Christophe Swinarski (ed) *Studies and Essays on International Humanitarian Law and Red Cross Principles in Honour of Jean Pictet* (Brill Nijhoff 1984); Forsythe (n 51) ch 5; Hans Haug, *Humanity for All: The International Red Cross and Red Crescent Movement* (Haupt 1993) 443–46. Note, however, Moorehead's important history of the Movement does not address the Fundamental Principles in any detail (Caroline Moorehead, *Dunant's Dream: War, Switzerland and the History of the Red Cross* (HarperCollins 1998)). The ICRC library's 'research guide' on the Fundamental Principles is available at: <https://blogs.icrc.org/cross-files/the-fundamental-principles-of-the-international-red-cross-and-red-crescent-movement/#_ftn1> accessed 13 June 2022.

volunteer response and, following his return to Geneva, authored an influential book about his experience.[60] Its ideas led to the founding in 1863 of the ICRC[61] and to the adoption in 1864 of the very first Geneva Convention on assistance to wounded combatants (the 1864 Geneva Convention).[62] Antecedents to the Fundamental Principles—and thus the core humanitarian principles—of neutrality, humanity, and impartiality are evident in this treaty. Article 1 of the 1864 Geneva Convention provides that '[a]mbulances and military hospitals shall be recognized as neutral', while article 2 relates to the neutrality of their personnel. Article 5 provides for the neutrality of local people who 'bring help to the wounded'; their assistance is sought based on appeals 'made to their *humanity*'.[63] Also neutral, under article 6, are evacuation parties collecting wounded combatants from the field. Article 7 establishes a distinctive flag and armlet to denote the neutrality of hospitals, ambulances, evacuation parties, and relevant individuals and personnel. Impartiality is evident in article 6, which provides that '[w]ounded or sick combatants, *to whatever nation they may belong*, shall be collected and cared for'.[64] These three principles inspired by the 1864 Geneva Convention, as well as additional principles drawn from other sources,[65] such as ICRC co-founder Gustave Moynier's 1874 pamphlet '*Ce que c'est que la Croix-Rouge*',[66] governed the Movement informally until 1921.

In 1921, Red Cross principles were written down for the first time in the ICRC's Revised Statutes. The 1921 Statutes list four principles: impartiality; political, religious, and economic independence; the Movement's universality; and the equality of its members.[67] In 1946, these four principles were affirmed and supplemented by thirteen additional principles and six rules of application at a meeting of the Board of Governors of the League of Red Cross Societies (the League, as the IFRC was then known) held in Oxford.[68] The seventeen 1946 principles were reaffirmed in 1952 at the XVIIIth International Conference of the Red Cross in Toronto.[69]

The 1952 principles were then analysed by ICRC official[70] Jean Pictet in his doctoral thesis on Red Cross doctrine. Pictet's thesis was supervised by Max Huber—who served as ICRC president from 1928 to 1944[71]—and was published in French

[60] Henri Dunant, *Un souvenir de Solférino* (1st edn, Imprimerie Jules-Guillaume Fick 1862).

[61] François Bugnion, 'Birth of an Idea: The Founding of the International Committee of the Red Cross and of the International Red Cross and Red Crescent Movement: from Solferino to the Original Geneva Convention (1859–1864)' (2012) 94 International Review of the Red Cross 1299, 1309. This history of the Red Cross and Red Crescent Movement is addressed in more detail in Chapter 6, Section 2.

[62] Convention for the Amelioration of the Conditions of the Wounded in Armies in the Field (adopted 22 August 1864, entered into force 22 June 1865).

[63] Emphasis added.

[64] Emphasis added.

[65] According to Glasman, there 'were twelve [Red Cross] principles (in the 1880s), then around twenty (circa 1900), and subsequently six (1920)' (Glasman (n 5)).

[66] Gustave Moynier, *Ce que c'est que la Croix-Rouge* (*B Soullier*, 1874) <https://library.icrc.org/library/search/notice?noticeNr = 1036> accessed 13 June 2022.

[67] Haug (n 59) 444.

[68] ICRC, 'The Fundamental Principles of the Red Cross and Red Crescent' (1996) ICRC publication ref. 0513 <https://www.icrc.org/en/doc/assets/files/other/icrc_002_0513.pdf> accessed 27 May 2022.

[69] ibid. The International Conference of the Red Cross is addressed in Chapter 6, Section 2.

[70] Pictet's job title in 1956 was 'Director for General Affairs' (Haug (n 59) 445).

[71] Yves Sandoz, 'Max Huber and the Red Cross' (2007) 18 European Journal of International Law 171, 176.

in 1955 and 1956 across several issues of the International Review of the Red Cross, as well as in English as a treatise.[72] Pictet divided the seventeen principles into two categories: seven 'fundamental principles' (humanity, equality, proportionality, impartiality, neutrality, independence, and universality) and ten 'organic principles' relating to the Movement's structure and functioning (selflessness, free service, voluntary service, auxiliarity, autonomy, multitudinism, equality of the National Societies, unity, solidarity, and foresight).

The 'whole Red Cross Movement took keen note of Pictet's work'.[73] The Japanese national society proposed that Pictet's principles become official Movement doctrine, leading to the establishment of a joint ICRC-League commission.[74] It 'worked out its own simplified draft and submitted it to the Standing Commission of the International Red Cross', which then proposed a slightly amended draft to the Council of Delegates of the International Red Cross.[75] The Council unanimously adopted the Standing Commission's draft with minor amendments in 1961.[76] The Fundamental Principles were formally 'proclaimed' by the whole Movement in 1965 at the XXth International Conference of the Red Cross in Vienna.[77] In 1979 and 1980, Pictet published a nine-part commentary on the Fundamental Principles,[78] making him both their architect and an important authority on their meaning.[79] The Fundamental Principles were reaffirmed at the XXVth International Conference of the Red Cross and Red Crescent in 1986, when they were incorporated into the preamble to the Movement Statutes.[80]

Glasman provides a rare *critical* account of Pictet's formulation of the Fundamental Principles within his monograph on the history of the principle of impartiality.[81] He explains that impartiality originates only partly in article 6 of the 1864 Geneva Convention. Quoted above,[82] this provision prohibits nationality-based discrimination. Glasman argues that impartiality's additional proportionality dimension—the principle dictates that humanitarian actors should provide assistance without discrimination *and* proportionate to need—originates not in the 1864 Geneva Convention but in Pictet's doctoral thesis.[83] The thesis clearly articulates the proportionality element: '*les hommes qui souffrent doivent être secourus; à détresse égale l'aide sera equivalente; à détresse inégale, elle sera conditionnée par l'importance des*

[72] Jean Pictet, *Red Cross Principles* (ICRC 1956) <https://library.icrc.org/library/docs/DOC/DOC_00028.pdf> accessed 13 June 2022.
[73] Haug (n 59) 445.
[74] ibid.
[75] ibid, 445–46. The Council of Delegates is addressed in Chapter 6, Section 2.
[76] ibid, 446.
[77] International Conference of the Red Cross, 'Resolutions Adopted by the XXth International Conference of the Red Cross' (1965) 5 International Review of the Red Cross 570 (XXth Conference Resolutions).
[78] Jean Pictet, 'The Fundamental Principles of the Red Cross: Commentary [parts 1–9]' (1979–1980) 210–18 IRRC; this Commentary was subsequently re-published by the IFRC as a stand-alone document; see note 54. Pictet's commentary is discussed in Section 4.2.2.
[79] A volume prepared to mark Pictet's seventieth birthday reflects this authority: Swinarski (n 59).
[80] Statutes of the International Red Cross and Red Crescent Movement (1986, as amended in 1995 and 2006) <https://www.icrc.org/en/doc/assets/files/other/statutes-en-a5.pdf> accessed 24 February 2022 (Movement Statutes) 5.
[81] Glasman (n 5).
[82] See text attached to note 64.
[83] Glasman (n 5).

besoins et leur urgence'.[84] The same is evident in the Fundamental Principles adopted in 1965: impartiality 'makes no discrimination as to nationality, race, religious beliefs, class or political opinions. It endeavours only to relieve suffering, giving priority to the most urgent cases of distress'.[85]

According to Glasman, the ICRC waged an ultimately successful 'moral and legal struggle for several years to ensure that Pictet's principles were adopted by the entire movement'.[86] Glasman explains that Pictet 'invented' impartiality's proportionality dimension, and the ICRC campaigned for it, not only 'to address ethical issues'—proportionality provides humanitarians with an ethical framework to apportion assistance in circumstances where not all urgent needs can be met—'but also to champion the interests of the ICRC itself in response to external attacks' from the League.[87] In 1946, the League proposed a reorganization of the Movement tantamount to 'an outright attack on the ICRC'.[88] According to Glasman, Pictet's 'thesis was the main weapon of choice' of the ICRC's 'counter-attack'.[89] Pictet

> formulated the principles in a way that could justify the moral authority of the [. . . ICRC] within both the humanitarian field and the Red Cross movement [. . .]. It is clear from Pictet's work that he considered 'impartiality' as a key tool to counter the [. . .] League's and National Societies' ambitions. The National Societies [. . .] acted on *national* scales, which did not allow them to be purely humanitarian: 'the National Societies of the Red Cross help above all those of their own nationality, which is normal, given the national character of these institutions'. The ICRC had the higher moral ground: It could allocate 'aid measured solely by the extent of distress'.[90]

Thus Pictet's framing of impartiality as including proportionality in addition to non-discrimination allowed the ICRC to maintain its supremacy within the Movement. The balance of this section demonstrates how this conceptualization ultimately extended to the whole humanitarian sector.

3.2. Non-governmental organizations

The core humanitarian principles came to govern humanitarian NGOs via the 1994 Code of Conduct, which propelled the core principles from the Movement to humanitarian NGOs more broadly. On the initiative of the French national society,[91] at

[84] 'Men who suffer shall be helped; with equal distress, the help will be equivalent; with unequal distress, it will be conditioned by the importance of the needs and their urgency' (author's translation; Jean Pictet, 'Les principes de la Croix-Rouge (III)' (1955) 37 International Review of the Red Cross 633, 636).

[85] XXth Conference Resolutions (n 77) 573.

[86] Glasman (n 5).

[87] ibid.

[88] ibid; see also Daniel Palmieri, 'Les principes fondamentaux de la Croix-Rouge: une histoire politique' (*ICRC*, 6 July 2015) <https://www.icrc.org/fr/document/les-principes-fondamentaux-de-la-croix-rouge-une-histoire-politique> accessed 8 February 2021.

[89] Glasman (n 6) 31.

[90] ibid, 31 and 33 (internal citations omitted).

[91] Dorothea Hilhorst, 'Dead Letter or Living Document? Ten Years of the Code of Conduct for Disaster Relief' (2005) 29 Disasters 351, 351.

its 1991 meeting in Budapest, the Movement's Council of Delegates adopted a resolution on the need for a code of conduct relating to '[h]umanitarian assistance in situations of natural and technological disasters'.[92] The resolution noted the Council of Delegates' concern 'for the respect for the Fundamental Principles' of the Movement and its awareness of the Movement's 'essential role in international humanitarian activities and related codification'.[93] The operative portion of the resolution 'asks' the IFRC, 'in consultation with the main relief organizations, to set up a group of experts to study the possibility of elaborating a Code of Conduct relative to humanitarian aid in situations of natural and technological disasters' and 'requests' the IFRC, 'after consultation with the main relief organizations, to report on the outcome of that study to the next Council of Delegates'.[94]

Around the same time, staff of several UK-based NGOs concluded separately that a code of conduct was needed to counter the threat the end of the Cold War posed to humanitarian operations, and Oxfam-GB began collaborating with the IFRC to draft what would become the Code of Conduct. Hugo Slim, who in 1991 worked for Save the Children, explained that he and colleagues at other British NGOs expected the end of the Cold War would change the impact of armed conflict on humanitarian actors. During the Cold War, conflicts were typically proxy wars involving major powers; their intensity confined humanitarian action to locations outside theatres of conflict, such as IDP and refugee camps. By contrast, humanitarian actors were often near the front lines of the civil wars that began or intensified following the end of the Cold War, such as in Bosnia, Liberia, and Sierra Leone.[95]

The next Council of Delegates was held in Birmingham in 1993. By this time, Peter Walker of IFRC and Tony Vaux of Oxfam-GB had consulted the Steering Committee for Humanitarian Response[96] and completed a draft of the code.[97] The Council of Delegates approved their draft and urged the IFRC and ICRC to 'take steps to promote the Code's implementation within the Movement and to disseminate the Code amongst disaster response agencies, encouraging them in turn to endorse the Code through their governing bodies'.[98]

In 1994, the IFRC, ICRC, and six NGOs—Caritas, Catholic Relief Services, the Lutheran World Federation, Oxfam, Save the Children, and the World Council of Churches—finalized the Code of Conduct. It includes the ten principles cited above,[99] three of which are essentially humanity, impartiality, and independence; there is also

[92] ICRC and IFRC, 'Verbatim Report: Council of Delegates, Budapest, 28–30 November 1991' (1992) <https://library.icrc.org/library/docs/CI/CD_1991_RAPPORT_ENG.pdf> accessed 11 July 2022, resolution 17, 221.

[93] ibid.

[94] ibid.

[95] Interview with Hugo Slim, Senior Research Fellow, Oxford Institute for Ethics, Law and Armed Conflict (via Zoom, 26 March 2021).

[96] Formed in 1972, the Steering Committee for Humanitarian Response is currently comprised of ACT Alliance, CARE, Caritas, the ICRC, the IFRC, the Lutheran World Federation, Oxfam International, Save the Children, and World Vision; see <www.schr.info> accessed 6 January 2022.

[97] Hilhorst (n 91) 351.

[98] 'Resolutions of the Council of Delegates (adopted at its session of 29–30 October 1993, in Birmingham)' <https://library.icrc.org/library/docs/CI/CD_1993_RESOLUTIONS_ENG.pdf> accessed 6 January 2022, resolution 6, 8.

[99] See text attached to note 27.

a principle similar to neutrality.[100] The XXVIth International Conference of the Red Cross and Red Crescent in 1995 took note of and welcomed the Code and invited states and National Societies to 'encourage NGOs to both abide by the principles and spirit of the Code and consider registering their support for the Code' with the IFRC.[101] As of 1 August 2025, the Code of Conduct had been signed by nearly 900 organizations.[102]

Strong evidence of the Code of Conduct's influence over the humanitarian principles employed in the NGO sector comes from other lists of principles adopted by groups of NGOs prior to and following 1994: there is a clear shift towards the core humanitarian principles after 1994. For example, a 'handbook for practitioners' published in 1993 articulates the Providence Principles: relieving life-threatening suffering, proportionality to need, non-partisanship, independence, accountability, appropriateness, contextualization, and subsidiarity of sovereignty.[103] By contrast, the 1995 Mohonk Criteria recognize humanity, impartiality, neutrality, independence, and empowerment.[104]

The Code of Conduct was 'strongly influenced by' the Fundamental Principles,[105] which is not surprising given that one of its lead drafters worked for the IFRC. After the Code of Conduct had been adopted by the six sponsoring organizations and other NGOs, these organizations would of course go on to incorporate its principles within their own operations, marking the beginning of the diffusion and then entrenchment of the core humanitarian principles outside of the Movement. There is thus a clear timeline that begins with the formal adoption by the Movement of its seven Fundamental Principles in 1965. In and after 1994, the Code of Conduct carried four of these Fundamental Principles beyond the Movement to humanitarian NGOs.

3.3. The United Nations

UN General Assembly resolution 46/182, which in 1991 reformed the UN's humanitarian architecture,[106] is the source of the humanitarian principles for the UN.[107] The committee that drafted resolution 46/182 spent a 'long time' discussing the principles.[108] Accounts of the origins of the humanitarian principles in resolution 46/182

[100] See note 27.

[101] 'Twenty-sixth International Conference of the Red Cross and Red Crescent: Resolutions' (1995) 36 International Review of the Red Cross 55, 73.

[102] <https://www.ifrc.org/code-conduct-signatories> accessed 1 August 2025.

[103] Larry Minear and Thomas G Weiss, *Humanitarian Action in Times of War: A Handbook for Practitioners* (Lynne Rienner Publishers 1993) 19.

[104] Jon Ebersole, 'The Mohonk Criteria for Humanitarian Assistance in Complex Emergencies' (1995) 17 Human Rights Quarterly 192, 196–97.

[105] Hugo Slim, 'Wonderful Work: Globalizing the Ethics of Humanitarian Action' in Roger Mac Ginty and Jenny H Peterson (eds), *The Routledge Companion to Humanitarian Action* (Routledge 2015) 17; see also Jérémie Labbé, 'Les principes de l'action humanitaire' in Sandra Szurek, Marina Eudes, and Philippe Ryfman (eds), *Droit et pratique de l'action humanitaire* (LGDJ 2019) 241. UN General Assembly resolution 46/182 (1991) may have also been influential. It provides that '[h]umanitarian assistance must be provided in accordance with the principles of humanity, neutrality and impartiality'; this is discussed in Section 3.3.

[106] See Chapter 5, Section 2.2.

[107] See Section 4.4.1.

[108] Interview with Jan Eliasson (via Zoom, 25 February 2022).

are rare, though Wynn-Pope and others state simply that humanity, impartiality, and neutrality were included based on the Fundamental Principles.[109] Jan Eliasson, who was the UN's first Under-Secretary-General for Humanitarian Affairs and Emergency Relief Coordinator—a position created by resolution 46/182—confirms that the principles were, indeed, 'picked [. . .] up from the International Red Cross'.[110] Edward Tsui, a now-retired UN official who was also involved in drafting resolution 46/182, recalls this was because the drafters did not want to 'reinvent the wheel'.[111] Rather, they looked to the ICRC for 'best practices' given its status as a highly respected humanitarian organization.[112] This link between the principles in resolution 46/182 and the Fundamental Principles is today widely known among OCHA personnel.[113] General Assembly resolution 45/100—the earlier (1990) resolution which also mentions humanity, neutrality, and impartiality and which may itself have been based on the Fundamental Principles—may have also been influential.[114] The origins of the core humanitarian principles, for NGOs as well as for the UN, can thus be definitively traced to the Fundamental Principles.

4. Legal character and normative content

Like their history, the core humanitarian principles' legal character is often incompletely understood. Mačák notes that impartiality and neutrality are 'sometimes described as binding on States and other humanitarian actors as a matter of international law',[115] citing several examples in this regard,[116] and further notes that 'such assertions are usually accompanied by little or no analysis as to their specific legal basis'.[117] This is true not only of impartiality and neutrality, but of all four core humanitarian principles. Wynn-Pope and others, for example, state that the core humanitarian principles 'are enshrined in modern-day international law as obligations of States and humanitarian actors',[118] without elaborating on the source of such obligations or how they might bind NGOs, which are not subjects of international

[109] Phoebe Wynn-Pope, Yvette Zegenhagen, and Fauve Kurnadi, 'Legislating Against Humanitarian Principles: A Case Study on the Humanitarian Implications of Australian Counterterrorism Legislation' (2015) 97 International Review of the Red Cross 235, 236.
[110] Eliasson interview (n 108).
[111] Tsui interview (n 34).
[112] ibid.
[113] Email from Aurelien Buffler (Chief, Policy Advice and Planning Section, Operations and Advocacy Division, OCHA) to author (25 October 2022).
[114] Res 45/100 (n 29).
[115] Mačák 2016 (n 7) 159. See also Emanuela-Chiara Gillard, 'Framing the Conversation: Humanitarian Principles and the Law' in Chatham House, 'The Normative Framework of Humanitarian Action in Armed Conflict' (2022) <https://chathamhouse.soutron.net/Portal/Public/en-GB/RecordView/Index/191239> accessed 10 November 2022.
[116] Mačák 2016 (n 7) 159. Examples cited by Mačák include Sylvain Beauchamp, 'Defining the Humanitarian Space Through Public International Law' (2008) On the Edges of Conflict Policy Paper; Vincent Chetail, 'The Contribution of the International Court of Justice to International Humanitarian Law' (2003) 85 International Review of the Red Cross 235.
[117] Mačák 2016 (n 7) 159.
[118] Wynn-Pope and others (n 109) 240.

law. Simm states that '[c]ustomary international law establishes humanitarian principles'.[119]

The issue is pronounced in relation to IHL. Gillard observes that the core humanitarian principles and IHL are 'frequently conflated' and that there is often 'an assumption that IHL is the source of the humanitarian principles'.[120] For example, a 'topic guide' commissioned by the UK presents the core humanitarian principles as if they are derived from IHL and does not distinguish between the principles and similarly-termed, but distinct, IHL concepts.[121]

The core humanitarian principles are also sometimes framed as international law in non-conflict contexts. The summary of the ILC's debate regarding draft article 6, on 'Humanitarian principles in disaster response', notes that the view was expressed that humanity, neutrality, and impartiality 'were well established in international law, as reflected in a number of international instruments'. However, there was also a contrary view that while the principles 'were important [. . .] for the International Red Cross Movement, it was not clear that they were principles of international law'.[122] Ultimately, the ILC did not resolve this question. Its commentary on draft article 6 notes that the principles 'are considered by the Commission to constitute humanitarian principles that underlie disaster relief and assistance' and on this basis, the ILC 'did not find it necessary to determine whether these principles are also general principles of international law'.[123] The Kampala Convention provides that '[i]nternational organizations and humanitarian agencies shall be bound by the principles of humanity, neutrality, impartiality and independence of humanitarian actors'.[124] This is problematic because just as a treaty cannot 'create either obligations or rights for a third State without its consent',[125] nor can it impose obligations on an international organization not party to the treaty in question, much less NGOs.

Given the frequency with which the core humanitarian principles are said to come from or constitute international law, particularly IHL, it is worth considering where this idea might originate. It is likely attributable to the use of 'humanitarian' and 'impartial' in the AP provisions on humanitarian relief operations.[126] Article 70(1) of API, which governs international armed conflict (IAC), provides that if 'the civilian population of any territory under the control of a Party to the conflict, other than occupied territory, is not adequately' supplied, 'relief actions which are *humanitarian* and *impartial* in character and conducted *without any adverse distinction* shall be undertaken'.[127] Article 18(2) of APII provides essentially the same in relation to

[119] Gabrielle Simm, 'Disaster Militarism? Military Humanitarian Assistance and Disaster Relief' (2019) 22 Max Planck Yearbook of United Nations Law Online 347, 350.

[120] Gillard (n 115) 12–13.

[121] GSDRC, 'International Legal Frameworks for Humanitarian Action' (2013) <https://gsdrc.org/wp-content/uploads/2015/07/ILFHA.pdf> accessed 25 January 2023, 25.

[122] ILC (n 38) para 309.

[123] ILC, 'Report of the International Law Commission on the Work of its 63rd Session' (26 April–3 June and 4 July–12 August 2011) A/66/10, para 289(1).

[124] Kampala Convention (n 20) art VI(3).

[125] Vienna Convention on the Law of Treaties (adopted 23 May 1969, entered into force 27 January 1980) 1155 UNTS 331, art 34.

[126] See Chapter 3, Section 4.

[127] API (n 9) emphasis added.

non-international armed conflict (NIAC).[128] 'Humanitarian' and 'impartial' in the senses of articles 70(1) and 18(2) are similar to the core principles of 'humanity' and 'impartiality'; 'without any adverse distinction' is a dimension of the principle of impartiality but could be confused with the humanitarian principle of neutrality. It is thus not surprising to come across references such as this: the 'humanitarian principles of impartiality and neutrality' have 'their legal basis in Art. 70' of API.[129] The statement is, however, inaccurate. For reasons explained below, the core humanitarian principles do not have any 'legal basis' in IHL.

Inaccurate claims that the principles are international law may also 'to some extent be explained by the[ir] perceived moral desirability'.[130] Nevertheless, it is important to counter the flawed idea that the principles constitute international law in some general sense. The analysis in this regard must proceed category-by-category because the principles' legal character depends on their source, which varies by category of humanitarian actor. First, however, the analysis demonstrates that 'principles' do not, on their own, create binding obligations. It then goes on to analyse the legal character, as well as the normative content, of the core humanitarian principles for the Movement, NGOs, the UN, and states.[131]

It must be noted at the outset that all humanitarian actors are bound to act in accordance with the core humanitarian principles if this is required by the domestic law of the state where humanitarian operations are taking place. Kälin notes that Peruvian law requires compliance with the core humanitarian principles and South Sudan has a draft law to this effect.[132]

4.1. Legal character of principles

The core humanitarian principles do not, in and of themselves, create binding obligations for humanitarian actors. A principle is 'a fundamental truth or proposition that serves as the foundation for a system of belief or behaviour or for a chain of reasoning'.[133] Principles are distinct from rules in that they do not themselves prescribe or proscribe conduct. Rather, a principle expresses a moral norm that may guide conduct and from which a rule or set of rules may be derived. In legal theory, principles refer 'to moral standards that do not apply in a conclusive and all-or-nothing fashion'; they 'vary in the weight they have'.[134] Principles are thus higher order norms that provide the rationale for rules but are not themselves binding. Thus, the core humanitarian principles do not themselves create legal obligations. They may,

[128] APII (n 9).

[129] Heike Spieker, 'Humanitarian Assistance, Access in Armed Conflict and Occupation' in Rüdiger Wolfrum (ed), *Max Planck Encyclopedia of Public International Law* (OUP 2015) para 1.

[130] Mačák 2016 (n 7) 159.

[131] This analysis is summarized in tabular form in Sharpe (n 17) Annex 2, which provides a snapshot of the source of the obligation to act in accordance with, or voluntary commitment to follow, humanitarian principles for select actors within each category.

[132] Kälin (n 23) 218.

[133] Definition from the Oxford English Dictionary, provided by Google on 10 June 2022.

[134] Brian Bix, *A Dictionary of Legal Theory* (OUP 2004) 165–66.

however, create obligations for a particular humanitarian actor if that actor has translated the humanitarian principles into a binding rule or rules, as will be shown below.

4.2. The International Red Cross and Red Crescent Movement

4.2.1. Legal character

The Movement's component organizations have had to act in accordance with the Fundamental Principles since 1965, when the XXth International Conference of the Red Cross proclaimed the 'fundamental principles on which Red Cross action is based'.[135] While the Fundamental Principles have been binding for the ICRC, IFRC, and national societies since 1965,[136] their character was clarified and affirmed by the Red Cross Statutes adopted in 1986. These provide that 'the Movement *shall be* guided by its Fundamental Principles'.[137] In addition to this mandatory language, Haug summarizes the other ways the 1986 Statutes impose the Fundamental Principles on Movement components:

> A National Society may only be recognised by the ICRC if it respects the Red Cross principles. The ICRC itself—as already in earlier years—is given the role of disseminating and preserving the principles. The Federation [IFRC] also shall fulfill its purpose of promoting National Societies and coordinating their activities, in particular in peacetime, in the context of the principles. The participants in Red Cross and Red Crescent Conferences and the members of the Council of Delegates of the Movement are expressly obliged to respect and maintain the principles during the meetings. New [in the 1986 Statutes] and specially important is the provision that the States parties to the Geneva Conventions have at all times to respect the fact that all components of the Movement are bound by its principles.[138]

Indeed, the Movement Statutes provide that states parties to the GCs 'shall at all times respect the adherence by all components of the Movement to the Fundamental Principles'.[139]

Several GC and AP provisions require states to grant certain facilities to Movement components operating in accordance with the Fundamental Principles. Under API, states undertake to grant their national societies 'the facilities necessary for carrying out their humanitarian activities [. . .] in accordance with [. . .] the Fundamental Principles' and to facilitate humanitarian assistance extended 'in accordance [. . .] with the fundamental principles'.[140] States also agree that in occupied territory, 'National Red Cross [. . .] Societies shall be able to pursue their activities in accordance with Red Cross principles'.[141] The Fundamental Principle of impartiality receives

135 XXth Conference Resolutions (n 77) 573.
136 Haug (n 59) 446.
137 Movement Statutes (n 80) preamble (emphasis added).
138 Haug (n 59) 447.
139 Movement Statutes (n 80) art 2(4).
140 API (n 9) art 81(2–3).
141 GCIV (n 8) art 63.

particular support through provisions on the ICRC's right of initiative,[142] which is its 'right to offer its services to all parties to any conflict, both international and non-international, on any matters that the ICRC considers as within its purview'.[143] The right of initiative is contingent on the ICRC acting impartially. Common article 3, which applies in NIAC, provides that an '*impartial* humanitarian body, such as the [... ICRC], may offer its services to the Parties to the Conflict'.[144] Article 9 common to GCI, GCII, and GCIII (article 10 in GCIV), which applies in IAC, states that the provisions of the GCs 'constitute no obstacle to the humanitarian activities which the [... ICRC] or any other *impartial* humanitarian organization may' undertake.[145]

Thus for the ICRC, IFRC, and national societies, the core humanitarian principles—as well as the three further Fundamental Principles—are binding via the Movement Statutes. Movement components' statutory obligations to act in accordance with the Fundamental Principles, in general, and the principle of impartiality, in particular, are supported by the GCs and the APs.

4.2.2. Normative content

Since the Movement Statutes are now the primary source of the principles for the Movement, they provide the authoritative statement of their meaning for the Movement. Each of the seven Fundamental Principles is briefly described in the Statutes' preamble in terms almost identical—there are a few minor grammatical changes—to those used when the Fundamental Principles were proclaimed in 1965.[146] Pictet provides more detailed explanations in his authoritative Commentary.[147]

Humanity is the Movement's 'essential principle'.[148] The Statutes do not define it as such. Rather, humanity is addressed entirely in terms of the Movement itself: the Movement, 'born of a desire to bring assistance without discrimination to the wounded on the battlefield, endeavours, in its international and national capacity, to prevent and alleviate human suffering wherever it may be found. Its purpose is to protect life and health and to ensure respect for the human being. It promotes mutual understanding, friendship, cooperation and lasting peace amongst all peoples'.[149] This self-referential explanation of humanity provides the Movement's 'ideal, its motivation and its objective'.[150] A less Red Cross-specific understanding of humanity can be found in the ICRC's Professional Standards for Protection Work, which define the principle of humanity as a directive: 'all people must be treated humanely in all circumstances'.[151]

The Movement Statutes explain that impartiality 'makes no discrimination as to nationality, race, religious beliefs, class or political opinions. It endeavours to relieve

[142] GCI (n 8) arts 3(2) and 9; GCII (n 8) arts 3(2) and 9; GCIII (n 8) arts 3(2) and 9; GCIV (n 8) arts 3(2) and 10; API (n 9) art 81(1).
[143] Emily Crawford and Alison Pert, *International Humanitarian Law* (3rd edn, CUP 2024) 305.
[144] Emphasis added.
[145] Emphasis added.
[146] XXth Conference Resolutions (n 77).
[147] Pictet (n 54).
[148] Pictet (n 54) 8.
[149] Movement Statutes (n 80) 5.
[150] Pictet (n 54) 14.
[151] ICRC, *Professional Standards for Protection Work* (3rd edn, ICRC 2018) 24.

the suffering of individuals, being guided solely by their needs, and to give priority to the most urgent cases of distress'.[152] It is thus evident, as explained in Section 3.1, that for the Movement, impartiality has two dimensions: non-discrimination (on the grounds listed) and proportionality. The latter means that 'help available shall be apportioned according to the relative importance of individual needs and in their order of urgency'.[153]

The principle of neutrality provides that in 'order to continue to enjoy the confidence of all, the Movement may not take sides in hostilities or engage at any time in controversies of a political, racial, religious or ideological nature'.[154] Pictet explains that while neutrality 'defines the attitude of the Red Cross towards belligerents and ideologies, it never determines its behaviour towards the human beings who suffer'.[155] The principle of neutrality explains then-ICRC President Peter Maurer's widely criticized but little understood meeting with Russian Foreign Minister Sergei Lavrov soon after Russia's illegal invasion of Ukraine in 2022.[156] In order to gain access to victims in the power of states—in this case in Russian controlled or occupied parts of Ukraine—the ICRC generally 'abstains from making public pronouncements about specific acts committed in violation of law and humanity and attributed to belligerents'.[157] The ICRC occasionally speaks out against conflict parties, and has at times made the wrong decision to remain neutral. Its decision 'not to issue a public appeal against abuses by the Third Reich was robustly debated within the ICRC, to the point that the text of such an appeal was drafted before the decision against this option was taken in October 1942'.[158]

Independence relates to the relationship between the Movement and other actors. The Statutes provide that the 'Movement is independent. The National Societies, while auxiliaries in the humanitarian services of their governments and subject to the laws of their respective countries, must always maintain their autonomy so that they may be able at all times to act in accordance with the principles of the Movement'.[159] Pictet identifies three dimensions of independence: economic, political, and religious.[160] Further, he clarifies that while the Statutes only mention independence from governments, the principle is in fact broader, referring to all 'outside forces'.[161] This includes (but is not limited to) 'public authorities',[162] 'intergovernmental organizations',[163] any 'class, pressure group or even public opinion',[164] and other humanitarian

152 Movement Statutes (n 80) 5.
153 Pictet (n 54) 27.
154 Movement Statutes (n 80) 5.
155 Pictet (n 54) 34.
156 Imogen Foulkes, 'Why the Red Cross has to be Neutral in the Ukraine Conflict' (*BBC*, 29 March 2022) <https://www.bbc.com/news/world-europe-60921567> accessed 6 July 2022.
157 Pictet (n 54) 39.
158 Eleanor Davey, John Borton, and Matthew Foley, 'A History of the Humanitarian System: Western Origins and Foundations' (2013) Humanitarian Policy Group Working Paper <https://odi.org/en/publications/a-history-of-the-humanitarian-system-western-origins-and-foundations/> accessed 1 August 2025.
159 Movement Statutes (n 80) 5.
160 Pictet (n 54) 40.
161 ibid.
162 ibid, 43–45.
163 ibid, 40.
164 ibid, 41.

organizations.[165] Pictet nevertheless focuses the majority of his commentary on independence from government. In this connection, he devotes considerable attention to the auxiliary status of national societies, explaining how they can be independent from governments while still supporting government humanitarian functions.[166]

While these articulations of the core humanitarian principles are specific to the Movement because they flow from the organization's Statutes and Pictet's commentary on the Fundamental Principles, they are also evident—given the origins described above—in the principles' normative content for other actors, which are addressed below.

4.3. Non-governmental organizations

4.3.1. Legal character

An NGO can only be bound by the core humanitarian principles through an internal governance document, such as its letters patent or by-laws, and/or via any voluntary sectoral document, such as the Code of Conduct, the organization may have signed. Both create obligations as a matter of institutional governance, but not as a matter of international law. For example, members of MSF agree to 'honour' the principles contained in the MSF Charter, which include to provide assistance 'irrespective of race, religion, creed or political convictions' (impartiality's non-discrimination dimension), to observe 'neutrality and impartiality in the name of universal medical ethics', and to 'maintain complete independence from all political, economic or religious powers';[167] they are also bound by the organization's Chantilly Principles.[168] These commitments are opposable by MSF vis-à-vis its staff, but not between third parties and MSF or between third parties and individual MSF staff members. NGOs that have committed to the core humanitarian principles or another set of humanitarian principles are often referred to as 'Dunantist', a term coined by Stoddard to describe organizations that 'seek to position themselves outside of state interests'.[169] As discussed in Section 2, not all humanitarian NGOs commit to the core humanitarian principles.

In armed conflict, an NGO may act in accordance with one or more of the core humanitarian principles not, or not only, because this is required by an internal governance document and/or by a sectoral document, but because doing so may have consequences in relation to the treaty obligations of conflict parties. For example, article 70(1) of API provides that if 'the civilian population of any territory under the control of a Party to the conflict, other than occupied territory, is not adequately provided with [... relief supplies], relief actions which are humanitarian and impartial in character and conducted without any adverse distinction shall be undertaken, subject

[165] ibid.
[166] ibid, 41–42.
[167] MSF, 'The MSF Charter', <https://www.msf.org/msf-charter> accessed 13 June 2022.
[168] MSF, 'Chantilly Principles' (4 October 1995) <https://www.msf.org/sites/default/files/Principles%20Chantilly%20EN.pdf> accessed 23 September 2022.
[169] Abby Stoddard, 'Humanitarian NGOs: Challenges and Trends' (2003) HPG Briefing No 12 <https://www.odi.org/sites/odi.org.uk/files/odi-assets/publications-opinion-files/349.pdf> accessed 11 September 2020, 2.

to the agreement of the Parties concerned'.[170] API is binding on the parties to the conflict in question but not NGOs. The effect of article 70(1) on the NGO is indirect: if its activities are humanitarian, impartial, and conducted without adverse distinction, and there are civilians in need, then the relevant conflict party cannot withhold consent to the NGO's humanitarian relief operation.[171] Thus, the NGO will act in accordance with the principles of humanity and impartiality not because it is treaty-bound to do so, but because acting in these ways privileges its operations under IHL. In short, a treaty can make it in an NGO's interests to act in accordance with humanitarian principles, but no treaty requires it.

There are additional practical reasons for NGOs to abide by the core humanitarian principles, such as operational security and effectiveness. Compliance may also be required to secure funding. For example, Cubie explains that the European Commission's Humanitarian Aid Department requires endorsement of the Code of Conduct (and hence of the core humanitarian principles) as a precondition of funding.[172]

4.3.2. Normative content

The meanings of the core humanitarian principles for an NGO bound by them pursuant to an internal governance document depend on how the principles are defined in that document or, if they are not defined, how they are commonly understood within the organization. Nevertheless, given the principles' common origins in the Fundamental Principles, the existence of sectoral documents such as the Code of Conduct, and the importance to humanitarian coordination of shared meanings, common understandings of the principles have emerged. These understandings common among NGOs are also shared with the UN; they are outlined in Section 4.4.2 below. Additionally, there is rich literature on the meanings of the core humanitarian principles and the tensions between them and practice,[173] which has influenced how NGOs understand the core humanitarian principles.

[170] API (n 9); see also: re. NIAC, APII (n 9) art 18(2); re. occupation, GCIV (n 8) art 59.

[171] See Chapter 3, Section 4.3.

[172] Dug Cubie, 'An Analysis of Soft Law Applicable to Humanitarian Action: Relative Normativity in Action?' (2011) 2 Journal of International Humanitarian Legal Studies 177, 195.

[173] See the sources cited elsewhere in this chapter, particularly at notes 3 and 4, and: Marion Harroff-Tavel, 'Neutrality and Impartiality: The Importance of these Principles for the International Red Cross and Red Crescent Movement and the Difficulties Involved in Applying Them' (1989) 29 International Review of the Red Cross 536; Hugo Slim, 'Relief Agencies and Moral Standing in War: Principles of Humanity, Neutrality, Impartiality and Solidarity' (1997) 7 Development in Practice 342; Andy Storey, 'Non-neutral Humanitarianism: NGOs and the Rwanda Crisis' (1997) 7 Development in Practice 384; Nicholas Leader, 'Proliferating Principles; Or How to Sup with the Devil without Getting Eaten' (1998) 22 Disasters 288; Larry Minear, 'The Theory and Practice of Neutrality: Some Thoughts on the Tensions' (1999) 81 International Review of the Red Cross 63; Robin Coupland, 'Humanity: What is it and How Does it Influence International Law?' (2001) 83 International Review of the Red Cross 969; Antonio Donini, 'Between a Rock and a Hard Place: Integration or Independence of Humanitarian Action' (2011) 93 International Review of the Red Cross 152; Antonio Donini (ed) *The Golden Fleece: Manipulation and Independence in Humanitarian Action* (Kumarian Press 2012); Scott Paul and Elizabeth Holland, 'Principled Humanitarian Organizations and the Use of Force: Is There Space to Speak Out?' (2015) 1 DePaul International Human Rights Law Journal 1; Heather Rysaback-Smith, 'History and Principles of Humanitarian Action' (2015) 15 Turkish Journal of Emergency Medicine 5; Andrew Thompson, 'Humanitarian Principles Put to the Test: Challenges to Humanitarian Action During Decolonization' (2015) 97 International Review of the

4.4. The United Nations

4.4.1. Legal character

Several provisions of General Assembly resolution 46/182 make clear that it applies to all UN entities. The fourth preambular paragraph notes that the Assembly is mindful of the need 'to strengthen further and make more effective the collective efforts of the international community, *in particular the [... UN] system*, in providing humanitarian assistance'.[174] The resolution's operative paragraph adopts the text in the annex to strengthen 'the coordination of emergency humanitarian assistance *of the [... UN] system*'.[175]

While resolution 46/182 applies to the whole UN system, whether a given UN entity is bound by the resolution in general and by the obligation to act 'in accordance with the principles of humanity, neutrality and impartiality' depends on its relationship with the General Assembly. This is determined by the UN Charter and, to a lesser extent, by established practice. The General Assembly is 'vested with an oversight role in relation to its fellow principal organs'; its ability to influence their actual functioning varies by organ.[176] The General Assembly 'has had a large influence on the functioning of the Secretariat, including the establishment and reform of its administrative structure'.[177] The General Assembly created, with resolution 46/182, the role of Emergency Relief Coordinator within the UN Secretariat and a secretariat, now known as OCHA, to support this high-level official.[178] As OCHA was essentially created by resolution 46/182,[179] it is clearly governed by the resolution.[180]

The General Assembly can create subsidiary organs.[181] Those relevant to humanitarian assistance include the UN Development Programme (UNDP),[182] the UN

Red Cross 45; Amelia B Kyazze, 'Walking the Walk: Evidence of Principles in Action from Red Cross and Red Crescent National Societies' (2016) 97 International Review of the Red Cross 211; Sophia Hoffmann, 'Impartiality' in Antonio De Lauri (ed), *Humanitarianism: Keywords* (Brill 2020); Jon Harald Sande Lie, 'The Humanitarian-Development Nexus: Humanitarian Principles, Practice, and Pragmatics' (2020) 5 Journal of International Humanitarian Action 1; Francesca Romeo, 'Humanity' in Antonio De Lauri (ed), *Humanitarianism: Keywords* (Brill 2020); Tristan Ferraro, 'International Humanitarian Law, Principled Humanitarian Action, Counterterrorism and Sanctions: Some Perspectives on Selected Issues' (2021) 103 International Review of the Red Cross 109.

174 Emphasis added.

175 Res 46/182 (n 30) para 1 (emphasis added).

176 Rosalyn Higgins and others, *Oppenheim's International Law: United Nations* (OUP 2017) 51; see also *Legal Consequences for States of the Continued presence of South Africa in Namibia (South West Africa) notwithstanding Security Council Resolution 276* Advisory Opinion, ICJ Rep 1971 (*South West Africa/Namibia*) para 105, in which the ICJ notes that 'it would not be correct to assume that, because the General Assembly is in principle vested with recommendatory powers, it is debarred from adopting, in specific cases within the framework of its competence, resolutions which make determinations or have operative design'.

177 Higgins and others (n 176) 53; Charter of the United Nations (adopted 26 June 1945, entered into force 24 October 1945) 1 UNTS XVI (UN Charter) art 101(1).

178 Res 46/182 (n 30) Annex, paras 34 and 36. See Chapter 5, Section 3.1.

179 See Chapter 5, Section 3.1.

180 Andrej Zwitter, 'United Nations' Legal Framework of Humanitarian Assistance' in Hans-Joachim Heintze and Andrej Zwitter (eds), *International Law and Humanitarian Assistance* (Springer 2011) 55–56.

181 UN Charter (n 177) arts 7(2) and 22.

182 UNGA Res 2029 (XX) (22 November 1965).

Population Fund (UNFPA),[183] UNHCR,[184] the UN Children's Fund (UNICEF),[185] the UN Relief and Works Agency for Palestine Refugees in the Near East (UNRWA),[186] and the World Food Programme (WFP); the latter was established jointly by the General Assembly and the Food and Agriculture Organization of the United Nations (FAO).[187]

Organs subsidiary to the General Assembly may be bound by resolution 46/182 if there is a basis for this in the organ's governance structure. UNHCR is bound by 46/182 pursuant to its Statute, which provides that the High Commissioner acts 'under the authority of the General Assembly' and must 'follow policy directives given [to] him by the General Assembly'.[188] Indeed, as a matter of practice, UNHCR aims to operate in accordance with the core four humanitarian principles.[189] UNRWA's Commissioner General is advised and assisted by an Advisory Commission composed of member states;[190] however, the Commissioner General is ultimately 'responsible to the General Assembly for the operation of the programme'.[191] UNRWA is thus also bound by resolution 46/182. UNICEF, UNDP, and UNFPA are not directly governed by the General Assembly, but by executive boards 'responsible for providing inter-governmental support to and supervision of the activities of each fund or programme *in accordance with the overall policy guidance of the General Assembly* and' the United Nations Economic and Social Council (ECOSOC).[192] Such policy guidance includes resolution 46/182. The core humanitarian principles are indeed apparent in the documentation of these subsidiary organs, such as UNICEF's 'Core Commitments for Children in Humanitarian Action'.[193] WFP is governed by an executive board composed of UN and FAO member states,[194] which is subject to policy guidance from the General Assembly and ECOSOC,[195] as well as from certain FAO bodies. WFP is thus also bound by resolution 46/182. Indeed, the core principles appear in WFP's ethics document, which specifies that its 'humanitarian response is rooted in the core humanitarian principles of humanity, neutrality, impartiality and operational independence'.[196]

General Assembly resolution 58/114 recognized in 2003 that independence 'is also an important guiding principle for the provision of humanitarian assistance'.[197] This lacks the mandatory language of resolution 46/182. Furthermore, independence is

[183] UNGA Res 2815 (XXVI) (14 December 1971).
[184] UNGA Res 428 (V) (14 December 1950) (Res 428).
[185] UNGA Res 57 (I) (11 December 1946).
[186] UNGA Res 302 (IV) (8 December 1949) (Res 302).
[187] UNGA Res 1714 (XVI) (19 December 1961).
[188] Res 428 (n 184) Annex, paras 1 and 3.
[189] UNHCR (n 19).
[190] Res 302 (n 186) para 8.
[191] ibid, para 9(a).
[192] UNGA Res 48/162 (14 January 1994) (Res 48/162) Annex, para 21 (emphasis added).
[193] (UNICEF, 2020) <https://www.unicef.org/emergencies/core-commitments-children> accessed 15 April 2025, 10.
[194] UNGA Res 50/8 (1 November 1995) para 1.
[195] Res 48/162 (n 192) Annex, para 30.
[196] WFP, 'Ethics in WFP' (*WFP*, 2020) <https://docs.wfp.org/api/documents/WFP-0000120630/download/> accessed 26 July 2022, 3.
[197] Res 58/114 (n 32) preambular para 5.

addressed in a preambular paragraph rather than in the operative portion of resolution 58/114. Thus, even components of the UN over which the General Assembly has binding authority were not initially required to act in accordance with the principle of independence. More recently, however, General Assembly resolutions routinely address independence alongside humanity, neutrality, and impartiality and do not distinguish among the four principles.[198] This practice suggests that independence is now equally binding in the UN. Indeed, the view among OCHA personnel is that member states expect UN humanitarian assistance to align with all four principles.[199]

General Assembly resolutions 46/182 and 58/114 are not, however, the only sources of the core humanitarian principles for UN entities. Specific entities may be required to act in accordance with one or more of the core principles, as well as with other principles, pursuant to other resolutions of the General Assembly. For example, UNHCR's Statute—a General Assembly resolution—provides that the 'work of the High Commissioner shall be of an entirely non-political character; it shall be humanitarian and social'.[200] Thus in addition to being bound to act in accordance with the principles in resolutions 46/182 and 58/114, UNHCR is also required to operate apolitically and to be humanitarian and social. These obligations are similar to, if not the same as, those imposed by the core humanitarian principles.[201]

4.4.2. Normative content

Neither General Assembly resolution 46/182 nor subsequent resolutions recalling and/or reaffirming resolution 46/182 define humanity, neutrality, or impartiality. Resolution 58/114 does, however, define independence, as 'the autonomy of humanitarian objectives from the political, economic, military or other objectives that any actor may hold with regard to areas where humanitarian action is being implemented'.[202] The same definition of independence is used in subsequent General Assembly resolutions.[203] The documentation of relevant UN entities uses the same, or substantively the same, definition of independence.[204]

While not defined in resolution 46/182, humanity, neutrality, and impartiality are defined in non-binding documentation published by OCHA, UNHCR, UNICEF, UNRWA, and WFP; UNDP and UNFPA do not define the humanitarian principles in publicly accessible documentation. These definitions demonstrate a system-wide UN understanding of these principles based on the Fundamental Principles. Of the three principles, there is the most variation in how humanity is defined, which can likely be attributed to the absence of a definition of humanity in the Movement Statutes. Despite these minor variations, the essential elements of humanity are the

198 See, for example, UNGA Res 76/124 (17 December 2021) para 5.
199 Buffler (n 113).
200 Res 428 (n 184) Annex, para 2.
201 On the meanings of these terms, see Sugino Kyoichi, 'The "Non-Political and Humanitarian" Clause in UNHCR's Statute' (1998) 17 Refugee Survey Quarterly 33.
202 Res 58/114 (n 32) preambular para 5.
203 See, for example, UNGA Res 59/141 (15 December 2004) preambular para 4; UNGA Res 60/125 (15 December 2005) preambular para 3; UNGA Res 60/124 (15 December 2005) preambular para 5.
204 See, for example, UNHCR (n 189) s 3; UNICEF (n 193) 10; UNRWA <https://www.unrwa.org/humanitarian-principles> accessed 26 September 2022; WFP (n 196) 3.

same: responding to human suffering and saving human lives. Neutrality means that UN entities will not engage in controversies of an ideological, political, racial, or religious nature, nor will they take sides in hostilities. Impartiality includes proportionality and non-discrimination dimensions.[205] The former requires that assistance be provided according to need alone. Non-discrimination means that assistance must be provided without distinction on the grounds of class, gender, nationality, political opinion, race, or religious belief. UNICEF distinguishes between sex and gender identity and specifies additional prohibited grounds of discrimination: ethnicity, language, disability, and sexual orientation. WFP also additionally specifies ethnic origin, but omits class.[206] Additionally, the ILC elaborates its understandings of humanity, neutrality, and impartiality in its commentary on draft article 6; however, these definitions are limited to the disaster context.[207]

4.5. States

4.5.1. Legal character

A state that provides humanitarian assistance in another country is not bound by international law to do so in accordance with the core humanitarian principles.[208] For the humanitarian principles to constitute international law, they would have to derive from one or more of the formal sources of international law: treaties, customary international law, and general principles of law.[209] Mačák has demonstrated that neither impartiality nor neutrality can be traced to any of these sources.[210] The same is true of humanity and independence.

While IHL treaties address humanitarian assistance in armed conflict and mention 'humanity', they do not mention the humanitarian principles of humanity or independence. Rather, 'humanity' features in terms of the principle of humane treatment[211] and in the Martens clause,[212] and it may constitute an autonomous principle of IHL,[213] but these usages are distinct from the humanitarian principle of humanity. The APs mention 'humanitarian' in relation to the characteristics of 'relief actions',[214] but not in the sense of imposing the principle of humanity on states in their humanitarian operations. Rather, as discussed above,[215] conflict parties may not withhold

[205] The humanitarian principle of impartiality is not the same as impartiality in UN peacekeeping; the latter is addressed in Chapter 5, Section 5.3.

[206] The OCHA, UNHCR, UNICEF, UNRWA, and WFP definitions of humanity, neutrality, and impartiality are reproduced in full in Sharpe (n 17) Annex 3.

[207] ILC (n 123) para 289(3–7).

[208] See Chapter 7.

[209] Statute of the International Court of Justice (24 October 1945) 961 UNTS 183, art 38(1).

[210] Mačák 2016 (n 7).

[211] The principle of humane treatment is expressed in Common Article 3 and at article 27 of GCIV (n 8) and requires that civilians are always treated humanely.

[212] Convention (II) with Respect to the Laws and Customs of War on Land and its Annex: Regulations concerning the Laws and Customs of War on Land (adopted 29 July 1899, entered into force 4 September 1900) preamble.

[213] See Crawford and Pert (n 143) 48–50.

[214] API (n 9) art 70(1); APII (n 9) art 18(2).

[215] See Section 4.3.1.

their consent to emergency relief operations for civilians in need if the operations are 'humanitarian' in character, as well as impartial and conducted without adverse distinction. Further, there is no widespread state practice and *opinio juris*, whether in armed conflict or in peacetime, that would elevate humanity and independence to the status of norms of customary international law. Finally, while there is no evidence that the independence of humanitarian assistance constitutes a general principle of law, it has been argued, further to the ICJ's judgment in *Corfu Channel*,[216] that 'elementary considerations of humanity' constitute one such general principle.[217] However, Mačák points out that in the *South West Africa* cases decided later, the ICJ rejected the notion that humanitarian considerations can generate legal obligations.[218] He notes further that in *Nicaragua*, also decided after *Corfu Channel*, the ICJ limited 'elementary considerations of humanity' to the narrower meaning contained in the GCs' Common Article 3.[219] Accordingly, like independence, humanity is not a general principle of law.

While the core humanitarian principles are not binding on states under international law, UN member states are required to 'consider' General Assembly resolutions.[220] Thus, the three principles in resolution 46/182, and resolution 58/114's addition of independence, are not irrelevant to states. Indeed, OCHA consistently stresses UN member states' responsibility—if not their legal obligation—to uphold the core four principles and promote their implementation within the UN.[221]

That the core humanitarian principles are not binding on states as a matter of international law is not to say that certain states have not committed to upholding them, though this is mostly in the sense of not impeding others' capacity to comply with the principles. EU member states have committed to humanitarian principles under the TFEU, which provides that '[h]umanitarian aid operations shall be conducted in compliance with [. . .] the principles of impartiality, neutrality and non-discrimination'.[222] States may also commit to upholding humanitarian principles as a matter of policy. For example, the UK's 2017 Humanitarian Reform Policy provided that humanitarian action 'should be guided by the principles of humanity [. . .] neutrality [. . .] impartiality [. . . and] independence'.[223] However, the UK's more recent 'Humanitarian Framework' does not mention the core principles.[224] The 'core values' of the now defunct Office of US [United States] Foreign Disaster Assistance were 'inspired by overarching and fundamental humanitarian principles of humanity, impartiality, and

[216] *Corfu Channel Case (United Kingdom v. Albania)* (Merits) [1949] ICJ Rep 4.
[217] Gerald Fitzmaurice, *The Law and Procedure of the International Court of Justice* (CUP 1986) 4 and Nils Melzer, *Targeted Killing in International Law* (OUP 2008) 187, cited in Mačák 2016 (n 7) 174.
[218] Mačák 2016 (n 7) 175.
[219] ibid; see also Kälin (n 23) 227.
[220] Jochen Frowein, 'United Nations' in Rüdiger Wolfrum (ed), *Max Planck Encyclopedia of Public International Law* (OUP 2013) para 34.
[221] Buffler (n 113).
[222] TFEU (n 43) art 214(2).
[223] UK Department for International Development, *Saving Lives, Building Resilience, Reforming the System: The UK Government's Humanitarian Reform Policy* (2017) 9 <https://assets.publishing.service.gov.uk/government/uploads/system/uploads/attachment_data/file/659965/UK-Humanitarian-Reform-Policy1.pdf> accessed 3 September 2022.
[224] UK Foreign, Commonwealth & Development Office, 'UK Humanitarian Framework' (10 November 2022) <https://www.gov.uk/government/publications/uk-humanitarian-framework/uk-humanitarian-framework> accessed 17 June 2025.

operational independence'.[225] Australia, Denmark, Finland, France, Germany, and the United Arab Emirates, for example, have also committed themselves to the core humanitarian principles via policy instruments.[226]

States would be bound to respect the humanitarian principles if required to do so by the UN Security Council, whose resolutions are binding when adopted under Chapter VII of the UN Charter or when mandatory language is used.[227] However, when Security Council decisions mention the principles, it is typically to require conflict parties to ensure humanitarian access so that humanitarian actors can deliver assistance in accordance with the principles;[228] the Security Council does not typically require state compliance with the humanitarian principles as such. OCHA reacted to Security Council decisions that have technically demanded state compliance with the principles—for example, resolutions on Darfur[229] and the Central African Republic[230]—by working with the Council to promote the use of more accurate language.[231]

More often, Security Council resolutions relating to the humanitarian principles do not use mandatory language. In relation to the Democratic Republic of the Congo, the Security Council called on 'all parties to respect the principles of neutrality and impartiality in the delivery of humanitarian assistance'.[232] The Security Council has also issued thematic resolutions mentioning the humanitarian principles. A 2009 resolution on the protection of civilians in armed conflict stressed 'the importance for all, within the framework of humanitarian assistance, of upholding and respecting the humanitarian principles of humanity, neutrality, impartiality and independence';[233] 'upholding' is addressed to states and 'respecting' to other humanitarian actors. More

[225] US Agency for International Development, Office of US Foreign Disaster Assistance, 'Policy for Humanitarian Action' (2015) <https://2012-2017.usaid.gov/sites/default/files/documents/1866/Humanitarian%20Policy%20Framework_digital.pdf> accessed 3 September 2022, 4.

[226] Australian Department of Foreign Affairs and Trade, 'Australia's Humanitarian Policy: Making a Difference for People in Crisis' (October 2024) <https://www.dfat.gov.au/sites/default/files/australian-humanitarian-policy.pdf> accessed 17 June 2025, 29; Ministry of Foreign Affairs of Denmark, 'The World We Share: Denmark's Strategy for Development Cooperation' (2021) <https://amg.um.dk/policies-and-strategies/stategy-for-danish-development-cooperation> accessed 17 June 2025, 8; Ministry of Foreign Affairs of Finland, 'Finland's Humanitarian Policy' (2012) <https://um.fi/documents/35732/48132/finlands_humanitarian_policy> accessed 24 September 2022, 11–12; French Minister for Europe and Foreign Affairs, 'France's Humanitarian Strategy (2023–2027)' <https://www.diplomatie.gouv.fr/en/french-foreign-policy/emergency-humanitarian-action/humanitarian-strategy-of-france-2023-2027/> accessed 17 June 2025, 6; German Federal Foreign Office, 'Federal Foreign Office Strategy for Humanitarian Assistance Abroad' (2024) <https://www.auswaertiges-amt.de/resource/blob/2672934/3052456b515f20acba6c60a35665cd1e/2024-strategie-huhi-data.pdf> accessed 17 June 2025, 12; United Arab Emirates Ministry of Foreign Affairs & International Cooperation, 'Promoting Global Peace and Prosperity: The United Arab Emirates Policy for Foreign Assistance 2022 Update' (2022) <https://www.mofa.gov.ae/en/The-Ministry/UAE-International-Development-Cooperation/UAE-Foreign-Aid-Policy> accessed 17 June 2025, 26.

[227] UN Charter (n 177) arts 25 and 103; *South West Africa/Namibia* (n 176) paras 113–14.

[228] See, for example, UNSC Res 2060 (25 July 2012) S/RES/2060, para 6; UNSC Res 2113 (30 July 2013) S/RES/2113, para 16; UNSC Res 2230 (14 July 2015) S/RES/2230, para 23; UNSC Res 2277 (30 March 2016) S/RES/2277, para 41; UNSC Res 2296 (29 June 2016) S/RES/2296, para 22. See Chapter 5, Section 4.4.2.

[229] UNSC Res 2113 (30 July 2013) S/RES/2113, para 16.

[230] UNSC Res 2134 (28 January 2014) S/RES/2134, para 26.

[231] Comment from Emanuela-Chiara Gillard (former OCHA staff) to author, 25 July 2023 (on file).

[232] UNSC Res 1341 (22 February 2001) S/RES/1341, para 12.

[233] UNSC Res 1894 (11 November 2009) S/RES/1894, para 13.

recently, the Security Council emphasized 'the importance of the principles of humanity, neutrality, impartiality and independence in the provision of humanitarian assistance' and reaffirmed 'the need for actors engaged in such assistance in situations of armed conflict to promote and fully respect these principles'.[234]

4.5.2. Normative content

The principles' content for states flows from applicable domestic or regional law or policy. Some states do not define the principles. Others, such as the UK, define the principles in terms based on those of the Movement and the same or substantially the same as those used in the UN.[235]

5. Conclusion

The core humanitarian principles are rooted in the Fundamental Principles, the first four of which are humanity, impartiality, neutrality, and independence. These principles diffused from the Movement to humanitarian NGOs via the Code of Conduct, which was prepared at the suggestion of the Movement's Council of Delegates and drafted by the IFRC and Oxfam-GB; the IFRC drafter presumably drew inspiration from his organization's own Fundamental Principles. The core principles govern UN humanitarian assistance pursuant to UN General Assembly resolution 46/182—whose drafters were also inspired by the Fundamental Principles—and resolution 58/114.

This common origin in the Fundamental Principles does not, however, imply that the core principles have the same legal character and normative content for all humanitarian actors. The principles' legal character varies depending on their source for the actor concerned. Their normative content also derives from the source of the principles for the actor in question. While in practice the principles' meanings are largely homogenous, reflecting their common origins in the Fundamental Principles, there are minor variations. These common origins and largely shared meanings may have contributed, in addition to the principles' evident value, to their common mischaracterization as binding as a matter of international law. The core humanitarian principles simply do not derive from any of the three sources of international law: treaties, customary international law, and general principles of law.

The fact that the core humanitarian principles do not come from international law should not be viewed as undermining them. While not derived from international law, the analysis above has demonstrated that, for most actors, the core humanitarian principles are indeed legally binding. For Movement components, this is by virtue of the Movement Statutes. NGOs may be bound by an internal governance document and/or by any sectoral document the organization has signed, such as the Code of

[234] UNSC Res 2474 (11 June 2019) S/RES/2474, preambular para 15; see also UNSC Res 2286 (3 May 2016) S/RES/2286, preambular para 15. For further examples of Security Council resolutions relating to the humanitarian principles, see OCHA, *Aide Memoire for the Consideration of Issues Pertaining to the Protection of Civilians in Armed Conflict* (2016) 94–98.

[235] Select state and regional definitions are reproduced in Sharpe (n 17) Annex 3.

Conduct. Since most UN humanitarian actors are subsidiary to the General Assembly, the principles are largely binding via its resolutions 46/182 and 58/114. For states, the source of the commitment to uphold the principles is national and/or regional law and/or policy. Additionally, while the GCs and their APs do not make the principles legally binding for states, at least impartiality is a constitutive element of humanitarian assistance under IHL. In addition to acting impartially because this is required by the Movement Statutes, the Code of Conduct, or General Assembly resolutions, humanitarian actors in armed conflict will act impartially because so doing privileges their assistance under IHL—on which the next chapter focuses.

3
Armed Conflict

1. Introduction

Armed conflict can generate significant humanitarian need among civilians, in several ways. Scarcity may be engendered by the conflict itself, which can disrupt the production, importation, and/or distribution of food, water, and other essential items. Scarcity may also arise from the military tactic of siege, in which a conflict party encircles a defined land area to isolate the enemy forces within it from reinforcements and supplies;[1] when a broader geographical area is isolated, especially by blocking coastal areas and ports and/or airspace and airports, this is known as blockade.[2] Hostilities may damage critical infrastructure, such as power plants and hospitals, and cause injuries that overwhelm health care capacity, particularly when heavy explosive weapons are used in populated urban areas.[3] Forced displacement disrupts normal patterns of life and affects livelihoods, communities, and their institutions, which can make it difficult for civilians to meet their basic needs. These effects of armed conflict, whether individually or in combination, mean that in most wars, many more deaths result from humanitarian crises created by the conflict than from kinetic military action.[4]

This chapter covers how international law governs the humanitarian assistance provided in response to such crises during armed conflict. Three regimes are particularly relevant. International humanitarian law (IHL) regulates the conduct of, and the protection of civilians and those *hors de combat* from, armed conflict. International human rights law (IHRL), which continues to apply during armed conflict,[5] underlies conflict parties' obligation to meet civilians' basic needs during armed conflict[6] and provides an additional basis, on top of IHL, for their obligation not to withhold consent to humanitarian assistance.[7] Finally, international criminal law (ICL) can

[1] James Kraska, 'Siege' in Rüdiger Wolfrum (ed), *Max Planck Encyclopedia of International Law* (OUP 2009).

[2] Wolff Heintschel von Heinegg, 'Blockade' in Rüdiger Wolfrum (ed), *Max Planck Encyclopedia of International Law* (OUP 2015).

[3] ICRC, 'Explosive Weapons with Wide Area Effects: A Deadly Choice in Populated Areas' (*ICRC*, 2022) <https://www.icrc.org/en/document/civilians-protected-against-explosive-weapons> accessed 5 July 2023, ch 1.

[4] Mohammed Jawad and others, 'Estimating Indirect Mortality Impacts of Armed Conflict in Civilian Populations: Panel Regression Analyses of 193 Countries, 1990–2017' (2020) 18 BMC Medicine 266.

[5] *Legality of the Threat or Use of Nuclear Weapons* (Advisory Opinion) [1996] ICJ Rep 226 (*Nuclear Weapons Advisory Opinion*) para 25; regarding economic, social, and cultural rights: *Legal Consequences of the Construction of a Wall in the Occupied Palestinian Territory* (Advisory Opinion) [2004] ICJ Rep 136 (*Wall Advisory Opinion*) para 106.

[6] See Chapter 1, Section 2.

[7] See Section 4.3.

Humanitarian Assistance in International Law. Marina Sharpe, Oxford University Press. © Marina Sharpe 2026.
DOI: 10.1093/9780198994695.003.0005

serve to hold individuals who have violated relevant rules accountable,[8] and certain ICL instruments are now being used to hold states responsible for conduct in armed conflict.[9]

1.1. Chapter structure

Among these regimes, IHL is the most relevant as well as the most specialized, so merits detailed introduction, which is where this chapter begins in Section 1.2. Section 1.2 also places IHL's regulation of humanitarian assistance in historical context. This is followed by a section of this introduction that provides armed conflict-specific definitions of key terms. The substance of the chapter then begins, in Section 2, with basic background: the primary responsibility of conflict parties to meet the needs of civilians within their control. Sections 3 through 6 are then structured around the distinct forms of and arrangements for the provision of relief. Section 3 covers humanitarian action in support of conflict parties' primary responsibility, particularly through impartial humanitarian organizations' right of initiative under IHL, and related IHL rules that facilitate humanitarian action, particularly by the International Red Cross and Red Crescent Movement (the Movement).[10] Section 4 then covers the IHL framework for emergency relief operations. It begins with an introductory overview of the rules on, and some of the modalities of and arrangements for, these operations: cross-border and cross-line operations, humanitarian corridors, airdrops, and protected zones. This is followed, for context, by a discussion of how real-world events and related policy literature have shaped how the rules on emergency relief operations have been understood since the early 2010s. Section 4 then addresses the rules' two-step framework—consent followed by implementation—in more detail, including the distinct issues that arise in international armed conflict (IAC) other than occupation, occupation, and non-international armed conflict (NIAC). Section 5 is devoted to relief regimes that benefit from specific rules under IHL: medical relief, food relief, relief for civilians deprived of their liberty, and relief for evacuated and displaced civilians. While it could equally have been addressed in Section 5, the IHL regime on assistance provided by third state civil defence organizations is covered in Chapter 7 on state humanitarian actors.[11] Section 6 then addresses the unlawful impeding of relief operations: withheld consent and violation of the obligation to allow and facilitate. The former includes a discussion of the 'arbitrary' and 'unlawful' approaches to withheld consent, which are evaluated in the context of consent withheld due to imperative considerations of military necessity. The latter includes a discussion of siege warfare. Section 6 also considers the operational consequences of unlawfully withheld strategic consent for United Nations (UN) and state humanitarian actors, on the one hand, and non-state actors, on the other. Section 7 covers individual accountability and international responsibility for unlawful impeding and attacks on humanitarian

[8] See Section 7.1.
[9] See Section 7.2.
[10] See Chapter 6, Section 2.
[11] See Chapter 7, Section 3.1.1.

personnel and protected zones. Section 8 concludes. Key IHL treaty provisions discussed in this chapter are reproduced in Appendix I and relevant customary IHL rules appear in Appendix II.

1.2. International humanitarian law and its historical regulation of humanitarian assistance

IHL is a set of treaty and customary rules that address humanitarian problems arising from IAC and NIAC. These rules protect persons and property that are, or may be, affected by armed conflict and limit the rights of conflict parties to use methods and means of warfare of their choice.[12] IHL binds all parties to armed conflict, including both states and organized armed groups (OAG).[13]

IHL is sometimes divided into two conceptual strands, Hague law and Geneva law, named for the cities where the major treaties of each strand were adopted. Hague law regulates the conduct of hostilities.[14] Geneva law aims to protect those who do not or no longer take part in hostilities—specifically, civilians; wounded, sick, and shipwrecked combatants; and prisoners of war (PoW)—from the ravages of war. Most IHL provisions related to humanitarian assistance form part of its Geneva strand. Today, Geneva law consists of the four Geneva Conventions (GC) of 1949;[15] their two Additional Protocols (AP), adopted in 1977 to update and fill gaps in the GCs;[16] and relevant customary international humanitarian law (CIHL), which the International Committee of the Red Cross (ICRC)[17] has articulated in 161 rules.[18] The first AP (API) also includes rules on means and methods of warfare, so the Hague and Geneva strands of IHL effectively merged in 1977. However, the Hague–Geneva dichotomy is useful here to highlight for those unfamiliar with IHL that this body of

[12] ICRC, 'International Humanitarian Law and International Human Rights Law: Similarities and Differences' (*ICRC*, 2021) Advisory Service on IHL Factsheet <https://www.icrc.org/en/document/international-humanitarian-law-and-international-human-rights-law-similarities-and> accessed 16 June 2023.

[13] *Prosecutor v Sam Hinga Norman* (Decision on Preliminary Motion Based on Lack of Jurisdiction) SCSL-2004-14-AR72(E) (31 May 2004) para 22.

[14] The 1899 and 1907 Hague Conventions remain in force. Today, the law on the means and methods of warfare also includes a range of treaties on specific issues, such as the prohibition of certain weapons and the protection of cultural property.

[15] Geneva Convention for the Amelioration of the Condition of the Wounded and Sick in Armed Forces in the Field (adopted 12 August 1949, entered into force 21 October 1950) 75 UNTS 31 (GCI); Geneva Convention for the Amelioration of the Condition of Wounded, Sick and Shipwrecked Members of Armed Forces at Sea (adopted 12 August 1949, entered into force 21 October 1950) 75 UNTS 85 (GCII); Geneva Convention Relative to the Treatment of Prisoners of War (adopted 12 August 1949, entered into force 21 October 1950) 75 UNTS 135 (GCIII); Geneva Convention Relative to the Protection of Civilian Persons in Time of War (adopted 12 August 1949, entered into force 21 October 1950) 75 UNTS 287 (GCIV).

[16] Protocol Additional to the Geneva Conventions of 12 August 1949, and relating to the Protection of Victims of International Armed Conflicts (adopted 8 June 1977, entered into force 7 December 1978) 1125 UNTS 3 (API); Protocol Additional to the Geneva Conventions of 12 August 1949, and relating to the Protection of Victims of Non-International Armed Conflicts (adopted 8 June 1977, entered into force 7 December 1978) 1125 UNTS 609 (APII).

[17] The ICRC is covered in Chapter 6, Section 2.1.

[18] Jean-Marie Henckaerts and Louise Doswald-Beck, *Customary International Humanitarian Law*, vol I (CUP 2005).

law is significantly broader than the Geneva law from which most of the rules analysed in this chapter are drawn.

The aspects of Geneva law that govern a given armed conflict depend on whether it is international or non-international. IACs are situations of declared war between states with or without actual hostilities; actual interstate armed conflict, which exists 'whenever there is a resort to armed force between States';[19] and situations of occupation.[20] The GCs (except Common Article 3), API, and almost all CIHL rules apply in IAC. A NIAC exists when violence rises to a certain level of intensity[21] and the OAG or OAGs involved are sufficiently organized.[22] Article 3 common to all four GCs (Common Article 3) applies in NIACs characterized by 'protracted armed violence between governmental authorities and [. . . OAGs] or between such groups'.[23] The second AP (APII) applies to a more limited set of NIACs: the affected state's armed forces must be involved and the OAG must be under responsible command and control sufficient territory to carry out sustained military operations and implement APII.[24] Thus, while Common Article 3 'applies to the whole range of internal armed conflict from short-lived rebellion to full civil war, APII applies only to the "upper segment" of this range'.[25] Of the 161 rules of CIHL, 140 apply in NIAC and a further eight arguably apply in NIAC.[26]

Prior to the adoption of the GCs in 1949, IHL did not contain any rules on humanitarian assistance for civilians. The ICRC first proposed provisions on civilian relief in 1921,[27] but states were only willing to agree to provisions for PoWs, adopted in 1929 within the first convention on the treatment of PoWs.[28] In 1934, the ICRC adopted draft rules on civilian relief at the XVth International Conference of the Red Cross,[29] and planned to submit them to a diplomatic conference in 1940, but the conference was cancelled due to the outbreak of World War II.[30] Given the lack of a treaty basis for civilian relief, humanitarian action by the ICRC and the League of Red Cross Societies (now the International Federation of Red Cross and Red Crescent Societies (IFRC)) during World War II was underpinned solely by the Movement's Statutes.[31]

[19] *Prosecutor v Tadić* (Appeal on Jurisdiction) ICTY-94-1 (2 October 1995) (*Tadić*) para 70.

[20] GCs (n 15) Common Article 2.

[21] Indicators of intensity include the 'number, duration and intensity of individual confrontations; the type of weapons and other military equipment used; the number and calibre of munitions fired; the number of persons and types of forces partaking in the fighting; the number of casualties; the extent of material destruction; and the number of civilians fleeing combat zones' (*Prosecutor v Haradinaj, Balaj and Brahimaj* (Judgement) IT-04-84-T (3 April 2008) para 49).

[22] Indicators of organization include the existence of headquarters; designated zones of operation; the ability of the group to procure, transport, and distribute arms; a command structure; the existence of an internal disciplinary system, uniforms, and military training; and the ability to control territory (Emily Crawford and Alison Pert, *International Humanitarian Law* (3rd edn, CUP 2024) 67–68).

[23] *Tadić* (n 19) para 70.

[24] APII (n 16) art 1(1).

[25] Crawford and Pert (n 22) 74.

[26] Henckaerts and Doswald-Beck (n 18).

[27] The ICRC's role in relation to IHL is addressed in Chapter 6, Section 2.1.

[28] This treaty has been superseded by GCIII.

[29] This conference is discussed in Chapter 6, Section 2.1.

[30] Denise Plattner, 'Assistance to the Civilian Population: the Development and Present State of International Humanitarian Law' (1992) 32 International Review of the Red Cross 249, 252.

[31] ibid, 253. These Statutes are addressed in Chapter 6, Section 2.

The ICRC's experience of negotiating access to civilians in Allied and German territories informed its drafting of the GCs, particularly GCIV's article 23 on items that should be allowed free passage, including through sieges and blockades, and its article 55 provision on an occupying power's duty to ensure that civilians in occupied territory are adequately supplied.[32] While a step forward, these provisions relate only to civilians in enemy or occupied territory; during the 1940s, the international community had 'a smaller appetite than today for making legally binding treaties protecting a State's citizens from the State itself'.[33] States did not have any obligations regarding external humanitarian assistance for their own nationals until the provisions on relief actions were adopted within the APs in 1977.[34] These AP provisions are at the core of this chapter.

1.3. Terminology

'Humanitarian assistance' was defined in Chapter 1. However, 'humanitarian' is used in both the GCs and the APs,[35] 'assistance' is employed in API,[36] and the related narrower notion of 'relief' features throughout the GCs and APs;[37] the ICRC has thus provided armed conflict-specific definitions of 'humanitarian activities', 'assistance activities', and 'relief activities'. The ICRC defines 'humanitarian' by reference to the Movement's fundamental principle of humanity.[38] 'Humanitarian activities' are thus 'all activities that prevent and alleviate human suffering wherever it may be found' in order 'to protect life and health and to ensure respect for the human being'.[39] 'Humanitarian activities' in armed conflict are 'those that seek to preserve the life, security, dignity and physical and mental well-being of persons affected by the conflict, or that seek to restore that well-being if it has been infringed upon'.[40] According to the ICRC, humanitarian 'assistance activities' refer to 'all activities, services, and delivery of goods, primarily in the fields of health, water, habitat and economic security and which seek to ensure that persons caught up in an armed conflict can survive and live in dignity'.[41] 'Relief' activities are strictly speaking a subset of assistance activities

[32] ibid, 255. These provisions are discussed in Section 4.

[33] Helen Durham and Phoebe Wynn-Pope, 'Protecting the "Helpers": Humanitarians and Health Care Workers During Times of Armed Conflict' in Michael Schmitt and Louise Arimatsu (eds), *Yearbook of International Humanitarian Law 2011*, vol 14 (TMC Asser Press 2012) 329.

[34] For a more detailed history of humanitarian assistance in IHL, see Flavia Lattanzi, 'Humanitarian Assistance' in Andrew Clapham, Paola Gaeta, and Marco Sassòli (eds), *The 1949 Geneva Conventions: A Commentary* (OUP 2015) 233–36.

[35] See, for example, GCs (n 15) Common Article 3(2); API (n 16) art 70(1); APII (n 16) art 18(2).

[36] API (n 16) art 81(1).

[37] See, for example, GCs (n 15) articles 9/9/9/10; GCIV (n 15) art 59; API (n 16) art 70; APII (n 16) art 18.

[38] ICRC, *Commentary on the First Geneva Convention: Convention (I) for the Amelioration of the Condition of the Wounded and Sick in Armed Forces in the Field* (CUP 2016) (ICRC 2016 Commentary GCI) para 811. See Chapter 2, Section 4.2.2.

[39] ibid.

[40] ibid, para 812.

[41] ICRC, 'ICRC Q&A and Lexicon on Humanitarian Access' (2014) 96 International Review of the Red Cross 359 (ICRC Lexicon) 367; see also ICRC 2016 Commentary GCI (n 38) para 1149.

aimed at addressing emergency situations.[42] Items that would be provided as part of a relief action include food, medical supplies, 'clothing, bedding, means of shelter, other supplies essential to the survival of the civilian population [...] and objects necessary for religious worship'.[43]

Relief is often used interchangeably with 'assistance'.[44] Here, however, 'assistance' and 'relief' are employed more deliberately in order to distinguish between the distinct legal regimes for *preventive* forms of *assistance* (addressed in Section 3) and *emergency* humanitarian *relief* operations (addressed in Sections 4–6). To further distinguish between preventive assistance, on the one hand, and emergency relief, on the other, what are typically termed 'humanitarian relief operations' are here termed 'emergency relief operations'; this terminological choice is discussed further in Section 3.

Humanitarian assistance in armed conflict is typically for civilians, rather than for combatants; combatants taken *hors de combat* by illness, injury, shipwreck, or having been taken prisoner; and individuals who directly participate in hostilities.[45] There are, however, two important exceptions. First, the ICRC is mandated to provide humanitarian assistance to both civilian and military victims of armed conflict or internal strife,[46] and in practice it provides individuals who are *hors de combat*, such as PoWs, with assistance. Second, universal medical ethics would preclude a humanitarian medical practitioner, such as a *Médecins Sans Frontières* (MSF) physician, from withholding care based on the patient having participated in hostilities. It is thus technically incorrect to conceive of humanitarian assistance in armed conflict as strictly limited to civilian beneficiaries. Most humanitarian actors do, however, aim their work at civilians; humanitarian assistance is therefore conceptualized here as limited to civilian beneficiaries, with the result that some armed conflict humanitarian assistance, such as for PoWs, is beyond the scope of this chapter.

The primary international humanitarian actors in armed conflict are UN operational bodies, such as the Office of the UN High Commissioner for Refugees (UNHCR) and the World Food Programme (WFP), and non-state actors: non-governmental organizations (NGOs) and Movement components, particularly the ICRC. These actors are addressed in detail in Part III of this book. 'Humanitarian organization' and 'humanitarian actor' as used here refer to UN entities, NGOs, and Movement components; where the context requires a distinction between international organizations and NGOs, this is drawn explicitly.

[42] ICRC Lexicon (n 41) 367.

[43] API (n 16) art 70(1) read with art 69(1).

[44] ICRC 2016 Commentary GCI (n 38) para 808; see also para 1136.

[45] There is no combatant status in NIAC. In NIAC, individuals who fight are termed persons directly participating in hostilities.

[46] Statutes of the International Committee of the Red Cross (adopted 21 December 2017, entered into force 1 January 2018) <https://www.icrc.org/en/document/statutes-international-committee-red-cross-0> accessed 10 July 2025, art 4(1)(d); Statutes of the International Red Cross and Red Crescent Movement (1986, as amended in 1995 and 2006) <https://www.icrc.org/en/doc/assets/files/other/statutes-en-a5.pdf> accessed 24 February 2022, art 5(2)(d). See also GCI–GCIII (n 15) Common Article 9.

2. Responsibility of conflict parties

Each conflict party has primary responsibility for meeting the needs of civilians in its territory or within its control.[47] The legal basis of this obligation differs depending on whether the conflict party in question is the territorial state, an occupying power, or an OAG. The obligation as it relates to territorial states was discussed in Chapter 1.[48]

The obligation in occupation is derived from IHL. Occupation is a transition phase of IAC in which a conflict party has overpowered an adversary and taken control of its territory, but the broader armed conflict remains ongoing.[49] Under IHL, territory 'is considered occupied when it is actually placed under the authority of the hostile army. The occupation extends only to the territory where such authority has been established and can be exercised'.[50] An occupying power has a duty to administer occupied territory for the benefit of the local population[51] and must 'ensure, as far as possible, public order and safety' and meet the needs of civilians in occupied territory.[52] Under GCIV, the occupying power must ensure to 'the fullest extent of the means available to it [. . .] the food and medical supplies of the population',[53] thereby incurring 'a definite obligation to maintain at a reasonable level the material conditions under which the population of the occupied territory lives'.[54] API broadened the list of items the occupying power must provide, adding, to food and medical supplies, 'clothing, bedding, means of shelter, other supplies essential to the survival of the civilian population [. . .] and objects necessary for religious worship'.[55] The occupying power has additional specific obligations in relation to hygiene and public health[56] and religious practice,[57] as well as to children[58] and in relation to humane treatment.[59] In addition to IHL, an occupying power also has obligations to meet the needs of civilians in occupied territory under IHRL.[60]

[47] ICRC Lexicon (n 41) 365; Dapo Akande and Emanuela-Chiara Gillard, 'Oxford Guidance on the Law Relating to Humanitarian Relief Operations in Situations of Armed Conflict' (2016) <https://www.elac.ox.ac.uk/wp-content/uploads/2022/06/oxfordguidancepdfpdf.pdf> accessed 2 May 2021 (Oxford Guidance) para 10; Nils Melzer, *International Humanitarian Law: A Comprehensive Introduction* (ICRC 2019) 250.

[48] See Chapter 1, Section 2.

[49] Sylvain Vité, 'Occupation' in Ben Saul and Dapo Akande (eds), *The Oxford Guide to International Humanitarian Law* (OUP 2020) 299.

[50] Convention (IV) respecting the Laws and Customs of War on Land (adopted 18 October 1907, entered into force 26 January 1910) Annex (Regulations) (Hague Regulations) art 42.

[51] *Legal Consequences arising from the Policies and Practices of Israel in the Occupied Palestinian Territory, including East Jerusalem* (Advisory Opinion) 2024 <https://www.icj-cij.org/sites/default/files/case-related/186/186-20240719-adv-01-00-en.pdf> accessed 20 June 2025 (*OPT AO*) para 105.

[52] Hague Regulations (n 50) art 43.

[53] GCIV (n 15) art 55(1).

[54] Jean Pictet and others, *Commentary: IV Geneva Convention Relative to the Protection of Civilian Persons in Time of War* (ICRC 1958) 310. See also *Obligations of Israel in Relation to the Presence and Activities of the United Nations, Other International Organizations and Third States in and in Relation to the Occupied Palestinian Territory* (Advisory Opinion) 2025 <https://www.icj-cij.org/sites/default/files/case-related/196/196-20251022-adv-01-00-en.pdf> accessed 31 October 2025 (*Israel Obligations AO*) para 92.

[55] API (n 16) art 69(1); see also art 68.

[56] GCIV (n 15) art 56(1).

[57] ibid, art 58.

[58] ibid, art 50.

[59] ibid, art 27.

[60] *OPT AO* (n 51) paras 99–101.

It is increasingly clear that OAGs in control of territory also have obligations to meet civilians' basic needs. For example, the Security Council exhorted an OAG in the DRC 'as the de facto authority responsible to bring to an end all extrajudicial executions, human rights violations and arbitrary harassment of civilians in Kisangani' and other areas under its control.[61] The Oxford Guidance[62] explains that where OAGs control territory in NIAC, 'they also have a responsibility to meet the needs of civilians under their effective control if the state party to the conflict is unable to or otherwise does not discharge its obligation in this regard'.[63] However, while it is settled that OAGs are bound by IHL, the legal basis of these obligations is less apparent.[64] Sutton and Gillard have called for more research on the source of OAGs' 'positive obligations to meet the basic needs of civilians and provide them access to services, coupled with case studies of how this has been implemented in practice'.[65] They cite a salient implementation modality: Geneva Call's 2021 Deed of Commitment for the Prevention of Starvation and Addressing Conflict-Related Food Insecurity,[66] which includes a commitment for OAGs to provide 'means of subsistence, for example through food or water distribution' to the extent of their capacity.[67] The 2023 Jeddah Declaration of Commitment to Protect the Civilians of Sudan constitutes another example. Among the commitments, the Rapid Support Forces, an OAG in Sudan, agrees, along with the Sudanese Armed Forces, that 'the interests and well-being of the Sudanese people are our top priority' and affirms its 'commitment to ensure that civilians are protected at all times'.[68]

3. The right of initiative and other provisions that support humanitarian assistance

If a conflict party has difficulty meeting its obligations to meet the basic needs of civilians within its control or wants support in this regard, it can request assistance from a humanitarian actor. Impartial humanitarian organizations can equally offer their services, as is their right under IHL in both IAC and NIAC.[69] This right, known as

[61] UNSC Res 1417 (14 June 2002) S/RES/1417, para 4. See generally, Françoise Bouchet-Saulnier, 'Consent to Humanitarian Access: An Obligation Triggered by Territorial Control, not States' Rights' (2014) 96 International Review of the Red Cross 207.

[62] The origins and importance of this document are discussed in Section 4.2.

[63] Oxford Guidance (n 47) para 15.

[64] See, generally, Tilman Rodenhäuser, 'The Legal Protection of Persons Living Under the Control of Non-State Armed Groups' (2020) 102 International Review of the Red Cross 991, 1011–14.

[65] Rebecca Sutton and Emanuela-Chiara Gillard, 'Beyond Compliance: International Humanitarian Law, Humanitarian Need and Civilian Harm in Armed Conflict' (*PeaceRep*, 2022) <https://peacerep.org/wp-content/uploads/2022/11/Beyond-Compliance-International-Humanitarian-Law-in-Armed-Conflict.pdf> accessed 4 May 2023, 29.

[66] Geneva Call is an NGO that 'endeavours to strengthen the respect of humanitarian norms and principles by armed groups and de facto authorities', notably by having OAGs sign deeds of commitment (<www.genevacall.org> accessed 11 May 2023).

[67] Sutton and Gillard (n 65) 28; see also Ezequiel Heffes, 'Armed Groups and the Protection of Health Care' (2019) 95 International Law Studies 226.

[68] US Department of State, 'Jeddah Declaration of Commitment to Protect the Civilians of Sudan' (11 May 2023) <https://www.state.gov/jeddah-declaration-of-commitment-to-protect-the-civilians-of-sudan/> accessed 18 May 2023.

[69] GCs (n 15) Common Article 3 and articles 9/9/9/10.

the 'right of initiative', is 'the legal entitlement given to impartial humanitarian organizations to propose their humanitarian activities to a party to the armed conflict'.[70] Although the provisions on the right of initiative in both IAC and NIAC mention the ICRC, the right is not limited to this organization. Rather, the right of initiative belongs to all impartial humanitarian organizations; states do not enjoy any right of initiative. The notion of an impartial humanitarian organization is not defined in IHL. The ICRC explains that it refers to 'the attitude to be adopted vis-à-vis the persons affected by the armed conflict when planning and implementing the proposed humanitarian activities'.[71] In other words, an impartial humanitarian organization is an organization that operates in line with the foundational humanitarian principles of humanity and impartiality.[72]

The right of initiative must be distinguished from the legal framework governing emergency relief operations, which is discussed in Section 4 below. Emergency relief operations occur in IAC when the civilian population is 'not adequately provided with' certain listed supplies[73] and in NIAC when 'the civilian population is suffering undue hardship owing to a lack of supplies essential for its survival'.[74] In other words, emergency relief operations take place, and the rules governing them take effect, when civilians have unmet needs. The right of initiative, by contrast, is always guaranteed during armed conflict.[75] The right of initiative thus underlies impartial humanitarian organizations' work to provide preventive assistance:[76] humanitarian assistance provided to prevent needs from going unfulfilled, which can avert the adverse consequences of unmet needs. Preventive assistance has been overlooked over the past decade given the analytical focus on the law governing emergency relief operations.[77] Indeed, the terminology of 'emergency relief operations' is used here in place of the more commonly used 'humanitarian relief operations' in order to clearly delineate between those rules that support emergency relief as well as preventive assistance (this section), on the one hand, and those relating exclusively to emergency relief (Section 4), on the other.

The right of initiative in IAC is guaranteed by the GCs' articles 9/9/9/10, which are the same except for the beneficiaries named. Article 10 of GCIV provides that the 'provisions of the present Convention constitute no obstacle to the humanitarian activities which the [. . . ICRC] or any other impartial humanitarian organization may, subject to the consent of the Parties to the conflict concerned, undertake for the protection of civilian persons and for their relief'. While the content of the humanitarian activities impartial humanitarian organizations may offer is stated as relief

[70] Tristan Ferraro, 'Relief Schemes and the Delivery of Humanitarian Activities in Situations of Armed Conflict: the ICRC's Perspective' in Fausto Pocar (ed), *The Additional Protocols 40 Years Later: New Conflicts, New Actors, New Perspectives* (FrancoAngeli 2018) 195.

[71] ICRC 2016 Commentary GCI (n 38) paras 794 (commentary on Common Article 3 (NIAC)) and 1160 (commentary on article 9 (IAC)).

[72] See Chapter 2, Section 4.

[73] API (n 16) art 70(1).

[74] APII (n 16) art 18(2).

[75] Though impartial humanitarian organizations are of course most likely to offer their services when civilians' needs are not being met by the conflict party with primary responsibility in this regard.

[76] ICRC Lexicon (n 41) 368.

[77] This focus and the reasons for it are addressed in Section 4.2.

and protection,[78] a 'specific feature' of the right of initiative is its recognition 'that impartial humanitarian organizations are legally entitled to offer to perform *any* humanitarian activity which they deem pertinent to meet the humanitarian needs engendered by the armed conflict'.[79]

The provisions on the right of initiative do not specifically mention the *right* of impartial humanitarian organizations to offer their services; however, this is implicit.[80] The requirement of state consent is stated explicitly. However, while consent is required, it may not be arbitrarily withheld.[81] The ICRC has provided guidance on what would constitute an arbitrary, and therefore unlawful, refusal. It notes that if 'humanitarian needs cannot be met otherwise, the refusal of an offer of services would be arbitrary'.[82] It further notes that while arbitrariness must be assessed in context, there 'are instances in which a refusal to grant consent will clearly not be considered arbitrary'. For example, 'if the State to which the offer is made is itself able and willing to address the humanitarian needs and, importantly, actually does so in an impartial manner'. Conversely, a refusal would be arbitrary 'if it entails a violation of the Party's legal obligations' under IHL or other fields of international law, such as IHRL. For example, a refusal will be arbitrary 'when the Party concerned is unable or unwilling to provide humanitarian assistance to the persons affected by the armed conflict, and even more so if their basic needs enabling them to live in dignity are not met'.[83]

The right of initiative is stated more explicitly in relation to NIAC. Common Article 3(2) provides that an 'impartial humanitarian body, such as the [. . . ICRC], may offer its services to the Parties to the conflict'.[84] In NIACs additionally covered by APII, the right of initiative extends explicitly to national relief societies, such as the national Red Cross or Red Crescent society, which 'may offer their services for the performance of their traditional functions in relation to the victims of armed conflict'.[85] Regarding the 'services' that may be offered, the ICRC notes that the right of initiative in NIAC includes 'all humanitarian activities'.[86] The right to offer services does not imply any corresponding obligation on the part of the conflict party to accept the offer; there is a requirement of state consent implicit in Common Article 3(2).[87] However, as with the IAC right of initiative, this consent may not be arbitrarily withheld.[88] The ICRC's analysis of what would constitute an 'arbitrary' withholding is essentially the same under Common Article 3(2) as under the articles 9/9/9/10 right of initiative.[89]

[78] Considering the often preventive nature of activities undertaken further to the right of initiative, articles 9/9/9/10 are an important instance of 'relief' being used interchangeably with the non-emergency notion of 'assistance'; see ICRC 2016 Commentary GCI (n 38) para 1148.

[79] ICRC 2016 Commentary GCI (n 38) para 1132.

[80] Tilman Rodenhäuser and Gilles Giacca, 'The International Humanitarian Law Framework for Humanitarian Relief During Armed Conflicts and Complex Emergencies' in Susan C. Breau and Katja L. H. Samuel (eds), *Research Handbook on Disasters and International Law* (Edward Elgar 2016) 134.

[81] ICRC 2016 Commentary GCI (n 38) paras 1173–74.

[82] ibid, para 1174.

[83] ibid, para 1175.

[84] GCs (n 15) Common Article 3(2).

[85] APII (n 16) art 18(1).

[86] ICRC Lexicon (n 41) 367.

[87] ICRC 2016 Commentary GCI (n 38) para 828; Oxford Guidance (n 47) para 22.

[88] ICRC 2016 Commentary GCI (n 38) para 834.

[89] See ibid, paras 834–35.

In the years leading up to the adoption of the Additional Protocols, national Red Cross and Red Crescent Societies wanted greater recognition of their role in IAC.[90] API article 81 thus includes rules obliging states to facilitate the humanitarian activities of the ICRC as well as those of national Red Cross and Red Crescent societies. Article 81(1) requires conflict parties to 'grant to the [. . . ICRC] all facilities within their power so as to enable it to carry out the humanitarian functions assigned to it by the Conventions and this Protocol in order to ensure protection and assistance to the victims of conflicts; the [. . . ICRC] may also carry out any other humanitarian activities in favour of these victims, subject to the consent of the Parties to the conflict concerned'. Article 81(2) sets out an equivalent obligation in favour of national Red Cross and Red Crescent societies. Article 81(3) provides these societies, as well as the IFRC, with further support, requiring conflict parties to 'facilitate in every possible way the assistance' they 'extend to the victims of conflicts'. Article 81(4) extends similar facilities to 'other humanitarian organizations', provided they are 'duly authorized by the respective Parties to the conflict' and 'perform their humanitarian activities in accordance with the' GCs and API. The facilities envisioned by article 81(4) include, in practice, 'permits for persons and goods, transport facilities for goods and other equipment, [and] exemptions from import taxes and customs duties'.[91] Additional GC provisions support Movement components' and other humanitarian organizations' work in occupied territories,[92] as well as in additional specific situations or in relation to particular categories of victim;[93] the latter provisions are addressed in Section 5.

The IHL provisions on 'Protecting Powers' provide an additional legal basis for humanitarian assistance.[94] A Protecting Power is a neutral third state that protects the interests of those who fall into the hands of an adverse power during IAC; its appointment depends on a third state volunteering its services and the conflict parties' consenting to it taking on this role. A Protecting Power 'safeguard[s] the interests of the Parties to the conflict'[95] and ensures the implementation of IHL.[96] In this connection, the Protecting Power can be empowered to, *inter alia*, visit detainees,[97] supervise the distribution of relief,[98] including in occupied territory,[99] and transmit information and documents.[100] In practice, however, Protecting Powers have only been appointed five times since 1949, because states rarely agree to third state supervision in armed conflict.[101] Perhaps anticipating this challenge, IHL provides for the possibility of entrusting 'to an organization which offers all guarantees of impartiality and

[90] Yves Sandoz, Christophe Swinarski, and Bruno Zimmermann (eds), *Commentary on the Additional Protocols of 8 June 1977 to the Geneva Conventions of 12 August 1949* (Martinus Nijhoff 1987) paras 3304–05.

[91] ibid, para 3331.

[92] GCIV (n 15) art 63.

[93] See generally, Michael A. Meyer, 'Humanitarian Action: A Delicate Balancing Act' (1987) 27 International Review of the Red Cross 485, 488–89.

[94] GCs (n 15) arts 8/8/8/9; API (n 16) art 5.

[95] GCs (n 15) arts 8(1)/8(1)/8(1)/9(1).

[96] API (n 16) art 5(1).

[97] GCIII (n 15) art 126; GCIV (n 15) art 143.

[98] API (n 16) art 70(3)(b).

[99] GCIV (n 15) art 59.

[100] ibid, art 137.

[101] Crawford and Pert (n 22) 304.

efficacy the duties incumbent on the Protecting Powers'.[102] The ICRC is specifically mentioned in this regard,[103] though this is 'without prejudice to the right of any other impartial humanitarian organization to [. . .] offer its good offices'.[104] The ICRC has, however, been reluctant to take on the Protecting Power role because it can fulfil most Protecting Power functions in its own right,[105] by relying on the provisions outlined in this section.

4. Emergency relief operations

Emergency relief operations respond to acute need among the civilian population. Also termed 'relief schemes' (in the GCs),[106] 'relief actions' (in the APs),[107] and 'humanitarian relief operations' (in most doctrine),[108] these operations refer to the 'provision of supplies and services that are exclusively humanitarian in nature and essential to the survival of the civilian population, such as food, water, medical supplies, clothing and means of shelter'.[109] The legal framework governing emergency relief operations in IAC (including occupation) consists primarily of articles 59 to 61 of GCIV and articles 69 to 71 of API.[110] In NIAC, the relevant law consists of Common Article 3(2) and article 18(2) of APII. CIHL applies alongside these treaty provisions in both IAC and NIAC and, critically for states not party to the APs, largely mirrors the AP rules.[111]

While there are minor variations in the treaty rules applicable in IAC other than occupation, occupation, and NIAC—these variations and the rules' details are addressed in Sections 4.3 and 4.4—in general the rules on emergency relief operations provide that where a conflict party is unable or unwilling to meet its primary responsibility to provide for the civilians within its control, third states and impartial humanitarian organizations may offer to conduct emergency relief operations. For the latter, this is in line with their right of initiative, discussed in Section 3 above.[112] Such operations proceed in two steps. At step one, the humanitarian actor seeks consent from the conflict party in control of the civilians in need.[113] This consent is 'the initial and general authorisation to carry out operations in a particular country';[114] it is

[102] GCs (n 15) arts 10(1)/10(1)/10(1)/11(1); see also API (n 16) art 5(3).
[103] GCs (n 15) arts 10(3)/10(3)/10(3)/11(3).
[104] API (n 16) art 5(3).
[105] Crawford and Pert (n 22) 304.
[106] GCIV (n 15) art 59(1).
[107] API (n 16) art 70; APII (n 16) art 18.
[108] On the decision to use 'emergency relief operations' instead of 'humanitarian relief operations', see Sections 1.3 and 3.
[109] Emanuela-Chiara Gillard, 'The Law Regulating Cross-Border Relief Operations' (2013) 95 International Review of the Red Cross 351, 352.
[110] Note, API article 70 does not apply to occupied territory.
[111] Henckaerts and Doswald-Beck (n 18) rules 31, 32, 55, and 56; see also Oxford Guidance (n 47) para 6. Rules 31, 32, 55, and 56 are cited in full in Section 4.4.5 and Appendix II.
[112] GCIV (n 15) arts 3(2) and 10.
[113] API (n 16) art 70(1); APII (n 16) art 18(2); Henckaerts and Doswald-Beck (n 18) 196–97.
[114] UK Foreign, Commonwealth & Development Office and Ministry of Defence, 'Conflict, Hunger and International Humanitarian Law: A Practitioner's Legal Handbook' (2025) <https://www.gov.uk/government/publications/conflict-hunger-and-international-humanitarian-law-a-practitioners-legal-handbook> accessed 23 May 2025 (Conflict & Hunger Handbook) 70.

often termed 'strategic' consent.[115] While strategic consent is required, it may not be—arbitrarily or unlawfully[116]—withheld.[117] After strategic consent has been obtained, practical implementation begins. At this second step, conflict parties must allow and facilitate the rapid and unimpeded passage of relief supplies, equipment, and personnel throughout their territory—often shortened to the 'obligation to allow and facilitate'—subject to their right of control.[118] The exercise of this right of control is sometimes termed 'operational consent'.[119] Conflict parties must also respect and protect emergency relief operations,[120] including their personnel.[121]

Article 23 of GCIV also bears mentioning. It was adopted to ensure the free passage through sieges and blockades of medical supplies and religious objects, as well as certain essential items, such as food, destined for certain vulnerable civilians (children under fifteen, pregnant women, and maternity cases); it covers humanitarian assistance as well as commercial goods.[122] Paragraph 2 of article 23, however, effectively relieves the relevant conflict party of its free passage obligation if it has 'serious reasons for fearing' that the relief in question will be diverted, not controlled effectively, or that it will provide the enemy with a definite advantage through the substitution of relief consignments 'for goods which would otherwise be provided or produced by the enemy or through the release of such material, services or facilities as would otherwise be required for the production of such goods'. This exception 'virtually allows the blockage of any relief action'.[123] API articles 69–71 now supplement GCIV article 23 (among other articles),[124] such that today, this more comprehensive and protective set of API provisions are widely viewed as having superseded GCIV article 23.[125] Article 23 is thus addressed here only where it is directly relevant, namely in Sections 5.1 on medical relief operations and 5.2 on food relief operations.

4.1. Practical modalities and arrangements

Emergency relief operations proceed according to three distinct modalities: cross-border, cross-line, or without crossing either. Cross-border operations originate in a

115 Matthias Vanhullebusch, 'Do Non-State Armed Groups Have a Legal Right to Consent to Offers of International Humanitarian Relief?' (2020) 25 Journal of Conflict & Security Law 317, 321.
116 See Sections 4.3.1 and 6.1.
117 Oxford Guidance (n 47) para 22; Henckaerts and Doswald-Beck (n 18) 196–97.
118 API (n 16) art 70(2–3); GCIV (n 15) arts 59 and 61; Henckaerts and Doswald-Beck (n 18) rules 55–56.
119 Vanhullebusch (n 115) 321.
120 API (n 16) art 70(4); GCIV (n 15) art 59(3).
121 API (n 16) art 71; Henckaerts and Doswald-Beck (n 18) rule 31.
122 Pictet and others (n 54) 178–79.
123 Sandoz and others (n 90) para 2850.
124 API (n 16) art 68.
125 Michael Bothe, Karl Josef Partsch, and Waldemar Solf (eds), *New Rules for Victims of Armed Conflicts: Commentary on the Two 1977 Protocols Additional to the Geneva Conventions of 1949* (Martinus Nijhoff 1982) 429; Sandoz and others (n 90) paras 2813–15 and 2848–51; Dapo Akande and Emanuela-Chiara Gillard, 'Promoting Compliance with the Rules Regulating Humanitarian Relief Operations in Armed Conflict: Some Challenges' (2017) 50 Israel Law Review 119, 128; Dapo Akande and Emanuela-Chiara Gillard, 'Conflict-induced Food Insecurity and the War Crime of Starvation of Civilians as a Method of Warfare: The Underlying Rules of International Humanitarian Law' (2019) 17 Journal of International Criminal Justice 753, 772.

country near the affected state.[126] They are used either because the most direct access route to civilians in need crosses an international border, as in Operation Lifeline Sudan from Kenya in the early 1990s, or because the affected state has refused to consent to operations for civilians in opposition territory, as was the case in Biafra in 1968 and in Syria from 2013.[127] By operating via an air bridge from São Tomé into Biafra and from points in Iraq, Jordan, and Türkiye into north-west Syria, humanitarian actors were able to reach civilians in need without setting foot in territory controlled by the governments of Nigeria or Syria.[128] Cross-line operations traverse the frontlines of armed conflict, moving relief from territory controlled by one belligerent into territory controlled by another. Emergency relief operations may equally cross neither borders nor conflict lines.

One or more of a range of practical arrangements may be used to facilitate an emergency relief operation and/or enhance its security.[129] These include humanitarian corridors, airdrops, protected zones, humanitarian notifications,[130] temporary ceasefires, and no-fly zones. The first three are addressed below; note, however, that while each is often used in emergency relief operations in armed conflict, they may also be employed in other contexts.

Humanitarian corridors, also termed 'relief corridors' or 'safe corridors', tend to be used when emergency relief operations take place in areas where hostilities are active. They were introduced in 1990 by the UN Secretary-General[131] and endorsed by the General Assembly later that same year.[132] The Secretary-General defined 'humanitarian corridor' in his 2012 Report on the Protection of Civilians in Armed Conflict as 'specific routes and logistical methods agreed upon by all relevant parties to allow the safe passage of humanitarian goods and/or people from one point to another in an area of active fighting'.[133] The report further specified that the corridor itself is 'typically a geographic route, often with a specified time frame'.[134] It lists the measures required to give effect to a humanitarian corridor: agreement by all relevant parties as to the use and conditions of the corridor; clear instructions to all relevant parties regarding the corridor's purpose, route, and time frame; and, regarding corridors for the delivery of relief, arrangements to facilitate the passage of humanitarian personnel

[126] See, generally, UNGA Res 43/131 (8 December 1988) A/RES/43/131, para 6; UNGA Res 45/100 (14 December 1990) A/RES/45/100 (Res 45/100) para 7.

[127] Hugo Slim and Emanuela-Chiara Gillard, 'Ethical and Legal Perspectives on Cross-Border Humanitarian Operations' [2013] Humanitarian Practice Network 6.

[128] The Syria case is discussed further in Chapter 5, Section 4.4.2.

[129] See Emanuela-Chiara Gillard, 'Enhancing the Security of Civilians in Conflict: Notifications, Evacuations, Humanitarian Corridors, Suspensions of Hostilities and Other Humanitarian Arrangements' (*Chatham House*, 30 April 2024) <https://www.chathamhouse.org/2024/04/enhancing-security-civilians-conflict> accessed 12 July 2024.

[130] Humanitarian notification arrangements are 'a voluntary system whereby humanitarian organizations share information, in a structured manner, with parties to an armed conflict on the location of facilities used for their operations, such as warehouses and offices, as well as on their movements, such as humanitarian convoys' (Gillard (n 129) 7).

[131] UN Secretary-General, 'Humanitarian Assistance to Victims of Natural Disasters and Similar Emergency Situations: Report of the Secretary-General' (24 October 1990) A/45/587, para 26.

[132] Res 45/100 (n 126) para 6.

[133] UNSC 'Report of the Secretary-General on the Protection of Civilians in Armed Conflict' (2012) S/2012/376, para 61.

[134] ibid.

and supplies through the corridor.[135] Examples of humanitarian corridors include the 'corridors of tranquility' through which Operation Lifeline Sudan relief passed in 1989,[136] and the land routes into north-west Syria authorized by the Security Council from 2014 to 2023.[137] Gillard explains that humanitarian organizations do not favour humanitarian corridors because they 'significantly restrict their activities and freedom of movement well beyond what is envisaged by IHL',[138] and notes that when stakeholders call for the creation of humanitarian corridors, often 'what is actually needed is better humanitarian access'.[139]

Airdrops are a rarely used delivery arrangement in which supplies are dropped into an area of severe need from planes, typically military aircraft. Relief is placed on pallets and secured with netting; the pallets are then attached to parachutes and pushed from the rear of aircraft.[140] This delivery method was first used by the UN in the Western Sahel region of Africa in 1973;[141] it has since been used in places such as Sri Lanka[142] and Gaza.[143] Airdrops are a last resort delivery arrangement, used only when others are insufficient or impossible, for several reasons. They are expensive, costing roughly eleven times as much per commodity compared to assistance delivered by truck.[144] They can only deliver small amounts of relief and limited types of aid, because of aircraft capacity restrictions, the expertise required to pilot planes, and the risk of certain items, like medicines, being destroyed by landing impact.[145] Airdrops can also be dangerous. Relief pallets of food can weigh up to 1,200 pounds, or 2,000 pounds if they include water; five Palestinians were killed by airdrops in Gaza in 2024.[146] Finally, airdrops mean there is no staff to manage delivery. Some of the July 2025 Gaza airdrops provoked 'chaos and violence' as people rushed to obtain supplies, and individuals on the ground took control of at least one drop site and began selling the aid; other drops landed in unsafe places or were lost.[147]

The idea to protect civilians from armed conflict at fixed locations emerged in 1929 when the French Surgeon-General proposed the creation of 'Geneva places' for non-combatants.[148] Since then, a range of other terms have been used to describe the same

135 ibid.
136 Gillard (n 129) 30.
137 See Chapter 5, Section 4.4.2.
138 Gillard (n 129) 32.
139 ibid, 37.
140 Pranav Baskar, 'Why Airdrops in Gaza Are Seen as a Risky Last Resort' (*The Seattle Times*, 29 July 2025) <https://www.seattletimes.com/nation-world/why-airdrops-in-gaza-are-seen-as-a-risky-last-resort/> accessed 30 July 2025.
141 Simona Beltrami, 'Humanitarian Airdrops: Light at the End of the Tunnel' (*WFP*, 14 July 2021) <https://www.wfp.org/stories/airdrops-humanitarian-emergency-un-world-food-programme-sudan-syria> accessed 28 July 2025.
142 Paul Costa and Peter Evans, 'The Indian Supply Drop into Sri Lanka: Nonmilitary Humanitarian Aid and the Troubling Idea of Intervention' (1988) 3 Connecticut Journal of International Law 417.
143 Aaron Boxerman, 'Israel to Allow Airdrops of Aid Amid Starvation' *The New York Times* (New York, 26 July 2025) A1. For details of the Sri Lanka and Gaza examples, see Chapter 7, Section 3.2.
144 Baskar (n 140).
145 ibid.
146 ibid.
147 Hasan Jaber and Janice Dickson, 'Gazans Describe Scenes of Chaos, Violence as Israel Allows Airdrops of Aid' (*The Globe and Mail*, 28 July 2025) <https://www.theglobeandmail.com/world/article-gaza-israel-airdrop-aid-supplies-food/> accessed 29 July 2025.
148 Karin Landgren, 'Safety Zones and International Protection: A Dark Grey Area' (1995) 7 International Journal of Refugee Law 442, 439.

idea: protected space, protection of civilians site, safe area, safe haven, safe zone, safety zone, security zone, and temporary security zone, among others. This discussion uses 'protected zone'; while not used in IHL, it is often used in discussions based on IHL because it reflects 'the reality that even if established and accorded special protection in law the areas might not in fact provide security to those sheltering there'.[149]

A protected zone is a place in a state experiencing armed conflict where civilians can gather for security and to receive humanitarian assistance. They are established by agreement among the conflict parties, are free of belligerent activity, and are open to all nationalities—including nationals of the conflict party opposed to the party on whose territory the zone is located. The conflict party administering the protected zone has a range of responsibilities. It must ensure that conditions respect fundamental guarantees of humane treatment under IHL,[150] as well as reception standards for evacuated and displaced persons.[151] In addition, if administration of the zone gives rise to effective control over the individuals sheltering there, the state has human rights obligations,[152] including in relation to food, water, shelter, health,[153] and the rights to life and security of the person.[154]

GCIV contemplates three different types of protected zone. Hospital zones and localities protect wounded and sick civilians,[155] and safety zones and localities are for certain vulnerable civilians, namely 'aged persons, children under fifteen, expectant mothers and mothers of children under seven'.[156] According to Gillard, 'it seems safe to assume that all civilians may seek shelter in [. . . safety] zones and localities, provided they do not pose' a threat.[157] Both hospital zones and localities and safety zones and localities are typically relatively permanent and located far from active hostilities.[158] Underlining the importance of agreement among the conflict parties on the establishment of protected zones, GCIV includes a draft model agreement for the establishment of hospital and safety zones and localities.[159]

GCIV also provides for 'neutralized zones' for the wounded and sick (whether military or civilian) and civilians who take no part in hostilities.[160] These zones are 'used

[149] Gillard (n 129) 46.

[150] GCs (n 15) Common Article 3; APII (n 16) art 75(1).

[151] See Section 5.4.

[152] Gillard (n 129) 51.

[153] International Covenant on Economic, Social and Cultural Rights (adopted 16 December 1966, entered into force 3 January 1976) 993 UNTS 3 (ICESCR) arts 11 and 12, read with: Committee on Economic, Social and Cultural Rights (CESCR), 'General Comment No. 4: The Right to Adequate Housing (Art. 11(1) of the Covenant)' (1991) E/1992/23; CESCR, 'General Comment No. 12: The Right to Adequate Food (Art. 11)' (12 May 1999) E/C.12/1999/5, paras 15, 17, 19, and 38; CESCR, 'General Comment No. 15: The Right to Water (Arts. 11 and 12 of the Covenant)' (20 January 2002) E/C.12/2002/11, para 25; CESCR, 'General Comment No. 14: The Right to the Highest Attainable Standard of Health (Art. 12)' (11 August 2000) E/C.12/2000/4, para 40.

[154] International Covenant on Civil and Political Rights (adopted 16 December 1966, entered into force 23 March 1976) 999 UNTS 171 (ICCPR) arts 6(1) and 9(1), read with Human Rights Committee, 'General Comment No. 6: Article 6 (Right to Life)' (30 April 1982) HR1/GEN/1/Rev.9, para 5.

[155] GCIV (n 15) art 14.

[156] ibid.

[157] Emanuela-Chiara Gillard, '"Safe Areas": The International Legal Framework' (2017) 99 International Review of the Red Cross 1075, 1079.

[158] ibid, 1082.

[159] See ibid, 1080–81.

[160] GCIV (n 15) art 15.

as quick temporary solutions when hostilities pose an immediate and serious risk to these individuals'.[161] They are typically temporary and located in conflict areas.[162] Gillard notes that the GCs' draft model agreements for the establishment of hospital and safety zones and localities can also be used to establish neutralized zones, particularly because these are located near active hostilities.[163] Despite the distinct forms of protected zones provided for by GCIV, in practice, the various types 'are likely to be combined, accommodating wounded and sick civilians and members of the armed forces, as well as other vulnerable people'.[164]

API added an additional type of protected zone:[165] the demilitarized zone (DMZ).[166] This is an area that may not be used by military forces or for military purposes.[167] The DMZ is similar to the GCIV notion of a neutralized zone, but while GCIV foresees 'the establishment of [neutralized] zones to which civilians and the wounded and sick can relocate, demilitarized zones operate by "fencing off" areas from military operations for the protection of all civilians'.[168] The agreement to establish a DMZ may be verbal or written and may be negotiated directly or through an impartial humanitarian organization;[169] in practice, the ICRC is usually involved.[170] Article 60(2) describes the elements a DMZ agreement should include: its boundaries and any methods of supervision. While both the API DMZ and the additional protected zones contemplated by GCIV relate exclusively to IAC, they may equally be established by agreement in NIAC, in line with Common Article 3's call for parties to NIAC to 'endeavour to bring into force, by means of special agreements, all or part of the other' GC provisions.

Classic IHL protected zones have only been used a handful of times since their codification in 1949. This is largely due to the difficulty of reaching agreement among belligerents. Safety zones were created in Dhaka in 1971 and Phnom Penh in 1975.[171] Neutralized zones were established in Nicosia in 1974, Saigon in 1975, for hospital ships at sea during the 1982 Falklands/Malvinas conflict (called the 'Red Cross Box'),[172]

[161] Michael Schmitt, 'Ukraine Symposium: Protected Zones in International Humanitarian Law' (*Articles of War*, 24 August 2022) <lieber.westpoint.edu/protected-zones-international-humanitarian-law> accessed 10 August 2023.

[162] Gillard (n 157) 1082.

[163] ibid.

[164] ibid, 1079.

[165] See, generally, Yves Sandoz, 'The Establishment of Safety Zones for Persons Displaced within their Country of Origin' in Najeeb Al-Nuaimi and Richard Meese (eds), *International Legal Issues Arising under the United Nations Decade of International Law* (Martinus Nijhoff 1995).

[166] API (n 16) art 60. API also provides, at article 59, for 'non-defended localities'. These have not been used recently (Gillard (n 157) 1082).

[167] API (n 16) art 60(3).

[168] Gillard (n 157) 1083.

[169] API (n 16) art 60(2).

[170] Schmitt (n 161).

[171] Landgren (n 148) 440.

[172] GCII does not provide for neutralized zones at sea. However, the San Remo Manual on International Law Applicable to Armed Conflict at Sea (San Remo Manual) indicates that conflict parties 'may agree, for humanitarian purposes, to create a zone in a defined area of the sea in which only activities consistent with those humanitarian purposes are permitted' (Louise Doswald-Beck, *San Remo Manual on International Law Applicable to Armed Conflict at Sea* (International Institute of Humanitarian Law 1995) para 160). The Red Cross Box was established by unwritten agreement between the conflict parties.

in Vukovar in 1991,[173] and in Dubrovnik in 1992.[174] Protected zones were used in Nicaragua in 1979 and Chad in 1980,[175] however, it is not clear how these were characterized. A DMZ was established in Côte d'Ivoire in 2003, though it was termed a 'zone of confidence'.[176]

In addition to these limited uses in their strict IHL senses, protected zones have also been established without the agreement of conflict parties, either pursuant to agreements among other relevant actors or by the UN Security Council. When the Security Council establishes protected zones, it is typically pursuant to Chapter VII so the zone's safety can (theoretically) be guaranteed by the threat or use of force by coalition forces or peacekeepers.[177] For example, in 1993 the Security Council established 'safe areas' under Chapter VII in six locations (including Srebrenica) in Bosnia and Herzegovina.[178] Protected zones may also emerge spontaneously as civilians congregate in places they expect will be secure, such as hospitals and UN compounds. For example, this occurred in South Sudan in 2013, when violence led civilians to gather in or near UNMISS bases. The Security Council subsequently gave UNMISS a Chapter VII mandate to protect these locations,[179] which became known as 'protection of civilians sites'.

The 1995 Srebrenica massacre, in which at least 7,000 Bosnian Muslim men and boys were killed by Bosnian Serb forces in the Srebrenica safe area, demonstrates that the threat or use of force does not necessarily ensure the safety of protected zones. In fact, it can 'compromise the safety of the zone, politicise its existence, and complicate humanitarian access'.[180] There is a clear consensus that the most effective way to guarantee the safety of a protected zone is to follow the IHL model,[181] which entails obtaining the conflict parties' consent to the creation of the zone and ensuring its civilian character.[182]

[173] Tristan Ferraro, Presentation to the IIHL's 46th Roundtable on Current Issues of International Humanitarian Law, 15 September 2023, San Remo, Italy.

[174] Landgren (n 148) 440.

[175] Jérémie Labbé, 'Are Safe Areas a Viable Way Out of the Humanitarian Deadlock in Syria?' (*IPI Global Observatory*, 30 August 2012) <https://theglobalobservatory.org/2012/08/are-safe-areas-a-viable-way-out-of-the-humanitarian-deadlock-in-syria> accessed 21 July 2023.

[176] Ferraro presentation (n 173).

[177] See Bruce Oswald, 'The Creation and Control of Places of Protection during United Nations Peace Operations' (2001) 83 International Review of the Red Cross 1013.

[178] Designation of Srebrenica: UNSC Res 819 (16 April 1993) S/RES/819, para 1; Designation of Sarajevo, Tuzla, Zepa, Gorazde and Bihac: UNSC Res 824 (6 May 1993) S/RES/824, para 3. In June 1993, the Security Council gave UNPROFOR a mandate to use force to defend these safe areas (UNSC Res 836 (4 June 1993) S/RES/836, para 5).

[179] UNSC Res 2155 (27 May 2014) S/RES/2155, para 4.

[180] Landgren (n 148) 442.

[181] See, for example, Landgren (n 148); Jennifer Hyndman, 'Preventive, Palliative or Punitive? Safe Spaces in Bosnia-Herzegovina, Somalia and Sri Lanka' (2003) 16 Journal of Refugee Studies 167; Labbé (n 175); Nathalie Weizmann, 'Trump's "Safe Areas" in Syria—An Explainer on International Law' (*Just Security*, 27 January 2017) <https://www.justsecurity.org/36889/trumps-safe-areas-syria-explainer-international-law> accessed 24 July 2023; Gillard (n 157); Gillard (n 129) 54.

[182] The Centre of Competence on Humanitarian Negotiation has identified 'essential lessons' for the negotiation of protected zones: see 'Six Essential Lessons to Remember while Negotiating "Safe Zones"' (*Frontline Negotiations*, 17 October 2023) <https://frontline-negotiations.org/blog-essential-lessons-negotiating-safe-zones/> accessed 17 October 2023.

While distinct modalities and arrangements may raise different legal, practical, and security issues, whether an emergency relief operation crosses a border, a conflict line, or neither, and whether it uses a humanitarian corridor, airdrops, or a protected zone, does not affect the legal framework of emergency relief operations. The evolution in understanding of this framework is addressed below.

4.2. Evolution

There was a significant shift in knowledge of the rules on emergency relief operations during the 2010s. This shift stemmed from practical humanitarian access challenges that arose after 11 September 2001 as a result of counterterrorism measures,[183] and worsened over time to include a range of other constraints on access. Access constraints can be divided into two categories: strategic and operational. The former are linked to step one in the legal framework outlined above, while operational factors are linked to the step two obligation to allow and facilitate passage. Strategic constraints include denial by the conflict party concerned of humanitarian need or of its duty to respond to such need by consenting to external assistance. Operational factors include bureaucratic impediments to the entry of supplies, equipment, and personnel; restrictions on or interference with the movement of supplies, equipment, and personnel within the affected state, including because of ongoing military operations; environmental constraints, such as a lack of passable roads, clean water, and communications infrastructure;[184] and insecurity, including from military operations.[185]

In practice, most humanitarian access challenges are operational. For example, the most recent report of the Independent International Fact-Finding Mission for the Sudan found that humanitarian organizations there are facing a range of operational access challenges, including delays in processing staff visa applications and authorizing internal movement.[186] New registration guidelines for international NGOs promulgated by Israel in March 2025 include 'broad and sweeping grounds for denying or revoking registration and work permits'.[187]

However, strategic access constraints became increasingly common in the early 2010s, prompting a response from the UN Secretary-General. In response to difficulties reaching civilians in need in armed conflicts in Sudan and Syria,[188] in 2013

[183] See Chapter 5, Section 4.4.3.

[184] Swiss Federal Department of Foreign Affairs, 'Humanitarian Access in Situations of Armed Conflict: Practitioners' Manual' (version 2, 2014) <https://reliefweb.int/report/world/humanitarian-access-situations-armed-conflict-handbook-international-normative> accessed 16 Nov 2023, 146-50.

[185] Romaric Ferraro, 'Challenges to Implementation of Humanitarian Access Norms in the Sahel' (2021) 103 International Review of the Red Cross 859, 871–72.

[186] Human Rights Council, 'Findings of the Investigations Conducted by the Independent International Fact-Finding Mission for the Sudan into Violations of International Human Rights Law and International Humanitarian Law, and Related Crimes, Committed in the Sudan in the Context of the Conflict that Erupted in mid-April 2023' (23 October 2024) A/HRC/57/CRP.6, para 281.

[187] Eitan Diamond, 'New Israeli Guidelines Threaten to Eliminate Humanitarian Action in the Occupied Palestinian Territory Almost Entirely' (*Just Security*, 8 April 2025) <https://www.justsecurity.org/109772/israel-humanitarian-ngo-guidelines/> accessed 4 May 2025.

[188] UNSC, 'Report of the Secretary-General on the Protection of Civilians in Armed Conflict' (22 November 2013) S/2013/689, para 57.

Secretary-General Ban Ki-moon underlined the 'continued failure of many parties to comply with' their obligation not to 'arbitrarily' withhold consent to relief operations.[189] He identified the need for further 'analysis and development' of the law in this area[190] and called on the UN Office for the Coordination of Humanitarian Affairs (OCHA) to engage stakeholders 'to examine the relevant rules' on 'the issue of arbitrary withholding of consent to relief operations and the consequences thereof'.[191] OCHA in turn convened a group of experts, led by University of Oxford scholars Dapo Akande and Emanuela-Chiara Gillard.[192] Then, in 2014, while the experts' work was ongoing, the Security Council responded to Syria's ongoing refusal to consent to assistance for civilians in its opposition-held north-west with an unprecedented decision imposing relief.[193] The outcome of the OCHA-convened work, now widely known as the Oxford Guidance, was published in 2016, with a disclaimer that it does not represent the official position of OCHA or the UN.[194] However, OCHA has subsequently described IHL on emergency relief operations using the same framing as the Oxford Guidance and with explicit reference to this Guidance.[195] Akande and Gillard subsequently published several scholarly articles that further analysed issues raised in the Oxford Guidance.[196]

While the current law on emergency relief operations has existed since the APs were adopted in 1977 and there is analysis of it predating the Secretary-General's 2013 call,[197] the developments outlined above, as well as a 'Lexicon' published by the ICRC in 2014,[198] have contributed significantly to understanding of the law on emergency relief operations. The Oxford Guidance is particularly valuable for its clear

[189] ibid, para 58.

[190] ibid.

[191] ibid, para 80.

[192] Oxford Guidance (n 47) 5.

[193] UNSC Res 2165 (14 July 2014) S/RES/2165, para 2. See Chapter 5, Section 4.4.2.

[194] On the legal status of the Oxford Guidance, see Rogier Bartels, 'Oxford Guidance on Relief Operations: Comments on Arbitrarily Withholding Consent and the Status of the Guidance' (*Just Security*, 15 December 2016) <https://www.justsecurity.org/35561/oxford-guidance-law-relating-humanitarian-relief-operations-situations-armed-conflict-comments-arbitrarily-withholding-consent-status-guidance/> accessed 16 May 2023.

[195] OCHA, 'Humanitarian Relief Operations in Armed Conflict: IHL Framework' (10 January 2019) <https://www.unocha.org/publications/report/world/humanitarian-relief-operations-armed-conflict-ihl-framework> accessed 15 May 2025.

[196] Dapo Akande and Emanuela-Chiara Gillard, 'Arbitrary Withholding of Consent to Humanitarian Relief Operations in Armed Conflict' (2016) 92 International Law Studies 483; Akande and Gillard 2017 (n 125); Akande and Gillard 2019 (n 125).

[197] See, for example, Charles Allen, 'Civilian Starvation and Relief During Armed Conflict: The Modern Humanitarian Law' (1989) 19 Georgia Journal of International & Comparative Law 1, 69–77; Katja Luopajärvi, 'Is There an Obligation on States to Accept International Humanitarian Assistance to Internally Displaced Persons under International Law?' (2003) 15 International Journal of Refugee Law 689; Rebecca Barber, 'Facilitating Humanitarian Assistance in International Humanitarian and Human Rights Law' (2009) 91 International Review of the Red Cross 371. See also the outputs of a Swiss initiative launched in 2009: Swiss Federal Department of Foreign Affairs, 'Humanitarian Access in Situations of Armed Conflict: Handbook on the International Normative Framework' (version 2, 2014) <https://reliefweb.int/report/world/humanitarian-access-situations-armed-conflict-handbook-international-normative> accessed 16 May 2023 and note 184; the normative framework manual is summarized in: Felix Schwendimann, 'The Legal Framework of Humanitarian Access in Armed Conflict' (2011) 93 International Review of the Red Cross 993.

[198] ICRC Lexicon (n 41); see also ICRC, 'Report: International Humanitarian Law and the Challenges of Contemporary Armed Conflicts' (2015) 32IC/15/11 (Challenges Report 2015) 26–30.

two-step—consent followed by implementation—framing of the rules. And while the Oxford Guidance, Akande and Gillard's related scholarly work, and the ICRC Lexicon are leading authorities, access challenges in Syria prompted a wave of scholarship on the law of emergency relief operations.[199]

The 2010s thus represented a turning point for the understanding and framing of the law on emergency relief operations. Prior to this decade, the first 'consent' step of these operations did not receive much or accurate attention. The requirement of consent features in both APs[200] and the interpretation that it cannot be arbitrarily withheld is—as will be shown in Section 4.3.1 below—traceable to the diplomatic conference where the Protocols were adopted and to early primary and secondary sources. Yet, in practice, consent was often framed as discretionary, with the focus on the step two obligation to allow and facilitate passage. For example, the UN Secretary-General's 2009 Report on the Protection of Civilians in Armed Conflict describes conflict parties' step one obligation as one in which they '*should* agree to relief operations that are humanitarian and impartial in character and conducted without any adverse distinction'.[201] Additionally, Henckaerts and Doswald-Beck note that the practice collected for the ICRC's CIHL study mostly does not mention consent.[202]

Before the 2010s, scholars and civil society actors attempted to explain or develop the law by focusing on the right of civilians to receive humanitarian assistance and the right of humanitarian actors to provide it,[203] without addressing the corresponding

[199] Cedric Ryngaert, 'Humanitarian Assistance and the Conundrum of Consent: A Legal Perspective' (2013) 5 Amsterdam Law Forum 5; Keiichiro Okimoto, 'Humanitarian Activities Carried Out Across Borders in Times of Armed Conflict' in Terry Gill and others (eds), *Yearbook of International Humanitarian Law 2014*, vol 17 (Springer 2016); Rodenhäuser and Giacca (n 80); Tom Gal, 'Territorial Control by Armed Groups and the Regulation of Access to Humanitarian Assistance' (2017) 50 Israel Law Review 25; Michael Bothe, 'Shedding Light on the Rules of Humanitarian Access: Reflections on the Occasion of the 40th Anniversary of the Protocols Additional to the Geneva Conventions' in Fausto Pocar (ed), *The Additional Protocols 40 Years Later: New Conflicts, New Actors, New Perspectives* (FrancoAngeli 2018); Ferraro (n 70); Eve Massingham and Kelisiana Thynne, 'Humanitarian Relief Operations' in Dapo Akande and Ben Saul (eds), *The Oxford Guide to International Humanitarian Law* (OUP 2020); Knut Dörmann and Tristan Ferraro, 'Humanitarian Assistance' in Dieter Fleck (ed), *The Handbook of International Humanitarian Law* (4th edn, OUP 2021); Emanuela-Chiara Gillard and Nathalie Weizmann, 'Humanitarian Relief in Situations of Armed Conflict' in Robin Geiß and Nils Melzer (eds), *The Oxford Handbook of the International Law of Global Security* (OUP 2021); Matthias Vanhullebusch, *The Law of International Humanitarian Relief in Non-International Armed Conflicts* (Brill 2021).

[200] API (n 16) art 70(1); APII (n 16) art 18(2).

[201] UNSC 'Report of the Secretary-General on the Protection of Civilians in Armed Conflict' (29 May 2009) S/2009/277, para 58 (emphasis added). By contrast, in the same paragraph the Secretary-General notes that parties '*must* allow and facilitate rapid and unimpeded passage of relief consignments' (emphasis added).

[202] Henckaerts and Doswald-Beck (n 18) 196.

[203] See, for example, Michael Bothe, 'Relief Actions' in Rudolf Bernhardt (ed), *Encyclopedia of Public International Law*, vol 1 (North-Holland 1982) 173; Boško Jakovljević, 'The Right to Humanitarian Assistance: Legal Aspects' (1987) 27 International Review of the Red Cross 469; Yves Beigbeder, *The Role and Status of International Humanitarian Volunteers and Organizations: The Right and Duty to Humanitarian Assistance* (Martinus Nijhoff 1991); Mario Bettati, 'Right of Humanitarian Intervention or the Right of Free Access to Victims?' (1992) 49 International Commission of Jurists Review 1; Yves Sandoz, '"*Droit*" or "*devoir d'ingérence*" and the Right to Assistance: the Issues Involved' (1992) 32 International Review of the Red Cross 215; Peter MacAlister-Smith, 'The Right to Humanitarian Assistance in International Law' (1998) 66 Revue de droit international de science diplomatiques et politiques 211; Yoram Dinstein, 'The Right to Humanitarian Assistance' (2000) 53 Naval War College Review 77; Joakim Dungel, 'A Right to Humanitarian Assistance in Internal Armed Conflicts Respecting Sovereignty, Neutrality and Legitimacy: Practical Proposals to Practical Problems' [2004] Journal of Humanitarian Assistance; Ruth

duties of the affected state. For instance, in 1993 the International Institute of Humanitarian Law (IIHL) in San Remo adopted the Guiding Principles on the Right to Humanitarian Assistance (the San Remo Principles). The San Remo Principles articulate the 'right to humanitarian assistance'[204] as 'the right to request and to receive such assistance, as well as to participate in its practical implementation.'[205] However, the Principles only note that the 'authorities of the States concerned, in the exercise of their sovereign rights, *should* extend their cooperation concerning the offer of humanitarian assistance.'[206] The San Remo Principles go on to note that when an offer of assistance is refused, 'the States and organizations concerned may undertake all necessary steps to ensure [...] access';[207] the steps focus on enforcement action by the Security Council and regional organizations, rather than on the duties of the affected state.[208] The current framing, based on the obligations of the affected conflict party rather than on inchoate rights, was not widely used by stakeholders until the Oxford Guidance and ICRC Lexicon were published and the Security Council adopted its Syria decision.

One result of better knowledge of the law on emergency relief operations was an increased role for diplomacy in securing humanitarian access. While IHL may figure little in real world humanitarian access negotiations,[209] once it became widely known that the conflict party in control of civilians in need cannot withhold consent to assistance for them in contravention of international law, third states became stronger advocates for humanitarian access. Gillard notes that the Syria experience led Security Council members supportive of the decision to impose relief on Syria 'to systematically emphasise the need for consent.'[210] Among the political commitments made at the 2016 World Humanitarian Summit,[211] Austria, Belgium, France, New Zealand, and Spain all committed to using 'their leverage and influence to prevent and end any

Abril Stoffels, 'Legal Regulation of Humanitarian Assistance in Armed Conflict: Achievements and Gaps' (2004) 86 International Review of the Red Cross 515; Henckaerts and Doswald-Beck (n 18) 199–200; David Fisher, 'The Right to Humanitarian Assistance' (2010) 41 Studies in Transnational Legal Policy 47; Heike Spieker, 'The Right to Give and Receive Humanitarian Assistance' in Hans-Joachim Heintze and Andrej Zwitter (eds), *International Law and Humanitarian Assistance: A Crosscut Through Legal Issues Pertaining to Humanitarianism* (Springer 2011).

204 International Institute of Humanitarian Law, 'Guiding Principles on the Right to Humanitarian Assistance' (1993) 33 International Review of the Red Cross 519 (San Remo Principles) principle 1, which provides that '[e]very human being has the right to humanitarian assistance in order to ensure respect for the human rights to life, health, protection against cruel and degrading treatment and other human rights which are essential to survival, well-being and protection in public emergencies.'

205 San Remo Principles (n 204) principle 2.

206 ibid, principle 5 (emphasis added).

207 ibid, principle 6.

208 ibid, principles 7 and 8.

209 Rob Grace, 'Humanitarian Negotiation with Parties to Armed Conflict: The Role of Laws and Principles in the Discourse' (2020) 11 Journal of International Humanitarian Legal Studies 68; Jori Breslawski, 'The Shortcomings of International Humanitarian Law in Access Negotiations: New Strategies and Ways Forward' (2022) 24 International Studies Review 1, 1.

210 Emanuela-Chiara Gillard, 'The United Nations Security Council and Humanitarian Operations in Syria: A Legal Analysis' (*Diakonia International Humanitarian Law Centre*, 2022) <https://www.diakonia.se/ihl/news/the-united-nations-security-council-and-humanitarian-operations-in-syria-a-legal-analysis-2/> accessed 2 August 2024, 29.

211 See Chapter 5, Section 4.1.

arbitrary withholding of consent to impartial humanitarian relief or to facilitate and ensure safe humanitarian access to all people in need in armed conflict'.[212] Barber has parlayed this progress into a role for the UN General Assembly in ensuring humanitarian access.[213]

In 2001, O'Connell identified four successive waves of rights, duties, and remedies related to humanitarian assistance, and predicted a fifth wave of retrenchment.[214] The foregoing demonstrates that we are now firmly within a subsequent sixth wave characterized by more widespread knowledge of conflict parties' duties in relation to emergency relief operations. With this context in place, the duties in detail—including their specificities in non-occupation IAC, occupation, and NIAC—are addressed below, beginning with step one: strategic consent.

4.3. Step one: strategic consent

As discussed in Chapter 1 and in Section 2 above, conflict parties have primary responsibility for meeting the needs of civilians within their control. The rules on emergency relief operations are triggered if the relevant conflict party fails in this regard. This is indicated in non-occupation IAC by the civilian population not being 'adequately provided with' essential items,[215] namely 'clothing, bedding, means of shelter, other supplies essential to the survival of the civilian population [. . .] and objects necessary for religious worship'.[216] The threshold in NIAC is the civilian population 'suffering undue hardship owing to a lack of the supplies essential for its survival, such as foodstuffs and medical supplies'.[217] In practice the question of whether a conflict party is failing to meet the needs of civilians in its control is assessed on a case-by-case basis, based on the 'essential character' of the unmet needs.[218]

Third states and impartial humanitarian organizations may respond to unmet civilian needs with offers to conduct relief operations. For the latter, such offers are in line with their right of initiative.[219] Two caveats are worth noting. First, as discussed in Section 3, impartial humanitarian organizations may always offer their services pursuant to their right of initiative; this is not contingent upon unmet civilian needs. Second, the conflict party with primary responsibility need not wait for an offer; it may request help, whether to respond to unmet needs or to prevent the situation from deteriorating to the point where needs go unfulfilled. Both caveats flow from the fact,

[212] Nathalie Weizmann, 'Ensuring Respect for IHL as it Relates to Humanitarian Activities' in Eve Massingham and Annabel McConnachie (eds), *Ensuring Respect for International Humanitarian Law* (Routledge 2020) 203.

[213] Rebecca Barber, 'Does International Law Permit the Provision of Humanitarian Assistance Without Host State Consent? Territorial Integrity, Necessity and the Determinative Function of the General Assembly' in Terry D. Gill and others (eds), *Yearbook of International Humanitarian Law 2020*, vol 23 (Springer 2022).

[214] Mary Ellen O'Connell, 'Humanitarian Assistance in Non-International Armed Conflict: the Fourth Wave of Rights, Duties and Remedies' (2001) 31 Israel Yearbook on Human Rights 183.

[215] API (n 16) art 70(1).

[216] ibid, art 69(1).

[217] APII (n 16) art 18(2).

[218] Oxford Guidance (n 47) para 18.

[219] GCIV (n 15) arts 3(2) and 10. See Section 3.

addressed in Sections 1 and 3 above, that humanitarian assistance can be preventive; indeed, as mentioned in Section 1.3, by definition, 'relief' responds to emergencies, but 'assistance' need not.

Once offers to conduct relief operations have been made, those that are 'humanitarian and impartial in character and conducted without adverse distinction shall be undertaken'.[220] 'Humanitarian' in this context has been described as meaning 'not political'[221] and as requiring simply that 'the action is aimed at bringing relief to victims' of armed conflict.[222] 'Impartial' has the same meaning as the humanitarian principle of impartiality.[223] However, the International Court of Justice (ICJ) recently opined that neutrality, in the sense of the humanitarian principle of neutrality,[224] 'plays a role in assessing the impartiality of the activities of humanitarian organizations', because an organization that is not neutral may have difficulty fulfilling impartiality's non-discrimination dimension.[225] Without 'adverse distinction' means without discrimination;[226] 'adverse' is included because some distinctions, such as distributing relief according to need, are required.[227] These three characteristics of relief actions serve to assure conflict parties that humanitarian assistance will not be instrumentalized to give one side a military advantage over the other. Operations with these three characteristics 'shall not be regarded as interference in the armed conflict or as unfriendly acts'.[228]

Because the foundational international law principle of sovereign equality prohibits interference with a state's political independence and safeguards its territorial integrity,[229] consent is a—if not the—major legal issue surrounding humanitarian assistance. Thus, even though the relevant provisions provide that relief operations with the requisite three characteristics 'shall be undertaken',[230] in both non-occupation IAC and NIAC, operations may not proceed without the consent of 'the Parties concerned in such relief actions'.[231] This refers primarily to the conflict party or parties 'for which the relief is intended';[232] in other words, the conflict party on whose territory the civilians in need are located.[233] However, provided there is need among the

[220] API (n 16) art 70(1); APII art 18(2) uses similar language: 'relief actions for the civilian population which are of an exclusively humanitarian and impartial nature and which are conducted without any adverse distinction shall be undertaken'.

[221] Michael Bothe, Karl Josef Partsch, and Waldemar Solf, *New Rules for Victims of Armed Conflicts: Commentary on the Two 1977 Protocols Additional to the Geneva Conventions of 1949* (2nd edn, Martinus Nijhoff 2013) 801 and 486.

[222] Sandoz and others (n 90) para 2798.

[223] ibid, para 2801. See Chapter 2, Section 4.4.2.

[224] See Chapter 2, Section 4.4.2.

[225] *Israel Obligations AO* (n 54) paras 115–16.

[226] Sandoz and others (n 90) para 2799.

[227] Other required distinctions are discussed in Section 4.4.1.

[228] API (n 16) art 70(1).

[229] Charter of the United Nations (adopted 26 June 1945, entered into force 24 October 1965) 1 UNTS XVI, art 2; UNGA Res 2625 (XXV) (24 October 1970) Annex, principle 1; *Military and Paramilitary Activities in and Against Nicaragua (Nicaragua v United States)* [1986] ICJ Rep 4 (*Nicaragua*) para 202.

[230] API (n 16) art 70(1) and APII (n 16) art 18(2).

[231] API (n 16) art 70(1). APII (n 16) art 18(2) mentions 'the High Contracting Party concerned'.

[232] Sandoz and others (n 90) para 2807; see also Oxford Guidance (n 47) para 23. Regarding NIAC, see Sandoz and others (n 90) para 4884 and Oxford Guidance (n 47) para 27.

[233] The issue of whose consent is required in NIAC with territorial control by an OAG is discussed in Section 4.3.2.

civilian population and the relief offered is humanitarian and impartial and will be distributed without discrimination, while this party's consent is required, it may not be withheld arbitrarily,[234] or perhaps even at all[235]—these distinct views are discussed in Sections 4.3.1 and 6.1 below. Put differently, the affected conflict party may refuse to consent to a relief action without the arbitrariness or lawfulness of its refusal even arising if civilians' needs are being met or if the relief action offered is not humanitarian, not impartial, or will be carried out in a discriminatory manner. For example, in *Popović*, the International Criminal Tribunal for the Former Yugoslavia's (ICTY) Appeals Chamber held, relying on CIHL, that the Bosnian Serb Army was not under any obligation to allow consignments that were not impartial.[236] However, if relief is needed and the relief offered is humanitarian, impartial, and non-discriminatory, as discussed further in Sections 4.3.1 and 6.1, the affected party's latitude to refuse consent is either very limited or non-existent.[237] Where the conflict party requests outside help, the request itself is tantamount to consent; in other words, consent is presumed.

In IAC, non-belligerent states where a cross-border relief operation may be initiated or through which it may transit have the same obligation as the affected conflict party.[238] Neither Common Article 3(2) nor APII imposes any obligation on third states in NIAC; however, there is 'an expectation that States not party to the NIAC will not oppose transit through their territory of impartial humanitarian organizations seeking to reach the victims of a NIAC'.[239] This expectation is, according to Ferraro,[240] based in states' obligation under the GCs to respect and ensure respect for IHL.[241]

While generally consent to relief actions cannot be withheld in violation of international law, there are two circumstances in which it can never be withheld. The first is occupation. If 'the whole or part of the population of an occupied territory is inadequately supplied', GCIV provides that 'the Occupying Power *shall agree* to relief schemes'.[242] The rationale for this is two-fold. First, an occupying power has no sovereignty over the territory it occupies, so cannot be concerned about relief actions infringing its sovereignty. Second, an occupying power has clear duties to the civilian population in the territory it occupies.[243] Given these obligations, the adequate provision of supplies to the population is the only ground on which an occupying power can validly withhold its consent to relief actions. Any non-belligerent state through whose territory a cross-border relief operation must transit to reach occupied territory has

234 Sandoz and others (n 90) para 2805; Oxford Guidance (n 47) para 44.

235 ICRC Lexicon (n 41) 369–70.

236 *Prosecutor v Popović* (Judgment, Appeals Chamber) IT-05-88-A (30 January 2015) para 615.

237 On the withdrawal of consent, see Emanuela-Chiara Gillard, 'Cross-Border Relief Operations: A Legal Perspective' (*OCHA Policy Series*, 2014) <https://www.unocha.org/sites/unocha/files/dms/Documents/Legal%20Perspective%20Cross-border%20relief%20operations.pdf> accessed 18 March 2024 (Gillard 2014) 26–27.

238 Sandoz and others (n 90) para 2807; Oxford Guidance (n 47) paras 104–05 (for a short survey and analysis of alternate views, see the Oxford Guidance (n 47) paras 99–103).

239 Ferraro (n 70) 202. See also UNGA Res 46/182 (19 December 1991) A/RES/46/182, Annex, para 7.

240 Ferraro (n 70) 202. See also Oxford Guidance (n 47) paras 106–07.

241 GCs (n 15) Common Article 1.

242 GCIV (n 15) art 59(1) (emphasis added). See *Israel Obligations AO* (n 54) para 94.

243 Hague Regulations (n 50) art 43; GCIV (n 15) arts 55(1) and 56(1); API (n 16) art 69(1). See *Israel Obligations AO* (n 54) para 92.

the same obligation as the occupying power: it must consent to passage.[244] The second circumstance is when the UN Security Council has imposed a relief action. This has occurred once: regarding Syria in 2014 and thereafter; this is discussed in Chapter 5.[245]

While the rules on strategic consent to emergency relief operations are largely settled, there is still disagreement surrounding two issues: the relevant conflict party's latitude to refuse to consent at step one, and which conflict party has the authority to consent in NIAC when the territory where civilians in need are located is controlled by an OAG and can be reached cross-border without transiting through areas controlled by the territorial state. Each is addressed in turn.

4.3.1. 'Arbitrary' vs 'unlawful' withholding of strategic consent

The interpretation that strategic consent may not be arbitrarily withheld first emerged at the diplomatic conference where the APs were drafted. Article 70(1) of API provides that relief actions 'shall be undertaken, subject to the agreement of the Parties concerned'.[246] The 'agreement' clause was added to protect the sovereignty of the state receiving relief.[247] However, the delegate from the Federal Republic of Germany stated that the addition 'did not imply that the Parties concerned had absolute and unlimited freedom to refuse their agreement to relief actions. A Party refusing its agreement must do so for valid reasons, not arbitrary or capricious ones'.[248] Similar comments were made regarding APII's article 18(2).[249]

The ICRC commentary and another important commentary are of the view that consent may not be arbitrarily withheld.[250] The same perspective can be found in an important early secondary source[251] and soft law,[252] including the Institute of International Law's 1989 Resolution on the Protection of Human Rights and the Principle of Non-Intervention in the Internal Affairs of States[253] and its 2003 Resolution on Humanitarian Assistance;[254] the Guiding Principles on Internal Displacement;[255] the ICRC CIHL study;[256] and the Council of Europe recommendation on IDPs.[257] The view has been affirmed recently in the Oxford Guidance,[258]

[244] GCIV (n 15) art 59(3); Oxford Guidance (n 47) para 98.

[245] See Chapter 5, Section 4.4.2.

[246] Interestingly, Okimoto notes that the drafter's intent regarding this language differs from the phrase's contemporary meaning ((n 199) 129).

[247] Sandoz and others (n 90) para 2805.

[248] Official Records, vol XII, CDDH/II/SR.87, para 27.

[249] Gillard (n 109) 356.

[250] Sandoz and others (n 90) paras 2805 and 4885–86; Bothe and others (n 125) 696.

[251] Michael Bothe, 'Relief Actions: The Position of the Recipient State' in Frits Kalshoven (ed), *Assisting the Victims of Armed Conflict and Other Disasters* (Martinus Nijhoff 1989) 94.

[252] Some of these soft law sources are drawn from a list compiled by Gillard ((n 109) 356–57).

[253] (1989) 63 Yearbook of the Institute of International Law 345, art 5.

[254] Institute of International Law, Bruges session (2003) <https://www.idi-iil.org/app/uploads/2017/06/2003_bru_03_en.pdf> accessed 18 May 2023, art VIII.

[255] ECOSOC, 'Report of the Representative of the Secretary-General, Mr Francis M Deng, Submitted Pursuant to Commission Resolution 1997/39, Addendum, Guiding Principles on Internal Displacement', E/CN.4/1998/53/Add.2 (11 February 1998) (Guiding Principles on Internal Displacement) principle 25(2).

[256] Henckaerts and Doswald-Beck (n 18) 196–97.

[257] Council of Europe Recommendation Rec (2006)6 of the Committee of Ministers to Member States on Internally Displaced Persons (5 April 2006) para 4.

[258] Oxford Guidance (n 47) s E.

by the UN Secretary-General[259] and UN bodies,[260] by states,[261] and in contemporary secondary sources.[262] It is thus now 'generally accepted that although the consent of the affected state to relief actions is required, it may not be arbitrarily withheld'.[263]

However, the ICRC now disagrees with the 'arbitrary' withholding interpretation of step one strategic consent. While the terminology of arbitrariness was 'introduced into parlance' by the ICRC in its 1987 commentary on the APs,[264] and the organization maintains that consent to offers of preventive assistance made pursuant to the right of initiative cannot be arbitrarily withheld,[265] the ICRC has recently sought to emphasize that besides a lack of need and the characteristics of the services offered, the Additional Protocols do 'not foresee other grounds justifying a general refusal to consent to' emergency relief operations.[266] As a result, when a conflict party withholds its consent to impartial and non-discriminatory humanitarian relief at step one notwithstanding unmet needs among the civilian population, the ICRC now terms this 'unlawful' rather than arbitrary.[267]

It is more than just a terminological difference: under the 'arbitrary withholding' interpretation of the law, if there are civilians in need and the relief action offered is humanitarian and impartial and does not discriminate, the range of circumstances in which a conflict party can legitimately withhold its consent is limited but not non-existent; for the ICRC, there are almost no such circumstances. This is addressed in detail in Section 6 on the unlawful impeding of emergency relief operations.[268]

4.3.2. Strategic consent in non-international armed conflict with territorial control by an organized armed group

The second controversial issue stems from distinct interpretations of both Common Article 3(2) and APII article 18(2) in circumstances where relief is destined for territory under the control of an OAG and such territory can be reached cross-border, without passing through areas controlled by the territorial state.[269] The Common Article 3(2) right of initiative, which provides that an 'impartial humanitarian body [. . .] may offer its services *to the Parties to the conflict*',[270] has been interpreted—most recently regarding opposition-held north-west Syria—as rendering the sole consent of the OAG sufficient.[271] The Oxford Guidance, by contrast, concludes that it is difficult

259 Report of the Secretary-General on the Protection of Civilians in Armed Conflict (n 188) para 58.

260 UN Human Rights Council, Group of Eminent International and Regional Experts on Yemen, 'Situation of Human Rights in Yemen, Including Violations and Abuses since September 2014' (3 September 2019) A/HRC/42/CRP.1, para 790; for other UN sources, see the Oxford Guidance (n 47) note 43.

261 Conflict & Hunger Handbook (n 114) 72.

262 Sandesh Sivakumaran, 'Arbitrary Withholding of Consent to Humanitarian Assistance in Situations of Disaster' (2015) 64 International & Comparative Law Quarterly 501, 512–14; Akande and Gillard 2016 (n 196).

263 Gillard (n 109) 356.

264 Bartels (n 194).

265 See Section 3.

266 ICRC Lexicon (n 41) 369; see also Challenges Report 2015 (n 198) 29.

267 ICRC Lexicon (n 41) 370; Ferraro (n 70) 201.

268 See Section 6.1.

269 See, generally, Vanhullebusch (n 199); Vijitha Veerakatty, *Arbitrary Withholding of Consent to Humanitarian Relief in Non-International Armed Conflict: Legal Regulations and Consequences* (Brill 2024).

270 Emphasis added.

271 Bouchet-Saulnier (n 61) 210; Payam Akhavan and others, 'There is no Legal Barrier to UN Cross-Border Operations in Syria' *The Guardian* (London, 28 April 2014); Bruno Simma and others, 'There is

to interpret Common Article 3(2) in this way, 'particularly in view of the significant infringement of territorial sovereignty' it entails.[272] Even if correct, since states do not enjoy the Common Article 3(2) right of initiative, the former (permissive) interpretation is limited to situations where assistance is provided by a humanitarian organization; if the humanitarian actor is a state, APII governs.

APII's article 18(2) provides that relief actions 'shall be undertaken subject to the consent of the High Contracting Party concerned'. One persistent interpretation, which originated in an important early commentary co-authored by Bothe,[273] is that the High Contracting Party (i.e. the affected state) is not 'concerned' by relief actions for civilians outside its control, so only the OAG's consent is required. Bothe reiterated this view in two subsequent analyses,[274] yet his most recent writing on this issue concludes that it is unsettled.[275] The weight of authority finds that the consent of the affected state is required.[276] Gillard notes that an early version of article 18(2) used 'the party or parties concerned', but this language was removed to ensure OAGs would not be empowered to consent to relief.[277] The ICRC Lexicon even concludes, based on APII article 18(2), that state consent is required even in NIACs governed only by Common Article 3.[278] This is in stark contrast to the organization's earlier commentary on article 18(2), in which it found that in 'exceptional cases when it is not possible to determine which are the authorities concerned'—such cases presumably relate to situations where there is no effective government—'consent is to be presumed in view of the fact that assistance for the victims is of paramount importance and should not suffer any delay'.[279] On balance, it seems that state consent is required, particularly considering APII's article 3, which provides that nothing in the Protocol 'shall be invoked for the purpose of affecting the sovereignty of a State'.

4.4. Step two: implementation

Once the strategic consent of the affected state has been obtained, implementation of the emergency relief operation by the humanitarian actor or actors concerned begins.

Still No Legal Barrier to UN Cross-Border Operations in Syria Without a UN Security Council Mandate' (10 February 2023) <https://www.crossborderislegal.org/_files/ugd/166212_e8342039d1794a5481238 6ec69b6906f.pdf> accessed 23 May 2023 (2023 Letter); Gillard lists additional proponents of this view (2014 (n 237) 13). This interpretation is not a panacea: there are examples of OAGs in Syria, Sudan, and Yemen depriving civilians under their control of humanitarian assistance (Vanhullebusch (n 115) 318).

272 Oxford Guidance (n 47) para 26.

273 Bothe (n 125) 696.

274 Bothe (n 251) 94; Bothe and others (n 221) 801.

275 Bothe (n 199) 189–90.

276 Sandoz and others (n 90) para 4884; Meyer (n 93) 221; Plattner (n 30) 260; Stoffels (n 203) 534–35; Oxford Guidance (n 47) para 30; Dire Tladi, 'The International Law Commission's Draft Articles on the Protection of Persons in the Event of Disasters: Codification, Progressive Development or Creation of Law from Thin Air?' (2017) 16 Chinese Journal of International Law 425, 446; Andreas Zimmermann, 'Humanitarian Assistance and the Security Council' (2017) 50 Israel Law Review 3, 18–19; contra: Vanhullebusch (n 115).

277 Gillard (n 109) 365–66.

278 ICRC Lexicon (n 41) 368–69.

279 Sandoz and others (n 90) para 4884.

IHL treaty provisions applicable in non-occupation IAC address priorities in the distribution of relief (API article 70(1)) and the obligation to allow and facilitate (API article 70(2–3)); the obligation to allow and facilitate relief in and en route to occupied territory is governed by GCIV (articles 59–61). The rules on relief personnel (API article 71) apply in both non-occupation IAC and in occupied territory. Implementation in NIAC is governed by APII (article 18). Each of these is addressed in turn.

4.4.1. Priorities in distribution in non-occupation international armed conflict

API imposes priorities in the distribution of relief in non-occupation IAC: 'priority shall be given to those persons, such as children, expectant mothers, maternity cases and nursing mothers, who, under the Fourth Convention or under this Protocol, are to be accorded privileged treatment or special protection'.[280] The list in API article 70(1) is not exhaustive; other categories of person privileged under GCIV and API include injured or sick civilians and persons deprived of their liberty.[281] The ICRC's commentary on API notes that the 'responsibility for ensuring that this obligation is fulfilled falls upon those responsible for the distribution of the relief',[282] which in practice will often be a humanitarian organization that is not itself directly governed by API. The affected state may therefore verify that the obligation regarding priorities in distribution is met, though by operation of API article 70(1) the humanitarian organization in question will be 'impartial', so accustomed to distributing relief according to beneficiaries' needs.

4.4.2. The obligation to allow and facilitate relief in non-occupation international armed conflict

The central obligation during implementation is conflict parties' obligation to allow and facilitate; this obligation arises in relation to all emergency relief operations that have been consented to. In IAC other than occupation, it requires that conflict parties 'allow and facilitate [the] rapid and unimpeded passage of all relief consignments, equipment and personnel' throughout the territory they control, even if the 'assistance is destined for the civilian population of the adverse' conflict party.[283] This obligation covers initial entry into the state and movement within it, and is not an obligation of means, but rather one of result.[284] Put simply, it is 'an obligation to cooperate and to take positive action to facilitate humanitarian operations'.[285]

While on its language alone the obligation is somewhat vague, its key elements can be further specified.[286] 'Allow and facilitate' means the parties 'are under an obligation to cooperate, and to take positive action to facilitate the operations', which includes facilitating the work of relief personnel.[287] 'Rapid' means as fast as possible in

[280] API (n 16) art 70(1); API art 77 sets the age of maturity at 18.
[281] See Sections 5.1 and 5.3.
[282] Sandoz and others (n 90) para 2816.
[283] API (n 16) art 70(2).
[284] ICRC Lexicon (n 41) 374.
[285] Tristan Ferraro, 'International Humanitarian Law, Principled Humanitarian Action, Counter-terrorism and Sanctions: Some Perspectives on Selected Issues' (2021) 103 International Review of the Red Cross 109, 135.
[286] For more detail, see ICRC Lexicon (n 41) 370–74.
[287] ICRC Lexicon (n 41) 370.

the circumstances.[288] 'Unimpeded' means without harassment or undue formality.[289] 'Passage' relates to the practicalities of entry into and movement within the country,[290] and may be over land or water or by air.[291]

The obligation to allow and facilitate governs the same issues that often arise in peacetime disasters, such as entry visas for relief personnel; restrictions on, delays in, and charges for the importation of relief goods and equipment; and the recognition of foreign professional qualifications.[292] While such issues are often challenging in peacetime relief operations, 'the strong general duty to facilitate relief in armed conflict dictates that appropriate accommodation must be found'.[293] Practical measures to give effect to the obligation to allow and facilitate may include waiving or simplifying and expediting entry procedures for humanitarian personnel; waiving, reducing, or expediting customs procedures; providing exemptions from taxes, customs duties, and fees; issuing permits for the passage of humanitarian supplies, equipment, and personnel; ensuring that bureaucratic formalities are met efficiently; and allowing telecommunications equipment to be imported.[294] UN officials in particular also enjoy facilities under the Convention on the Privileges and Immunities of the United Nations,[295] which is discussed in Chapter 5.[296]

The obligation to allow and facilitate applies equally to non-belligerent transit states.[297] According to the Oxford Guidance, it 'seems reasonable to assume that passage should be simpler and swifter through' these states than through conflict parties.[298] Transit states party to the Convention on the Safety of United Nations and Associated Personnel (UN Safety Convention), discussed in Chapter 5,[299] have an additional obligation to facilitate 'the unimpeded transit of United Nations and associated personnel and their equipment to and from the host State'.[300]

Conflict parties and non-belligerent transit states retain 'the right to prescribe technical arrangements' for the passage of supplies, equipment, and personnel.[301] This is often referred to as their right of control. The right of control is 'limited',[302] and serves distinct purposes: to verify the humanitarian nature of relief supplies, to prevent relief convoys from interfering with or being affected by military operations, and to ensure equipment and supplies meet health and safety standards.[303] While conflict parties and non-belligerent transit states have discretion in the prescription of

[288] Sandoz and others (n 90) para 2829.
[289] ibid.
[290] Oxford Guidance (n 47) para 59.
[291] Sandoz and others (n 90) para 2829.
[292] See Chapter 4, Section 2.
[293] David Fisher, 'Domestic Regulation of International Humanitarian Relief in Disasters and Armed Conflict: A Comparative Analysis' (2007) 89 International Review of the Red Cross 345, 369.
[294] OCHA (n 195) 2.
[295] (Adopted 13 February 1946; entered into force 17 September 1946) 1 UNTS 15.
[296] See Chapter 5, Section 5.1.
[297] API (n 16) art 70(2).
[298] Oxford Guidance (n 47) para 121.
[299] See Chapter 5, Section 5.4.
[300] (Adopted 9 December 1994, entered into force 15 January 1999) 2051 UNTS 363, art 5.
[301] API (n 16) art 70(3)(a).
[302] *Israel Obligations AO* (n 54) para 91.
[303] Oxford Guidance (n 47) para 66.

technical arrangements, this latitude is subject to their central obligation to allow and facilitate: a conflict party may not interfere with relief consignments under the guise of its right to prescribe technical arrangements.[304] In other words, conflict parties may not abuse their right of control.[305] Examples of technical arrangements include consignment searches and the prescription of specific distribution routes at specific times of day. In addition to their right of control, conflict parties and non-belligerent transit states may require that relief be distributed under the supervision of an impartial humanitarian organization.[306] States and organizations have published practical guidance regarding engaging with conflict parties around technical arrangements.[307]

After stating the central obligation to allow and facilitate at article 70(2) and reserving the right of control at article 70(3)(a), API article 70(3) goes on to specify conduct required by the obligation to allow and facilitate. Conflict parties and non-belligerent transit states have a specific obligation not to 'divert relief consignments from the purpose for which they are intended nor delay their forwarding, except in cases of urgent necessity in the interest of the civilian population concerned'[308] and must 'encourage and facilitate effective international coordination' of relief actions.[309] Conflict parties, in particular, are required to 'protect relief consignments and facilitate their rapid distribution'.[310]

4.4.3. The obligation to allow and facilitate relief in and en route to occupied territory

As discussed in Section 4.3, an occupying power has an absolute obligation to consent to relief for civilians in occupied territory if 'whole or part of the population [. . .] is inadequately supplied'.[311] The nature of the occupying power's obligation to allow and facilitate such relief, and transit and co-belligerent states' obligations regarding relief en route to occupied territory, are similar to the obligations in non-occupation IAC, though the sources are GCIV and articles 69 and 71 of API,[312] rather than API article 70—which does not apply to occupied territory.[313]

[304] *Prosecutor v Tolimir* (Judgement, Appeals Chamber) IT-05-88/2-A (8 April 2015) (*Tolimir*) para 329.

[305] Ferraro (n 70) 203; Tzvi Mintz, 'Substantive Technicalities: Understanding the Legal Framework of Humanitarian Assistance in Armed Conflicts through the Prescription of Technical Arrangements' (2019) 227 Military Law Review 275, 305.

[306] API (n 16) art 70(3)(b); this provision refers to a 'Protecting Power', which is discussed in Section 3.

[307] Deborah Mancini-Griffoli and André Picot, 'Humanitarian Negotiation: A Handbook for Securing Access, Assistance and Protection for Civilians in Armed Conflict' (*Centre for Humanitarian Dialogue*, 2004) <https://hdcentre.org/wp-content/uploads/2016/07/Humanitarian-Negotiationn-A-handbook-October-2004.pdf> accessed 25 May 2023; Swiss Federal Department of Foreign Affairs, Practitioners' Manual (n 197); Centre of Competence on Humanitarian Negotiation, *CCHN Field Manual on Frontline Humanitarian Negotiation* (2nd edn, 2019) <https://frontline-negotiations.org/wp-content/uploads/2019/11/CCHN-Field-Manual-EN.pdf> accessed 5 June 2023; see also Oxford Guidance (n 47) s F.2.

[308] API (n 16) art 70(3)(c).

[309] ibid, art 70(5).

[310] ibid, art 70(4).

[311] GCIV (n 15) art 59(1).

[312] API (n 16) art 69(2).

[313] ibid, arts 70(1) and 69(2), which notes that relief 'actions for the benefit of the civilian population of occupied territories are governed by Articles 59, 60, 61, 62, 108, 109, 110 and 111 of the Fourth Convention, and by Article 71 of this Protocol'.

API article 69(2) provides that relief 'actions for the benefit of the civilian population of occupied territories' must 'be implemented without delay', which underlines the urgent character of such actions.[314] GCIV provides that an occupying power must facilitate relief schemes 'by all the means at its disposal'.[315] GCIV goes on to specify some elements of this clear and unambiguous obligation. The occupying power must facilitate the rapid distribution of relief,[316] including by not subjecting relief consignments to taxes, charges, or customs duties, unless these are 'necessary in the interests of the economy of the [occupied] territory'.[317] Additionally, the occupying power 'shall in no way whatsoever divert relief consignments from the purpose for which they are intended, except in cases of urgent necessity, in the interests of the population of the occupied territory'.[318] This notion of diversion is broad, 'covering a change of destination of relief consignments of any kind'; the 'specific conditions for allowing diversion [. . .] are cumulative and such action may be taken only in the interests of the local population'.[319] The ICJ has opined that overall, 'an occupying Power must do more than simply allow the passage of essential items into the occupied territory. It must also use all means at its disposal so that these items are distributed in a regular, fair and non-discriminatory manner, including by facilitating access to them and refraining from threats of use of violence or lethal force against the civilian population seeking to access such humanitarian relief'.[320] The occupying power may subject the distribution of relief to the supervision of an impartial humanitarian organization.[321]

All 'Contracting Parties', meaning both transit and co-belligerent states, 'shall permit the free passage of [. . . relief] consignments' en route to occupied territory 'and shall guarantee their protection'.[322] Non-belligerent transit states must also 'endeavour to permit the transit and transport, free of charge, of [. . .] relief consignments on their way to occupied territories'.[323]

GCIV does not mention the occupying power's right of control; however, 'it follows from the occupying Power's control over territory that it is also entitled to exercise these rights'.[324] Non-belligerent transit states also enjoy an implied right of control,[325] and GCIV specifies a right of control for any co-belligerent transit state.[326] Specifically, the co-belligerent transit state has the right to 'search the consignments, to regulate their passage according to prescribed times and routes, and to be reasonably satisfied through the Protecting Power' or an impartial humanitarian organization[327] 'that

314 Sandoz and others (n 90) para 2788.
315 GCIV (n 15) art 59(1).
316 ibid, art 61(2).
317 ibid.
318 ibid, art 60.
319 *Israel Obligations AO* (n 54) para 99.
320 ibid, para 101.
321 GCIV (n 15) art 61(1).
322 GCIV (n 15) art 59(3).
323 ibid, art 61(3).
324 *Israel Obligations AO* (n 54) para 97.
325 Oxford Guidance (n 47) para 98.
326 GCIV (n 15) art 59(4).
327 See Section 3.

these consignments are to be used for the relief of the needy population and are not to be used for the benefit of the Occupying Power'.[328]

4.4.4. Relief personnel in international armed conflict

Article 71 of API imposes further specific measures regarding all personnel participating in relief actions. It binds both the affected state in IAC generally and the occupying power in situations of occupation.[329] The participation of personnel in general and of particular individuals is subject to the approval of the affected state or, in situations of occupation, the occupying power.[330] However, this approval is not distinct from the more general provision of consent at step one, as it would be absurd for the affected state or occupying power to consent to a relief action but not to its staffing. As the ICRC's commentary on API notes, 'there are not two decisions but an overall agreement, and it is understood that participation of personnel is in itself an important element of such an agreement'.[331] Personnel must be generally respected and protected,[332] where the negative notion of 'respect' means 'to spare, not to attack' and the positive notion of 'protect' means 'to come to someone's defence, to lend help and support'.[333] The affected state or occupying power must also assist approved relief personnel in carrying out their mission.[334] This general duty implies that the affected state or occupying power must 'do its utmost to facilitate the task of relief personnel'.[335] They may, however, temporarily limit the activities or movements of relief personnel for reasons of imperative military necessity,[336] such as to prevent them from entering areas of kinetic warfare. Relief personnel must comply with the technical arrangements prescribed by the affected state or occupying power, or their individual approval to participate in the relief operation could be rescinded.[337]

Relief personnel also benefit from more general protections under both the Hague and Geneva strands of IHL. Humanitarians are protected as civilians under Geneva law, including the foundational principle of distinction, which prohibits the targeting of civilians and civilian objects,[338] and fundamental IHL guarantees, which include

[328] GCIV (n 15) art 59(4). The issue of a co-belligerent transit state blocking commercial and relief supplies on their way to occupied territory was addressed by the ICJ in a case brought by Armenia against Azerbaijan. However, for jurisdictional reasons, the case was brought and thus decided under the International Convention on the Elimination of All Forms of Racial Discrimination rather than under IHL. The ICJ ordered Azerbaijan to 'take all measures at its disposal to ensure unimpeded movement of persons, vehicles and cargo along the Lachin Corridor [to the Nagorno-Karabakh region] in both directions' (*Application of the International Convention on the Elimination of All Forms of Racial Discrimination (Armenia v Azerbaijan)* (Request for the Indication of Provisional Measures: Order) [2023] ICJ Rep 36, para 67).

[329] API (n 16) art 69(2); Sandoz and others (n 90) para 2876.

[330] API (n 16) art 71(1); Sandoz and others (n 90) paras 2881 and 2883.

[331] Sandoz and others (n 90) para 2882.

[332] API (n 16) art 71(2); Henckaerts and Doswald-Beck (n 18) rules 31 and 32.

[333] Pictet and others (n 54) 146.

[334] API (n 16) art 71(3); Henckaerts and Doswald-Beck (n 18) rule 56.

[335] Sandoz and others (n 90) para 2892.

[336] API (n 16) art 71(3); Henckaerts and Doswald-Beck (n 18) rule 56.

[337] API (n 16) art 71(4).

[338] API (n 16) art 48.

prohibitions on the taking of hostages.[339] Additionally, humanitarian vehicles and equipment are civilian objects so they may not be targeted.[340] Certain Hague law provisions relate exclusively to humanitarian personnel.[341] Humanitarian personnel also continue to enjoy the protection of IHRL during armed conflict. Several UN General Assembly and Security Council resolutions have called for better protection of UN and other humanitarian relief personnel, and many relief personnel are protected by the UN Safety Convention; these are addressed in Chapters 5 and 6.[342]

4.4.5. Implementation in non-international armed conflict

Neither Common Article 3 nor APII speaks to the implementation of emergency relief operations in NIAC. However, the API rules applicable in IAC are considered customary and applicable in both IAC and NIAC.[343] Indeed, the relevant rules of CIHL largely reflect the API treaty provisions outlined above. Rule 55 states the general obligation that the 'parties to the conflict must allow and facilitate rapid and unimpeded passage of humanitarian relief for civilians in need, which is impartial in character and conducted without any adverse distinction, subject to their right of control'.[344] The step two obligation to allow and facilitate is self-evident within rule 55.[345] Rule 55 does not address the implementation obligations of non-belligerent transit states in NIAC. However, as mentioned above regarding their consent in NIAC,[346] non-belligerent transit states' GC undertakings to ensure respect for IHL, as well as their IHRL obligations, would suggest that they should endeavour to allow and facilitate rapid and unimpeded passage of relief supplies, equipment, and personnel on their way to victims of NIAC.[347]

Regarding equipment and supplies, rule 32 provides that '[o]bjects used for humanitarian relief operations must be respected and protected'.[348] Regarding personnel, rule 31 provides that '[h]umanitarian relief personnel must be respected and protected'.[349] Rule 56 provides that the 'parties to the conflict must ensure the freedom of movement of authorised humanitarian relief personnel essential to the exercise of their functions. Only in case of imperative military necessity may their movements be temporarily restricted'.[350]

[339] ibid, art 75(2)(c); APII (n 16) art 4(2)(c). See also GCs (n 15) Common Article 3.
[340] API (n 16) art 48.
[341] Convention on Prohibitions or Restrictions on the Use of Certain Conventional Weapons which may be Deemed to be Excessively Injurious or to have Indiscriminate Effects (with Protocols I, II and III) (adopted 10 October 1980, entered into force 2 December 1983) 1342 UNTS 134, Protocol II, art 12.
[342] See Chapter 5, Section 5.4 and Chapter 6, Section 3.3.
[343] Oxford Guidance (n 47) para 6; Henckaerts and Doswald-Beck (n 18) rules 55 and 56.
[344] Henckaerts and Doswald-Beck (n 18) 193.
[345] Less clear from the language of the rule alone, but also part of it, is the requirement of consent at step one. In their commentary on rule 55, Henckaerts and Doswald-Beck note that it is 'self-evident that a humanitarian organization cannot operate without the consent of the party concerned. However, such consent must not be refused on arbitrary grounds' (Henckaerts and Doswald-Beck (n 18) 196–97).
[346] See Section 4.3.
[347] Oxford Guidance (n 47) para 123; see also Henckaerts and Doswald-Beck (n 18) 198–99.
[348] Henckaerts and Doswald-Beck (n 18) 109.
[349] ibid, 105.
[350] ibid, 200.

5. Privileged types of relief and relief for civilians in specific circumstances

In addition to addressing emergency relief operations in general, IHL also includes provisions on medical and food relief. The general provisions discussed in Section 4 above apply equally to these types of assistance; this section outlines the additional privileges accorded to medical and food relief.[351] IHL also covers relief for individuals in specific circumstances: civilians deprived of their liberty and evacuated and displaced civilians. Each is discussed in turn.

5.1. Medical relief

Medical relief operations may respond to injuries sustained by civilians in the conflict and/or they may address armed conflict's incidental effects on health, such as malnutrition and the spread of infectious disease. This work may reinforce existing civilian health infrastructure, such as clinics and hospitals, and/or involve establishing new temporary facilities, such as mobile clinics and field hospitals.

In both IAC and NIAC, wounded and sick civilians must be respected and protected and are entitled to be searched for, collected, and evacuated, and to receive the medical care and attention required by their condition to the fullest extent practicable and with the least possible delay, without any adverse distinction.[352] This absolute entitlement creates, for the relevant conflict party, an obligation under IHL to consent to medical relief operations if the wounded and sick would not otherwise receive the care required by their condition.[353] The obligation to consent to medical relief operations can, for states at least, also be derived from IHRL, particularly the ICCPR article 6(1) right to life and the ICESCR article 12(1) right to the highest attainable standard of health.[354]

GCIV article 23(1) provides that conflict parties and transit states must allow the free passage of medical supplies 'intended only for civilians of another High Contracting Party, even if the latter is its adversary'. As mentioned in Section 4 above, article 23 has now been superseded by the broader API articles 69-71 regime on emergency relief operations.[355] However, the article 23 free passage obligation remains relevant regarding preventive relief—which the API regime does not cover—because

351 The protection of medical relief operations is addressed in Chapter 6 (Section 3.3.1) on non-state humanitarian actors, because most humanitarian medics are Movement or NGO personnel.

352 GCIV (n 15) art 16; API (n 16) art 10; GCs (n 15) Common Article 3; APII (n 16) arts 7 and 8; Henckaerts and Doswald-Beck (n 18) rule 110.

353 Bouchet-Saulnier (n 61) 212–13; Oxford Guidance (n 47) para 114; Akande and Gillard 2019 (n 125) 771.

354 For more on how IHRL relates to medical relief operations in armed conflict, see Durham and Wynn-Pope (n 33) 341–42; Alexander Breitegger, 'The Legal Framework Applicable to Insecurity and Violence Affecting the Delivery of Health Care in Armed Conflicts and Other Emergencies' (2013) 95 International Review of the Red Cross 83; Brigit Toebes, 'Health and Humanitarian Assistance: Towards an Integrated Norm under International Law' (2013) 18 Tilburg Law Review 133, 137–41.

355 See sources cited at note 125.

article 23 is not contingent on civilians being inadequately supplied. Conflict parties and any transit states must thus allow the free passage of medical supplies, even if they are for civilians of an adversary. This is subject to several limitations related to military considerations.[356] They must also ensure that medical supplies are 'forwarded as rapidly as possible', subject to their right of control.[357]

5.2. Food relief

GCIV article 23, discussed immediately above, also mentions 'essential foodstuffs, clothing and tonics intended for children under fifteen, expectant mothers and maternity cases'. The beneficiary group was limited for military reasons: the items listed could conceivably reinforce the war economy, whereas the medical supplies also mentioned in article 23 could not.[358] The legal framework here is the same as above regarding medical supplies: article 23 has for the most part been overtaken by the API article 69-71 regime on emergency relief operations, which is not limited to children, pregnant women, and new mothers—although, as mentioned in Section 4.4.1, they must be prioritized in the distribution of relief—and does not include the limitations related to military considerations set out at article 23(2).[359] However, GCIV article 23 remains relevant to preventive relief because its applicability is not contingent on civilians being inadequately supplied. Preventive food relief is particularly important because once malnutrition sets in, it may be too late to prevent irreparable harm, particularly to young children.[360] Pursuant to GCIV article 23, conflict parties and any transit states must allow the free passage of relief consignments comprising food, clothing, and tonics destined for children, pregnant women, and new mothers,[361] subject to certain limitations related to military considerations.[362] They must also forward the consignment 'as rapidly as possible', subject to their right of control.[363]

IHRL is also relevant to food relief during armed conflict. This has been analysed in detail elsewhere.[364]

[356] GCIV (n 15) art 23(2). Again, in circumstances where API article 70 also applies, these limitations are effectively obsolete and conflict parties and any transit states 'have an absolute obligation to allow and facilitate rapid and unimpeded passage of medical relief supplies and equipment' (Oxford Guidance (n 47) para 88).

[357] GCIV (n 15) art 23(4).

[358] Pictet and others (n 54) 180.

[359] Oxford Guidance (n 47) para 92.

[360] Cesar Victoria and others, 'Maternal and Child Undernutrition: Consequences for Adult Health and Human Capital' (2008) 371 The Lancet 340.

[361] GCIV (n 15) art 23(1).

[362] ibid, art 23(2).

[363] ibid, art 23(4).

[364] Simone Hutter, 'Starvation in Armed Conflicts: An Analysis Based on the Right to Food' (2019) 17 Journal of International Criminal Justice 723; Simone Hutter, 'The Right to Food in Armed Conflict' in Bridget Conley and others (eds), *Accountability for Mass Starvation: Testing the Limits of the Law* (OUP 2022).

5.3. Civilians deprived of their liberty

Civilians detained for reasons related to an armed conflict are particularly vulnerable. As Sivakumaran notes, they 'have been deprived of their liberty; they are in the hands of the adverse party, the very entity against which the armed conflict is being fought; and they are at the mercy of their captors'.[365] There are several forms of civilian detention during armed conflict: internment; detention for reasons other than internment, such as criminal detention; and, in NIAC, detention by an OAG. IHL only governs detention related to the armed conflict. If a person is detained during an armed conflict for reasons unrelated to the conflict, IHRL applies. IHL protects the right of those detained in IAC or NIAC to receive humanitarian assistance.[366] Each type of armed conflict is addressed in turn.

5.3.1. International armed conflict

Civilians deprived of their liberty in IAC are protected by GCIV. Part II of GCIV (articles 13–26) protects all civilians, while part III (articles 27–141), which constitutes the bulk of GCIV, relates specifically to 'Protected Persons'. These are defined as all 'those who, at a given moment and in any manner whatsoever, find themselves, in case of a conflict or occupation, in the hands of a Party to the conflict or Occupying Power of which they are not nationals'.[367] Within part III, some provisions apply to all Protected Persons (articles 27–34), while others apply only to certain subsets of Protected Persons: civilians in the power of a conflict party of which they are not a national (also known as 'enemy aliens', articles 35–46), civilians in occupied territory (articles 47–78), and civilian internees (articles 79–135).[368] Because of this structure, a detained civilian's entitlement to relief depends on whether they are an enemy alien, in occupied territory, or interned.

Enemy aliens detained for any reason other than internment 'shall be enabled to receive the individual or collective relief that may be sent to them' and must receive any medical attention required 'to the same extent as the nationals' of the detaining power.[369]

Criminal detainees in occupied territory have the same right to relief as other civilians in occupied territory.[370] They thus have the right to be visited by the ICRC and to receive 'at least one relief parcel monthly'.[371] Pictet and others recommend 'that the Occupying Power should allow a higher number of parcels in view of the exclusively humanitarian character of the relief' and note that relief parcels do 'not in any way

365 Sandesh Sivakumaran, 'Armed Conflict-Related Detention of Particularly Vulnerable Persons: Challenges and Possibilities' (2018) 94 International Law Studies 39, 40.

366 On the protection of detainees more broadly, particularly vulnerable detainees, see Sivakumaran (n 365).

367 GCIV (n 15) art 4.

368 Internment is a specific type of deprivation of liberty without criminal charge ordered by the conflict party's executive branch (rather than by its judiciary) for non-punitive security reasons. Conflict parties' power to intern civilians is not unlimited (GCIV (n 15) art 79).

369 ibid, art 38(1–2). These rights to relief and medical care do not pertain to civilians detained in occupied territory, for which there is a distinct provision, discussed below.

370 See Sections 4.3 and 4.4.

371 GCIV (n 15) art 76(6–7).

mean that the Occupying Power is not called upon to supply the minimum amount of food and attention'[372] it must provide pursuant to the other provisions for civilians detained in occupied territory.[373]

Civilian internees in IAC have a range of rights relating to relief, outlined in GCIV articles 108–111. The detaining power must allow internees to receive individual and collective relief—including food, clothing, medical supplies, and religious, educational, or recreational books and objects—by post or other means.[374] Reinforcing the primary responsibility of conflict parties to meet the needs of civilians within their control,[375] internees' right to relief does not 'free the Detaining Power from the obligations imposed on it by' GCIV,[376] of which there are several.[377] The detaining power may temporarily limit the size of relief shipments for reasons of military necessity if the shipments are placing 'exceptional strain on transport or communications'.[378] If limits are imposed, the detaining power must notify the ICRC or 'any other organization giving assistance to the internees'[379]—the range of such 'other organizations' is addressed in the discussion of article 142 later in this section. The modalities for sending and receiving collective relief to civilian internees are regulated either by special agreement between the conflict parties or, in the absence of such an agreement, by the 'Draft Regulations Concerning Collective Relief' annexed to GCIV (annex II).[380] Internees organized as a committee have a right to receive and distribute relief and the ICRC and any other assisting organization are entitled to supervise distribution to prevent discrimination.[381] Neither of these rights may be abrogated by agreement between the conflict parties.[382] Relief for civilian internees must be completely exempt from import, customs and other dues, and postal charges,[383] and shipment costs must 'be borne by the Detaining Power in all the territories under its control'.[384] GCIV article 111 establishes that in the first instance, responsibility for transporting relief to internees resides with the detaining power. Nevertheless, if the detaining power is unable to fulfil this obligation for military reasons, article 111 provides that transport may be arranged by the ICRC or 'any other organization duly approved by the Parties to the conflict'.

Articles 30 and 142–143 of GCIV, when read in conjunction,[385] give effect to the protections described immediately above by ensuring Protected Persons' access to

[372] Pictet (n 54) 365–66.
[373] GCIV (n 15) art 76(1).
[374] ibid, art 108(1).
[375] See Chapter 1, Section 2 and Section 2 above.
[376] GCIV (n 15) art 108(1).
[377] See GCIV (n 15) arts 27, 79–135; Henckaerts and Doswald-Beck (n 18) rule 118. The treatment of civilian detainees was addressed by the ICTY in *Čelebići* (*Prosecutor v Delalic et al* (Judgement) IT-96-21-T (16 November 1998) and *Prosecutor v Aleksovski* (Judgement) IT-95-14/1-T (25 June 1999) paras 154–82.
[378] Pictet and others (n 54) 455.
[379] GCIV (n 15) art 108(2).
[380] ibid, art 109(1).
[381] Pictet and others (n 54) 458.
[382] GCIV (n 15) art 109(2–3).
[383] ibid, art 110(1–2).
[384] ibid, art 110(3).
[385] Iris van der Heijden, 'Other Issues Relating to the Treatment of Civilians in Enemy Hands' in Andrew Clapham, Paola Gaeta, and Marco Sassòli (eds), *The 1949 Geneva Conventions: A Commentary* (OUP 2015) 1254.

humanitarian organizations,[386] and vice versa,[387] in all places where such persons are located, particularly places of internment, detention, and work.[388] All impartial humanitarian organizations enjoy such access.[389] The detaining power must provide them with 'all facilities' for visiting Protected Persons and for distributing relief supplies,[390] subject to the measures the detaining power may consider essential to ensure its security or to meet any other reasonable need.[391] The detaining power may limit the number of organizations providing relief to Protected Persons, but not at the expense of 'effective and adequate relief to all' such persons.[392] The 'special position' of the ICRC in relation to Protected Persons 'shall be recognized and respected at all times'.[393] In view of this requirement, GCIV article 143 guarantees the ICRC's access to all places where Protected Persons are located;[394] this is also CIHL.[395]

While the specific provisions on relief for civilians deprived of their liberty discussed above are located in GCIV, there is no reason why the API regime on emergency relief operations would not apply equally to individuals deprived of their liberty. Consequently, relief actions may be undertaken in accordance with API article 70 if detainees in non-occupation IAC are not provided with adequate food, medical supplies, clothing, bedding, means of shelter, religious objects, and other supplies essential for their survival.

5.3.2. Non-international armed conflict

Civilians whose liberty has been restricted in NIAC,[396] including internees and individuals detained for other reasons,[397] must be allowed to 'receive individual or collective relief'.[398] As in IAC, this right does not diminish the conflict party's primary obligations to persons deprived of their liberty, which include humane treatment,[399] providing food and drinking water, and safeguarding health and hygiene to the same extent as the local civilian population.[400] Additionally, persons whose liberty has been restricted are entitled to medical examinations.[401] Wounded and sick detainees, in particular, must be 'respected and protected' and treated humanely,[402] and must receive 'to the fullest extent practicable and with the least possible delay, the medical care and attention required by their condition'.[403]

386 GCIV (n 15) art 30(1).
387 ibid, art 142(1).
388 ibid, art 143(1). See *Israel Obligations AO* (n 54) para 142.
389 Durham and Wynn-Pope (n 33) 335.
390 GCIV (n 15) arts 30(2) and 142(1).
391 ibid, art 142(1).
392 ibid, art 142(2).
393 ibid, art 142(3).
394 ibid, art 143(5).
395 Henckaerts and Doswald-Beck (n 18) rule 124A.
396 See generally Lawrence Hill-Cawthorne, *Detention in Non-International Armed Conflict* (OUP 2016) ch 3.
397 APII (n 16) art 5(1).
398 ibid, art 5(1)(c).
399 GCs (n 15) Common Article 3.
400 APII (n 16) art 5(1)(b); Henckaerts and Doswald-Beck (n 18) rules 118 and 121.
401 APII (n 16) art 5(2)(d); Henckaerts and Doswald-Beck (n 18) rule 118.
402 APII (n 16) arts 5(2)(a) and 7(a)–(b).
403 ibid, arts 5(2)(a) and 7(b).

Neither Common Article 3 nor APII requires conflict parties in NIAC to accept detention visits by the ICRC or any other humanitarian actor. In other words, there is no NIAC analog of GCIV articles 142–143. Nevertheless, as in IAC, there is no reason why APII article 18(2), covered in Section 4 above, cannot provide the basis for access to civilians detained in NIAC and who are 'suffering undue hardship owing to a lack of the supplies essential' for their survival.[404]

Civilians in NIAC may be detained by an OAG.[405] The ICRC estimates that in 2021, over 100 armed groups held detainees.[406] Such detention 'often presents legal and practical challenges, ranging from a lack of knowledge of international rules and standards [. . .] to practical challenges such as how to ensure humane conditions of detention'.[407] The ICRC's study of detention by OAGs provides examples of measures OAGs have taken to give effect to their IHL obligations towards detained persons, several of which involve collaboration with humanitarian organizations.[408]

5.4. Evacuated and displaced civilians

Evacuations 'are arrangements to remove people protected by IHL from locations where they are insecure, either because they face risks from military operations or because they cannot access adequate food, water and other basic goods and services'.[409] IHL includes several provisions on civilian evacuation, including regarding the evacuation of children;[410] civilians in the vicinity of military objectives;[411] persons detained or interned near a combat zone in NIAC;[412] Protected Persons in occupied territory;[413] and the wounded, sick, elderly, children, and pregnant women in besieged areas.[414] Evacuations must not amount to forced displacement, which is prohibited in occupied territory[415] and NIAC.[416] Forced displacement can in certain circumstances constitute a war crime (in both IAC and NIAC),[417] as well as a crime against humanity.[418] The distinction between lawful evacuation and unlawful forced

[404] ibid, art 18(2).
[405] See generally Ezequiel Heffes, *Detention by Non-State Armed Groups Under International Law* (CUP 2022).
[406] ICRC, 'Detention by Non-State Armed Groups: Obligations under International Humanitarian Law and Examples of How to Implement Them' (*ICRC*, 2023) <https://www.icrc.org/en/publication/4687-detention-non-state-armed-groups-obligations-under-international-humanitarian-law> accessed 29 June 2023, 8.
[407] ibid.
[408] ibid, 29.
[409] Gillard (n 129) 19.
[410] GCIV (n 15) arts 17 and 24(2); API (n 16) art 78; APII (n 16) art 4(3)(e).
[411] API (n 16) art 58(a); APII (n 16) art 17 (this provision refers to relocation orders rather than to evacuation); Henckaerts and Doswald-Beck (n 18) rule 24.
[412] APII (n 16) art 5(2)(c).
[413] GCIV (n 15) art 49(2–3).
[414] GCIV (n 15) art 17; Henckaerts and Doswald-Beck (n 18) rule 109.
[415] GCIV (n 15) art 49(1); Henckaerts and Doswald-Beck (n 18) rule 129A; see Mélanie Jacques, *Armed Conflict and Displacement* (CUP 2015) ch 1.
[416] APII (n 16) art 17(2); Henckaerts and Doswald-Beck (n 18) rule 129B; see Jacques (n 415) ch 2.
[417] Rome Statute of the International Criminal Court (adopted 17 July 1998, entered into force 1 July 2002) 2187 UNTS 3 (Rome Statute) arts 8(2)(b)(viii) and 8(2)(e)(viii).
[418] ibid, art 7(1)(d).

displacement turns on several factors, primarily whether the purpose is protective or illicit,[419] such as ethnic cleansing.

In practice, evacuations can be conducted by an impartial humanitarian organization.[420] For example, in 2023 the ICRC moved more than 300 children and 71 caretakers from the Mygoma Orphanage in Khartoum, Sudan, to the safer Sudanese city of Wad Madani.[421] Evacuations by humanitarian organizations typically proceed further to an agreement or arrangement between the organization and the relevant conflict party or parties, as contemplated by several IHL provisions on evacuation.[422]

Some of the IHL provisions on evacuation specify standards that must be met in receiving evacuated civilians. GCIV article 49(3) provides that in evacuating civilians from occupied territory, the occupying power must 'ensure, to the greatest practicable extent, that proper accommodation is provided to receive the protected persons, that the removals are effected in satisfactory conditions of hygiene, health, safety and nutrition, and that members of the same family are not separated'. Regarding evacuations effectuated in NIAC for the security of civilians or imperative military reasons, APII article 17(1) provides that 'all possible measures shall be taken in order that the civilian population may be received under satisfactory conditions of shelter, hygiene, health, safety and nutrition'. CIHL includes a similar rule, applicable in both IAC and NIAC, stated in stronger terms: in 'case of displacement, all possible measures must be taken in order that the civilians concerned are received under satisfactory conditions of shelter, hygiene, health, safety and nutrition and that members of the same family are not separated'.[423] This customary rule benefits not only civilians displaced internally pursuant to an evacuation notice but all individuals internally displaced by armed conflict.[424] If the state in control of the area to which people are displaced cannot meet this obligation, then it has a customary 'obligation to permit the free passage of humanitarian assistance to internally displaced persons'.[425] This customary obligation is akin to that under CIHL rule 55[426] and includes both the step one consent obligation and the step two implementation obligation discussed in Section 4 above.[427]

6. Unlawful impeding of emergency relief operations

Relief operations are impeded unlawfully when there are civilians in need and: (i) an occupying power does not consent to relief offered by third states or impartial

[419] See Yousuf Syed Khan, 'The Directive to Evacuate Northern Gaza: Advance Warning or Forced Displacement?' (*Just Security*, 19 October 2023) <https://www.justsecurity.org/89617/the-directive-to-evacuate-northern-gaza-advance-warning-or-forced-displacement/> accessed 16 November 2023.

[420] See Gillard (n 129) 28–29.

[421] ICRC, 'Sudan: Relief as ICRC Evacuates 300 Children "Towards Safety, Away from the Sounds of Gunfire"' (*ICRC*, 9 June 2023) <https://www.icrc.org/en/document/sudan-relief-icrc-evacuates-300-children> accessed 10 August 2023.

[422] GCIV (n 15) art 17; API (n 16) art 78; APII (n 16) art 4(3)(e).

[423] Henckaerts and Doswald-Beck (n 18) rule 131.

[424] ibid, 463–68.

[425] ibid, 467.

[426] ibid.

[427] Guiding Principles on Internal Displacement (n 255) principle 25.

humanitarian organizations; (ii) a conflict party subject to a relevant Security Council decision does not allow the relief operation to proceed according to the decision; (iii) a conflict party or transit state withholds its consent to offers of relief in violation of international law; or (iv) a conflict party or transit state violates its obligation to allow and facilitate and related implementation obligations.[428] The first and second situations are straightforward: if an occupying power cannot provide for civilians in occupied territory, it must consent to emergency relief operations,[429] and a conflict party ordered by the Security Council to accept emergency relief must comply with that decision.[430] The third and fourth situations, however, are more complex; each is addressed in turn.

6.1. Withholding of strategic consent

As explained in Section 4.3 above, if there is need among the civilian population and the relief offered meets the criteria set by IHL, the affected conflict party's consent to relief operations is required and may not be—either arbitrarily or unlawfully—withheld.[431] Until recently, a conflict party's latitude in this regard—in other words, what would amount to justified withholding of consent—was barely theorized. No judicial body had addressed the issue. Among the few commentators who had briefly or incidentally covered it, some viewed the conflict party as having wide discretion,[432] while for others, there was little room for manoeuvre.[433]

Two distinct views are now competing to fill this void. As introduced in Section 4.3.1 above, the alternative interpretations of withheld consent as either arbitrary or unlawful stem from the approach of Akande and Gillard and the Oxford Guidance on the one hand, and the ICRC on the other. Each is addressed in turn in this section, which concludes with analysis of the two approaches grounded in the reason conflict parties in practice invoke to justify withholding consent to relief: imperative considerations of military necessity.

6.1.1. Arbitrary withholding of strategic consent

The lack of clarity around consent to relief operations contributed to the UN Secretary-General's 2013 call for 'analysis and development' of the law,[434] which resulted in the 2016 publication of the Oxford Guidance. One of the background studies commissioned in connection with the Guidance's development was published, also in 2016, by Akande and Gillard as an academic article.[435] The Oxford Guidance and

[428] These typologies of unlawful impeding are based on those used in the Oxford Guidance ((n 47) para 131).
[429] See Section 4.3.
[430] UN Charter (n 229) art 25. See Chapter 5, Section 4.4.2.
[431] On the arbitrary withholding of consent by non-belligerent states, see Oxford Guidance (n 47) paras 108–19.
[432] Dinstein (n 203) 84; Durham and Wynn-Pope (n 33) 334 and 337.
[433] Jelena Pejic, 'The Right to Food in Situations of Armed Conflict: The Legal Framework' (2001) 83 International Review of the Red Cross 1097, 1103.
[434] UNSC (n 188) para 58. See Section 4.2.
[435] Akande and Gillard 2016 (n 196).

this article are important sources regarding consent to relief operations. Both adopt the 'arbitrary' framing, finding that a conflict party withholds its consent arbitrarily in three sets of circumstances: if the withholding (i) violates the party's international law obligations regarding the civilian population in question; (ii) violates the principles of necessity and proportionality; or (iii) is 'unreasonable, unjust, lacking in predictability or otherwise inappropriate'.[436]

Regarding the first set of circumstances, Akande and Gillard provide a non-exhaustive list of examples of conflict parties' international law obligations to civilians:[437] the prohibition of starvation of civilians as a method of warfare and the related obligation to protect objects indispensable to their survival;[438] the obligation to consent to medical relief operations;[439] the prohibitions of discrimination under IHL[440] and IHRL;[441] and IHRL obligations more generally, such as the obligation to meet the 'minimum core' of relevant economic, social, and cultural rights.[442] The principles of necessity and proportionality in the second set of circumstances are drawn from IHRL. Human rights judicial bodies have consistently found that for conduct not to be arbitrary, it must 'be necessary for achieving legitimate ends and a proportionate means of achieving those ends'.[443] Finally, Akande and Gillard draw their notion of unreasonableness from international human rights decisions, which have found that arbitrariness includes 'elements of inappropriateness, injustice, lack of predictability' and unreasonableness in the circumstances.[444] They explain that applied to emergency relief operations, 'withholding of consent will be regarded as arbitrary [. . .] if the reasons for withholding consent, though not inherently unlawful, fail to accord with the values that underpin IHL and IHRL' or if the manner of the withholding 'leads to injustice or lack of predictability'.[445] For example, consent would be withheld arbitrarily if no reasons are provided or if reasons are based on factual errors, such as a denial of need without a proper assessment.[446]

6.1.2. Unlawful withholding of strategic consent

On the ICRC view, when a conflict party has not fulfilled its primary obligation to meet the needs of the population and appropriate offers of services have been made, there are no lawful grounds to withhold strategic consent.[447] While the 'arbitrary' approach outlined above invokes IHRL, the ICRC's 'unlawful' approach

436 Akande and Gillard 2016 (n 196) 494.
437 ibid, 496–97; for additional examples, see Oxford Guidance (n 47) para 51.
438 API (n 16) art 54; APII (n 16) art 14; Henckaerts and Doswald-Beck (n 18) rule 53. The same authors analysed this obligation in depth in Akande and Gillard 2019 (n 125).
439 API (n 16) art 10; APII (n 16) art 7. See Section 5.1.
440 GCIV (n 15) art 13 and API (n 16) art 75(1); GCs (n 15) Common Article 3 and API (n 16) art 4(1).
441 ICESCR (n 153) art 2(2); ICCPR (n 154) arts 2(1) and 26.
442 CESCR, 'General Comment No. 3: The Nature of States Parties' Obligations (Art. 2, Para. 1, of the Covenant)' (14 December 1990) E/1991/23, para 10.
443 Akande and Gillard 2016 (n 196) 498.
444 ibid.
445 ibid, 500.
446 ibid, 501.
447 ICRC Lexicon (n 41) 369.

limits itself to IHL. This divergence reflects the broader debate regarding how IHL and IHRL interact when both bodies of law apply.[448] Akande and Gillard explicitly acknowledge that their 'arbitrary' approach is grounded in the Vienna Convention on the Law of Treaties' (VCLT) notion of systemic integration,[449] which provides that treaties should be interpreted in light of 'any relevant rules of international law applicable in the relations between the parties'.[450] As a result, they and the Oxford Guidance interpret IHL in light of IHRL.[451] In contrast, the ICRC considers only IHL—possibly as the *lex specialis*, an interpretive maxim which, when invoked to resolve a specific norm conflict,[452] indicates that specialist law trumps more general law.[453]

IHRL and IHL are for the most part complementary and thus the simultaneous applicability of both bodies of law rarely raises any need to resort to *lex specialis* in the sense of a provision of IHL setting a norm of IHRL aside.[454] Indeed, the maxim should only be invoked in relation to genuine norm conflicts,[455] and only to the extent required to resolve the conflict.[456] It seems that the crux of the divergence between the 'arbitrary' and 'unlawful' approaches to withheld consent is whether a true norm conflict exists in relation to military necessity, the reason typically raised by conflict parties to justify withholding strategic consent. For Akande and Gillard and under the Oxford Guidance, IHL can be interpreted in light of IHRL because this does not produce a norm conflict. For the ICRC, interpreting IHL on this issue in light of IHRL produces a result incompatible with IHL and thus IHL must be applied alone as the *lex specialis*. Alternatively, it may be that the ICRC simply sees no basis on which to invoke IHRL in relation to API article 70(1) and APII article 18(2)—this is explored in practical terms below.

[448] On this debate, see Marko Milanović, *Extraterritorial Application of Human Rights Treaties: Law, Principles, and Policy* (OUP 2011) ch 5; Derek Jinks, 'International Human Rights Law in Time of Armed Conflict' in Andrew Clapham and Paola Gaeta (eds), *The Oxford Handbook of International Law in Armed Conflict* (OUP 2014); Jens David Ohlin (ed), *Theoretical Boundaries of Armed Conflict and Human Rights* (CUP 2016). Additionally, and more generally, the 'arbitrariness' approach gives more weight to the foundational international law principles of sovereignty and non-intervention than does the ICRC's 'unlawfulness' approach. For a critique of placing too much weight on the principle of non-intervention in relation to emergency relief operations, see Barber ((n 213) 92–99).

[449] Akande and Gillard 2016 (n 196) 495.

[450] (Adopted 23 May 1969, entered into force 27 January 1980) 1155 UNTS 331 (VCLT) art 31(3)(c).

[451] Watts criticizes the Oxford Guidance in this regard but fails to acknowledge the approach's legal basis in the VCLT, arguing instead that the Oxford Guidance 'whether by error, or by clever turn' misapplies *lex specialis* (Sean Watts, 'Humanitarian Logic and the Law of Siege: A Study of the Oxford Guidance on Relief Actions' (2019) 95 International Law Studies 1, 36).

[452] *Lex specialis* can also be used to assist in the interpretation of a general provision applicable to a matter also governed by a more specific norm.

[453] This was the approach taken in, for example, the *Nuclear Weapons Advisory Opinion* (n 5) para 25 and the *Wall Advisory Opinion* (n 5) para 106.

[454] Cordula Droege, 'The Interplay between International Humanitarian Law and International Human Rights Law in Situations of Armed Conflict' (2007) 40 Israel Law Review 310.

[455] On the distinction between apparent and genuine norm conflicts, see Joost Pauwelyn, *Conflict of Norms in Public International Law: How WTO Law Relates to Other Rules of International Law* (CUP 2003) 178.

[456] Marko Milanović, 'The Lost Origins of *Lex Specialis*: Rethinking the Relationship Between Human Rights and International Humanitarian Law' in Ohlin (n 448) 104.

6.1.3. Military necessity

The 'arbitrary' and 'unlawful' approaches produce two distinct views of whether military necessity may be invoked as a valid ground to refuse to consent to relief at step one. On the former approach, military necessity is a valid reason to withhold strategic consent, provided it is not 'withheld beyond what military necessity demands'.[457] Here Akande and Gillard invoke IHRL necessity and proportionality, finding that limitations 'in terms of time, duration, location, and affected goods and services must not go beyond what is absolutely necessary to achieve the legitimate' military necessity aim of the conflict party withholding consent.[458] Bothe and others,[459] as well as some states,[460] also view military necessity as a legitimate reason for a conflict party to withhold strategic consent to relief.

The ICRC, however, finds that this systemic interpretation of IHL in line with IHRL necessity and proportionality produces a result irreconcilable with IHL itself. According to the ICRC, military necessity can 'be invoked in exceptional circumstances in order to regulate—but not prohibit—humanitarian access, and can only *temporarily* and *geographically* restrict the freedom of movement of humanitarian personnel. Military necessity cannot be used under IHL to turn down a valid offer of services or to deny in their entirety the humanitarian activities proposed by impartial humanitarian organizations'.[461] In other words, for the ICRC, a conflict party may invoke military necessity at step two (implementation) in the context of its right of control, but there is no basis in IHL for a conflict party to invoke it at step one. Thus, for the ICRC, either systemic integration produces a result incompatible with IHL so the issue is properly analysed under IHL alone as the *lex specialis*, or there is simply no basis for systemic integration in relation to this issue because IHRL does not address strategic consent to emergency relief operations.

Evaluating the 'arbitrary' and 'unlawful' approaches is essentially an assessment of two distinct interpretations of the underlying treaty rules, API article 70(1) and APII article 18(2). In other words, it is a question of treaty interpretation. The two approaches should thus be evaluated from the perspective of which reflects 'the ordinary meaning' of these rules, 'in their context and in light of' their 'object and purpose'.[462] If the rules' ordinary meaning was clear, the two distinct approaches would not both exist. Their object and purpose is to ensure that undersupplied civilians receive the relief they need, without relief actions infringing state sovereignty. The 'unlawful' approach is more likely to fulfil this object and purpose, as both approaches require state consent, but under the 'arbitrary' approach, civilians can be lawfully deprived of relief until their suffering becomes disproportionate to the military considerations of the conflict party withholding it. The 'unlawful' approach is thus easier to reconcile with the object and purpose of the underlying treaty rules. Moreover, it does not discount

[457] Akande and Gillard 2016 (n 196) 499; see also Oxford Guidance (n 47) para 52.

[458] ibid.

[459] Bothe and others (n 125) 434; Bothe and others (n 221) 485; Bothe (n 251) 95.

[460] See, for example, United Kingdom Ministry of Defence, *The Joint Service Manual of the Law of Armed Conflict* (Joint Service Publication 383, 2004) (UK Military Manual) para 9.12.1.

[461] ICRC Lexicon (n 41) 364 (emphasis in original).

[462] VCLT (n 450) art 31(1).

military necessity entirely, it merely addresses it in the context of operational (rather than strategic) consent.

An additional object and purpose of the rules is to lay out a clear legal framework for relief actions. The 'arbitrary' approach can produce what amounts to legal distinctions that are of no practical effect—the opposite of a clear framework. Recall that emergency relief operations are conducted when civilians are inadequately supplied with essential items and that strategic consent is 'the initial and general authorisation to carry out operations in a particular country'.[463] It is hard to imagine circumstances in which civilians lack basic items such as food and the relevant conflict party could withhold this initial and general authorization for reasons of military necessity *without* it violating its international legal obligations to the civilians in question or the principles of necessity and proportionality, or without the withholding being unreasonable, unjust, lacking in predictability, or otherwise inappropriate. The distinction between the 'arbitrary' and 'unlawful' approaches to step one strategic consent thus looks more like a theoretical legal distinction rather than one that will make any real practical difference. In other words, if strategic consent withheld for reasons of military necessity will almost always be arbitrary, then there is no real difference in practice between this approach and that of the ICRC. And this legal framework 'will not be used in litigation, where an independent and impartial judicial body makes a determination of the relative merits of the legal arguments of those wishing to provide assistance and of affected states'.[464] Rather, it 'will be the background to guide negotiations with affected states'.[465] With this in mind, it is hard to imagine that the drafters of the Additional Protocols intended to craft a framework that permits legal wrangling with little to no practical effect. They more likely intended to articulate a clear framework: when civilians are in need and relief actions that are impartial in character and conducted without adverse distinction have been offered, the offer must be accepted, with practical concerns such as military necessity addressed as a matter of implementation.

For these reasons, the ICRC's 'unlawful' interpretation seems the more accurate one. In what may amount to the same preference, the Security Council, which has in the past used the terminology of arbitrariness,[466] has more recently used 'unlawful'.[467] A recent United Kingdom (UK) parliamentary committee report took the same approach.[468]

[463] Conflict & Hunger Handbook (n 114) 70.

[464] Gillard (n 109) 354.

[465] ibid.

[466] UNSC Res 2139 (22 February 2014) S/RES/2139, preambular para 10; UNSC Res 2165 (n 193) preambular para 15.

[467] UNSC Res 2417 (24 May 2018) S/RES/2417, paras 4 and 6.

[468] House of Commons International Development Committee, 'Protection Not Permission: The UK's Role in Upholding International Humanitarian Law and Supporting the Safe Delivery of Humanitarian Aid' (12 June 2025) Fifth Report of Session 2024–25, HC 526 <https://committees.parliament.uk/publications/48324/documents/252895/default/> accessed 17 June 2025, which noted that the 'parties to the conflict must consent to . . . [humanitarian] activities when the needs of the population under their control are not met' (6). The report elaborates in a footnote, where it explains that when 'a party to an armed conflict is unable or unwilling to fulfil its primary obligation to meet the needs of its population and when offers of services have been made by impartial humanitarian organisations, there are no lawful grounds to withhold or deny consent to the undertaking of humanitarian activities' (footnote 8).

6.2. Violation of the obligation to allow and facilitate relief

Emergency relief operations are also unlawfully impeded if a conflict party fails to comply with its central obligation to allow and facilitate. IHL prescribes several specific sub-obligations related to this central obligation, which were detailed in Section 4.4.2 above. The negative obligations are particularly relevant to unlawful impeding. These are the prohibitions against diverting relief supplies from their intended purpose or delaying their forwarding, unless there is urgent necessity in the interest of the civilians in need;[469] limiting the activities of relief personnel or temporarily restricting their movement beyond what is required for reasons of imperative military necessity;[470] and, in situations of occupation, levying charges, taxes, or customs duties on relief supplies, unless these are necessary in the interests of the occupied territory's economy.[471] Akande and Gillard's analysis suggests that a clear violation of any of these negative obligations would amount to a violation of the obligation to allow and facilitate.[472]

Beyond this, it is not easy 'to determine the point at which the effect of constraints, impediments or delays to humanitarian relief operations is of such a nature and extent as to amount to a violation of the obligation to allow and facilitate' because 'IHL instruments do not provide guidance on this issue and to date it has not been addressed by any national or international tribunal'.[473] Akande and Gillard go on to explain that the 'issue should not be analysed in terms of the bilateral relationship between' the actors concerned, but rather in terms of 'the outstanding needs of the civilian population'.[474] If all or part of the civilian population is left 'without essential relief items or specific services for prolonged periods of time', then the conflict party in question can be considered to have violated the obligation to allow and facilitate and thus to have unlawfully impeded emergency relief operations.[475]

6.2.1. Siege and blockade

As mentioned in the introduction, siege is a military tactic in which the besieging party cuts people in a defined area, such as a city, off from life-sustaining supplies to facilitate the capture of or operations in the place in question. Although aimed at combatants, civilians are often caught up in sieges, such as in Gaza (2023, 2025),[476] Mariupol (2022),[477]

469 API (n 16) art 70(3)(c).
470 ibid, art 71(3).
471 GCIV (n 15) art 61(2).
472 Akande and Gillard 2017 (n 125) 124–25; Akande and Gillard 2019 (n 125) 773–74.
473 Akande and Gillard 2017 (n 125) 126.
474 ibid.
475 ibid.
476 Tom Dannenbaum, 'The Siege of Gaza and the Starvation War Crime' (*Just Security*, 11 October 2023) <https://www.justsecurity.org/89403/the-siege-of-gaza-and-the-starvation-war-crime/> accessed 12 October 2023; Erika Solomon and Rawan Sheikh Ahmad, 'As Gaza Siege Grinds On, Gazan Children Go Hungry and Patients Die' (*The New York Times*, 4 May 2025) <https://www.nytimes.com/2025/05/04/world/europe/israel-gaza-blockade-humanitarian-crisis.html> accessed 4 May 2025.
477 Michael Schwirtz, 'Last Stand at the Steelworks: Inside an 80-Day Siege' *The New York Times* (New York, 24 July 2022) A1.

Tigray (2020–2022),[478] Aleppo[479] (2016) and Eastern Ghouta (2018),[480] Mosul (2016–2017),[481] Grozny (1994–1995, 1999–2000), and Sarajevo (1992–1996)[482] and Srebrenica (1992–1995).[483] Siege is not prohibited by IHL unless the tactic's sole or primary purpose is to starve civilians or destroy objects essential to their survival.[484] It is also unlawful for an occupying power to besiege the territory it occupies, as this violates the occupying power's absolute obligation to provide for civilians in occupied territory.[485]

As the party in control of the civilian population in the besieged area, the besieged party bears primary responsibility for meeting their needs.[486] However, scarcity engendered by the siege may prevent it from fulfilling this obligation, giving rise to need among the civilian population. There are two views regarding whether the besieging party can invoke military necessity—the necessity of maintaining the siege—as a reason to limit humanitarian access in these circumstances. Dinstein, Gillard, and the ICRC view this as impermissible,[487] although Dinstein is critical of the law in this regard.[488] Watts, by contrast, contends that the military imperative of maintaining a

[478] Kenneth Roth, 'Confronting Ethiopia's Abusive Siege' (*Human Rights Watch*, 31 August 2022) <https://www.hrw.org/news/2022/08/31/confronting-ethiopias-abusive-siege> accessed 4 July 2025.

[479] Maks Czuperski, Emma Beals, Faysal Itani, Eliot Higgins, and Ben Nimmo, 'Breaking Aleppo' (*Atlantic Council*, 2017) <https://www.atlanticcouncil.org/in-depth-research-reports/report/breaking-aleppo/> accessed 26 September 2023.

[480] Independent International Commission of Inquiry on the Syrian Arab Republic, 'Sieges as a Weapon of War: Encircle, Starve, Surrender, Evacuate' (29 May 2018) <https://www.ohchr.org/sites/default/files/Documents/HRBodies/HRCouncil/CoISyria/PolicyPaperSieges_29May2018.pdf> accessed 26 March 2025.

[481] Amos C Fox, 'The Mosul Study Group and the Lessons of the Battle of Mosul' (2020) *The Association of the United States Army, Land Warfare* Paper 130 <https://www.ausa.org/sites/default/files/publications/LWP-130-The-Mosul-Study-Group-and-the-Lessons-of-the-Battle-of-Mosul.pdf> accessed 26 September 2023.

[482] *Prosecutor v Milošević* (Judgement) ICTY-98-29/1-T, T Ch III (12 December 2007), para 415.

[483] Kraska (n 1) para 3.

[484] API (n 16) art 54; APII (n 16) art 14; Gloria Gaggioli, 'Joint Blog Series on International Law and Armed Conflict: Are Sieges Prohibited under Contemporary IHL?' (*EJIL:Talk!*, 30 January 2019) <https://www.ejiltalk.org/joint-blog-series-on-international-law-and-armed-conflict-are-sieges-prohibited-under-contemporary-ihl/> accessed 26 September 2023; Gloria Gaggioli and Nils Melzer, 'Methods of Warfare' in Ben Saul and Dapo Akande (eds), *The Oxford Guide to International Humanitarian Law* (OUP 2020) 248–49; San Remo Manual (n 172) para 102.

[485] GCIV (n 15) arts 55 and 59.

[486] See Chapter 1, Section 2 and Section 2 above, as well as Emanuela-Chiara Gillard, 'Sieges, the Law and Protecting Civilians' (*Chatham House*, June 2019) <https://www.chathamhouse.org/2019/06/sieges-law-and-protecting-civilians> accessed 22 September 2023, 11.

[487] Yoram Dinstein, 'Siege Warfare and the Starvation of Civilians' in Astrid Delissen and Gerard Tanja (eds), *Humanitarian Law of Armed Conflict Challenges Ahead: Essays in Honour of Frits Kalshoven* (Martinus Nijhoff 1991) 143; Gillard (n 486) 11; ICRC, 'International Humanitarian Law and the Challenges of Contemporary Armed Conflicts: Recommitting to Protection in Armed Conflict on the 70th Anniversary of the Geneva Conventions' (*ICRC*, 2019) <https://www.icrc.org/en/publication/4427-international-humanitarian-law-and-challenges-contemporary-armed-conflicts> accessed 26 September 2023, 25. See also Laurie R Blank, 'Joint Blog Series: Sieges, Evacuations and Urban Warfare: Thoughts from the Transatlantic Workshop on International Law and Armed Conflict' (*EJIL:Talk!*, 17 January 2019) <https://www.ejiltalk.org/joint-blog-series-sieges-evacuations-and-urban-warfare-thoughts-from-the-transatlantic-workshop-on-international-law-and-armed-conflict/> accessed 25 September 2023 and Kraska (n 1) para 10.

[488] Dinstein (n 487) 150–52.

siege is a valid basis for denying humanitarian access.[489] Some states, such as the UK, Denmark, and Israel, also take this view.[490] The UK military manual, for example, states that as 'long as the besieging commander left open his offer to allow civilians and the wounded and sick to leave the besieged area, he would be justified in preventing any supplies from reaching that area'.[491]

These divergent views depend on the step at which access is considered. Because emergency relief operations would typically already be underway in the state where the siege is taking place, Dinstein, Gillard, and the ICRC address relief to besieged civilians in terms of the step two obligation to allow and facilitate. For the same reason, siege is addressed in this section rather than as part of the withheld consent analysis at Section 6.1 above. Because the obligation to allow and facilitate is an obligation of the 'Parties to the conflict'[492] (i.e. both the besieged and the besieging forces) and because it is an obligation not just of means but also one of result,[493] the besieging party must allow relief to reach civilians in the besieged area.[494] While this is subject to both parties' right of control—which allows the imposition of 'temporary and geographically limited restrictions required by military necessity at the time and place of on-going hostilities'[495]—an attempt by the besieging force to block relief entirely in order to maintain the siege would not be temporary.

Watts, by contrast, addresses the issue as one of step one strategic consent.[496] This approach is problematic for three reasons. First, if emergency relief operations are already underway in the state where the siege is taking place, step one strategic consent—as the initial authorization to conduct relief operations in a particular state—simply does not arise; access to civilians in need is a question of the step two obligation to allow and facilitate, which as just mentioned is an obligation of all parties to the conflict. Indeed, article 23 of GCIV, which was drafted in response to the cognate blockade context,[497] imposes a free passage obligation, rather than one relating to initial access to territory.

The second and third issues arise in the factual scenario in which relief operations are *not* already underway in the state where people are in need. Watts's approach of requiring the consent of both belligerents, including the besieging force,[498] is difficult

489 Watts (n 451). See also Michael Schmitt, Kieran Tinkler, and Durward Johnson, 'The UN Yemen Report and Siege Warfare' (*Just Security*, 12 September 2019) <https://www.justsecurity.org/66137/the-un-yemen-report-and-siege-warfare/> accessed 22 September 2023.

490 UK Military Manual (n 460) s 5.34.3.; Danish Ministry of Defence, *Military Manual on International Law Relevant to Danish Armed Forces in International Operations* (2020) 419; Israel Defence Forces, Military Advocate-General's Corps Command, IDF School of Military Law, *Rules of Warfare on the Battlefield* (2nd edn, 2006) 37.

491 UK Military Manual (n 460) s 5.34.3.

492 API (n 16) art 70(2).

493 ICRC Lexicon (n 41) 374.

494 Dinstein (n 487) 150; Gillard (n 486) 11; ICRC (n 487) 25; see also Abby Zeith, 'Trapped in Conflict: Urban Sieges and Encirclement' (*ICRC Humanitarian Law & Policy*, 20 June 2024) <https://blogs.icrc.org/law-and-policy/2024/06/20/trapped-in-conflict-urban-sieges-and-encirclement/> accessed 4 July 2024. Also note that conflict parties must 'endeavour to conclude local agreements [. . .] for the passage of [. . .] medical personnel and medical equipment on their way to' besieged areas (GCIV (n 15) art 17).

495 ICRC (n 487) 25.

496 Watts (n 451).

497 Dinstein (n 203) 81.

498 Watts notes: '[c]onsent of the belligerent parties appears to be a precondition to deliveries of humanitarian relief under Article 70(1)' (Watts (n 451) 22).

to reconcile with article 70(1) of API. This provision subjects emergency relief operations to the consent of 'the Parties concerned in such' actions; the besieging force is not among those 'concerned' within the meaning of article 70(1). According to Sandoz and others, in IAC 'an adverse party to that receiving relief'—in this case, this besieging force—'is not among *the Parties concerned* in the sense of' article 70(1).[499] For example, if during the 2022 siege of Mariupol impartial humanitarian actors not already present in Ukraine offered to provide relief, only Ukrainian—and not Russian—consent would be required.

The law in NIAC refers to the 'High Contracting Party concerned'.[500] This refers to 'the government in power' or,[501] in other words, the state party to the NIAC on whose territory relief is needed.[502] Where a state besieges its own citizens, as occurred in Iraq (Mosul) and north-west Syria during the 2010s, this implies that the besieging force's consent is required, though it would be rare in such circumstances for humanitarian actors to not already be present in-country—in which case, as discussed above, consent would be a matter of step two operational consent. Indeed, in the Syria case, the Security Council determined that Syria was required to consent to relief, and when it refused, the Council imposed relief actions.[503] Finally, Watts's approach is impossible to reconcile with the ICRC's 'unlawfulness' approach to strategic consent, in which military necessity—including the military necessity of maintaining a siege—may not be invoked at step one.[504]

Additionally, Watts's conclusion that a besieging force may withhold strategic consent to relief is difficult to reconcile with the prohibition of the starvation of civilians as a method of warfare,[505] although the scope of this prohibition is not settled.[506] It also does not account for how API superseded GCIV article 23.[507] Article 23 allows a besieging or blockading force to block relief from entering the encircled area if there are 'serious reasons for fearing [. . .] that a definite advantage may accrue to the military efforts or economy of the enemy through the substitution of [. . .] consignments for goods which would otherwise be provided or produced by the enemy'.[508] Sandoz

[499] Sandoz and others (n 90) para 2806. See also Oxford Guidance (n 47) para 23.
[500] APII (n 16) art 18(2).
[501] Sandoz and others (n 90) para 4884.
[502] Oxford Guidance (n 47) para 27.
[503] See Chapter 5, Section 4.4.2.
[504] See Sections 4.3.1 and 6.1.2.
[505] API (n 16) art 54; APII (n 16) art 14; Henckaerts and Doswald-Beck (n 18) rule 53.
[506] The disagreement relates to whether only the intentional starvation of civilians is prohibited, or whether the prohibition also includes starvation incidental to any deliberate deprivation of objects indispensable to the survival of the civilian population. See Akande and Gillard 2019 (n 125); Gloria Gaggioli, 'Besieging Cities and Humanitarian Access: How to Accommodate Humanitarian Needs, Legal Obligations and Operational Constraints?' (2020) Proceedings of the 20th Bruges Colloquium: Legal Challenges for Protecting and Assisting in Current Armed Conflicts <https://www.coleurope.eu/sites/default/files/uploads/page/collegium_50_lowres.pdf> accessed 26 September 2023, 122–26; Tom Dannenbaum, 'Criminalizing Starvation in an Age of Mass Deprivation in War: Intent, Method, Form, and Consequence' (2022) 55 Vanderbilt Journal of Transnational Law 681, 748–49; Tom Dannenbaum, 'Siege Starvation: A War Crime of Societal Torture' (2022) 22 Chicago Journal of International Law 368; Rosa-Lena Lauterbach, 'Humanitarian Relief as a Bargaining Chip' (*Articles of War*, 25 March 2025) <https://lieber.westpoint.edu/humanitarian-relief-bargaining-chip/> accessed 14 August 2025.
[507] See authorities cited at note 125.
[508] GCIV (n 15) art 23(2)(c).

and others note that with the adoption of API article 70, there is now 'no way one could weigh the humanitarian considerations of an action destined to ensure the survival of a civilian population lacking essential supplies against the military advantage that such an action could have for the receiving Party'.[509]

Technical guidance on this issue in the cognate context of blockade—in which a broader geographical area is isolated—mostly aligns with the Dinstein/Gillard/ICRC view. Both the San Remo Manual and the Harvard *Manual on International Law Applicable to Air and Missile Warfare* provide that a blockading party must allow the free passage of essential supplies through naval and aerial blockades respectively.[510] The UK Military Manual says the same regarding naval blockades.[511] Additionally, the Report of the Secretary-General's Panel of Inquiry on the 31 May 2010 Flotilla Incident—in which a ship forming part of the Freedom Flotilla Coalition, which was attempting to break Israel's naval blockade of Gaza, was intercepted by Israeli forces,[512] who killed 10 crew members—concluded that 'the blockading power has an obligation to allow for [... humanitarian] assistance to be provided where necessary'.[513] However, the *Newport Manual on the Law of Naval Warfare* states that there 'is no exemption from blockade enforcement for vessels carrying humanitarian materials intended for the civilian population of a blockaded area'.[514]

While weight of authority regarding both siege and blockade suggests that relief must be allowed to reach civilians in need, the law in this area needs clarification. Bellal and Casey-Maslen have suggested that the General Assembly should adopt a resolution in this regard.[515]

6.3. Operational consequences of withheld strategic consent

If a conflict party withholds strategic consent unlawfully, this does not give rise to an entitlement to conduct unauthorized operations.[516] In the absence of Security Council

509 Sandoz and others (n 90) paras 2850–51.

510 San Remo Manual (n 172) paras 103–04 (contra: Phillip J. Drew, 'Can We Starve the Civilians? Exploring the Dichotomy Between the Traditional Law of Maritime Blockade and Humanitarian Initiatives' (2019) 95 International Law Studies 302); Harvard University Program on Humanitarian Policy and Conflict Research, *Manual on International Law Applicable to Air and Missile Warfare* (CUP 2013) para 158. See also Tom Dannenbaum, 'Encirclement, Deprivation, and Humanity: Revising the San Remo Manual Provisions on Blockade' (2021) 97 International Law Studies 307 and Martin Fink, 'Delivery of Humanitarian Aid from the Sea' (*Articles of War*, 13 December 2023) <https://lieber.westpoint.edu/delivery-humanitarian-aid-from-sea/> accessed 5 January 2024.

511 UK Military Manual (n 460) para 13.75.

512 A similar incident occurred in June 2025, when Israel intercepted the Freedom Flotilla Coalition's ship *Madleen*, which was carrying relief supplies bound for Gaza. The 12 activists on board, including Swedish climate activist Greta Thunberg, were detained and some were deported (Amnesty International, 'What Happened to the Madleen and Why Were They Trying to Reach Gaza' (11 June 2025) <https://amnesty.ca/features/what-happened-to-the-madleen-and-why-were-they-trying-to-reach-gaza/> accessed 17 June 2025).

513 (2011) <https://digitallibrary.un.org/record/720841?ln = en> accessed 25 September 2023, para 161.

514 (2023) 101 International Law Studies, para 7.4.5; this paragraph goes on to note that 'the blockading State may make and declare arrangements for the provision of humanitarian support to a blockaded area, whether by sea or by land'.

515 Annyssa Bellal and Stuart Casey-Maslen, *The Additional Protocols to the Geneva Conventions in Context* (OUP 2022) 232.

516 ICRC Lexicon (n 41) 370.

intervention,[517] humanitarian actors confronted with unlawfully withheld strategic consent face a difficult choice between the legal and operational risks of delivering relief without the cooperation of the relevant conflict party and the human costs of not conducting the operation. The parameters of this dilemma differ for UN entities and states, which are governed by international law, and for operations by NGOs, which are not subjects of international law.[518] Each is addressed in turn.

6.3.1. International organizations and states

There is a broad consensus that UN and state emergency relief operations undertaken without affected state consent violate its territorial integrity, even if consent is withheld unlawfully.[519] This view is not, however, universally held; there are three main counterarguments. First, some detractors point to the possibility that in NIAC, the consent of an OAG with territorial control is sufficient; this was addressed above.[520] Second, some have pointed to the ICJ's decision in *Nicaragua*,[521] which held that there 'can be no doubt that the provision of strictly humanitarian aid to persons or forces in another country, whatever their political affiliations or objectives, cannot be considered as unlawful intervention, or as in any other way contrary to international law'.[522] This decision does not, however, support the proposition that UN and state relief operations that proceed without the consent of the affected state do not violate its territorial integrity. Gillard notes that the ICJ was contrasting humanitarian assistance with military support, rather than addressing the issue of withheld consent as such. She further notes that the assistance in question was not even distributed in Nicaragua; rather, relief items were distributed in neighbouring Honduras to actors operating inside Nicaragua.[523]

Third, Barber has challenged the conventional view that humanitarian assistance provided without the consent of the affected state violates its territorial integrity on three bases. First, she argues 'that conduct only amounts to a violation of territorial integrity if the conduct encroaches upon a State's *domaine réservé*—matters in relation to which a State is entitled to decide freely, by virtue of its sovereignty—and does so in a coercive way'. Second, she argues 'that a State's territorial integrity/*domaine réservé* does not encompass an unlimited freedom to violate human rights' and therefore 'humanitarian assistance provided solely for the purpose of protecting human rights—at least those rights corresponding with obligations *erga omnes*—does not encroach upon territorial integrity'. Third, she argues 'that even if humanitarian assistance is regarded as encroaching upon a State's territorial integrity, such encroachment ought not to be regarded as "coercive"—the second component of the test of a prohibited

[517] See Chapter 5, Section 4.4.2.
[518] See Chapter 6, Section 3.1.
[519] See, for example, Bothe (n 251) 95; Stoffels (n 203) 535; Ryngaert (n 199) 14; ICRC Lexicon (n 41) 370; Oxford Guidance (n 47) para 143.
[520] See Section 4.3.2.
[521] 2023 Letter (n 271).
[522] *Nicaragua* (n 229) para 242.
[523] Gillard 2014 (n 237) 29. See also Dietrich Schindler, 'Humanitarian Assistance, Humanitarian Interference and International Law' in Ronald MacDonald (ed), *Essays in Honour of Wang Tieya* (Martinus Nijhoff 1994) 698–99.

intervention'.[524] This is, however, a minority view; as noted above, most authors see unauthorized relief operations as violating territorial integrity.

The International Law Commission's (ILC) Articles on Responsibility of States for Internationally Wrongful Acts (ARSIWA) and its Articles on the Responsibility of International Organizations (ARIO) recognize six circumstances that may preclude the wrongfulness of conduct that would otherwise breach an international obligation: consent, self-defence, countermeasures, *force majeure*, distress, and necessity. Two of these, necessity and countermeasures, might preclude the wrongfulness of UN or state relief operations that proceed without the affected state's consent.[525] Each is addressed in turn.

Necessity 'may be invoked by a state or an international organisation to justify an otherwise wrongful act, if that act was the only way for it to safeguard an essential interest against a grave and imminent peril; and it does not seriously impair an essential interest of the injured state or of the international community'.[526] While circumstances that meet these criteria could arguably arise in the context of unauthorized relief operations, the question is largely academic. As Barber notes, since these issues are unlikely to be litigated in court, 'the theoretical possibility of a successful plea of necessity is unlikely to assuage the concerns of States and international organisations about the *prima facie* illegality of humanitarian assistance provided without consent'.[527] Indeed, it seems that precisely such concerns informed the UN Office of Legal Affairs' position that UN humanitarian actors could not operate in opposition-held north-west Syria without the consent of the Assad government.[528]

Countermeasures are non-forcible measures that a state or international organization may take in response to a state's breach of an international obligation. These measures would normally breach an obligation owed by the aggrieved state or organization to the responsible state. However, if several conditions are met,[529] the measures can be characterized as 'countermeasures' and their wrongfulness precluded. Four of these conditions are relevant here.[530] First, countermeasures only apply in the relations between the aggrieved state or organization and the responsible state. According to the Oxford Guidance, if the 'increasingly accepted notion of "third party" countermeasures'[531] is invoked, this first condition is met.[532] Barber, however,

[524] Barber (n 213) 97.

[525] See, regarding necessity and countermeasures: Gillard 2014 (n 237) 31–33 and Oxford Guidance (n 47) paras 146–56. Regarding necessity: Barber (n 213) 99–104. Regarding countermeasures: Bothe (n 251) 96–97; cf Okimoto (n 199) 137–38, who rejects the possibility of both necessity and countermeasures precluding the wrongfulness of unauthorized relief operations.

[526] Oxford Guidance (n 47) para 146, drawing on UNGA Res 56/83 (28 January 2002) A/RES/56/83, Annex (ARSIWA) art 25 and ILC, 'Report of the International Law Commission on the Work of its 63rd Session' (26 April—3 June and 4 July—12 August 2011) A/66/10, paras 87–88 (ARIO and associated Commentary) art 25.

[527] Barber (n 213) 104.

[528] Note from Patricia O'Brien, Under Secretary-General for Legal Affairs, to Jeffrey Feltman, Under Secretary-General for Political Affairs (21 March 2013), reproduced in part in Gillard 2022 (n 210) 7–8.

[529] ARSIWA (n 526) arts 49–54; ARIO and associated Commentary (n 526) arts 51–57.

[530] Oxford Guidance (n 47) para 153.

[531] These allow for the possibility of states or international organizations taking countermeasures in response to violations of obligations owed to the international community as a whole (obligations *erga omnes*).

[532] Oxford Guidance (n 47) para 154.

dismisses the possibility of characterizing unauthorized emergency relief operations as countermeasures, noting that the ILC has reasoned that countermeasures do not include measures taken to ensure compliance with obligations *erga omnes*.[533] Second, countermeasures must aim to induce the responsible state to comply with its international obligations. While this would not initially appear to be the purpose of unauthorized emergency relief operations, such operations do aim to induce cessation of and reparation for unlawfully impeded operations. For this reason, the Oxford Guidance concludes that the second condition is met.[534] Third, countermeasures must be proportionate to the injury caused by the initial breach. For unauthorized emergency relief operations to satisfy this condition, 'it will need to be shown that the unlawful impeding [. . .] amounts to a particularly serious breach of international law with severe consequences for those in need of assistance'.[535] Finally, with regard to international organizations, an international organization cannot invoke countermeasures unless they 'are not inconsistent with the rules of the organization'.[536] This means that 'the constituent instruments, decisions, resolutions and other acts of the international organization adopted in accordance with those instruments, and established practice of the organization' must be taken into account.[537] Regarding the UN, Okimoto finds that the General Assembly resolution 46/182 requirement that 'humanitarian assistance should be provided with the consent of the affected country'[538] prevents the UN from invoking countermeasures for unauthorized emergency relief operations.[539] In any case, as with necessity, the characterization of an unauthorized relief operation as a countermeasure in order to preclude its wrongfulness is largely an academic exercise. A state or international organization facing unlawful impeding will be more concerned with how to deliver relief securely than with undertaking an unauthorized operation that could perhaps later be justified in legal proceedings.[540]

6.3.2. Non-state actors

Non-state humanitarian actors—Movement components and NGOs—have at times responded to unlawfully withheld strategic consent by conducting unauthorized emergency relief operations.[541] For example, during the Nigeria-Biafra war, the ICRC operated for several months without the consent of either conflict party, until an ICRC plane was shot down by Nigerian forces.[542] NGOs also airlifted relief into Biafra

[533] Barber (n 213) 99.
[534] Oxford Guidance (n 47) para 155.
[535] ibid, para 156.
[536] ARIO (n 526) art 22(2)(b).
[537] ibid, art 2(b).
[538] UNGA Res 46/182 (19 December 1991) A/RES/46/182, Annex, para 3; see Chapter 5, Section 3.
[539] Okimoto (n 199) 137; see also Oxford Guidance (n 47) para 145.
[540] Gillard discusses a range of practical options for states and international organizations wishing to deliver relief in the face of unlawful impeding (Gillard 2014 (n 237) 35–41).
[541] Bouchet-Saulnier (n 61) 215.
[542] Eleanor Davey, John Borton, and Matthew Foley, 'A History of the Humanitarian System: Western Origins and Foundations' (2013) Humanitarian Policy Group Working Paper <https://odi.org/en/publications/a-history-of-the-humanitarian-system-western-origins-and-foundations/> accessed 1 August 2025, 11.

without government consent.[543] MSF has established a limited number of clandestine field hospitals,[544] such as in Syria in 2012.[545] When certain Security Council-imposed border crossings into north-west Syria were not re-authorized,[546] some international NGOs continued to operate via these crossings.[547] However, unauthorized relief operations are rare, for both legal and practical reasons.

Legally, an NGO is bound by the domestic law of any state in which it operates.[548] Unauthorized relief operations may violate a state's civil and/or criminal laws. For example, the act of unauthorized entry is a crime in Syria.[549] Domestic law penalties for unauthorized emergency relief operations may include the deportation of personnel and the confiscation of organizational property.[550] Practically, unauthorized operations raise serious security risks.[551] Additionally, NGOs often serve as UN implementing partners and rely on OCHA for coordination and other technical support. Without any UN presence, opportunities for NGO operations may be limited or operations may become significantly more difficult. Finally, many NGOs rely on states for funding. States may be unwilling to fund unauthorized emergency relief operations, in part for fear that such funding violates international law, though Gillard has concluded that it does not.[552]

7. Accountability and responsibility for unlawful impeding and attacking humanitarian personnel and protected zones

Impeding relief operations and attacking humanitarian personnel or protected zones may violate IHL and IHRL. A range of consequences may ensue: the UN Security Council may respond, either by imposing relief operations on the state or sanctions on the individuals responsible; relevant individuals may be held accountable under ICL;[553] and/or conflict parties may be held internationally responsible. Individual accountability and international responsibility are addressed in turn; Security Council involvement is addressed in Chapter 5.[554]

[543] ibid.
[544] Ryngaert (n 199) 11.
[545] Elizabeth Rose Donnelly, 'Towards Greater Legal Protection for Medical-Humanitarian NGOs in Situations of Armed Conflict' (2018) 3 Cambridge Law Review 144, 155.
[546] See Chapter 5, Section 4.4.2.
[547] Gillard 2022 (n 210) 27.
[548] The ICRC may enjoy privileges and immunities; see Chapter 6, Section 2.3.
[549] Gillard 2022 (n 210) 25.
[550] Ryngaert (n 199) 11.
[551] Bothe (n 199) 191.
[552] Gillard 2022 (n 210) 25–27.
[553] Experts have, however, advised caution in the use of ICL and targeted sanctions while access negotiations are ongoing: 'it is questionable whether early threats of criminal responsibility or of the imposition of sanctions for impeding humanitarian relief operations is likely to promote compliance [. . .] there is the real risk that it may entrench positions and close the space for dialogue rather than assist the confidence-building exercise' (Akande and Gillard 2017 (n 125) 133).
[554] See Chapter 5, Sections 4.4.2 and 4.4.3.

7.1. Individual accountability

Conduct such as obstructing relief operations or attacking humanitarian personnel and protected zones may give rise to international criminal responsibility, potentially qualifying as war crimes, crimes against humanity, or even genocide; each category of crime is examined in turn.

7.1.1. War crimes

War crimes are serious violations of IHL. Several war crimes within the International Criminal Court's (ICC) jurisdiction are relevant. 'Intentionally using starvation of civilians as a method of warfare by depriving them of objects indispensable to their survival, including wilfully impeding relief supplies as provided for under the Geneva Conventions' is a war crime in IAC.[555] There are a range of views on whether the reference to the 'Geneva Conventions' includes the API rules on emergency relief operations;[556] Dannenbaum's is persuasive. He argues that the Rome Statute's mention of the 'Geneva Conventions' should be understood as a reference to 'the form of humanitarian action "provided for," but not specifically protected from impediment, in common Articles 9, 9, 9, and 10 of the four conventions'.[557] This focuses 'attention on "humanitarian activities" pursued by the ICRC or "any other impartial humanitarian organization" for the "protection of civilian persons and for their relief"', such that 'the Geneva Conventions are referenced not to limit or define the scope of proscribed deprivation [. . .] but to clarify the kind of relief operations that are to be protected against impediment'.[558] In short, the reference to the Geneva Conventions in article 8(2)(b)(xxv) does not limit its scope; rather, it identifies the type of relief operations protected as those that are humanitarian and impartial. The Rome Statute was amended in 2019[559] to include a similar crime in NIAC, which does not refer to any underlying IHL rules.[560]

For both the IAC and NIAC crimes, relief supplies are wilfully impeded when the obligations outlined above are violated.[561] However, impeding is not on its own sufficient to constitute either crime; both require that impeding be in order to deprive civilians of objects indispensable to their survival, in order to intentionally starve them as a method of warfare.[562] Doctrine on what exactly this means has only just begun to emerge,[563] and the ICC has yet to decide a relevant case. The crime was first charged

555 Rome Statute (n 417) art 8(2)(b)(xxv).
556 For a survey, see Dannenbaum (Vanderbilt) (n 506) 751–52.
557 Dannenbaum (Vanderbilt) (n 506) 754. On articles 9/9/9/10, see Section 3.
558 ibid.
559 Assembly of States Parties to the Rome Statute, Resolution ICC-ASP/18/Res.5 (6 December 2019). On the need for this amendment, see Rogier Bartels, 'Denying Humanitarian Access as an International Crime in Times of Non-International Armed Conflict: The Challenges to Prosecute and Some Proposals for the Future' (2015) 48 Israel Law Review 281.
560 Rome Statute (n 417) art 8(2)(e)(xix).
561 See Sections 6.1 and 6.2. For more detail, see Akande and Gillard 2019 (n 125) 772–75.
562 See Geoff Corn and Emanuela-Chiara Gillard, 'The War Crime of Starvation: The Irony of Grasping at Low Hanging Fruit' (*Articles of War*, 15 May 2024) <https://lieber.westpoint.edu/war-crime-starvation-irony-grasping-low-hanging-fruit/> accessed 4 August 2025.
563 See ibid and sources cited at note 506.

in 2024, when the ICC Prosecutor applied for warrants of arrest for Israeli Prime Minister Benjamin Netanyahu and then Minister of Defense Yoav Gallant—as well as three Hamas leaders—under, *inter alia*, article 8(2)(b)(xxv). While the Prosecutor's application and the Pre-Trial Chamber's decision to issue warrants are sealed, the ICC press release announcing the warrants noted that the Pre-Trial Chamber 'considered that there are reasonable grounds to believe that both individuals intentionally and knowingly deprived the civilian population in Gaza of objects indispensable to their survival, including food, water, and medicine and medical supplies, as well as fuel and electricity'. The release went on to note that this 'finding is based on the role of Mr Netanyahu and Mr Gallant in impeding humanitarian aid in violation of' IHL and their failure to facilitate relief by all means at their disposal.[564]

The NIAC and IAC war crime of '[i]ntentionally directing attacks against personnel, installations, material, units, or vehicles involved in a humanitarian assistance or peacekeeping mission [. . .] as long as they are entitled to the protection given to civilians or civilian objects' is also relevant.[565] The limitation to civilians and civilian objects means military providers of humanitarian assistance are not covered by the provision.[566] Bieńczyk-Missala and Grzebyk argue that it is 'superfluous' to criminalize attacks against humanitarian personnel,[567] because these individuals are usually civilians, whom it is of course also unlawful to attack.[568] Sutton has, however, demonstrated the unique character of humanitarian personnel,[569] and it is relevant to criminalize attacks on them specifically in light of the rising number of attacks they face.[570] The war crime of '[i]ntentionally directing attacks against material, medical units and transport, and personnel using the distinctive emblems of the Geneva Conventions'[571] is also relevant; however, it will in practice only cover the ICRC, as this is the only humanitarian organization generally authorized to use the distinctive emblems.[572]

The Rome Statute also prohibits attacks on hospitals and protected zones. Articles 8(2)(b)(ix) and 8(2)(e)(iv) provide that '[i]ntentionally directing attacks against [. . .] hospitals and places where the sick and wounded are collected' is a war crime in IAC and NIAC respectively, 'provided they are not military objectives'. A civilian object can become a military objective if it makes an effective contribution to military action through its nature, location, purpose, or use and its destruction offers a definite

[564] ICC, 'Situation in the State of Palestine: ICC Pre-Trial Chamber I Rejects the State of Israel's Challenges to Jurisdiction and Issues Warrants of Arrest for Benjamin Netanyahu and Yoav Gallant' (Press Release, 21 November 2024) <https://www.icc-cpi.int/news/situation-state-palestine-icc-pre-trial-chamber-i-rejects-state-israels-challenges> accessed 4 August 2025 (ICC Press Release).

[565] Rome Statute (n 417) arts 8(2)(b)(iii) (IAC) and 8(2)(e)(iii) (NIAC).

[566] See Chapter 7, Section 3.2.

[567] Agnieszka Bieńczyk-Missala and Patrycja Grzebyk, 'Safety and Protection of Humanitarian Workers' in Pat Gibbons and Hans-Joachim Heintze (eds), *The Humanitarian Challenge: 20 Years European Network on Humanitarian Action* (Springer 2015) 240.

[568] Rome Statute (n 417) arts 8(2)(b)(i) (IAC) and 8(2)(e)(i) (NIAC). See also Rome Statute (n 417) art 8(2)(b)(ii) regarding civilian objects in IAC; there is no Rome Statute war crime of intentionally directing attacks against civilian objects in NIAC.

[569] Rebecca Sutton, 'Enacting the "Civilian Plus": International Humanitarian Actors and the Conceptualization of Distinction' (2020) 33 Leiden Journal of International Law 429.

[570] See Chapter 5, Section 5.4.

[571] Rome Statute (n 417) arts 8(2)(b)(xxiv) (IAC) and 8(2)(e)(ii) (NIAC).

[572] See Chapter 6, Section 2.3.

military advantage.[573] A medical unit in particular loses its protection if it is used to commit acts harmful to the enemy, though a warning must be given before it may be targeted. [574]

In addition to individual accountability under the Rome Statute, individuals may be held accountable for unlawful impeding or attacking humanitarian personnel or a protected zone in IAC under IHL's regime to suppress violations, pursuant to which states parties must adopt domestic legislation criminalizing grave breaches of the GCs and API as war crimes, search for individuals who have committed such crimes, and either prosecute them or extradite them to another state for prosecution.[575] Unlawful impeding could be covered by the grave breach of 'wilfully causing great suffering or serious injury to body or health' to protected persons.[576] Attacking a protected person is covered by the grave breach of wilfully killing protected persons,[577] while attacking a protected zone could be covered by the grave breach of wilfully making a DMZ the object of attack if the attack causes 'death or serious injury to body or health'.[578]

7.1.2. Crimes against humanity

Crimes against humanity can, but need not, be committed in the context of an armed conflict. As defined in the Rome Statute, crimes against humanity are certain enumerated acts when committed with the required chapeau elements: with knowledge and 'as part of a widespread or systematic attack directed against any civilian population'.[579] '[D]irected against any civilian population' means the acts in question were 'pursuant to or in furtherance of a State or organizational policy'.[580]

Several Rome Statute crimes against humanity are relevant to the unlawful impeding of emergency relief operations. Several authors have identified the article 7(1)(b) crime against humanity of extermination as relevant to unlawful impeding.[581] It 'includes the intentional infliction of conditions of life, *inter alia* the deprivation of access to food and medicine, calculated to bring about the destruction of part of a population'.[582] However, extermination has a high threshold, requiring the 'mass killing of members of a civilian population'.[583] As a result, unlawful impeding is

573 API (n 16) art 53.
574 ibid, art 13; APII (n 16) art 11.
575 GCI (n 15) art 49; GCII (n 15) art 50; GCIII (n 15) art 129; GCIV (n 15) art 146; API (n 16) arts 11(4) and 85.
576 GCIV (n 15) art 147.
577 ibid.
578 API (n 16) art 85(3)(d).
579 Rome Statute (n 417) art 7(1).
580 ibid, art 7(2)(a).
581 Christa Rottensteiner, 'The Denial of Humanitarian Assistance as a Crime Under International Law' (1999) 81 International Review of the Red Cross 555, 573; Bartels (n 559) 302; Okimoto (n 199) 135; Allard K Lowenstein International Human Rights Clinic at Yale Law School, '"All of Us are in Constant Hunger": Ethiopia's Responsibility for Starvation in Tigray' (2023) <https://law.yale.edu/sites/default/files/area/center/schell/document/all_of_us_are_in_constant_hunger.pdf> accessed 15 August 2023 (Lowenstein Clinic Report) 113–16.
582 Rome Statute (n 417) art 7(2)(b).
583 Assembly of State Parties to the Rome Statute, 'The ICC Elements of Crimes' (9 September 2002) ICC-ASP/1/3, art 7(1)(b) (Elements of Crimes) element 2.

unlikely to amount to the crime against humanity of extermination. Indeed, the ICC Prosecutor charged Netanyahu and Gallant with the crime against humanity of extermination, but the Pre-Trial Chamber 'could not determine that all elements of the crime against humanity of extermination were met'.[584] The Pre-Trial Chamber did, however, find that the same conduct alleged in connection with extermination—intentionally limiting or preventing medical supplies and medicine from entering Gaza—amounted to the article 7(1)(a) crime against humanity of murder.[585] This crime could also be used to prosecute an attack on a protected zone.

Other crimes against humanity relevant to unlawful impeding include '[o]ther inhumane acts', which are acts of a similar character to those underlying other crimes against humanity that intentionally cause 'great suffering, or serious injury to body or to mental or physical health',[586] and persecution,[587] which means 'the intentional and severe deprivation of fundamental rights contrary to international law by reason' of a group or collectivity's identity.[588] The Netanyahu and Gallant arrest warrants include these charges; the Pre-Trial Chamber found that 'by intentionally limiting or preventing medical supplies from getting into Gaza, in particular anaesthetics and anaesthesia machines, the two individuals are [. . .] responsible for inflicting great suffering by means of inhumane acts on persons in need of treatment'.[589] Additionally, the Pre-Trial Chamber found reasonable grounds to believe that the same conduct 'deprived a significant portion of the civilian population in Gaza of their fundamental rights, including the rights to life and health, and that the population was targeted based on political and/or national grounds. It therefore found that the crime against humanity of persecution was committed'.[590]

7.1.3. Genocide

Like crimes against humanity, genocide need not be committed in the context of an armed conflict. Genocide occurs when one or more of certain enumerated acts are 'committed with intent to destroy, in whole or in part, a national, ethnical, racial or religious group, as such'.[591] Unlawful impeding could be characterized as the enumerated act of '[d]eliberately inflicting on the group conditions of life calculated to bring about its physical destruction in whole or in part'.[592] Indeed, the ICC Elements of Crimes notes that 'conditions of life' may include 'deliberate deprivation of resources indispensable for the survival of members of one of the protected groups, such as food or medical services'.[593] Attacking a protected zone could be characterized as the

584 ICC Press Release (n 564).
585 ibid.
586 Rome Statute (n 417) art 7(1)(k).
587 ibid, art 7(1)(h).
588 ibid, art 7(2)(g).
589 ICC Press Release (n 564).
590 ibid.
591 Rome Statute (n 417) art 6. See also Convention on the Prevention and Punishment of the Crime of Genocide (adopted 9 December 1948, entered into force 12 January 1951) 78 UNTS 277 (Genocide Convention) art II.
592 Rome Statute (n 417) art 6(c); Genocide Convention (n 591) art II(c).
593 Elements of Crimes (n 583) art 6(c), note to element 4.

enumerated act of '[k]illing members of the group'[594] or '[c]ausing serious bodily or mental harm to members of the group'.[595]

Genocide is difficult to prove because of the requirement to establish the intent to destroy the targeted group; this may be demonstrated through express statements or inferred from a pattern of conduct. The unlawful impeding of humanitarian assistance was among the genocide allegations made by the ICC Prosecutor against Sudanese President Omar Al Bashir. However, the Pre-Trial Chamber found that the 'hindrance of humanitarian assistance, as well as cutting off supplies of food and other essential goods, can be carried out for a variety of reasons other than intending to destroy' the targeted group.[596] Similarly, the ICTY Appeals Chamber found that military directives regarding the blocking of humanitarian assistance destined for Muslims in Bosnia were 'insufficiently clear to establish that there was a genocidal intent on the part of the members of the Main Staff who issued them'.[597] International criminal tribunals have, however, found that depriving a group of humanitarian items such as food can amount to '[d]eliberately inflicting on the group conditions of life calculated to bring about its physical destruction', within the meaning of provisions cognate to article II(c) of the Genocide Convention.[598] Genocidal intent may be easier to establish in the case of an attack on a protected zone. In the foregoing[599] and several other ICTY cases,[600] individuals were convicted of genocide or aiding and abetting genocide in relation to the attack on the Srebrenica safe area.

7.2. International responsibility

It is a general principle of international law that the breach by a state of an international obligation of that state constitutes an internationally wrongful act, giving rise to the state's responsibility.[601] Responsibility entails the state's primary obligation to cease the breach if it is ongoing and secondary obligations to make full reparation for

594 Rome Statute (n 417) art 6(a).

595 ibid, art 6(b).

596 *In the Case of the Prosecutor v Omar Hassan Ahmad Al Bashir* (Decision on the Prosecution's Application for a Warrant of Arrest) ICC-02/05-01/09 (4 March 2009) para 181.

597 *Prosecutor v Krstić* (Judgement, Appeals Chamber) IT-98-33-A (19 April 2004) (*Krstić* Appeal) para 90. Military directive 7 declared that 'the relevant State and military organs responsible for the work of UNPROFOR and humanitarian organisations shall, through planned and unobtrusively restrictive issuing of permits, reduce and limit the logistics support of UNPROFOR to the enclaves and the supply of material resources to the Muslim population, making them dependent on our good will while at the same time avoiding the condemnation of the international community and international public opinion' (cited in *Krstić* Appeal, para 89).

598 *Prosecutor v Jean-Paul Akayesu* (Judgement, Trial Chamber) ICTR-96-4-T (2 September 1998) para 506; *Prosecutor v Clément Kayishema and Obed Ruzindana* (Judgement, Trial Chamber) ICTR-95-1-T (21 May 1999) paras 115–16; *Prosecutor v Brđanin* (Judgement, Trial Chamber) IT-99-36-T (1 September 2004) para 691; *Prosecutor v Stakić* (Judgement, Trial Chamber) IT-97-24-T (31 July 2003) para 517; *Tolimir* (n 304) paras 225–28.

599 *Prosecutor v Krstić* (Judgement, Trial Chamber) IT-98-33-T (2 August 2001); *Krstić* Appeal (n 597).

600 See, for example, *Prosecutor v Popović* (Judgement, Appeals Chamber) IT-05-88-A (30 January 2015); *Prosecutor v Karadžić* (Appeals Judgement) MICT-13-55-A (20 March 2019); *Prosecutor v Mladić* (Appeals Judgement) MICT-13-56-A (8 June 2021).

601 ARSIWA (n 526) art 1.

any injuries caused by the breach and to offer assurances of non-repetition if required in the circumstances.[602]

As shown above, states have obligations under IHL not to withhold strategic consent to emergency relief operations and to allow and facilitate such operations;[603] they also have obligations in relation to particular forms of relief and regarding relief for particular beneficiaries.[604] Additionally, they have obligations not to attack humanitarian personnel and protected zones.[605] States also have relevant obligations under IHRL, such as in relation to the rights to life, food, water, and the highest attainable standard of health.[606] If a state violates any of these obligations, it will have committed an internationally wrongful act giving rise to its responsibility under international law.

Many IHL and IHRL treaty obligations are obligations *erga omnes partes*. If the obligation in question is an obligation *erga omnes partes*, then every state party to the treaty setting it out has standing to enforce the responsibility of the state in breach by initiating proceedings in a forum with jurisdiction. However, until recently, no state had taken steps in this regard, either because no state considered itself sufficiently injured,[607] because states have chosen to focus their limited resources on bilateral and/or multilateral diplomatic channels,[608] or because of the lack of fora with jurisdiction—none of the relevant IHL treaties contains a compromissory clause.[609] However, since the escalation in 2023 of the armed conflict between Israel and Hamas, states have sought to hold Israel responsible for impeding humanitarian assistance (*inter alia*) under the Genocide Convention.[610]

The Genocide Convention contains a compromissory clause.[611] This jurisdictional hook, coupled with the *erga omnes partes* nature of obligations under the Genocide Convention, enabled South Africa to institute ICJ proceedings against Israel relating, *inter alia*, to its '[d]eprivation of access to adequate food and water to Palestinians in Gaza', including by limiting humanitarian access to the Strip.[612] South Africa alleges that this amounts to 'deliberately inflicting on Palestinians conditions of life calculated to bring about their destruction', within the meaning of article II(c) of the Genocide Convention.[613] The case is pending; however, the ICJ has three times ordered provisional measures to preserve Palestinians' plausible right to be protected from

602 ibid, arts 30–31.
603 See Section 4.
604 See Section 5.
605 API (n 16) arts 48, 51, and 52; APII (n 16) art 13; Henckaerts and Doswald-Beck (n 18) rules 1 and 7. See Section 4.4.4.
606 See Chapter 1, Section 2.
607 Gillard 2014 (n 237) 34.
608 See Chapter 5, Sections 4.3 and 4.4.
609 A compromissory clause allows states party to the treaty in question to refer disputes about its interpretation or application to the ICJ.
610 See, generally, Marko Milanović, 'State Responsibility for Genocide' (2006) 17 European Journal of International Law 553.
611 Genocide Convention (n 591) art IX.
612 *Application of the Convention on the Prevention and Punishment of the Crime of Genocide in the Gaza Strip* (*South Africa v Israel*) (Application Instituting Proceedings containing a Request for the Indication of Provisional Measures) General List No 192 [2023] ICJ 1, 94.
613 ibid, para 70.

genocide. First, it ordered Israel to take measures including enabling 'the provision of urgently needed basic services and humanitarian assistance to address the adverse conditions of life faced by Palestinians in the Gaza Strip'.[614] The Court subsequently ordered Israel to take 'all necessary and effective measures to ensure, without delay, in full co-operation with the United Nations, the unhindered provision at scale by all concerned of urgently needed basic services and humanitarian assistance, including food, water, electricity, fuel, shelter, clothing, hygiene and sanitation requirements, as well as medical supplies and medical care to Palestinians throughout Gaza, including by increasing the capacity and number of land crossing points and maintaining them open for as long as necessary' and to ensure 'that its military does not commit acts which constitute a violation of any of the rights of the Palestinians in Gaza [. . .] including by preventing, through any action, the delivery of urgently needed humanitarian assistance'.[615] Most recently, the ICJ ordered Israel to take measures including maintaining 'open the Rafah crossing for unhindered provision at scale of urgently needed basic services and humanitarian assistance'.[616] Since South Africa instituted proceedings in 2023, several states, such as Colombia, Ireland, and Mexico, have intervened to offer their views regarding the Genocide Convention,[617] mostly in support of one or more of South Africa's positions.

South Africa v Israel is not the first time a state has alleged that impeding humanitarian assistance may amount to genocide. In the past, however, the state instituting proceedings did not rely on *erga omnes partes* standing; rather, it was itself directly injured by the alleged breach. In *Bosnia and Herzegovina v Serbia and Montenegro*, the ICJ considered, *inter alia*, whether blocking humanitarian assistance could amount to creating 'conditions of life calculated to bring about' the 'physical destruction in whole or in part' of civilians in Sarajevo.[618] While the Court determined that the acts in question were not carried out with the intent required to sustain a charge of genocide, it refused to rule out the possibility that they could be calculated to create 'conditions of life' that would lead to the destruction of the group.[619] Similarly, in *Croatia v Serbia*, the Court found that depriving a group of food, medical care, shelter, or clothing can constitute the '[d]eliberate infliction on the group of conditions of life calculated to bring about its physical destruction in whole or in part', within the meaning of article II(c) of the Genocide Convention.[620]

[614] *Application of the Convention on the Prevention and Punishment of the Crime of Genocide in the Gaza Strip* (*South Africa v Israel*) (Request for the Indication of Provisional Measures: Order of 26 January 2024) General List No 192 [2024] ICJ 3, para 80.

[615] *Application of the Convention on the Prevention and Punishment of the Crime of Genocide in the Gaza Strip* (*South Africa v Israel*) (Request for the Indication of Provisional Measures: Order of 28 March 2024) General List No 192 [2024] ICJ 513, para 51.

[616] *Application of the Convention on the Prevention and Punishment of the Crime of Genocide in the Gaza Strip* (*South Africa v Israel*) (Request for the Modification of the Order of 28 March 2024: Order of 24 May 2024) General List No 192 [2024] ICJ 649, para 57.

[617] Statute of the International Court of Justice (24 October 1945) 961 UNTS 183, art 63.

[618] Genocide Convention (n 591) art II(c).

[619] *Case Concerning Application of the Convention on the Prevention and Punishment of the Crime of Genocide (Bosnia and Herzegovina v Serbia and Montenegro)* (Merits) [2007] ICJ Rep 43, para 328.

[620] *Application of the Convention on the Prevention and Punishment of the Crime of Genocide (Croatia v Serbia)* (Merits) [2015] ICJ Rep 3, para 161.

Alongside the general regime of state responsibility, IHL has its own reparations regime[621] aimed at preventing 'the vanquished from being compelled in an armistice agreement or peace treaty to renounce all compensation due for breaches committed by persons in the service of the victor'.[622] It should be noted that OAGs party to an armed conflict have the same IHL obligations as states. The international responsibility of OAGs for the violation of their IHL obligations is a nascent but developing area of law.[623]

8. Conclusion

This chapter has outlined and contextualized the legal framework of humanitarian assistance in armed conflict. Conflict parties have primary responsibility to ensure that the needs of civilians within their control are met. Several IHL rules, including the right of initiative, support impartial humanitarian organizations' work to help conflict parties in meeting this obligation. If, however, a conflict party is unable or unwilling to discharge this obligation and civilians are inadequately supplied, the rules on emergency relief operations apply. Impartial humanitarian actors may offer to conduct relief actions; strategic consent to such actions cannot be withheld unlawfully—or, for operations in occupied territory, at all. At the implementation phase, conflict parties, as well as any transit states, must fulfil their obligation to allow and facilitate relief—including relief for besieged civilians—subject to their right of control, within which conflict parties may address considerations relating to military necessity. Conflict parties must also protect relief consignments and facilitate their rapid distribution, and respect and protect relief personnel. Conflict parties have additional obligations in relation to medical and food relief, and when relief is destined for civilians deprived of their liberty or for evacuated or displaced civilians. Individual accountability for violations of rules within this framework may be addressed via ICL. States can also be held responsible for violations; the Genocide Convention's compromissory clause has recently made the ICJ a forum where states pursue responsibility for egregious violations.

While this legal framework is contained across a range of IHL treaties and customary rules and has developed over time, it has nevertheless been cohesive and largely complete since the APs were adopted in 1977, even if it was not elucidated comprehensively until much more recently. The same cannot be said of the regime in peacetime. It has only just begun to develop towards a comprehensive treaty framework for humanitarian assistance on land, while states are at the same time increasingly abdicating their humanitarian obligations at sea. The next chapter explores these developments, as well as how the framework outlined here applies when disaster and armed conflict coincide.

[621] GCIV (n 15) art 148 (GCI-GCIII include identical provisions); API (n 16) art 91; Henckaerts and Doswald-Beck (n 18) rule 150.

[622] Sandoz and others (n 90) para 3649.

[623] See Ezequiel Heffes and Brian E Frenkel, 'The International Responsibility of Non-State Armed Groups: In Search of the Applicable Rules' (2017) 8 Goettingen Journal of International Law 39.

4
Peacetime

1. Introduction

Chapter 3 outlined the legal framework for humanitarian assistance in situations of armed conflict. This chapter covers peacetime. People have many of the same basic needs in peacetime as they do during armed conflict, such as for food, clean water, medical care, and shelter. Yet whereas international humanitarian law (IHL) provides a clear set of rules on humanitarian assistance, there is not yet a generally applicable legal framework regarding peacetime humanitarian assistance. This is because the distinct contexts give rise to at least two fundamentally different sets of concerns. First, in armed conflict, the principle of equality of belligerents means that all conflict parties are governed by the same IHL rules; the law did not develop around sovereign interests. In international law applicable in peacetime, by contrast, state sovereignty is of paramount importance, and it limits external actors' involvement in states' internal affairs and breach of their territorial integrity. Second, in armed conflict, conflict parties are concerned that humanitarian assistance could be diverted by one side, giving it a military advantage over its enemy or enemies. Taken together, and at the risk of oversimplification, these two differences have allowed for the development of a set of wartime rules on humanitarian assistance that take military necessity into account, while they have precluded the development of a coherent peacetime legal framework—though there have recently been major developments in this regard.

This chapter surveys, in Section 2, international disaster response law (IDRL) as it currently stands—a patchwork of rules drawn from sectoral, contextual, regional, sub-regional, and bilateral treaties—and outlines the significant work undertaken by the International Federation of Red Cross and Red Crescent Societies (IFRC) and the International Law Commission (ILC) to transform this patchwork into something more coherent. Section 2 concludes with a discussion of the legal framework applicable in mixed situations: when a disaster strikes during armed conflict or an armed conflict erupts in a disaster zone. The chapter also addresses the other non-war contexts that can give rise to significant humanitarian need: violence not amounting to armed conflict (Section 3) and maritime migration (Section 4), which has since the early 2010s made the sea a major new theatre of humanitarian operations.

In all of these contexts, the starting point is the same: the state has primary responsibility for meeting the needs of individuals in its territory or within its effective control. The basis of this obligation in disasters, mixed situations, and violence not amounting to armed conflict was addressed in Chapter 1.[1] Its basis in relation to individuals in

[1] See Chapter 1, Section 2.

Humanitarian Assistance in International Law. Marina Sharpe, Oxford University Press. © Marina Sharpe 2026.
DOI: 10.1093/9780198994695.003.0006

distress at sea is the distinct law of the sea framework, which is addressed at the outset of Section 4.[2]

2. International disaster response law

A disaster is an event, or series of events, other than armed conflict that seriously disrupts the functioning of society.[3] This definition is based on those used by the IFRC and the ILC in their respective disaster initiatives.[4] Drawing on the definition used in the Tampere Convention on the Provision of Telecommunication Resources for Disaster Mitigation and Relief Operations (Tampere Convention),[5] the IFRC defines a disaster as 'a serious disruption of the functioning of society, which poses a significant, widespread threat to human life, health, property or the environment, whether arising from accident, nature or human activity, whether developing suddenly or as the result of long-term processes, but excluding armed conflict'.[6] The ILC defines a disaster as 'a calamitous event or series of events resulting in widespread loss of life, great human suffering and distress, mass displacement, or large-scale material or environmental damage, thereby seriously disrupting the functioning of society'.[7]

Three points are worth making to clarify the scope of, and terminology surrounding, the notion of a disaster. First, while neither the IFRC nor ILC definitions exclude public health, technological,[8] or slow-onset disasters—indeed the IFRC definition explicitly includes the last of these—in practice, most international disaster responses relate to sudden-onset climate or geophysical events,[9] such as cyclones, hurricanes, floods, earthquakes, and landslides. Examples of such events include the 2004 Indian Ocean tsunami, the 2010 earthquake in Haiti, the 2014 Badakhshan mudslides in Afghanistan, Cyclone Pam in the South Pacific in 2015, the 2023 Türkiye-Syria earthquake, and the 2023 flooding in Libya following Cyclone Daniel. Additionally, since World Health Organization member states agreed during the COVID-19 pandemic to negotiate an international instrument on pandemic prevention, preparedness, and response,[10] the field of public health response has been evolving as a separate legal

[2] See Sections 4.1–4.2.

[3] For a survey of the range of ways a disaster has been defined in international law, see Rosalyn Higgins and others, *Oppenheim's International Law: United Nations* (OUP 2017) 702–04.

[4] These initiatives are discussed in Section 2.3.

[5] (Adopted 18 June 1998, entered into force 8 January 2005) 2296 UNTS 5 (Tampere Convention) art 1(6).

[6] IFRC, 'Guidelines for the Domestic Facilitation and Regulation of International Disaster Relief and Initial Recovery Assistance' (2011) <https://www.icrc.org/en/doc/assets/files/red-cross-crescent-movement/31st-international-conference/idrl-guidelines-en.pdf> accessed 11 June 2024 (IFRC Guidelines) s 2.1.

[7] ILC, 'Report of the International Law Commission on the Work of its 68th Session' (2 May–10 June and 4 July–12 August 2016) A/71/10, 13 (ILC Draft Articles) art 3(a). Unlike the IFRC, the ILC does not explicitly exclude armed conflict from its definition of disaster. Instead, it deals with the role of IDRL in armed conflict as a substantive issue rather than a definitional one; this is addressed in Section 2.4.

[8] Technological disasters may be industrial (e.g. the nuclear accidents at Chernobyl in 1986 and Fukushima in 2011) or transport-related (e.g. the 2013 Lac Mégantic rail disaster in Québec, Canada).

[9] Kirsten Nakjavani Bookmiller, 'Closing "The Yawning Gap"? International Disaster Response Law at Fifteen' in Susan Carolyn Breau and Katja Samuel (eds), *Research Handbook on Disasters and International Law* (Edward Elgar Publishing 2016) 47.

[10] International Treaty on Pandemic Prevention, Preparedness and Response (adopted 20 May 2025, not yet in force).

regime. The second point relates to the terms used to describe humanitarian assistance in disasters. As explained in Chapters 1[11] and 3,[12] humanitarian relief is a subtype of humanitarian assistance responsive to emergency situations. Because sudden-onset disasters typically produce emergencies, humanitarian assistance for disaster victims is often termed 'humanitarian relief' or 'disaster relief'. Finally, disasters are sometimes termed 'natural' disasters. This qualifier is not used here because many disasters stem at least in part from human-generated phenomena such as climate change.[13]

Disasters are a relatively new subject of public international law (PIL), so there is not yet any agreed terminology to describe the PIL regime concerned with disasters. However, several authors and actors have attached terms to the field and its subfields. Aronsson-Storrier and da Costa describe 'international disaster law' (IDL) as 'an "overarching umbrella"' term.[14] The IFRC also uses IDL in this way: in 2012, it changed the name of its disaster programme from 'International Disaster Response Laws, Rules and Principles Programme' (IDRL Programme) to 'Disaster Law Programme' to cover not just disaster response, but also disaster risk reduction and disaster recovery.[15] This change reflected contemporaneous recognition by states and by humanitarian and development organizations that more emphasis and funding should be devoted to preventing and reducing vulnerability to disasters, instead of relying solely on emergency response.[16] The 'overarching umbrella' of IDL includes three subfields: IDRL,[17] disaster risk reduction (DRR), and post-disaster recovery. This chapter focuses on IDRL, which is considered the most established part of IDL,[18] because it contains the rules on disaster relief. DRR and recovery are beyond the scope of this chapter because the international assistance provided for these is, strictly speaking, not humanitarian but development assistance.[19] It should, however, be noted that the importance of collaboration between humanitarian and

[11] See Chapter 1, Section 2.

[12] See Chapter 3, Section 1.3.

[13] Maarten Van Aalst, 'The Impacts of Climate Change on the Risk of Natural Disasters' (2006) 30 Disasters 5; Peter Stott and others, 'Attribution of Extreme Weather and Climate-Related Events' (2015) 7 WIREs Climate Change 23.

[14] Marie Aronsson-Storrier and Karen da Costa, 'Regulating Disasters? The Role of International Law in Disaster Prevention and Management' (2017) 26 Disaster Prevention and Management 502, 502.

[15] Emika Tokunaga, 'Evolution of International Disaster Response Law: Toward Codification and Progressive Development of the Law' in David D. Caron, Michael J. Kelly, and Anastasia Telesetsky (eds), *The International Law of Disaster Relief* (CUP 2014) 57.

[16] David Fisher, 'The Future of International Disaster Response Law' (2012) 55 German Yearbook of International Law 87, 115.

[17] This has also been termed the 'international law of disaster relief' (e.g. in Sandesh Sivakumaran, 'Arbitrary Withholding of Consent to Humanitarian Assistance in Situations of Disaster' (2015) 64 International & Comparative Law Quarterly 501); however, IDRL is the more widely used term.

[18] Aronsson-Storrier and da Costa (n 14) 503.

[19] On DRR, see the three successive global risk reduction strategies: Yokohama Strategy and Plan of Action for a Safer World: Guidelines for Natural Disaster Prevention, Preparedness and Mitigation (United Nations, Report of the World Conference on Natural Disaster Reduction, Yokohama, Japan, 23–27 May 1994 (1994) <https://www.preventionweb.net/files/8241_doc6841contenido1.pdf> accessed 27 June 2024); Hyogo Framework for Action 2005–2015: Building the Resilience of Nations and Communities to Disasters (United Nations, 'Final Report of the World Conference on Disaster Reduction' (16 March 2005) A/CONF.206/6) (Hyogo Framework); Sendai Framework for Disaster Risk Reduction 2015–2030 (United Nations Office for Disaster Risk Reduction, 'Proceedings: Third UN World Conference on Disaster Risk Reduction' (2015) <https://www.undrr.org/publication/proceedings-third-un-world-conference-disaster-risk-reduction> accessed 11 June 2024). See also ILC Draft Articles (n 7) art 9.

development actors has been recognized for some time, particularly in terms of the 'humanitarian-development nexus',[20] which gained prominence following the 2016 World Humanitarian Summit.[21]

Disaster response proceeds, at least in theory, in sequential phases. While it may not always be possible to clearly delineate these phases from each other in practice, for the sake of exposition, five phases are identified.[22] First, the response is initiated, which includes a request for and/or offers of assistance and the determination, among the parties concerned, of how the response will proceed, including its modalities and any conditions placed on the provision of relief. Some of the same modalities used to deliver humanitarian assistance in situations of armed conflict, such as humanitarian relief corridors and protected zones,[23] may also be used in disaster response. Second, humanitarian access is negotiated, including as it relates to humanitarian personnel (entry visas, work visas, and the recognition of professional qualifications), goods and equipment (customs and duties), freedom of movement (within the affected state and through any transit states), and overflight and landing rights. Third, issues of status are addressed, including the identification of humanitarian personnel and the privileges, immunities, and facilities to be granted to each category of humanitarian worker (international organization, non-governmental organization (NGO), and state). The fourth phase relates to the actual provision of humanitarian assistance, which raises a range of issues, such as the protection of humanitarian personnel, the coordination of humanitarian activities, quality control, any use of military or civil defence assets, and the allocation of liability and compensation for any harm caused. In the final phase, the response is terminated. Termination is often followed by a recovery period and then a development phase.[24]

While IDRL is a new subfield of PIL, international disaster relief itself is not new. The response to the 1755 Lisbon earthquake is widely recognized as the first major international disaster response.[25] Early efforts to formalize such response, led by Italian Red Cross official Giovanni Ciraolo,[26] gave rise to the creation in 1927 of the International Relief Union (IRU) within the League of Nations.[27] However, the IRU never played a significant role in any disaster and folded in 1967.[28] In 1984, following a 1977 study by the IFRC and the United Nations Disaster Relief Organization[29] (UNDRO),[30] which was noted by the Economic and Social Council (ECOSOC)

[20] For a critical appraisal of this nexus, see Jon Harald Sande Lie, 'The Humanitarian-Development Nexus: Humanitarian Principles, Practice, and Pragmatics' (2020) 5 Journal of International Humanitarian Action 1.

[21] See Chapter 5, Section 4.1.

[22] These phases are based on the four 'aspects' described in: United Nations (UN), 'Protection of Persons in the Event of Disasters: Memorandum by the Secretariat' (11 December 2007) A/CN.4/590 (UN Secretariat Memo).

[23] See Chapter 3, Section 4.1.

[24] See UNGA Res 46/182 (19 December 1991) A/RES/46/182 (Res 46/182) Annex, paras 40–42.

[25] Saptarishi Bandopadhyay, *All is Well: Catastrophe and the Making of the Normal State* (OUP 2022) ch 4.

[26] Bookmiller (n 9) 49.

[27] Convention Establishing an International Relief Union (adopted 12 July 1927, entered into force 27 December 1932) 135 LNTS 247.

[28] See Chapter 5, Section 2.1.

[29] See Chapter 5, Section 2.2.

[30] UNGA, 'Report of the Secretary-General' (12 May 1977) A/32/64.

and endorsed by the General Assembly,[31] UNDRO proposed the draft Convention on Expediting the Delivery of Emergency Assistance.[32] It focused on reducing entry barriers for relief personnel, goods, and equipment. The draft convention was presented to ECOSOC, which referred it on to the General Assembly's Economic and Financial (Second) Committee. However, the draft did not receive broad support, due in large part to concern that its over-specificity might actually impede relief,[33] and the Second Committee never acted on it.[34] Then, at the end of the twentieth century, the emergence of disaster studies as an area of academic inquiry[35] and improved data collection, which demonstrated the extensive human and economic costs of disasters, increased stakeholders' focus on international roles and responsibilities in disaster response and brought about increased calls for an attendant legal regime.[36] However, as a result of the IRU's ineffectiveness, a comprehensive disaster response treaty was no longer considered feasible.[37] Instead, a new approach emerged: sectoral treaties—regulating matters such as customs, the transport of goods, and waste management—began to include provisions on states' duties in the event of a disaster.[38] These rules constitute a large part of the current IDRL treaty framework, which is surveyed in the next section.

2.1. Instruments

As mentioned above, there is no comprehensive disaster response treaty. Instead, the current IDRL framework consists of a patchwork of instruments,[39] which can be grouped into five distinct categories.[40] The first category is comprised of sectoral treaties that cover a range of issues, including disaster response. This category includes the Convention on Civil Aviation,[41] the Convention on Facilitation of International

[31] ECOSOC Res 2102 (LXIII) (3 August 1977); UNGA Res 32/56 (8 December 1977).

[32] UNGA, ECOSOC, and UNDRO, 'Report of the Secretary-General' (18 June 1984) A/39/267/Add.2, Annex.

[33] Bookmiller (n 9) 54.

[34] Fisher (n 16) 114.

[35] See generally David Alexander, 'The Study of Natural Disasters, 1977–1997: Some Reflections on a Changing Field of Knowledge' (1997) 21 Disasters 284.

[36] Bookmiller (n 9) 52.

[37] Andrea de Guttry, 'Surveying the Law' in Andrea de Guttry, Marco Gestri, and Gabriella Venturini (eds), *International Disaster Response Law* (TMC Asser Press 2012) 34.

[38] ibid, 35.

[39] For a more complete survey of this patchwork, see IFRC, 'Law and Legal Issues in International Disaster Response: A Desk Study' (*IFRC*, 2007) <https://disasterlaw.ifrc.org/sites/default/files/media/disaster_law/2020-08/113600-idrl-deskstudy-en.pdf> accessed 12 June 2024; UN Secretariat Memo (n 22); de Guttry (n 37); David D Caron, Michael K Kelly, and Anastasia Telesetsky (eds), *The International Law of Disaster Relief* (CUP 2014); Dug Cubie, *The International Legal Protection of Persons in Humanitarian Crises: Exploring the Acquis Humanitaire* (Hart 2017) ch 8; Flavia Zorzi Giustiniani, *International Law in Disaster Scenarios* (Springer 2021).

[40] For reasons of space, this chapter cannot list every instrument in each category. For a complete (up to 2007) list of all multilateral, regional, sub-regional, and bilateral instruments related to both disaster response and disaster risk reduction, see UN Secretariat, 'Protection of Persons in the Event of Disasters: Memorandum by the Secretariat, Annex II (List of Instruments)' (11 December 2007) A/CN.4/590/Add.2.

[41] (Adopted 7 December 1944, entered into force 4 April 1947) 15 UNTS 295; Chapter 8 of its Annex 9 on facilitation addresses relief flights following disasters.

Maritime Traffic,[42] the Food Assistance Convention,[43] and instruments adopted under World Customs Organization (WCO) auspices, such as the Convention on Temporary Admission[44] and the amended Convention on the Simplification and Harmonization of Customs Procedures (the Kyoto Convention).[45]

The second category is comprised of context-specific treaties, meaning agreements that address disaster response but are limited to either a specific type of disaster or a particular aspect of disaster response. Such treaties include the Convention on Early Notification of a Nuclear Accident,[46] the Convention on Assistance in the Case of a Nuclear Accident or Radiological Emergency,[47] the International Convention on Oil Pollution Preparedness, Response and Cooperation,[48] the Convention on the Protection and Use of Transboundary Watercourses and International Lakes,[49] the Tampere Convention,[50] the Framework Convention on Civil Defence Assistance,[51] and the Charter on Cooperation to Achieve the Coordinated Use of Space Facilities in the Event of Natural or Technological Disasters.[52] Most of the treaties in this category address only state-to-state assistance, even though much disaster relief is now delivered via UN bodies and NGOs.[53]

Third are regional and sub-regional disaster response treaties and mechanisms. The regionalization of disaster response cooperation is a well-established trend,[54] especially in relation to coordination. Fisher notes a 'very gradual shift of coordination authority from the global to the regional level'.[55] For example, Caribbean states established a regional disaster response agency in 2008,[56] and the African Union (AU) is currently working towards the full operationalization of the African Humanitarian Agency.[57] While the regional and sub-regional planes are beyond the scope of this

[42] (Adopted 9 April 1965, entered into force 5 March 1967) 591 UNTS 265; sections 7.8–7.20 address facilitating the arrival and departure of ships involved in disaster response.

[43] (Adopted 25 April 2012, entered into force 1 January 2013) 2884 UNTS 3; see Chapter 7, Section 2.

[44] (Adopted 26 June 1990, entered into force 27 November 1993) 1762 UNTS 121; its Annex B.9. provides that goods 'imported for humanitarian purposes shall be granted temporary admission in accordance with' the Convention's article 2.

[45] (Adopted 26 June 1999, entered into force 3 February 2006) 1545 UNTS 316; article 2 of Annex J(5) recommends that relief consignments be prioritized in clearance processes and article 5 of the same Annex requires receiving states to waive financial import/export requirements.

[46] (Adopted 26 September 1986, entered into force 27 October 1986) 1439 UNTS 275.

[47] (Adopted 26 September 1986, entered into force 26 February 1987) 1457 UNTS 133.

[48] (Adopted 30 November 1990, entered into force 13 May 1995) 1891 UNTS 77.

[49] (Adopted 17 March 1992, entered into force 6 October 1996) 1936 UNTS 269.

[50] Tampere Convention (n 5).

[51] (Adopted 22 May 2000, entered into force 23 September 2001) 2172 UNTS 213.

[52] (Adopted 25 April 2000). Also known as the International Charter on Space and Major Disasters, this is a mechanism for collaboration among space agencies through which satellite-derived information is made available to support disaster response.

[53] Fisher (n 16) 92.

[54] David Fisher, 'A Glass Half Full: The International Law Commission's Draft Articles and the Operational Challenges of International Disaster Response' (2020) 1 Yearbook of International Disaster Law 93, 106.

[55] ibid, 108.

[56] Agreement Establishing the Caribbean Disaster Emergency Management Agency (adopted 2 July 2008, entered into force 4 July 2013) <https://caricom.org/treaties/agreement-establishing-the-caribbean-disaster-management-agency/> accessed 13 June 2024.

[57] The African Humanitarian Agency's statute was adopted in 2023 (AU Assembly of Heads of State and Government, 'Decisions on Draft Legal Instruments' (18–19 February 2023) Assembly/AU/Dec.856(XXXVI) para 2(iii)).

book, it is worth noting that *comprehensive* disaster response treaties do exist at these levels;[58] however, they tend to cover state-to-state cooperation and not assistance from outside the region or from non-state actors.[59] Regional and sub-regional instruments include the Arab Cooperation Agreement on Regulating and Facilitating Relief Operations,[60] the Inter-American Convention to Facilitate Disaster Assistance,[61] the Agreement among the Governments of the Participating States of the Black Sea Economic Cooperation on Collaboration in Emergency Assistance and Emergency Response to Natural and Man-Made Disasters,[62] and the ASEAN Agreement on Disaster Emergency Management and Emergency Response.[63]

The fourth category consists of bilateral treaties. Such treaties, which number well over 100,[64] make up the majority of disaster relief treaties.[65] They were adopted in waves during the 1950s, 1970s, and 1990s, on the assumption that most relief would come from geographically proximate countries.[66] De Guttry has identified three general types of bilateral disaster response treaty: those that regulate all types of major disasters; those that regulate a specific type of disaster, such as forest fires; and those that regulate disasters in a defined thematic or geographic area, such as at sea.[67]

The treaties in these four categories—sectoral, context-specific, regional or sub-regional, and bilateral—generally aim to modify or harmonize national rules to expedite relief operations. A request for assistance under a particular treaty triggers the processes and procedures established by that agreement. Given the range of treaties potentially applicable to any one disaster, it is possible that several different agreements will govern distinct aspects of the response to the same disaster.

Beyond treaty-based rules, there are very few other international disaster response rules, whether drawn from custom or general principles of law.[68] The IFRC reported that it found no evidence of 'the existence of a system of customary IDRL'.[69] The ILC, however, determined that when a disaster manifestly exceeds a state's national response capacity, that state's duty to seek assistance is based, in part, on its obligations under customary international law.[70]

[58] For a survey of regional and sub-regional disaster response treaties, see de Guttry (n 37) 17–33.
[59] Fisher (n 16) 111.
[60] (Adopted 3 September 1987) <https://disasterlaw.ifrc.org/media/3123> accessed 13 June 2024.
[61] (Adopted 7 June 1991, entered into force 16 October 1996) <http://www.oas.org/juridico/english/treaties/a-54.html> accessed 13 June 2024.
[62] (Adopted 15 April 1998) <https://www.bsec-organization.org/UploadedDocuments/StatutoryDocumentsAgreements/Emergencyagreement071116.pdf> accessed 13 June 2024.
[63] (Adopted 26 July 2005, entered into force 24 December 2009) <https://agreement.asean.org/media/download/20220330063139.pdf> accessed 13 June 2024.
[64] Fisher (n 16) 90.
[65] Sandesh Sivakumaran, 'Techniques in International Law-Making: Extrapolation, Analogy, Form and the Emergence of an International Law of Disaster Relief' (2018) 28 European Journal of International Law 1097, 1102.
[66] Fisher (n 16) 108.
[67] de Guttry (n 37) 11–12.
[68] Sivakumaran (n 65) 1105.
[69] Michael Hoffman, 'What is the Scope of International Disaster Response Law?' in IFRC (ed) *International Disaster Response Laws, Principles and Practice: Reflections, Prospects and Challenges* (IFRC 2003) 16.
[70] ILC, 'Report of the International Law Commission on the Work of its 68th Session' (2 May–19 June and 4 July–12 August 2016) A/71/10 (ILC Commentary) commentary to art 11, para 3.

The fifth and final category consists of soft law instruments. Cubie defines these as 'authoritative norm creating texts and practices which are not "law" in the sense of creating enforceable obligations [. . .] but which may directly influence international law through the creation of consistent practices and consensus within the international community'.[71] Soft law is made with varying degrees of state involvement; Bartolini has described IDRL sources with minimal state involvement as 'even softer than soft law'.[72] Soft law instruments are directed at states, non-state humanitarian actors, or both.[73] Examples of soft law addressed to states include the Recommendation of the Customs Co-operation Council to Expedite the Forwarding of Relief Consignments in the Event of Disasters[74] and the Model Agreement on Customs Facilitation in International Emergency Humanitarian Assistance produced by the UN Office for the Coordination of Humanitarian Affairs (OCHA) and the WCO.[75] Several associations of, or organizations for, international law professionals have promulgated soft law related to disaster relief, including: the International Law Association's Draft Model Agreement Relating to Humanitarian Relief Operations;[76] the Max Planck Institute's International Guidelines for Humanitarian Assistance Operations;[77] the International Institute of Humanitarian Law's Guiding Principles on the Right to Humanitarian Assistance (San Remo Principles);[78] and the Institute of International Law's Bruges Resolution on humanitarian assistance.[79] An additional important soft law instrument made by non-state actors and addressed to both states and non-state actors is the International Search and Rescue Advisory Group's Guidelines (INSARAG Guidelines).[80] These were developed to promote the coordination of urban search-and-rescue teams among themselves and with affected states; they have been recognized by the General Assembly.[81] Additional soft law made by and for non-state actors include the UNDRO and League of Red Cross and Red Crescent Societies'

[71] Dug Cubie, 'An Analysis of Soft Law Applicable to Humanitarian Action: Relative Normativity in Action?' (2011) 2 Journal of International Humanitarian Legal Studies 177, 189.

[72] Giulio Bartolini, 'A Universal Treaty for Disasters? Remarks on the International Law Commission's Draft Articles on the Protection of Persons in the Event of Disasters' (2017) 99 International Review of the Red Cross 1103, 1109.

[73] For a list of soft law instruments related to disaster response, see de Guttry (n 37) 36.

[74] (8 June 1970) T2-423; para 5 recommends that states exempt relief from import duties, taxes, and prohibitions or restrictions, and para 6 recommends that states facilitate the temporary admission of equipment used in relief operations; see also Customs Co-operation Council, 'Resolution of the Customs Co-operation Council on the Role of Customs in Natural Disaster Relief' (June 2011) <https://www.wcoomd.org/en/about-us/legal-instruments/~/media/A0C1DEE96F944E08BCD48FFDD1A7D4B7.ashx> accessed 17 June 2024.

[75] OCHA, 'Model Agreement on Customs Facilitation in International Emergency Humanitarian Assistance' (1996) ST/DHA/96/134 <https://digitallibrary.un.org/record/230021?ln=&v=pdf> accessed 3 October 2024.

[76] International Law Association, 'Report of the Fifty-Ninth Conference Held at Belgrade, 17–23 August 1980' (1981) 520.

[77] Peter MacAlister-Smith, 'International Guidelines for Humanitarian Assistance Operations' (Max Planck Institute for Comparative Law and International Law 1991).

[78] International Institute of Humanitarian Law, 'Guiding Principles on the Right to Humanitarian Assistance' (1993) 33 International Review of the Red Cross 519 (San Remo Principles).

[79] Institute of International Law, Bruges Session, Sixteenth Commission, Humanitarian Assistance, 'Resolution' (2 September 2003) (Bruges Resolution).

[80] INSARAG, Guidelines 2020 (INSARAG 2020) <https://insarag.org/methodology/insarag-guidelines/> accessed 4 February 2025.

[81] UNGA Res 57/150 (27 February 2003) A/RES/57/150, preambular para 16.

(now IFRC) Measures to Expedite International Relief,[82] the Code of Conduct for the International Red Cross and Red Crescent Movement and Non-Governmental Organizations in Disaster Relief,[83] and the Sphere Humanitarian Charter.[84] Some of these soft law instruments address the notion of a human right to humanitarian assistance, which is discussed in the next section.

The IDRL instruments across these five categories together number in the hundreds[85] and make up a 'fragmented and incomplete' patchwork of norms.[86] It would take a separate book to summarize them all and, in any case, the more useful approach is to map the most significant principles and rules derived from the universe of IDRL instruments onto the five phases of disaster response outlined above: initiation, access, status, relief delivery, and termination. The UN Secretariat took this approach in a memorandum it prepared for the ILC in connection with its work on the protection of persons in the event of disasters.[87] The ILC then incorporated the most significant areas of convergence into its Draft Articles on the Protection of Persons in the Event of Disasters (the Draft Articles), which are discussed below.[88]

2.2. Human rights, a right to assistance, the responsibility to protect, and humanitarian access

Beyond the disaster-specific instruments outlined above, individuals affected by disasters are also protected by international human rights law (IHRL).[89] Under IHRL, and consistent with the principle of sovereignty, the affected state bears 'responsibility first and foremost to take care of the victims of natural disasters [. . .] occurring on its territory'.[90] The rights to food, water, shelter, and health are especially significant during disaster,[91] but may become more difficult for the affected

[82] UNGA and UNDRO, 'Report of the Secretary-General' (12 May 1977) A/32/61, Annex II.

[83] IFRC and ICRC, 'The Code of Conduct for the International Red Cross and Red Crescent Movement and Non-Governmental Organizations (NGOs) in Disaster Relief' (1994) <https://www.icrc.org/en/doc/assets/files/publications/icrc-002-1067.pdf> accessed 30 June 2025; see Chapter 2, Section 3.2.

[84] Sphere Association, *The Sphere Handbook* (4th edn, Sphere Association 2018) 27; see Chapter 6, Section 3.2.

[85] UN Secretariat (n 40).

[86] David Fidler, 'Disaster Relief and Governance After the Indian Ocean Tsunami: What Role for International Law?' (2005) 6 Melbourne Journal of International Law 458, 465; Fisher (n 16) 91.

[87] UN Secretariat Memo (n 22).

[88] See Section 2.3.2.

[89] ILC Draft Articles (n 7) arts 5 and 18(1).

[90] Res 46/182 (n 24) Annex, para 4; see also ILC Draft Articles (n 7) art 10 and IFRC Guidelines (n 6) s I.3.1.

[91] International Covenant on Economic, Social and Cultural Rights (adopted 16 December 1966, entered into force 3 January 1976) 993 UNTS 3 (ICESCR) arts 11 and 12, read with: Committee on Economic, Social and Cultural Rights (CESCR), 'General Comment No. 4: The Right to Adequate Housing (Art. 11(1) of the Covenant)' (1991) E/1992/23; CESCR, 'General Comment No. 12: The Right to Adequate Food (Art. 11)' (12 May 1999) E/C.12/1999/5, paras 15, 17, 19, and 38; CESCR, 'General Comment No. 15: The Right to Water (Arts. 11 and 12 of the Covenant)' (20 January 2002) E/C.12/2002/11, para 25; CESCR, 'General Comment No. 14: The Right to the Highest Attainable Standard of Health (Art. 12)' (11 August 2000) E/C.12/2000/4, para 40; Convention on the Rights of the Child (adopted 20 November 1989, entered into force 2 September 1990) 1577 UNTS 3, art 24.

state to fulfill;[92] the rights to life and security of the person are also particularly relevant.[93]

In addition to these specific human rights, there was for a time debate among IDRL experts regarding whether disaster-affected individuals also enjoy a right to humanitarian assistance. Advocates of this right argue that it could resolve practical issues when affected states refuse or delay external assistance, such as in Myanmar after Cyclone Nargis in 2008[94] and in Iran following the 1990 earthquake in Gilan province.[95] They also suggest that a dedicated right to humanitarian assistance would elevate the needs of disaster-affected individuals and drive political and legal change. As Fisher explains, recognition of a right to humanitarian assistance 'would put the needs of affected persons much closer to the centre of debates about whether and how to facilitate international relief efforts. It could also help to shape political dialogue around difficult operations'.[96] He also notes that in the longer term, 'it could lead to a cultural shift in expectations around international assistance to disaster affected persons and also nudge domestic law on the question of international assistance in a more permissive direction'.[97]

Early scholarship on this issue derived a dedicated right to humanitarian assistance from the human rights to food, water, shelter, and health,[98] or from customary international law.[99] Soft law sources have also recognized a right to humanitarian assistance. For example, the Bruges Resolution notes that leaving 'victims of disaster without humanitarian assistance constitutes a threat to human life and an offence to human dignity and therefore a violation of fundamental human rights',[100] thus they 'are entitled to request and receive humanitarian assistance'.[101] The first San Remo Principle similarly provides that every 'human being has the right to humanitarian assistance in order to ensure respect for the human rights to life, health, protection against cruel and degrading treatment and other human rights which are essential to survival, well-being and protection in public emergencies'.[102] For the International Red Cross and Red Crescent Movement (the Movement),[103] it is 'a fundamental right of all people to both offer and receive humanitarian assistance'.[104] The Guiding

[92] See generally, Dug Cubie and Marlies Hesselman, 'Accountability for the Human Rights Implications of Natural Disasters: A Proposal for Systemic International Oversight' (2015) 33 Netherlands Quarterly of Human Rights 9.

[93] International Covenant on Civil and Political Rights (adopted 16 December 1966, entered into force 23 March 1976) 999 UNTS 171 (ICCPR) arts 6(1) and 9(1), read with Human Rights Committee, 'General Comment No. 6: Article 6 (Right to Life)' (30 April 1982) HR1/GEN/1/Rev.9, para 5.

[94] Craig Allan and Therese O'Donnell, 'An Offer You Cannot Refuse? Natural Disasters, the Politics of Aid Refusal and Potential Legal Implications' (2013) 5 Amsterdam Law Forum 36, 36–37.

[95] Rohan Hardcastle and Adrian Chua, 'Victims of Natural Disasters: The Right to Receive Humanitarian Assistance' (1997) 1 The International Journal of Human Rights 37, 41.

[96] Fisher (n 54) 99.

[97] ibid, 100.

[98] Boško Jakovljević, 'The Right to Humanitarian Assistance: Legal Aspects' (1987) 27 International Review of the Red Cross 469; Hardcastle and Chua (n 95).

[99] Rohan Hardcastle and Adrian Chua, 'Humanitarian Assistance: Towards a Right of Access to Victims of Natural Disasters' (1998) 38 International Review of the Red Cross 589.

[100] Bruges Resolution (n 79) art II(1).

[101] ibid, art II(2).

[102] San Remo Principles (n 78).

[103] See Chapter 6, Section 2.

[104] Report of the XXVIth International Conference of the Red Cross and Red Crescent, Annex IV: The Principles and Rules for Red Cross and Red Crescent Disaster Relief (1995) <https://library.icrc.org/library/docs/CI/CI_1995_RAPPORT_ENG.pdf> accessed 24 June 2024, para 2.1.

Principles on Internal Displacement provide that internally displaced persons 'have the right to request and to receive protection and humanitarian assistance'.[105] Other early scholars of this issue, by contrast, found no dedicated right to humanitarian assistance in disasters.[106] More recent scholarship has concluded there is a dedicated but derivative right to humanitarian assistance,[107] or that one may be emerging.[108] Most of the sources that find a right to humanitarian assistance do not specify who bears the corresponding duty—whether the affected state or third states. For sources that do identify a duty-bearer, such as the Movement,[109] the Guiding Principles on Internal Displacement,[110] and some scholars,[111] it is the affected state.

This debate regarding whether there is a dedicated right to humanitarian assistance in disasters is ultimately a distraction from the real issue of humanitarian access. As Kälin points out, a right to receive humanitarian assistance is more a shorthand for a complex legal situation than a statement of any clear or enforceable right.[112] In the aftermath of a disaster, a state typically requires assistance because it lacks sufficient resources to respond on its own. An individual right to humanitarian assistance opposable against that under-resourced state is of little practical benefit, unless the real problem is that the state refuses assistance, for example, due to discrimination against marginalized groups or a fear of losing control of the response. The only human right to assistance that makes practical sense is one that leads to a state duty to request or accept assistance from the international community. It is thus more straightforward to simply bypass individual rights and approach the issue as a matter of affected state duty.

Other scholars have argued that a third state can provide disaster relief without the affected state's consent further to the responsibility to protect (R2P). UN member states endorsed R2P at the 2005 World Summit. It rests on three pillars. First is each state's responsibility to protect its population from genocide, war crimes, ethnic cleansing, and crimes against humanity.[113] Second is the international community's responsibility to use peaceful means to support states to meet their pillar one responsibility. Third is the international community's willingness 'to take collective action, in a timely and decisive manner, through the Security Council, in accordance with the Charter, including Chapter VII, [. . .] should peaceful means be inadequate and [if]

[105] ECOSOC, 'Report of the Representative of the Secretary-General, Mr Francis M Deng, Submitted Pursuant to Commission Resolution 1997/39, Addendum, Guiding Principles on Internal Displacement', E/CN.4/1998/53/Add.2 (11 February 1998) (Guiding Principles on Internal Displacement) principle 3(2).

[106] Nigel Rodley, 'Interventions des participants' in UNESCO, '*Le droit à l'assistance humanitaire: actes du colloque international organisé par l'UNESCO*' (1995) SHS-95/Conf.86/6, 146–52; Peter MacAlister-Smith, 'The Right to Humanitarian Assistance in International Law' (1998) 66 Revue de droit international de science diplomatiques et politiques 211, 224–25; Yoram Dinstein, 'The Right to Humanitarian Assistance' (2000) 53 Naval War College Review 77, 77.

[107] Annalisa Creta, 'A (Human) Right to Humanitarian Assistance in Disaster Situations? Surveying Public International Law' in Andrea de Guttry, Marco Gestri, and Gabriella Venturini (eds), *International Disaster Response Law* (Springer 2012) 360–61; Emilie Kuijt, *Humanitarian Assistance and State Sovereignty in International Law: Towards a Comprehensive Framework* (Intersentia 2015) ch V.

[108] Cubie (n 39) 325; Guglielmo Verdirame, *The UN and Human Rights: Who Guards the Guardians?* (CUP 2011) 159–61.

[109] IFRC (n 39) 35.

[110] Guiding Principles on Internal Displacement (n 105) principle 3(2).

[111] Creta (n 107) 361.

[112] Walter Kälin, *Internal Displacement and the Law* (OUP 2023) 204.

[113] UNGA Res 60/1, '2005 World Summit Outcome' (24 October 2005) A/RES/60/1, para 138.

national authorities are manifestly failing to protect their populations from genocide, war crimes, ethnic cleansing and crimes against humanity'.[114] The argument is that a denial by the affected state of external assistance could amount to a crime against humanity and therefore activate pillar three.[115] There are two problems with this argument, both related to the fact that intervention under pillar three requires Security Council authorization. First, the aid denial would have to amount to a threat to international peace and security to engage the Security Council's competence.[116] Second, the Security Council has only ever authorized intervention pursuant to R2P once, in Libya in 2011, and its reliance on R2P in that context was tenuous at best.[117]

The debates about a right to humanitarian assistance and R2P have now largely resolved around the more accurate state consent framing. Today, the issue is for the most part no longer framed in terms of individuals' right to assistance[118] or R2P, but rather in terms of the affected state's duty to seek assistance or to consent to assistance offered by external actors.[119] Indeed, as will be shown below, this is how the issue was ultimately addressed by the ILC in its work to progressively develop IDRL.[120] IDRL's increasing coherence in this and other regards owes much to the ILC's work, and to the work of the IFRC before it. Their efforts are outlined below.

2.3. Progressive development

The IFRC's World Disasters Report 2000 identified a 'yawning gap' at the centre of IDRL.[121] Reflecting on the nature of the IDRL framework outlined above, Hoffman

[114] ibid, para 139.

[115] Rebecca Barber, 'The Responsibility to Protect the Survivors of Natural Disaster: Cyclone Nargis, a Case Study' (2009) 14 Journal of Conflict & Security Law 3; Jürgen Haacke, 'Myanmar, the Responsibility to Protect and the Need for Practical Assistance' (2009) 1 Global Responsibility to Protect 156; Stuart Ford, 'Is the Failure to Respond Appropriately to a Natural Disaster a Crime Against Humanity? The Responsibility to Protect and Individual Criminal Responsibility in the Aftermath of Cyclone Nargis' (2010) 38 Denver Journal of International Law and Policy 227; Francesca Russo, 'Disasters Through the Lens of International Criminal Law' in Andrea de Guttry, Marco Gestri, and Gabriella Venturini (eds), *International Disaster Response Law* (TMC Asser Press 2012).

[116] Charter of the United Nations (adopted 26 June 1945, entered into force 24 October 1945) 1 UNTS XVI (UN Charter) art 24.

[117] UNSC Res 1973 (17 March 2011) S/RES/1973, preambular paras 4–5 and para 4. See also UNSC Res 1970 (26 February 2011) S/RES/1970, preambular para 9.

[118] This is not to say that there is no longer legal scholarship on the right to assistance in disaster; see, for example, the sources cited above (notes 107 and 108) and Marlies Hesselman, 'A Right to International (Humanitarian) Assistance in Times of Disaster: Fresh Perspectives from International Human Rights Law' in Flavia Zorzi Giustiniani and others (eds), *Routledge Handbook of Human Rights and Disaster* (Routledge 2018).

[119] For literature that approaches the issue in this way, see Chan Leng Sun, 'Humanitarian Assistance by International Organisations: A Question of Compulsory Access to Victims' (1991) Singapore Journal of Legal Studies 320; Michael Eburn, 'International Law and Disaster Response' (2010) 36 Monash University Law Review 162; J Benton Heath, 'Disasters, Relief, and Neglect: the Duty to Accept Humanitarian Assistance and the Work of the International Law Commission' (2011) 43 NYU Journal of International Law and Policy 419; Sivakumaran (n 17); Hans-Joaquim Heintze, 'Access to Victims and Humanitarian Assistance' in Hans-Joaquim Heintze and Pierre Thielbörger (eds), *From Cold War to Cyber War: The Evolution of the International Law of Peace and Armed Conflict over the Last 25 Years* (Springer 2016).

[120] See Section 2.3.2.1.

[121] Michael Hoffman, 'Towards an International Disaster Response Law' in Peter Walker and Jonathan Walter (eds), *World Disasters Report 2000* (IFRC 2000) 145.

observed that there was 'no definitive, broadly accepted source of international law which spells out legal standards, procedures, rights and duties pertaining to disaster response and assistance'.[122] He further noted that no 'systematic attempt has been made to pull together the disparate threads of existing law, to formalize customary law or to expand and develop the law in new ways'.[123] This lack of a comprehensive legal framework gives rise to practical challenges in disaster response, which Fisher has grouped in two categories.[124] First, legal obstacles to the entry and operation of international relief items, equipment, and personnel. For example, a year after the 2004 Indian Ocean tsunami, over 400 containers of relief were still waiting to clear customs in Jakarta and Medan, Indonesia.[125] Second, issues of quality and coordination. One important problem in this regard is the arrival of large quantities of unneeded or inappropriate relief items, such as used winter clothing in tropical climates and expired medicines.[126] Hoffman's observation was the 'legal clarion call'[127] that galvanized efforts to map the range of IDRL instruments and transform them from a patchwork of norms into a comprehensive body of international law on disaster relief, with a view to resolving these practical challenges. Two actors conducted much of the work: the IFRC and the ILC. Working separately but in what could be termed a conversation, they shaped IDRL into a structured body of law. This section covers their efforts and achievements, starting with the IFRC,[128] whose work began first.

2.3.1. International Federation of Red Cross and Red Crescent Societies initiatives

While the IFRC's involvement with IDRL dates back to the 1920s,[129] its IDRL Programme was launched in 2001 with the goal of strengthening states' legal preparedness for disasters and exploring the role of law in disaster response. More specifically, the Programme aimed to support states by providing technical assistance and capacity building in, and research on, the legal regulation of disaster response.[130] That same year, the Movement's Council of Delegates[131] endorsed the IFRC's initiative to advocate for the development of IDRL and encouraged the IFRC to continue its work.[132] Two years later, in 2003, the IFRC's work was mentioned in the International Conference of the Red Cross and Red Crescent's (International Conference) Agenda

[122] ibid.

[123] ibid.

[124] David Fisher, 'The Law of International Disaster Response: Overview and Ramifications for Military Actors' (2008) 38 Israel Yearbook on Human Rights 115, 131.

[125] ibid, 133.

[126] ibid, 135.

[127] Bookmiller (n 9) 46.

[128] On the IFRC generally, see Chapter 6, Section 2.2.

[129] See Rachel Macleod, 'The Evolution of the International Federation of Red Cross and Red Crescent Societies' Work in Disaster Law' in Marie Aronsson-Storrier and Susan Breau (eds), *Research Handbook on Disasters and International Law* (2nd edn, Edward Elgar 2024) 300–02 and Jiří Toman, 'Towards a Disaster Relief Law: Legal Aspects of Disaster Relief Operations' in Frits Kalshoven (ed), *Assisting the Victims of Armed Conflict and Other Disasters* (Martinus Nijhoff 1989).

[130] This section is limited to IFRC initiatives in relation to IDRL. The IFRC's involvement in disaster law is, however, broader, also encompassing elements such as disaster risk reduction. For a more detailed treatment of IFRC disaster law initiatives, see Macleod (n 129).

[131] This and other aspects of Movement governance are discussed in Chapter 6, Section 2.

[132] Council of Delegates of the International Red Cross and Red Crescent Movement, 'Resolutions, Geneva, 11–14 November 2001' (2002) 84 International Review of the Red Cross 263, Resolution 5.

for Humanitarian Action, which focused in part on reducing the risk and impact of disasters.[133]

The IFRC's IDRL Programme has taken a largely bottom-up approach, focusing on helping states make their domestic law and policy frameworks more open to external disaster relief. It has produced five principal outputs. The first was a major research report authored by David Fisher and published in 2007 in both full[134] and summary[135] versions. The report maps relevant institutions, legal regimes,[136] and international, regional, and bilateral instruments, and identifies key legal issues related to disaster response.[137] This research underpins the IDRL Programme's other main outputs: the IFRC Guidelines for the Domestic Facilitation and Regulation of International Disaster Relief and Initial Recovery Assistance (IFRC Guidelines),[138] the IFRC Model Act for the Facilitation and Regulation of International Disaster Relief and Initial Recovery Assistance (IFRC Model Act),[139] the IFRC Model Emergency Decree for the Facilitation and Regulation of International Disaster Relief and Initial Recovery Assistance (IFRC Model Emergency Decree),[140] and the Checklist on the Facilitation and Regulation of International Disaster Relief and Initial Recovery Assistance (IDRL Checklist).[141]

The second output, the IFRC Guidelines, was approved at the Movement's XXXth International Conference in 2007.[142] These guidelines provide recommendations to states for addressing aspects of national law that may unintentionally hamper disaster relief operations. Organized into five parts—core responsibilities, early warning and preparedness, initiation and termination of assistance, eligibility for legal facilities, and legal facilities for entry and operations—the IFRC Guidelines emphasize the central role of domestic authorities and actors in disaster response. Parts I and III reflect the law on humanitarian access introduced above.[143] The affected state has primary

[133] XXVIIIth International Conference of the Red Cross and Red Crescent (2–6 December 2003) 'Agenda for Humanitarian Action' <https://www.icrc.org/en/doc/assets/files/other/icrc_002_1103.pdf> accessed 24 June 2024, general objective 3.

[134] IFRC (n 39).

[135] IFRC, 'Law and Legal Issues in International Disaster Response: A Desk Study (summary version)' (*IFRC*, 2007) <https://disasterlaw.ifrc.org/sites/default/files/media/disaster_law/2021-02/IDRL%20Desk%20Study%20Summary%20%28English%29.pdf> accessed 12 June 2024.

[136] The report identifies human rights law, IHL, refugee and internally displaced persons law, privileges and immunities law, customs law, transport law, telecommunications law, donor law, civil defence and military law, health law, environmental and industrial accident law, weapons control law, space law, and humanitarian personnel security law.

[137] The issues are grouped in categories: initiation and termination; goods and equipment; personnel, transport, and movement; operations; quality and accountability; coordination; involvement of militaries; and mixed situations.

[138] IFRC (n 6).

[139] IFRC, OCHA, and IPU, 'Model Act for the Facilitation and Regulation of International Disaster Relief and Initial Recovery Assistance (with Commentary)' (2013) <https://disasterlaw.ifrc.org/media/1772> accessed 24 June 2024, 12.

[140] IFRC and OCHA, 'Model Emergency Decree for the Facilitation and Regulation of International Disaster Relief and Initial Recovery Assistance' (2017) <https://disasterlaw.ifrc.org/sites/default/files/media/disaster_law/2020-09/Model-Decree_EN-LR.pdf> accessed 25 June 2024.

[141] IFRC, 'The Checklist on the Facilitation and Regulation of International Disaster Relief and Initial Recovery Assistance' (2017) <https://disasterlaw.ifrc.org/sites/default/files/media/disaster_law/2020-09/IDRL-Checklist-EN-LR-1.pdf> accessed 25 June 2024.

[142] Report of the XXXth International Conference of the Red Cross and Red Crescent (2007) <https://www.icrc.org/en/doc/assets/files/2011/bluebook-2007-english.pdf> accessed 24 June 2024, resolution 4.

[143] See Section 2.2.

responsibility for ensuring disaster relief within its territory.[144] If the affected state's response capacity is exceeded, it should request international assistance,[145] which should only be initiated with the affected state's consent and, in principle, following its request.[146]

The Guidelines go on to make recommendations regarding the effective delivery and coordination of international assistance, primarily with respect to legal facilities. They include guidance on selecting states and organizations eligible for legal facilities[147] and propose measures to prevent relief from being delayed or restricted.[148] These measures relate to personnel (e.g. to expedite the provision of visas and work permits and the recognition of professional qualifications),[149] goods and equipment (e.g. to exempt them from customs duties, taxes, and tariffs),[150] transport (e.g. to grant overflight and landing rights),[151] domestic legal status (e.g. to provide temporary authorization to operate),[152] taxation (to offer tax exemptions),[153] security,[154] extended hours,[155] and costs.[156] Since 2008, the UN General Assembly has regularly encouraged states to use the IFRC Guidelines,[157] and they are viewed as having made a significant contribution to state responses to disasters.[158]

In 2009, the IFRC, along with OCHA and the Inter-Parliamentary Union, began developing the third output—the IFRC Model Act—in response to states' requests for model legislative language to implement the Guidelines domestically.[159] A pilot version was launched in 2011 at the Movement's XXXIst International Conference,[160] and the final IFRC Model Act was published in 2013. It contains detailed provisions on the initiation and termination of international disaster relief (Chapter II), the coordination of preparedness for such assistance (Chapter III), the responsibilities of assisting actors (Chapter IV), eligibility for legal facilities (Chapter V), legal facilities for eligible actors (Chapter VI), supervision and sanctioning of, and reporting by, assisting actors (Chapter VII), and the transit of international disaster relief (Chapter VIII).[161] The IFRC Model Act is designed to form the basis for a dedicated domestic disaster relief law, or it can be 'used as inspiration for amendments to other existing

[144] IFRC (n 6) s I.3.1.
[145] ibid, s I.3.2.
[146] ibid, s III.10.1.
[147] ibid, s IV.
[148] ibid, s V.16-24.
[149] ibid, s V.16.
[150] ibid, s V.17-18.
[151] ibid, s V.19.
[152] ibid, s V.20.
[153] ibid, s V.21.
[154] ibid, s V.22.
[155] ibid, s V.23.
[156] ibid, s V.24.
[157] See, for example, UNGA Res 71/127 (24 January 2017) A/RES/71/127, para 27.
[158] Claire Clement, 'International Disaster Response Laws, Rules, and Principles: A Pragmatic Approach to Strengthening International Disaster Response Mechanisms' in David D. Caron, Michael J. Kelly, and Anastasia Telesetsky (eds), *The International Law of Disaster Relief* (CUP 2014).
[159] IFRC, OCHA, and IPU (n 139) 7.
[160] Report of the 31st International Conference of the Red Cross and Red Crescent (2011) <https://rcrcconference.org/app//uploads/2019/03/R7_Disaster_Laws_EN.pdf> accessed 24 June 2024, resolution 7, para 5.
[161] IFRC, OCHA, and IPU (n 139) 12–15.

laws or rules, such as legislation or regulations concerning disaster management, immigration, customs, taxation, health, telecommunications or transport'.[162]

During the piloting of the IFRC Model Act, some stakeholders expressed a preference for an emergency decree over a dedicated law.[163] In response, the IFRC and OCHA developed the IFRC Model Emergency Decree, as 'a complementary tool' to the IFRC Guidelines and Model Act. The Model Emergency Decree is intended for situations where no legal framework exists prior to the onset of a disaster.[164] Published in 2017, the IFRC Model Emergency Decree assumes that the affected state has already declared a state of emergency. It aims to inform 'a subsequent decree, based on the special powers of the state of emergency, to provide specific rules for managing' incoming relief over a set period.[165] Around the same time as the Model Emergency Decree, the IFRC also published the IDRL Checklist as an additional tool to help states make use of the IDRL Guidelines. The IDRL Checklist outlines a self-assessment process states can follow to examine their existing legal framework in light of the recommendations contained in the IDRL Guidelines.[166]

The IFRC Guidelines, Model Act, Model Emergency Decree, and Checklist have helped align domestic laws and policies with swift international disaster relief. As of 2017, thirty states had amended their national laws or policies in light of the IFRC Guidelines.[167] But the IFRC's approach focused on the domestic legal plane has been criticized as 'time-consuming and lacking in coherence'.[168] Work on the international plane, with the potential to circumvent these problems, was undertaken by the ILC. This is addressed below.

2.3.2. International Law Commission Draft Articles on the Protection of Persons in the Event of Disasters

The UN General Assembly created the ILC in 1947 to deliver on its mandate to 'initiate studies and make recommendations' to encourage 'the progressive development of international law and its codification'.[169] In 2006, during its 58th session, the 'protection of persons in the event of disasters' was added to the ILC's long-term programme of work.[170] This decision was influenced by challenges that arose during the international response to the 2004 Indian Ocean tsunami,[171] the adoption of the Hyogo Framework on disaster risk reduction in 2005,[172] and the ongoing work of the IFRC's IDRL Programme.[173] In 2007, the protection of persons in the event of disasters was

[162] ibid, 9.
[163] IFRC and OCHA (n 140) 5.
[164] ibid.
[165] ibid.
[166] IDRL Checklist (n 141) 4.
[167] IFRC, OCHA, and IPU (n 139) 4.
[168] Bartolini (n 72).
[169] UN Charter (n 116) art 13(1).
[170] ILC, 'Report of the International Law Commission on the Work of its 58th Session' (1 May–9 June and 3 July–11 August 2006) A/61/10, para 257.
[171] See Fidler (n 86).
[172] Hyogo Framework (n 19).
[173] Dug Cubie, 'An Enchanted Tool? Humanitarian Assistance and the ILC Draft Articles on the Protection of Persons in the Event of Disasters' (2012) 4 Irish Yearbook of International Law 119, 133.

added to the ILC's current programme of work and Eduardo Valencia-Ospina was appointed Special Rapporteur.[174]

The ILC tends not to explicitly distinguish between the aspects of its work that relate to the codification of international law and those that relate to its progressive development. In this case, however, the ILC acknowledged that its work would largely relate to progressive development. This acknowledgement was based on 'the fragmentary nature of existing instruments and uncertainties about the legal significance to attribute to State practice'.[175] The ILC set a 'pragmatic goal' of establishing 'a framework of legal rules, guidelines or mechanisms' to facilitate practical international cooperation in disaster response.[176] Ultimately, the ILC described the Draft Articles' purpose as facilitating 'adequate and effective response to disasters, and reduction of the risk of disasters, so as to meet the essential needs of the persons concerned, with full respect for their rights'.[177]

The ILC's substantive disasters work began in 2008 and ran until the Draft Articles were adopted in August 2016. During this time, the Special Rapporteur produced eight reports and the Drafting Committee issued seven. These and other aspects of the ILC's work are detailed in the ILC's online 'analytical guide'.[178] The focus here is not on the process leading to the adoption of the Draft Articles but rather on the Draft Articles themselves.[179]

Unlike the first and second categories of IDRL instruments outlined in Section 2.1 above—which only apply in specific sectors or contexts—the Draft Articles apply broadly to all types of disaster, whether natural or human-made,[180] and to all forms of external disaster relief.[181] The Draft Articles identify two types of humanitarian actor: third states, termed 'assisting State',[182] and a category termed 'other assisting actor', which means 'a competent intergovernmental organization, or a relevant non-governmental organization or entity, providing assistance to an affected State with its consent'.[183] They define 'relief personnel' as 'civilian or military personnel sent' by either type of humanitarian actor.[184] The Draft Articles thus do not distinguish between state and UN personnel, on the one hand, and NGO personnel, on the other. They do, however, exclude local and national NGO personnel; because the Draft Articles are concerned with humanitarian assistance originating from outside the affected

[174] ILC, 'Report of the International Law Commission on the Work of its 59th Session' (7 May–5 June and 9 July–10 August 2007) A/62/10, para 375.

[175] Fisher (n 54) 94.

[176] ILC, 'Report of the International Law Commission on the Work of its 60th Session' (5 May–6 June and 7 July–8 August 2008) A/63/10, para 257.

[177] ILC Draft Articles (n 7) art 2.

[178] ILC, Analytical Guide to the Work of the International Law Commission <https://legal.un.org/ilc/guide/6_3.shtml> accessed 26 June 2024.

[179] For a more detailed summary of the Draft Articles, see Bartolini (n 72).

[180] See the ILC's definition of disaster cited above (text attached to n 7).

[181] The Draft Articles do not define 'relief' as such, but they define 'equipment and goods' broadly as 'supplies, tools, machines, specially trained animals, foodstuffs, drinking water, medical supplies, means of shelter, clothing, bedding, vehicles, telecommunications equipment, and other objects for disaster relief assistance' ((n 7) art 3(g)).

[182] ILC Draft Articles (n 7) art 3(c).

[183] ibid, art 3(d).

[184] ibid, art 3(f).

state, the term 'other assisting actor' does not include 'domestic non-governmental organizations'.[185]

The Draft Articles' substantive provisions can be viewed along two dimensions: the vertical (articles 4–6) and the horizontal (articles 7–17).[186] The former relates to relationships between victims, the affected state, and assisting actors, while the latter covers cooperation between the affected state and assisting actors.[187] The provisions along the Draft Articles' vertical dimension cover respect for victims' inherent human dignity[188] and human rights,[189] as well as the humanitarian principles.[190] Three sets of issues arise along the horizontal dimension: the initiation and termination of relief (articles 10–14 and 17); the facilitation and coordination of relief operations (articles 7–8, 10, and 15); and the protection of relief personnel, equipment, and goods (article 16). Each is addressed in turn.

2.3.2.1. Initiation and termination of relief

The Draft Articles' provisions on the initiation and termination of relief represent the ILC's views on the right to assistance and humanitarian access issue introduced above in Section 2.2. Their starting point, based in state sovereignty,[191] is the affected state's 'primary role [. . .] in providing disaster relief assistance'[192] and its 'duty to ensure' the 'provision of disaster relief assistance in its territory'.[193] If needs manifestly exceed the affected state's response capacity, it 'has the duty to seek assistance from, as appropriate, other States, the United Nations, and other potential assisting actors'.[194] While these actors must give such requests 'due consideration',[195] they often offer assistance unilaterally, as is their right.[196] In view of state sovereignty, the actual provision of external relief 'requires the consent of the affected State',[197] but this consent 'shall not be withheld arbitrarily'.[198] The affected state can, however, place conditions on the provision of external assistance[199] and terminate it at any time,[200] unless termination would amount to an arbitrary withholding of consent. Fisher views these provisions—that the affected state must seek external assistance when its response capacity is exceeded and may not arbitrarily withhold its consent to offers of assistance—as the Draft Articles' 'most daring advance'.[201] Tladi, who was a member of the ILC when the Draft Articles were adopted, is more critical, finding 'virtually

185 ibid, commentary to art 3, para 21.
186 Bartolini (n 72) 1111.
187 ibid.
188 ILC Draft Articles (n 7) art 4.
189 ibid, art 5.
190 ibid, art 6. See Chapter 2.
191 ILC Commentary (n 70) commentary to art 10, para 2.
192 ILC Draft Articles (n 7) preambular para 5.
193 ibid, art 10(1).
194 ibid, art 11.
195 ibid, art 12(2).
196 ibid, art 12(1).
197 ibid, art 13(1).
198 ibid, art 13(2).
199 ibid, art 14.
200 ibid, art 17.
201 Fisher (n 54) 99.

no State practice to support any duty to accept assistance (or not to arbitrarily refuse consent).'[202]

Another critique relates to the ILC's initial failure to explain what makes a withholding of consent arbitrary.[203] Sivakumaran's 2015 study of affected state consent to humanitarian relief operations in disasters attempted to fill this gap. He finds that arbitrariness is essentially a synonym for 'unjustified'.[204] Thus a state withholding consent to relief must provide a reason, and this reason must be assessed by a relevant third party, such as the UN Emergency Relief Coordinator.[205] The third party should consider 'the necessity of the withholding, the proportionality of the withholding, and compliance with the affected State's human rights obligations'.[206] These factors are clearly inspired by IHRL's justification test, in which states can generally limit human rights if the restriction is established by law, serves a legitimate aim, and is necessary and proportionate in a democratic society. In practice, Sivakumaran's approach implies that consent can be validly withheld when 'there are no unmet needs, the offered assistance does not match the needs, or the offers emanate from questionable actors or actors with (perceived or actual) questionable motives'.[207] Outside such scenarios, in 'situations where there are unmet needs, with correlating offers of assistance from impartial humanitarian actors, there are very few instances in which the withholding of consent will be' valid.[208]

Sivakumaran's analysis aligns with the ILC's commentary on the Draft Articles, which was published a year after his paper. The ILC identifies three principles that can assist in determining whether an instance of withheld consent is arbitrary. Consent is not withheld arbitrarily if the affected state is willing and able to respond adequately and effectively with its own resources; if it has accepted sufficient assistance from another source; or if the relevant offer is not made in accordance with the Draft Articles, such as if it does not respect the humanitarian principles.[209] Thus the legal position on consent to external humanitarian assistance in peacetime disasters is similar to the position in armed conflict,[210] although it was argued that the rules applicable in armed conflict place an even more onerous obligation on the affected state: its withholding of strategic consent will in all but a very limited set of circumstances be unlawful.[211]

2.3.2.2. Facilitation and coordination of relief operations

The Draft Articles locate overall responsibility for disaster relief with the affected state, which 'has the primary role' in its 'direction, control, coordination and supervision'.[212]

[202] Dire Tladi, 'The International Law Commission's Draft Articles on the Protection of Persons in the Event of Disasters: Codification, Progressive Development or Creation of Law from Thin Air?' (2017) 16 Chinese Journal of International Law 425, 450.
[203] Sivakumaran (n 17) 516.
[204] ibid, 519.
[205] ibid, 528–30.
[206] ibid, 531.
[207] ibid, 525.
[208] ibid.
[209] ILC Commentary (n 70) commentary to art 13, para 8.
[210] ibid, commentary to art 13, para 9; see Chapter 3, Section 4.3.
[211] See Chapter 3, Section 6.1.
[212] ILC Draft Articles (n 7) art 10(2).

This lead role relates to any assistance the affected state provides itself and to international assistance.[213] While the affected state may cede overall coordination to an external actor,[214] it must still cooperate with assisting actors.[215] This central role contrasts starkly with the position of territorial states in armed conflict, where the territorial state merely retains a right of control in humanitarian operations largely implemented by impartial humanitarian actors.[216]

Once the affected state and external relief actors agree on the provision of assistance, the affected state must facilitate and coordinate relief operations. Facilitation relates to the entry of relief personnel, equipment, and supplies, and their movement and operation within the affected state. Key personnel issues relate to entry and work visas and the recognition of foreign professional qualifications, especially in the medical field.[217] Equipment and supply issues often relate to restrictions on, delays in, and charges (i.e. customs duties) for the importation of relief equipment and supplies.[218] Additional issues that arise after equipment and supplies are landed include technical barriers such as restrictions on the operation of certain types of vehicles, denial of overflight and landing rights, carriage permit requirements, and transport-specific charges and taxes, such as wharfage, demurrage and landing fees, and road tolls.[219] NGOs, which do not typically enjoy privileges, immunities, and facilities under existing IDRL instruments, face additional challenges.[220]

The Draft Articles respond to this range of challenges in broad terms, providing that the affected state must 'take the necessary measures, within its national law, to facilitate the prompt and effective provision of external assistance, in particular regarding: (a) relief personnel, in fields such as privileges and immunities, visa and entry requirements, work permits, and freedom of movement; and (b) equipment and goods, in fields such as customs requirements and tariffs, taxation, transport, and the disposal thereof'.[221] Fisher notes that many IDRL treaties are more prescriptive than this.[222] He cites the Kyoto and Tampere Conventions, along with regional treaties for the Americas, the Black Sea, the Caribbean, the Middle East, and South-East Asia, all of which require signatories to provide customs exemptions for relief goods and equipment.[223] Some of these treaties even go further, requiring expedited customs processing and particular facilities for items that often pose difficulties, such as telecommunications equipment and vehicles.[224]

On coordination, the Draft Articles require that states 'cooperate among themselves' and with the UN, Movement components, and other assisting actors,[225] in particular

[213] ILC Commentary (n 70) commentary to art 10, para 7.
[214] ibid, para 6.
[215] ibid, para 7.
[216] See Chapter 3, Section 4.4.
[217] IFRC (n 135) 14–15.
[218] ibid, 13–14.
[219] ibid, 15.
[220] IFRC (n 135) 15. See Chapter 6, Section 3.1.
[221] ILC Draft Articles (n 7) art 15(1).
[222] Fisher (n 54) 101.
[223] ibid, 102.
[224] ibid.
[225] ILC Draft Articles (n 7) art 7.

in relation to 'humanitarian assistance, coordination of international relief actions and communications, and making available relief personnel, equipment and goods, and scientific, medical and technical resources'.[226] Fisher locates another important innovation here, finding that 'the most important advance in the Draft Articles is their expansive inclusion of non-state entities among the international actors whose aid should be facilitated and regulated, and even among those with whom States have a duty to cooperate'. He notes that this is 'unusual among existing global and regional treaties', but not uncommon in soft law.[227]

2.3.2.3. Protection of relief personnel, equipment, and goods

The Draft Articles address the protection of relief personnel, equipment, and goods in a single provision.[228] It provides that the 'affected State shall take the appropriate measures to ensure the protection of relief personnel and of equipment and goods present in its territory, or in territory under its jurisdiction or control, for the purpose of providing external assistance'.[229] This provision applies to all foreign relief personnel, making it more protective than most IDRL instruments, which for the most part do not explicitly apply to NGO staff.[230] However, as mentioned above, 'relief personnel' does not include domestic personnel; relief personnel are individuals sent 'by an assisting State or other assisting actor',[231] and 'other assisting actor' is limited to actors 'external to the affected State'.[232]

2.3.2.4. A comprehensive international disaster response law treaty

When the ILC adopted the Draft Articles in 2016, it recommended that the General Assembly draw on them to elaborate a convention on the protection of persons in the event of disasters.[233] This was far from the first call for a treaty on disaster relief. A 1975 Movement report noted that an 'international Relief Convention' could 'establish a set of reasonable criteria outlining when and through what administrative mechanisms states would be expected to accept humanitarian aid on behalf of their populations'.[234] Early scholars issued similar calls. Jakovljević, for example, argued in 1987 that it was 'high time that serious effort was made to arrive at an international instrument for regulating humanitarian assistance in peacetime'.[235]

In 2016 and again in 2018, the General Assembly invited states to comment on the ILC's recommendation of a treaty.[236] There was no significant

[226] ibid, art 8.
[227] Fisher (n 54) 96–97.
[228] This section is limited to the Draft Articles' treatment of this issue; the protection of relief personnel is addressed in more detail in Part III, with analysis of UN (Chapter 5, Sections 5.1 and 5.4), Movement (Chapter 6, Section 2.3), and NGO (Chapter 6, Section 3.3) personnel.
[229] ILC Draft Articles (n 7) art 16.
[230] IFRC (n 135) 16. See Chapter 6, Section 3.3.
[231] ILC Draft Articles (n 7) art 3(f).
[232] ibid, commentary to art 3, para 21.
[233] ibid, para 46.
[234] Donald Tansley, *Final Report: An Agenda for the Red Cross* (Joint Committee for the Reappraisal of the Role of the Red Cross 1975) 80.
[235] Jakovljević (n 98) 482; see also Hardcastle and Chua (n 95).
[236] UNGA Res 71/141 (13 December 2016) A/RES/71/141, para 2; UNGA Res 73/209 (20 December 2018) A/RES/73/209, para 3.

response.[237] A turning point was, however, reached in 2021, when, with support from a core group of states,[238] the General Assembly resolved to consider the treaty through a working group of its Sixth (Legal) Committee.[239] This working group met for four days during each of the Assembly's 78th (2023) and 79th (2024) sessions. Based on these deliberations, in 2024, the Sixth Committee recommended the conclusion of a legally binding instrument on the protection of persons in the event of disasters by the end of 2027,[240] and set out several steps to achieve this.[241] The General Assembly went on to adopt this recommendation.[242] States have thus decided to negotiate a treaty that will establish one unified international legal framework on disasters, based on the Draft Articles.

2.4. Mixed situations

Disasters sometimes strike during armed conflict, whether by coincidence—such as when an earthquake hit north-west Syria (and Türkiye) in 2023[243]—or due to indiscriminate means or methods of warfare or scorched earth tactics.[244] Disasters may also cause armed conflict by creating competition for scarce resources.[245] When a disaster and armed conflict occur in the same place simultaneously, this is known as a 'mixed situation'. The term 'complex emergency' is sometimes also used, though this involves more than the coincidence of disaster and armed conflict.[246]

Mixed situations raise the question of which body of law—IHL, IDRL, or both—governs relief operations. IHL does not limit its applicability to needs generated directly by armed conflict. Rather, its provisions on humanitarian relief are triggered whenever there is a need among the civilian population during armed conflict, regardless of its cause.[247] Before addressing the question of applicable law, it is worth considering the distinct logics underlying the IDRL and IHL frameworks. Rodenhäuser and Giacca explain that under the former, a

237 Giulio Bartolini, 'Towards a Universal Treaty on "Protection of Persons in the Event of Disasters"' (*EJIL:Talk!*, 17 December 2024) <https://www.ejiltalk.org/toward-a-universal-treaty-on-protection-of-persons-in-the-event-of-disasters/> accessed 13 January 2025.

238 The Bahamas, Bangladesh, Colombia, Croatia, Hungary, Italy, Nigeria, and Thailand.

239 UNGA Res 76/119 (9 December 2021) A/RES/76/119, para 4.

240 UNGA Sixth Committee (79th Session) 'Protection of Persons in the Event of Disasters' (15 November 2024) A/C.6/79/L.16, para 4.

241 ibid, paras 5–7.

242 UNGA Res 79/128 (12 December 2024) A/RES/79/128, para 4.

243 Rebecca Barber, 'What Blocked the UN's Response to the Earthquakes in Northwest Syria? Reflections on a Humanitarian System Premised on Government Consent' (2023) 15 Journal of International Humanitarian Legal Studies 83.

244 Gabriella Venturini, 'Disasters and Armed Conflict' in Andrea de Guttry, Marco Gestri, and Gabriella Venturini (eds), *International Disaster Response Law* (TMC Asser Press 2012) 252.

245 ibid.

246 'Complex emergency' is defined in Chapter 7, Section 3.3.2.

247 David Fisher, 'Domestic Regulation of International Humanitarian Relief in Disasters and Armed Conflict: A Comparative Analysis' (2007) 89 International Review of the Red Cross 345, 368; IFRC (n 39) 157; Tilman Rodenhäuser and Gilles Giacca, 'The International Humanitarian Law Framework for Humanitarian Relief During Armed Conflicts and Complex Emergencies' in Susan C. Breau and Katja L. H. Samuel (eds), *Research Handbook on Disasters and International Law* (Edward Elgar 2016) 147.

> balance is drawn between, on the one hand, the territorial state's sovereignty, and, on the other hand, the affected individuals' need to receive, as well as the international community's humanitarian interest to provide, humanitarian relief. In contrast, during armed conflict, the balancing of interests is different. During armed conflict, states continue to be concerned with their sovereignty, and this concern may be reinforced by legitimate and important security interests. At the same time, during times of conflict considerations of reciprocity might be important. For example, all parties have a respective interest that 'their civilians' receive fundamental humanitarian relief even when they are under the control of the adversary, especially during occupation. Thus, one party may be inclined to grant passage for humanitarian relief for the adversary's civilian population with the expectation that the adversary does the same. Last, but not least, the international community has a well-established interest and concern for civilians affected by armed conflict. Therefore, the provision of humanitarian relief during armed conflicts is no longer considered as interference in the *domaine réservé* of states.[248]

As a result of these underlying differences, as outlined above, IDRL is premised on the affected state leading and coordinating any international assistance.[249] IHL, by contrast, ensures the humanitarian access of external actors; beyond its right of control, the affected state does not under IHL lead or coordinate emergency relief operations.[250]

The ILC's answer to the question of the law applicable in mixed situations is provided by article 18(2), which states that the Draft Articles 'do not apply to the extent that the response to a disaster is governed by the rules of' IHL. This establishes IHL as the *lex specialis*.[251] Crucially, however, as a tool to resolve norm conflicts, *lex specialis* 'operates at the level of individual norms and not of regimes'.[252] Thus IHL does not simply displace IDRL whenever a disaster occurs during armed conflict. Rather, if there is a norm conflict between a provision of IHL and one from IDRL, IHL governs. And such conflicts are rare because IHL provisions are typically more general than those of IDRL.[253] IDRL applies in respect of any legal issue raised by a disaster taking place during an armed conflict that is not covered by IHL,[254] with the result that the two regimes are often complementary.

IDRL will also apply when IHL does not apply for geographical reasons, of which there are at least two. First, while IHL applies across conflict parties' territory in international armed conflict (IAC), its geographic scope is less clear in non-international armed conflict (NIAC). There are competing views regarding whether IHL applies only to theatres of combat or to the whole territory of the state where the NIAC occurs.[255] Second, if the armed conflict is confined to a particular part of the affected

[248] Rodenhäuser and Giacca (n 247) 151.
[249] See Sections 2.3.2.1 and 2.3.2.2.
[250] See Chapter 3, Section 4.
[251] ILC Commentary (n 70) commentary to art 18, para 9.
[252] Giustiniani (n 39) 43. See, generally, Marko Milanović, *Extraterritorial Application of Human Rights Treaties: Law, Principles, and Policy* (OUP 2011) ch V.
[253] Giustiniani (n 39) 49.
[254] ILC Commentary (n 70) commentary to art 18, para 9.
[255] See Michael Schmitt, 'Charting the Legal Geography of Non-International Armed Conflict' (2014) 90 International Law Studies 1.

state, far from the location of the disaster, then 'it is difficult to see how the applicable *lex specialis* could be IHL'.[256]

In sum, the question of which legal regime governs a mixed situation must be answered on a case-by-case and issue-by-issue basis.[257] The overall case analysis involves determining the extent of the nexus between the conflict, on the one hand, and the disaster, on the other. Rodenhäuser and Giacca explain that this nexus should be construed broadly, as an armed conflict in one part of a state's territory is likely to affect its ability to respond to a disaster in another.[258] In circumstances where there is a nexus between the armed conflict and the disaster, the issue-by-issue analysis involves determining whether there is an IHL norm applicable to the issue at hand and, if not, proceeding to look to IDRL. IHL only displaces IDRL when both bodies of law address the issue in question and produce a norm conflict.

3. Violence not amounting to armed conflict

Disasters are not the only trigger of humanitarian need during times of relative peace. Such need can also result from so-called grey-zone conflicts, which are situations of violence—such as internal tensions, riots, disturbances, and low-intensity conflicts—that do not trigger the application of IHL.[259] Individuals in grey-zone conflicts are protected by IHRL. However, if the violence amounts to a public emergency, the affected state may derogate from all except a core of non-derogable international human rights obligations,[260] creating a legal protection gap.[261] On top of this gap, there is no international legal basis for humanitarian access, as IHL does not apply.

The international community has sought to fill this gap with a non-derogable instrument, which has become known as a Declaration on Fundamental Standards of Humanity. In 1990, experts met at Åbo Akademi University in Turku, Finland, and drafted the 'Declaration of Minimum Humanitarian Standards' (the Turku Declaration). This non-binding instrument restates existing standards drawn from IHRL and IHL but provides that they apply 'in all situations, including internal violence, disturbances, tensions, and public emergency' and 'cannot be derogated from under any circumstances'.[262] The Turku Declaration provides that in such situations,

[256] Rodenhäuser and Giacca (n 247) 148. See also Sarah Williams and Gabrielle Simm, 'Assistance to Disaster Victims in an Armed Conflict' in Flavia Zorzi Giustiniani and others (eds), *Routledge Handbook of Human Rights and Disasters* (Routledge 2018) 53.

[257] Daniela Gavshon, 'The Applicability of IHL in Mixed Situations of Disaster and Conflict' (2009) 14 Journal of Conflict & Security Law 243; Rodenhäuser and Giacca (n 247) 148; Giustiniani (n 39) 50.

[258] Rodenhäuser and Giacca (n 247) 148–49.

[259] The threshold criteria for NIAC and IAC are outlined in Chapter 3, Section 1.2.

[260] ICCPR (n 93) art 4; the following rights are non-derogable: right to life (art 6), prohibition of torture and cruel, inhuman, or degrading treatment or punishment (art 7), prohibition of slavery and servitude (art 8(1–2)), prohibition of imprisonment for breach of contract (art 11), non-retroactivity of criminal law (art 15), right to recognition as a person before the law (art 16), and freedom of thought, conscience, and religion (art 18). The ICESCR does not contain a derogation clause because of its standard of progressive realization ((n 91) art 2(1)).

[261] Theodor Meron, 'On the Inadequate Reach of Humanitarian and Human Rights Law and the Need for a New Instrument' (1983) 89 American Journal of International Law 589.

[262] 'Declaration of Turku: Internal Disturbances and Tensions—Declaration of Minimum Humanitarian Standards' (1991) 282 International Review of the Red Cross 328, art 1.

'humanitarian organizations shall be granted all the facilities necessary to enable them to carry out their humanitarian activities'.[263] Additionally, much like IHL, the Turku Declaration privileges certain types of relief operations in terms of the mission itself or its beneficiaries, including medical and religious personnel,[264] the wounded and sick,[265] individuals deprived of their liberty,[266] and displaced persons.[267] The Turku Declaration was transmitted to the UN Commission on Human Rights with a view to its eventual adoption as a UN declaration;[268] however, this never materialized.[269] Efforts towards the adoption of a global Declaration on Fundamental Standards of Humanity are currently stalled, in no small part because states are concerned about potential infringements of their sovereignty.[270]

Chapter 6 explains that the Movement's statutes are adopted in part by states.[271] The legal effect of this is particularly important in situations of violence not amounting to armed conflict, where there is no IHL legal basis for humanitarian access. Because states conferred each Movement component's mandate, they are obliged to cooperate with Movement components in the exercise of those mandates. The International Committee of the Red Cross (ICRC), in particular, has a mandate to provide humanitarian assistance in situations of 'internal strife' and to 'take any humanitarian initiative which comes within its role as a specifically neutral and independent institution and intermediary'.[272] This provides a basis for the ICRC to access individuals in need of humanitarian assistance in situations of violence not amounting to armed conflict. Indeed, the ICRC offers 'its humanitarian services to states even where there is no armed conflict, and there is corresponding practice of states to accept this'.[273]

4. Humanitarian assistance at sea

Like grey-zone conflicts, maritime migration is another peacetime phenomenon that generates significant humanitarian need. The number of people travelling by sea in search of international protection or a better life began to increase sharply in the early 2010s, especially along the central Mediterranean migration route from North Africa to Italy and Malta. Their travel is often facilitated by smugglers or human

[263] ibid, art 15 (cf Chapter 3, Section 3).
[264] ibid, art 14 (cf Chapter 3, Section 5.1).
[265] ibid, arts 12–13 (cf Chapter 3, Section 5.1).
[266] ibid, art 4(4) (cf Chapter 3, Section 5.3).
[267] ibid, art 7(1) (cf Chapter 3, Section 5.4).
[268] Report of the Secretary-General Prepared Pursuant to Commission Resolution 1995/29 (28 November 1995) E/CN.4/1996/80, Annex.
[269] See Emily Crawford, 'Road to Nowhere? The Future for a Declaration on Fundamental Standards of Humanity' (2012) 3 Journal of International Humanitarian Legal Studies 43, 53–55.
[270] ibid, 58.
[271] See Chapter 6, Section 2.
[272] Statutes of the International Red Cross and Red Crescent Movement (1986, as amended in 1995 and 2006) <https://www.icrc.org/en/doc/assets/files/other/statutes-en-a5.pdf> accessed 24 February 2022, arts 5(2)(d) and 5(3).
[273] Nishat Nishat, 'The Right of Initiative of the ICRC and Other Impartial Humanitarian Bodies' in Andrew Clapham, Paola Gaeta, and Marco Sassòli (eds), *The 1949 Geneva Conventions: A Commentary* (OUP 2015) 506.

traffickers,[274] who may employ unseaworthy and/or overcrowded vessels; such journeys can end catastrophically. For example, in 2015, more than a million people arrived in Europe by sea, and nearly 4,000 died en route.[275] At the same time, states have become increasingly unwilling to rescue refugees and migrants in distress at sea. One well-known incident, which has become known as the "left-to-die" boat, illustrates this tragic dynamic. In 2011, 72 people left Libya aboard a rubber boat bound for Italy. Within hours of their departure, they ran out of fuel and issued a distress call. Despite receipt of the distress call by several states and interaction with at least one warship and one military helicopter, the boat was left to drift. When it landed back in Libya after 14 days, only nine passengers were still alive.[276] According to the International Organization for Migration's Missing Migrants Project, nearly 40,000 migrants drowned between 2014 and 2024, with more than half of these deaths occurring along the central Mediterranean route.[277]

NGOs have responded by supporting or running maritime search-and-rescue operations. This section outlines the legal framework governing, and state responses to, this relatively new form of peacetime humanitarian work. It begins with an overview of the law of the sea, including maritime jurisdiction, maritime zones, and some key freedoms within each zone. It then outlines captains' duty to rescue, states' duty to provide search-and-rescue services, and the duties owed to rescued individuals. Finally, with this legal background established, it moves on to the nature and legality of state responses to NGOs' rescue at sea operations.

4.1. Maritime jurisdiction and zones

Jurisdiction at sea derives from both nationality and territoriality. Under the former, a state has jurisdiction over a vessel with its nationality, that is, a vessel registered in that state (the flag state). Territorial jurisdiction, on the other hand, differs by maritime zone, as delineated in the United Nations Convention on the Law of the Sea

[274] Both smuggling and trafficking are regulated by protocols to the UN Convention against Transnational Organized Crime. Article 3(a) of The Protocol against the Smuggling of Migrants by Land, Sea and Air (Smuggling Protocol) defines smuggling as the 'procurement, in order to obtain, directly or indirectly, a financial or other material benefit, of the illegal entry of a person into a State Party of which the person is not a national or a permanent resident' ((adopted 15 November 2000, entered into force 28 January 2004) 2241 UNTS 507). Article 3(a) of The Protocol to Prevent, Suppress and Punish Trafficking in Persons, Especially Women and Children defines trafficking in persons as 'the recruitment, transportation, transfer, harbouring or receipt of persons, by means of the threat or use of force or other forms of coercion, of abduction, of fraud, of deception, of the abuse of power or of a position of vulnerability or of the giving or receiving of payments or benefits to achieve the consent of a person having control over another person, for the purpose of exploitation' ((adopted 15 November 2000, entered into force 25 December 2003) 2237 UNTS 319). The key distinction between smuggling and trafficking is the latter crime's exploitative purpose.

[275] Daniel Ghezelbash and others, 'Securitization of Search and Rescue at Sea: The Response to Boat Migration in the Mediterranean and Offshore Australia' (2018) 67 International & Comparative Law Quarterly 315, 318.

[276] Charles Heller, Lorenzo Pezzani, and Situ Studio, 'Report on the "Left-to-Die Boat"' (*Forensic Oceanography*, 2014) <https://content.forensic-architecture.org/wp-content/uploads/2019/06/FO-report.pdf> accessed 13 August 2024.

[277] <https://missingmigrants.iom.int/data> accessed 16 August 2024.

(UNCLOS). These zones are measured from a coastal state's baseline (similar to its coastline), with the extent of a coastal state's jurisdiction decreasing in each maritime zone further from its baseline. The area extending to a maximum of 12 nautical miles from the coastal state's baseline is the territorial sea. This area is subject to the coastal state's exclusive territorial jurisdiction.[278] However, any vessel in the territorial sea—or indeed within any maritime zone—also comes within the flag state's jurisdiction.[279] The waters beyond the territorial sea extending to a maximum of 24 nautical miles from the coastal state's baseline constitute the contiguous zone.[280] Within this zone, the coastal state may exercise the jurisdiction necessary to 'prevent infringement of its customs, fiscal, immigration or sanitary laws within its territory or territorial sea'.[281] The area of sea extending 200 nautical miles from the coastal state's baseline is its exclusive economic zone (EEZ).[282] A state has rights to explore, exploit, conserve, and manage the resources within its EEZ.[283] Vessels beyond the contiguous zone but within the EEZ are generally under the exclusive jurisdiction of the flag state. The international waters beyond the EEZ are known as the high seas.[284] Vessels on the high seas are also generally under the exclusive jurisdiction of the flag state.[285] As a result of the dual nationality and territoriality bases of jurisdiction at sea, there is no marine space where a single state enjoys exclusive jurisdiction.

Vessels generally enjoy freedom of navigation at sea,[286] except in the territorial sea. Within this zone, foreign vessels enjoy a right of innocent passage,[287] subject to limited exceptions related to the legal meaning of 'passage'[288] and what constitutes 'innocent passage'.[289]

4.2. The duties to rescue, to provide search-and-rescue services, and to survivors

As a result of the centuries-old duty to save life at sea,[290] all ship captains, including both state vessels (predominantly naval and coast guard vessels) and private vessels (e.g. merchant shipping vessels and pleasure craft), have a duty to rescue at sea. This duty is found in a range of legal sources. Among treaty sources, under UNCLOS each state party must use its domestic law to require the captains of ships flying its flag '(a) to render assistance to any person found at sea in danger of being lost; [and] (b) to

[278] United Nations Convention on the Law of the Sea (adopted 10 December 1982, entered into force 16 November 1994) 1833 UNTS 3, arts 2–3 (UNCLOS).
[279] ibid, art 94.
[280] ibid, art 33(2).
[281] ibid, art 33(1).
[282] ibid, art 57.
[283] ibid, art 56.
[284] ibid, art 86.
[285] ibid, art 92(1).
[286] ibid, arts 58 and 87.
[287] ibid, art 17.
[288] ibid, art 18.
[289] ibid, art 19.
[290] Irini Papanicolopulu, 'The Duty to Rescue at Sea, in Peacetime and in War: A General Overview' (2016) 98 International Review of the Red Cross 491, 494.

proceed with all possible speed to the rescue of persons in distress, if informed of their need of assistance'.[291] Under the Convention for the Safety of Life at Sea (SOLAS), the captain 'of a ship at sea which is in a position to be able to provide assistance, on receiving a signal from any source that persons are in distress at sea, is bound to proceed with all speed to their assistance'.[292] The International Convention on Maritime Search and Rescue (SAR) provides that states parties must 'ensure that assistance be provided to any person in distress at sea'.[293]

Some of these treaties permit limited exceptions. Under UNCLOS, the duty does not apply if performing the rescue poses a serious danger to the rescuing ship, its crew, or its passengers.[294] Similarly, SOLAS provides that assistance is not required if it is not possible to render aid or if the ship receiving the distress alert determines that providing assistance would be unreasonable or unnecessary.[295] In addition to these treaty sources, the duty to rescue is customary international law and therefore binding upon all states, even those without relevant treaty obligations.[296] The duty to rescue applies in all maritime jurisdiction zones and to all persons in distress at sea, including refugees and migrants.[297] If a state vessel does not discharge its duty to rescue, this entails the flag state's international responsibility.

The duty to rescue is backed by the duty of coastal states to establish search-and-rescue services.[298] These services take the form of rescue coordination centres, which are equipped with vessels, aircraft, rescue gear, and communications infrastructure.[299] SAR divides the sea into search-and-rescue areas, with each area under the designated responsibility of a particular coastal state.[300] A state's rescue coordination centre receives distress calls, looks out for vessels in distress, and coordinates—sometimes with neighbouring coastal states—rescue operations within its area of responsibility. Rescues may be performed by state vessels operating for this purpose[301] or by private vessels discharging their duty to rescue, whether further to communication with

[291] UNCLOS (n 278) art 98(1).

[292] International Convention for the Safety of Life at Sea, as amended (adopted 1 November 1974, entered into force 25 May 1980) 1184 UNTS 278, ch V, reg 33.1 (SOLAS).

[293] International Convention on Maritime Search and Rescue, as amended (adopted 27 April 1979, entered into force 22 June 1985) 1405 UNTS 118, reg 2.1.10 (SAR).

[294] UNCLOS (n 278) art 98(1).

[295] SOLAS (n 292) ch V, reg 33.1.

[296] Richard Barnes, 'The International Law of the Sea and Migration Control' in Bernard Ryan and Valsamis Mitsilegas (eds), *Extraterritorial Immigration Control: Legal Challenges* (Martinus Nijhoff 2010) 136; David Testa, 'Safeguarding Human Life and Ensuring Respect for Fundamental Human Rights: A Consequential Approach to the Disembarkation of Persons Rescued at Sea' (2014) 28 Ocean Yearbook 555, 556–57; Papanicolopulu (n 290) 494.

[297] Both SOLAS and SAR are explicit in this regard. SOLAS provides that the 'obligation to provide assistance applies regardless of the nationality or status of such persons or the circumstances in which they are found' ((n 292) ch V, reg 33.1). SAR provides that the duty to rescue applies 'regardless of the nationality or status' of the person in distress at sea, 'or the circumstances in which that person is found' ((n 293) reg 2.1.10).

[298] UNCLOS (n 278) art 98(2); SOLAS (n 292) ch V, reg 7.1; SAR (n 293) reg 2.1.1.

[299] The International Maritime Organization and the International Civil Aviation Organization jointly publish the International Aeronautical and Maritime Search and Rescue Manual, which 'provides guidelines for a common aviation and maritime approach to organizing and providing search and rescue' services (<https://www.imo.org/en/OurWork/Safety/Pages/IAMSARManual.aspx> accessed 16 August 2024).

[300] SAR (n 293) regs 2.1.4–2.1.5.

[301] This constitutes an important component of state humanitarian action; see Chapter 7.

a rescue coordination centre or of the captain's own initiative. Neighbouring coastal states typically cooperate in search and rescue through bilateral agreements, which are published in an International Maritime Organization (IMO) database.[302]

The captain of a rescuing ship has two duties to survivors. First, the rescued individuals must be treated humanely. For state-operated vessels, this duty derives from IHRL, as a state's international human rights obligations attach whenever it has de jure or de facto jurisdiction over individuals.[303] At sea, de jure jurisdiction is based on flag state jurisdiction,[304] while de facto jurisdiction arises from a state's 'power or effective control' over the individuals aboard its vessel.[305] SOLAS also addresses humane treatment.[306] For private vessels, the duty of humane treatment is articulated in a non-binding resolution of the IMO's Maritime Safety Committee.[307]

The captain's second duty to survivors is to disembark them in a place of safety.[308] A place of safety is 'a location where rescue operations are considered to terminate' and where 'the survivors' safety is no longer threatened and where their basic human needs (such as food, shelter and medical needs) can be met'.[309] Additionally, a place of safety is a 'place from which transportation arrangements can be made for the survivors' next or final destination'.[310] Several places might fulfil these criteria, such as the rescuing vessel's next planned port of call, the port closest to the location where the rescue occurred, a port chosen by survivors, or another port where assistance is available.

SAR regulates disembarkation by specifying that the state responsible for the search and rescue area where the rescue occurred 'shall exercise primary responsibility for ensuring' coordination and cooperation so that survivors 'are disembarked from the assisting ship and delivered to a place of safety'.[311] This provision stops short of specifying that survivors should be disembarked at a port in the search and rescue area where they were rescued. In practice, captains often have difficulty finding a state that will allow survivors to disembark,[312] especially if they are likely to apply for refugee

302 The IMO is the UN specialized agency responsible for the safety and security of shipping and the prevention of pollution by ships.

303 ICCPR (n 93) art 2(1).

304 *Hirsi Jamaa and Others v Italy* App no 27765/09 (ECHR, 23 February 2012) (*Hirsi*).

305 Human Rights Committee, 'General Comment No. 31: The Nature of the General Legal Obligation Imposed on States Parties to the Covenant' (26 May 2004) CCPR/C/21/Rev.1/Add.13 (General Comment 31) para 10; see also Milanović (n 252) 160–70 and *Hirsi* (n 304) paras 81–82.

306 SOLAS (n 292) reg 33.6, which provides that captains 'who have embarked persons in distress at sea shall treat them with humanity, within the capabilities and limitations of the ship'.

307 IMO, Maritime Safety Committee, Resolution MSC.167(78): Guidelines on the Treatment of Persons Rescued at Sea, IMO Doc. MSC 78/26/Add.2 (20 May 2004) (MSC Resolution) para 5.1.2, which provides that captains should 'do everything possible, within the capabilities and limitations of the ship, to treat the survivors humanely and to meet their immediate needs'.

308 SOLAS (n 292) ch V, reg 33.1-1; SAR (n 293) reg 3.1.9.

309 MSC Resolution (n 307) para 6.12.

310 ibid.

311 SAR (n 293) reg 3.1.9.

312 See generally, Douglas Guilfoyle and Efthymios Papastavridis, 'Mapping Disembarkation Options: Towards Strengthening Cooperation in Managing Irregular Movements by Sea' (*UNHCR and The Bali Process*, 2014) <https://www.refworld.org/reference/confdoc/unhcr/2014/en/98791> accessed 13 August 2024, 16–17; Kristof Gombeer, 'Human Rights Adrift? Enabling the Disembarkation of Migrants to a Place of Safety in the Mediterranean' in Fiona de Londras and Siobhán Mullally (eds), *Irish Yearbook of International Law 2015*, vol 10 (Hart 2017).

status.[313] For example, in 2001, Australia refused to allow the merchant vessel *Tampa*, which had 433 rescued refugees and migrants on board, to enter its territorial waters or to disembark the survivors on the nearby Australian territory of Christmas Island.[314] In 2018, Italy stopped allowing rescued refugees and migrants to disembark in its ports.[315]

In the absence of complete rules on disembarkation, two international law principles apply: state sovereignty and *non-refoulement*.[316] The former applies equally in the territorial sea; as a result, no vessel has a right to enter a state's port merely because it has survivors on board. At the same time, *non-refoulement* prohibits state vessels from disembarking survivors in states where their life or freedom would be threatened for reasons of their race, religion, nationality, membership of a particular social group, or political opinion.[317] *Non-refoulement* also prohibits state vessels from disembarking survivors in states where they might be subject to torture or other cruel, inhuman, or degrading treatment or punishment.[318] As a customary norm,[319] *non-refoulement* binds all states, even those that have not ratified relevant treaties.

4.3. Non-governmental organizations and rescue at sea

States have viewed increasing maritime migration as a security and political threat,[320] prompting a shift in affected states—predominantly Australia and European Union (EU) member states—from the 'fundamentally humanitarian mission' of search and rescue 'to a complex, securitized response to boat migration'.[321] The shift began in the early 2010s with a drastic reduction of search-and-rescue capacity among EU Mediterranean coastal states, resulting in mass drownings.[322] In response, Italy

[313] On disembarkation and refugee protection, see Guy Goodwin-Gill and Jane McAdam, *The Refugee in International Law* (4th edn, OUP 2021) 344–45.

[314] Penelope Mathew, 'Australian Refugee Protection in the Wake of the *Tampa*' (2002) 96 American Journal of International Law 661, 661.

[315] Violeta Moreno-Lax, 'Towards a Thousand Little Morias: The EU (Non-)Rescue Scheme—Criminalizing Solidarity, Structuralising Defection' in Daniel Thym (ed), *Reforming the Common European Asylum System: Opportunities, Pitfalls, and Downsides of the Commission Proposals for a New Pact on Migration and Asylum* (Nomos 2022) 166.

[316] Papanicolopulu (n 290) 500.

[317] Convention relating to the Status of Refugees (adopted 28 July 1951, entered into force 22 April 1954) 189 UNTS 137, art 33(1); for detailed analysis of *non-refoulement* at sea, see Goodwin-Gill and McAdam (n 313) 331–42.

[318] Convention against Torture and Other Cruel, Inhuman or Degrading Treatment or Punishment (adopted 10 December 1984, entered into force 26 June 1987) 1465 UNTS 85, art 3(1); ICCPR (n 93) art 7, read with General Comment 31 (n 305) para 12. See, generally, Jane McAdam, *Complementary Protection in International Refugee Law* (OUP 2007) chs 3–4.

[319] Cathryn Costello and Michelle Foster, 'Non-refoulement as Custom and *Jus Cogens*? Putting the Prohibition to the Test' (2016) 46 Netherlands Yearbook of International Law 2015, 273.

[320] Ghezelbash and others (n 275) 330–32. See, generally, Violeta Moreno-Lax and Efthymios Papastavridis (eds), *"Boat Refugees" and Migrants at Sea: A Comprehensive Approach* (Brill Nijhoff 2016).

[321] Ghezelbash and others (n 275) 317.

[322] Moreno-Lax (n 315) 165. For a detailed overview of the shift in Europe, see Violeta Moreno-Lax and others, 'The EU Approach on Migration in the Mediterranean' (*European Parliament*, 2021) <https://www.europarl.europa.eu/RegData/etudes/STUD/2021/694413/IPOL_STU(2021)694413_EN.pdf> accessed 30 August 2024.

launched the joint Navy and Air Force operation *Mare Nostrum* in October 2013.[323] While it rescued at least 150,000 people, Italy viewed *Mare Nostrum* as a 'pull factor',[324] and it was replaced after just one year by European Border and Coast Guard Agency (Frontex) missions oriented towards border control and interdiction rather than search and rescue.[325] Other measures to deter maritime migration include cooperative migration control agreements, such as deals between Italy and Libya and between Australia and Indonesia.[326]

Since 2014, NGOs, including existing organizations and dedicated start-ups, have worked to fill the search-and-rescue gap left by states' increasingly securitized response to maritime migration.[327] Some NGOs run their own search-and-rescue operations, while others respond to emergencies at sea with essentials—such as life jackets, drinking water, and medical care—without necessarily taking people on board their vessel.[328] For example, in 2016, *Médecins Sans Frontières* (MSF) and its partner *SOS MEDITERRANEE*—a search-and-rescue NGO founded in 2015—began operating the *Aquarius*. The vessel assisted nearly 30,000 people in the international waters between Italy, Libya, and Malta before it was forced to cease operations at the end of 2018 because of a difficult law and policy environment (discussed below).[329] MSF operated other vessels between 2015 and 2017, and as of August 2024 operated one, the *Geo Barents*, in international waters north of Libya.[330] In December 2024, MSF announced that the *Geo Barents* had ceased operations and it had ended its search-and-rescue operations in the Central Mediterranean, due to Italian law and policy.[331] The IFRC also has a partnership with *SOS MEDITERRANEE*, providing services aboard the latter's *Ocean Viking* ship.[332] In addition to *SOS MEDITERRANEE*, other dedicated maritime search-and-rescue NGOs include Jugend Rettet, Open Arms, Sea-Eye,

[323] Martina Tazzioli, 'Border Displacements: Challenging the Politics of Rescue between Mare Nostrum and Triton' (2016) 4 Migration Studies 1.

[324] Frédéric Mégret, 'Activists on the High Seas: Reinventing International Law for the Mare Liberum?' (2021) 23 International Community Law Review 367, 372.

[325] Violeta Moreno-Lax, 'The EU Humanitarian Border and the Securitization of Human Rights: The "Rescue-through-Interdiction/Rescue-without-Protection" Paradigm' (2018) 56 Journal of Common Market Studies 119.

[326] Francesca Mussi and Nikolas Feith Tan, 'Comparing Cooperation on Migration Control: Italy-Libya and Australia-Indonesia' in Fiona de Londras and Siobhán Mullally (eds), *Irish Yearbook of International Law 2015*, vol 10 (Hart 2017).

[327] Eugenio Cusumano and James Pattison, 'The Non-Governmental Provision of Search and Rescue in the Mediterranean and the Abdication of State Responsibility' (2018) 31 Cambridge Review of International Affairs 53.

[328] Kristof Gombeer and Melanie Fink, 'Non-Governmental Organisations and Search and Rescue at Sea' (2018) 4 Maritime Safety and Security Law Journal 1, 2.

[329] MSF, 'Aquarius Forced to End Operations as Europe Condemns People to Drown' (6 December 2018) <https://www.msf.org/aquarius-forced-end-operations-europe-condemns-people-drown> accessed 13 August 2024.

[330] <https://searchandrescue.msf.org> accessed 13 August 2024.

[331] MSF, 'MSF Forced to End Search and Rescue Operations in the Central Mediterranean' (13 December 2024) <https://msf.org.uk/article/msf-forced-end-search-and-rescue-operations-central-mediterranean> accessed 21 July 2025.

[332] IFRC, 'With Warmer Temperatures Approaching, IFRC Braces for New Year of Danger on Central Mediterranean Sea Migration Route' (5 March 2024) <https://www.ifrc.org/press-release/warmer-temperatures-approaching-ifrc-braces-new-year-danger-central-mediterranean-sea> accessed 26 September 2024.

Sea-Watch, and SOS Humanity. Cusumano and Pattison counted 11 NGOs conducting their own fully fledged search-and-rescue operations in the Mediterranean between 2014 and 2018.[333] 'The Righteous of the Med Sea' campaign for the 2018 Nobel Peace Prize listed over 50 NGOs involved in search-and-rescue work on the Mediterranean.[334]

States have responded to this new NGO activity by attempting to limit their search-and-rescue activities in three main ways. First, they have sought to limit NGO navigation in both territorial waters and on the high seas.[335] For example, in 2017, Italy introduced a code of conduct for NGO search-and-rescue operations, which aimed to prohibit NGOs from entering Libyan territorial waters except in situations of grave and imminent danger.[336] Interference has also occurred on the high seas. In one instance in 2017, a Libyan Coast Guard vessel obstructed the navigation of a Dutch-flagged NGO ship, attempting to push it away from the Libyan coast and compel it to transfer survivors to the Libyan ship.[337] Gombeer and Fink's analysis demonstrates that states have no legal right to restrict NGO navigation, whether in territorial waters or on the high seas.[338] All vessels enjoy a right of innocent passage through territorial waters.[339] Additionally, SAR provides that coastal states should authorize 'immediate entry into or over its territorial sea [. . .] solely for the purpose of searching for the position of maritime casualties' and rescuing survivors.[340] In waters beyond the territorial sea, vessels enjoy freedom of navigation.[341]

Second, states have sought to control how NGOs conduct search-and-rescue operations by issuing instructions through search-and-rescue coordination centres. For example, the Italian Maritime Rescue Coordination Centre has, on several occasions, instructed NGO vessels to either leave a distress scene or refrain from providing assistance.[342] The EU 'Commission Guidance on the Implementation of EU Rules on Definition and Prevention of the Facilitation of Unauthorised Entry, Transit and Residence' provides that '[e]veryone involved in search and rescue activities must observe the instructions received from the coordinating authority when intervening in search and rescue events'.[343] However, as Gombeer and Fink explain, such instructions only bind NGOs operating in the instructing state's territorial sea. Outside of this zone, a vessel is under the jurisdiction of its flag state. As a result, under international law, search-and-rescue instructions issued by national authorities to foreign vessels 'can only be considered as "requests for cooperation"' reminding them 'to comply with their obligations under the domestic law of the flag state concerning the duty to assist'.[344] Certain search-and-rescue instructions may

[333] Cusumano and Pattison (n 327) 56.
[334] <http://www.nobel-righteous-mediterraneansea.info/the-righteous-of-the-mediterranean-sea/> accessed 15 August 2024.
[335] Gombeer and Fink (n 328) 2.
[336] ibid; Italy's 2017 code of conduct is appended to Gombeer and Fink (n 328).
[337] ibid.
[338] Gombeer and Fink (n 328).
[339] UNCLOS (n 278) art 17; see Gombeer and Fink (n 328) 9–14.
[340] SAR (n 293) reg 3.1.2.
[341] UNCLOS (n 278) arts 58 and 87.
[342] Gombeer and Fink (n 328) 2.
[343] [2020] OJ C 323, s 3 (Commission Guidance).
[344] Gombeer and Fink (n 328) 17; see also Moreno-Lax (n 315) 175.

also be substantively non-compliant with international law. In particular, instructions to avoid or leave a distress scene, or to refrain from providing assistance run counter to international law on search and rescue.[345] Additionally, when issued in relation to a distress scene within the instructing state's territorial sea, such instructions may violate the right to life of the individuals in distress.[346] When faced with unlawful instructions, captains have what has been termed 'a right to obey international law'.[347]

States have also tried to control NGO search and rescue by promulgating rules in this regard. In 2023, Italy issued a new code of conduct for rescue at sea, which effectively prohibits simultaneous rescues by demanding that vessels with survivors on board proceed 'without delay' to the assigned disembarkation port.[348] This is irreconcilable with the duty to rescue treaty provisions outlined above.[349] Indeed, a joint statement by affected NGOs points out that Italy's new code contradicts the law of the sea.[350]

Third and finally, some states have criminalized NGO search-and-rescue operations. This criminalization originates in international cooperation to suppress smuggling. Under the Smuggling Protocol, smuggling is essentially a *commercial* transaction between someone who wants to travel internationally and another person who facilitates this.[351] While smuggling is not always exploitative and can ensure refugees' access to international protection,[352] the Smuggling Protocol led to the EU's 2002 adoption of the significantly broader Facilitation Directive. The Facilitation Directive requires EU member states to sanction 'any person who intentionally assists a person who is not a national of a Member State to enter, or transit across, the territory of a Member State in breach of the laws of the State concerned',[353] regardless of whether the assisting person was motivated by profit.[354] The Facilitation Directive does, however, allow member states to 'decide not to impose sanctions [...] where the aim of the behaviour is to provide humanitarian assistance'.[355] Similarly, anti-smuggling laws in Australia, Canada, and the United States all characterize certain assistance to migrants as smuggling even where no financial gain is involved.[356]

345 Gombeer and Fink (n 328) 22.
346 ibid.
347 Massimo Starita, 'The Duty to Rescue at Sea and the Shipmaster's "Right to Obey" (International) "Law"' (2019) 7 Diritti umani e diritto internazionale 5, cited in Moreno-Lax (n 315) 175.
348 France24, 'Italy's Migrant Rules "Contradict" International Law, say Charities' (5 January 2023) <https://www.france24.com/en/live-news/20230105-italy-s-migrant-rules-contradict-international-law-say-charities> accessed 25 September 2024 (France24).
349 See notes 291–293.
350 France24 (n 348).
351 Smuggling Protocol (n 274) art 3(a); the definition of smuggling is provided at note 274.
352 James Hathaway, 'The Human Rights Quagmire of "Human Trafficking"' (2008) 49 Virginia Journal of International Law 1, 5.
353 Council Directive 2002/90/EC defining the facilitation of unauthorised entry, transit and residence [2002] OJ L 328 (Facilitation Directive) art 1(1)(a).
354 See generally, Violeta Moreno-Lax, 'Solidarity Crimes, Legitimacy Limits' (*Verfassungsblog*, 17 April 2024) <https://verfassungsblog.de/solidarity-crimes-legitimacy-limits/> accessed 25 September 2024.
355 Facilitation Directive (n 353) art 1(2).
356 Miriam Bradley, *The Politics and Everyday Practice of International Humanitarianism* (OUP 2023) 263–64.

Many European states, most notably Italy, have not implemented the Facilitation Directive's humanitarian assistance exception.[357] Instead, Italy has used its criminal law to suppress the provision of humanitarian assistance at sea.[358] For example, *Sea-Watch 3* captain Carola Rackete was arrested in 2019 after she rammed her vessel, with 53 rescued migrants on board, into an Italian border control ship that was trying to prevent her from docking in Lampedusa. The broader reason for her arrest was Italy's long-standing opposition to *Sea-Watch*'s search-and-rescue activities.[359] Rackete was charged with several offences, including Italy's Facilitation Directive-based crime of facilitating irregular migration.[360] Rackete was in 2020 found not criminally liable, with the preliminary investigative judge recognizing that she had been fulfilling her duty to rescue under international law.[361] However, in 2022, Italy laid similar charges against four crew members of Jugend Rettet's vessel *Iuventa*.[362] These charges were dropped in 2024. In addition to charging the facilitating irregular migration offence in the context of NGO search and rescue, Italy has also taken steps to specifically criminalize rescue at sea.[363]

In 2020, the European Commission issued guidance on the implementation of the Facilitation Directive. The guidance states that the 'criminalisation of NGOs or any other non-state actors that carry out search and rescue operations at sea, while complying with the relevant legal framework, amounts to a breach of international law, and therefore is not permitted by EU law'.[364] Moreno-Lax points out that the 'while complying with' the law qualifier leaves states 'ample margin' for manoeuvre.[365]

[357] Joan David Janer Torrens, 'Migrant Search and Rescue Operations in the Mediterranean by Humanitarian Organizations: Migrant Smuggling or Humanitarian Assistance?' (2020) 8 Paix et Sécurité Internationales 381, 400.

[358] See Adam Smith, 'Uncertainty, Alert and Distress: The Precarious Position of NGO Search and Rescue Operations in the Central Mediterranean' (2017) 5 Journal of International Law and International Relations 29; Eugenio Cusumano and Matteo Villa, 'From "Angels" to "Vice Smugglers": the Criminalization of Sea Rescue NGOs in Italy' (2021) 27 European Journal on Criminal Policy and Research 23.

[359] Mégret (n 324) 368.

[360] Cathryn Costello and Stefano Zirulia, 'Pushing Back: How to Limit Overcriminalisation of Assistance to Those in Need of Protection' (*Verfassungsblog*, 29 February 2024) <https://verfassungsblog.de/pushing-back/> accessed 25 September 2024.

[361] Zara Freudenberg and others, 'The Island of Hope in a Sea of Misery' (*Verfassungsblog*, 10 March 2020) <https://verfassungsblog.de/the-island-of-hope-in-a-sea-of-misery/> accessed 25 September 2024.

[362] UN Office of the High Commissioner for Human Rights, 'Italy: Criminalisation of Human Rights Defenders Engaged in Sea Rescue Missions Must End, Says Expert' (9 February 2023) <https://www.ohchr.org/en/press-releases/2023/02/italy-criminalisation-human-rights-defenders-engaged-sea-rescue-missions> accessed 25 September 2024. Italy impounded the *Iuventa* in 2017 after Jugend Rettet refused to sign its 2017 code of conduct for search-and-rescue NGOs (Moreno-Lax (n 315) 166).

[363] Joint Communication from UN Special Procedures to His Excellency Mr Gian Lorenzo Cornado, Permanent Representative, Permanent Mission of Italy to the UN and other international organizations in Geneva (15 May 2019) <https://www.avvenire.it/c/attualita/Documents/ONUdirittiViolati.pdf> accessed 25 September 2024.

[364] Commission Guidance (n 343) s 4(ii).

[365] Moreno-Lax (n 354).

5. Conclusion

This chapter has explored the patchwork of rules that make up current IDRL, how the IFRC and ILC have worked to bring coherence to this area of law, and the prospect of a comprehensive IDRL treaty based on the ILC's Draft Articles. It has also addressed mixed situations, violence not amounting to armed conflict, and humanitarian assistance at sea, including the law of the sea framework for search and rescue, how states are increasingly failing to fulfil their obligations in this regard, how NGOs have stepped in to fill the gap, and how states have responded. It completes Part II on the international legal framework for humanitarian assistance. However, this legal framework is useless without the humanitarian actors who operate within it. Part III is devoted to them: UN, non-state, and state humanitarian actors, beginning with the UN in Chapter 5.

PART III
HUMANITARIAN ACTORS

5
The United Nations

1. Introduction

The United Nations (UN) is comprised of six principal organs: the General Assembly, the Security Council, the Economic and Social Council (ECOSOC), the Secretariat, the International Court of Justice (ICJ), and the Trusteeship Council,[1] as well as their subsidiary organs.[2] It has a general humanitarian mandate: to 'achieve international co-operation in solving international problems of an economic, social, cultural, or humanitarian character'.[3] This chapter surveys how the UN has discharged this mandate in relation to humanitarian assistance. It frames the UN's humanitarian assistance functions in terms of three distinct roles: coordination and funding (Section 3), normative (Section 4), and operational (Section 5).

This tripartite range of engagement is, however, relatively new, as the UN's humanitarian assistance role has expanded over time. The chapter thus begins with a historical overview at Section 2, spanning relevant international organizations that existed prior to 1945 until the end of 1991, when the UN's humanitarian architecture was overhauled. Section 3 then covers the main coordination and funding structures created in 1991, which still exist today. These are the Under-Secretary-General for Humanitarian Affairs and Emergency Relief Coordinator and the office within the UN Secretariat that supports this official, now called the UN Office for the Coordination of Humanitarian Affairs (OCHA); the Inter-Agency Standing Committee (IASC); the Central Emergency Response Fund (CERF); and country-level coordination and funding mechanisms. Section 4 addresses post-1991 initiatives of major norm-generating actors and organs: the Secretary-General; ECOSOC; the General Assembly; and the Security Council.[4] The section on the Security Council outlines its thematic agenda on the protection of civilians in armed conflict and a key dimension of humanitarian assistance the Council has taken up: humanitarian access. It also covers how counterterrorism measures, particularly sanctions, can impede access, and what the Security Council has done to address this issue. Section 4 does not consider UN Charter-based human rights mechanisms; their relatively minor

[1] The operations of the Trusteeship Council have been suspended since 1994.

[2] cf the 'UN system', which refers to the UN plus its related organizations (e.g. the International Organization for Migration (IOM)) and specialized agencies (e.g. the Food and Agriculture Organization of the United Nations (FAO)).

[3] Charter of the United Nations (adopted 26 June 1945, entered into force 24 October 1945) 1 UNTS XVI (UN Charter) art 1(3).

[4] Other UN entities, notably the Office of the United Nations High Commissioner for Refugees (UNHCR) and the United Nations Children's Fund (UNICEF), also have normative roles (see Sections 5.2.1 and 5.2.2). However, in light of UNHCR's and UNICEF's more significant operational functions, they are addressed in Section 5 on operational humanitarian entities.

Humanitarian Assistance in International Law. Marina Sharpe, Oxford University Press. © Marina Sharpe 2026.
DOI: 10.1093/9780198994695.003.0008

role in humanitarian assistance has been addressed elsewhere.[5] Section 5 is devoted to the UN's operational humanitarian entities. It begins by addressing UN privileges and immunities. This is followed by coverage of certain semi-autonomous subsidiary organs of the General Assembly—UNHCR, UNICEF, the World Food Programme (WFP), and the UN Relief and Works Agency for Palestine Refugees in the Near East (UNRWA)—as well as UN peacekeeping operations and special political missions (SPM).[6] Finally, Section 5 addresses the protection of UN humanitarian operations and personnel. This chapter does not address UN accountability for conduct in humanitarian response that may infringe international law, as this broad topic has been addressed extensively elsewhere.[7] Section 6 concludes.

2. History

2.1. International initiatives before 1945

Even before the UN was created, states cooperated on humanitarian issues.[8] Many of these initiatives related specifically to refugees and other displaced persons.[9] However, two pre-UN international organizations had broader humanitarian mandates: one focused on disasters and the other on civilians affected by armed conflict.

The disaster-focused organization was the International Relief Union (IRU),[10] which was conceptualized in 1927 further to a proposal put to the League of Nations by Italian Red Cross President Giovanni Ciraolo.[11] The IRU was primarily a 'clearing house' for international assistance,[12] funded by initial contributions and then

[5] Marlies Hesselman, 'A Right to International (Humanitarian) Assistance in Times of Disaster: Fresh Perspectives from International Human Rights Law' in Flavia Zorzi Giustiniani and others (eds), *Routledge Handbook of Human Rights and Disaster* (Routledge 2018) 73–77.

[6] The role of non-UN military operations, including individual state and allied operations, is addressed in Chapter 7.

[7] See, for example, ILC, 'Report of the International Law Commission on the Work of its 63rd Session' (26 April–3 June and 4 July–12 August 2011) A/66/10, s V; Guglielmo Verdirame, *The UN and Human Rights: Who Guards the Guardians?* (CUP 2011) ch 8; Kristen Boon, 'The United Nations as Good Samaritan: Immunity and Responsibility' (2016) 16 Chicago Journal of International Law 341; Carla Ferstman, *International Organizations and the Fight for Accountability: The Remedies and Reparations Gap* (OUP 2017); Rosalyn Higgins and others, *Oppenheim's International Law: United Nations* (OUP 2017) ch 13; Jan Klabbers, *An Introduction to International Organizations Law* (4th edn, CUP 2022) ch 14.

[8] On the history of humanitarianism more generally, see Michael Barnett, *Empire of Humanity: A History of Humanitarianism* (Cornell University Press 2011); Eleanor Davey, John Borton, and Matthew Foley, 'A History of the Humanitarian System: Western Origins and Foundations' (2013) HPG Working Paper <https://odi.org/en/publications/a-history-of-the-humanitarian-system-western-origins-and-foundations/> accessed 14 March 2022; Bruno Cabanes, *The Great War and the Origins of Humanitarianism 1918–1924* (CUP 2014).

[9] See Peter MacAlister-Smith, *International Humanitarian Assistance: Disaster Relief Actions in International Law and Organization* (Springer 1985) 15–16; Gilbert Jaeger, 'On the History of the International Protection of Refugees' (2001) 83 International Review of the Red Cross 727.

[10] Convention Establishing an International Relief Union (adopted 12 July 1927, entered into force 27 December 1932) 135 LNTS 247 (IRU Statute).

[11] Michael Eburn, 'International Law and Disaster Response' (2010) 36 Monash University Law Review 162, 165.

[12] ibid, 166.

voluntary grants from states.[13] States in need of assistance could apply to the IRU for 'funds, resources and assistance of all kinds',[14] so that aid would flow through the IRU rather than bilaterally, thereby ensuring that it 'was seen as humanitarian only, and did not create any bonds of obligation'.[15] The IRU also had coordination and research roles.[16]

However, the IRU struggled to operate effectively due to insufficient funding, state ambivalence, and institutional tensions.[17] These factors were a result of the global climate when the organization's statute entered into force in 1932, namely the Great Depression and the lead-up to World War II.[18] The IRU provided assistance in just two disasters, earthquakes in South Asia in 1934 and 1935,[19] before falling dormant. Efforts to revive the organization during the UN's early years ultimately failed.[20] The IRU was formally terminated in 1967 when its assets and obligations were transferred to ECOSOC further to its request.[21]

The second major international organization for humanitarian assistance formed prior to the creation of the UN was the United Nations Relief and Rehabilitation Administration (UNRRA).[22] It was created during World War II (in 1943) by forty-four states to provide relief for civilians in areas liberated from Axis powers and to promote inter-state cooperation to this end.[23] UNRRA was terminated in 1947 because, as the iron curtain came down, the United States (US) refused to work through the organization.[24] When UNRRA was wound down, its assets and functions were divided among the UN's agencies, funds, and programmes, with most of the money going to the UN International Children's Emergency Fund (now UNICEF).[25]

2.2. 1945 to 1991

The UN's engagement with humanitarian assistance can be roughly divided into six periods, the first two of which predate the 1991 reforms. During the first period, which spans the organization's founding in 1945 until late in the Cold War, three main factors

[13] IRU Statute (n 10) arts 9, 11, and 12.
[14] ibid, art 2(1).
[15] Eburn (n 11) 166.
[16] IRU Statute (n 10) art 2(2).
[17] Sandesh Sivakumaran, 'Techniques in International Law-Making: Extrapolation, Analogy, Form and the Emergence of an International Law of Disaster Relief' (2018) 28 European Journal of International Law 1097, 1109.
[18] MacAlister-Smith (n 9) 21.
[19] Peter MacAlister-Smith, 'The International Relief Union: Reflections on Establishing an International Relief Union of July 12, 1927' (1986) 54 Legal History Review 363, 370.
[20] MacAlister-Smith (n 9) 95.
[21] ECOSOC Res 1153 (XLI) (4 August 1966).
[22] See generally Katherine Rossy and Samantha Knapton (eds), *Rehabilitation Among the Ruins: The United Nations Relief and Rehabilitation Administration* (Bloomsbury 2023).
[23] Agreement for United Nations Relief and Rehabilitation Administration [1943] NZTS 2, art 2.
[24] Andrej Zwitter, 'United Nations' Legal Framework of Humanitarian Assistance' in Hans-Joachim Heintze and Andrej Zwitter (eds), *International Law and Humanitarian Assistance: A Crosscut Through Legal Issues Pertaining to Humanitarianism* (Springer 2011) 53.
[25] MacAlister-Smith (n 9) 14.

precluded sustained involvement in humanitarian assistance. Two were a function of prevailing realities. In the immediate aftermath of World War II, the UN was focused on reconstruction and assisting individuals displaced by the war.[26] Later, the organization concentrated on development in newly decolonized states.[27] The third factor was state sovereignty, which meant that 'strikingly little was said or done about giving the UN a role in providing emergency humanitarian assistance'.[28] However, crises in the early 1970s—a major earthquake in Peru in 1970 and the third Indo-Pakistani war in 1971—prompted a re-evaluation. Yet after 'considerable soul-searching', the Secretariat concluded in 1971 that the UN should leave humanitarian assistance to the International Red Cross and Red Crescent Movement (the Movement) and non-governmental organizations (NGOs).[29]

The General Assembly did not, however, agree. In 1970, it had requested that the Secretary-General consider establishing a permanent office within the UN Secretariat 'responsible for the co-ordination of action related to natural disasters, epidemics, famines and similar emergency situations'.[30] In 1971, the General Assembly adopted resolution 2816, which created the position of Disaster Relief Coordinator and this official's office, the UN Disaster Relief Organization (UNDRO).[31] UNDRO began operations in March 1972.[32] The Disaster Relief Coordinator was endowed with a broad mandate that included internal and external resource mobilization, coordination, and the provision of response and prevention assistance to affected states.[33] Among its initiatives, in 1984, UNDRO proposed a draft convention on the expediting and delivery of relief. However, UNDRO experienced a range of challenges. A 1980 evaluation by the UN Joint Inspection Unit concluded that its mandate in relation to disasters was unclear and other UN agencies had obstructed its coordination role.[34] Similarly, according to Tsui and Myint-U, 'UNDRO's main weaknesses were its inability actually to direct other parts of the UN system in times of crisis and the reluctance of the UN's agencies, funds and programmes to see their independence or funding limited by a centralised structure in Geneva'.[35] Although efforts were made to address these weaknesses,[36] UNDRO was terminated in 1992 when it was incorporated into the Department of Humanitarian Affairs (DHA), which was created as part of the 1991 reforms discussed below.[37]

[26] Jeff Crisp, 'Humanitarian Action and Coordination' in Thomas G Weiss and Sam Daws (eds), *The Oxford Handbook on the United Nations* (2nd edn, OUP 2018) 585.
[27] ibid.
[28] Edward Tsui and Thant Myint-U, 'The Institutional Response: Creating a Framework in Response to New Challenges' in *The Humanitarian Decade: Challenges for Humanitarian Assistance in the last Decade and into the Future*, vol 2 (OCHA 2004) 2.
[29] ibid, 2–3; Barnett (n 8) 169.
[30] UNGA Res 2717 (XXV) (15 December 1970) para 4(c).
[31] UNGA Res 2816 (XXVI) (14 December 1971) (Res 2816).
[32] Zwitter (n 24) 55.
[33] Res 2816 (n 31) para 1.
[34] UN Joint Inspection Unit, 'Evaluation of the Office of the United Nations Disaster Relief Co-Ordinator' (1980) JIU/REP/80/11 <https://www.unjiu.org/sites/www.unjiu.org/files/jiu_document_files/products/en/reports-notes/JIU%20Products/JIU_REP_1980_11_English.pdf> accessed 28 January 2025.
[35] Tsui and Myint-U (n 28) 3.
[36] See, for example, UNGA, 'Strengthening of the Office of the United Nations Disaster Relief Co-ordinator', Res 45/221 (21 December 1990) A/RES/45/221.
[37] See Section 3.

UNDRO was not the only humanitarian assistance body established during this first period. Additional offices were created in response to the consequences of drought in sub-Saharan Africa. The Secretary-General created the UN Office for Emergency Operations for Africa in 1984.[38] The UN Office for Emergency Operations in Ethiopia, which coordinated the response to the 1983–1985 famine there, followed soon after.[39] Unlike UNDRO, these initiatives were viewed as successful, and set 'the precedent of a "slim" coordinating body close to the Secretary-General'.[40] And improved humanitarian response was on the General Assembly's agenda throughout the 1980s.[41]

Also during the 1980s, following an address by Crown Prince Hassan of Jordan to the General Assembly, the Permanent Representative of Jordan wrote to the Secretary-General to request that an item on a 'New International Humanitarian Order' be added to the agenda of the General Assembly's 36th session in 1981.[42] The Jordanian proposal highlighted the 'essentially *ad hoc* and fragmentary' nature of international responses to 'major natural and man-made disasters in virtually all parts of the world'.[43] An explanatory memorandum annexed to the letter attributed this to 'a deep conflict between the prerogatives of the State and the rights of the individual'.[44] The item was added to the agenda of the General Assembly's 37th session in 1982[45] and remained on the Assembly's agenda for several years.[46] The Jordanian initiative also led to the creation of the Independent Commission on International Humanitarian Issues[47] in 1983 and its successor, the Independent Bureau for Humanitarian Issues.[48] While the work of these autonomous bodies did not produce any concrete institutional developments, their reports advanced the global conversation around international cooperation on humanitarian issues.[49]

The fall of the Berlin Wall in 1989 marked the beginning of the end of the Cold War and ushered in the second period, during which the UN overhauled its institutional architecture for humanitarian assistance with the critical General Assembly resolution 46/182.[50] Two factors led to this milestone resolution. First, in the early 1990s, the UN became involved in the humanitarian aspects of military operations

[38] Charles-Henri LaMunière, 'Managing the UN's Emergency Operations in Africa: Lessons for Organizational Development' (1987) 7 Public Administration and Development 195, 196.

[39] Randolph Kent, 'The United Nations' Humanitarian Pillar: Re-Focusing the UN's Disaster and Emergency Roles and Responsibilities' (2004) 28 Disasters 216, 217.

[40] Tsui and Myint-U (n 28) 3.

[41] See, for example, UNGA Res 42/121 (7 December 1987); UNGA Res 43/130 (8 December 1988).

[42] UNGA, 'Letter Dated 28 October 1981 from the Permanent Representative of Jordan to the United Nations Addressed to the Secretary-General' (30 October 1981) A/36/245.

[43] ibid, 1.

[44] ibid, Annex, 1.

[45] UNGA Res 36/136 (14 December 1981) para 2.

[46] See, for example, UNGA Res 51/74 (12 December 1996).

[47] Ignaz Seidl-Hohenveldern, 'Reviewed Work: *Les Garanties Fondamentales de la Personne en Droit Humanitaire et Droits de L'Homme*' (1987) 81 AJIL 974, 974.

[48] Peter MacAlister-Smith, 'Protection of the Civilian Population and the Prohibition of Starvation as a Method of Warfare: Draft Texts on International Humanitarian Assistance' (1991) 31 International Review of the Red Cross 440, 453.

[49] See, for example, Sadruddin Aga Khan, *Winning the Human Race? The Report of the Independent Commission on International Humanitarian Issues* (Zed Books 1988).

[50] UNGA, 'Strengthening of the Coordination of Humanitarian Emergency Assistance of the United Nations', Res 46/182 (19 December 1991) A/RES/46/182 (Res 46/182).

in the Persian Gulf (1990–1991)[51] and northern Iraq (1991),[52] where it encountered significant challenges, including poor coordination and an approach based almost entirely on experience in disasters.[53]

The second factor was the civil wars that seemed likely to follow the end of the Cold War. Former UN Deputy Secretary-General (2012–2016) Jan Eliasson described this factor, and the reform process it gave rise to, in a research interview.[54] His account provides the first and only unofficial 'drafting history' of resolution 46/182. Eliasson became Sweden's Permanent Representative to the UN in New York in 1988. Around 1989, he and other UN ambassadors began to discuss the challenges that would likely emerge following the end of the Cold War. They predicted that conflicts would increasingly occur within—rather than between—states,[55] and such non-international armed conflicts (NIAC) would particularly affect civilians, but state sovereignty would complicate any UN humanitarian response. The solution, they concluded, was to reform the UN's humanitarian architecture.[56]

The challenge in this regard was twofold: first, to get the reform idea on the General Assembly's agenda, and second, to shape the resulting Assembly resolution.[57] The first challenge was addressed through the European Council of what was then the European Community. In June 1991, the European Council issued its 'Declaration on the Improvement of Emergency Assistance within the United Nations Framework', which recommended the 'appointment of a high-level coordinator for emergency humanitarian aid' who would, among other things, chair 'an inter-agency standing committee' to 'coordinate assistance efforts'.[58] At the July 1991 G7 summit in London, leaders agreed to push for the 'designation of a high level [UN] official to coordinate future international emergency operations'.[59] Subsequently, a 16 August 1991 letter to the Secretary-General from the Permanent Representative of the Netherlands, writing on behalf of all European Community member states, requested that strengthening 'the coordination of [UN] humanitarian emergency assistance' be added to the agenda for the General Assembly's 46th session, to be held in the fall of 1991.[60] The agenda item was added.[61]

[51] Thomas G Weiss, 'Humanitarian Shell Games: Whither UN Reform?' (1998) 29 Security Dialogue 9, 10–11.

[52] David Scheffer, 'The Expanding UN Role in Humanitarian Relief Operations' (1992) 86 American Society of International Law Proceedings 313, 314.

[53] Gita Swamy Meier-Ewert, 'Humanitarian Assistance' in Helmut Volger (ed), *A Concise Encyclopedia of the United Nations* (Brill 2010) 342; see also UNGA Res 45/100 (14 December 1990) A/RES/45/100.

[54] Author's interview of Jan Eliasson (via Zoom, 25 February 2022) (Eliasson interview). An account of this interview was previously published in Marina Sharpe, 'It's All Relative: The Origins, Legal Character and Normative Content of the Humanitarian Principles' (2024) 106 International Review of the Red Cross 12.

[55] See, generally, Mary Kaldor, *New and Old Wars: Organized Violence in a Global Era* (3rd edn, Stanford University Press 2012).

[56] Eliasson interview (n 54).

[57] ibid.

[58] UNGA, 'Letter dated 1 July 1991 from the Chargé d'affaires a.i. of the Permanent Mission of the Netherlands to the United Nations addressed to the Secretary-General' (8 July 1991) A/46/288, Annex.

[59] Tsui and Myint-U (n 28) 7.

[60] UNGA 'Letter dated 16 August 1991 from the Permanent Representative of the Netherlands to the United Nations addressed to the Secretary-General' (19 August 1991) A/46/194 (1991).

[61] UNGA 'Provisional Verbatim Record of the 3rd Meeting' (20 September 1991) A/46/PV.3; UNGA 'Annotated Agenda of the Forty-Sixth Regular Session of the General Assembly' (30 September 1991) A/46/100/Add.1, para 142.

With the UN's humanitarian architecture now on the General Assembly's agenda, the second challenge was to shape the deliberations. To tackle this, Eliasson and his ambassador colleagues decided that, given Sweden's established interest in humanitarian affairs, Eliasson should run for the ECOSOC vice-presidency. ECOSOC makes or initiates 'studies and reports with respect to international economic, social, cultural, educational, health, and related matters' and makes 'recommendations with respect to any such matters to the General Assembly'.[62] The vice-presidency would, accordingly, allow Eliasson to influence ECOSOC's, and thus the General Assembly's, deliberations regarding the UN's humanitarian architecture.[63] Eliasson was elected in 1991. The agenda of ECOSOC's Second Regular Session of 1991, held in Geneva in July, thus included 'Coordination Questions', including the 'Response of the United Nations to Emergencies'.[64]

The UN response to emergencies was addressed by ECOSOC's Third (Programme and Coordination) Committee from 8 to 11 July 1991. The Third Committee produced an 'outline for a [UN humanitarian] mandate', 'with the elements to be decided by the General Assembly'.[65] This outline is contained in the Chairman's Summary annexed to ECOSOC's 1991 annual report,[66] which was provided to General Assembly member states to background the deliberations that ultimately led to resolution 46/182. The Summary covers four main topics: 'prevention; preparedness; coordination and cooperation; and the relationship between emergency relief and development'.[67] Eliasson described the drafting of resolution 46/182 as a 'two-stage rocket', with the Chairman's Summary that emerged from the ECOSOC Third Committee meetings representing the first stage.[68] Indeed, the Third Committee topics, and a handful of others, are reflected in resolution 46/182. The additional topics originated in a report of the Secretary-General.[69]

Back in New York, Eliasson asked General Assembly President (and Permanent Representative of Saudi Arabia) Samir Shihabi to convene an *ad hoc* General Assembly committee to negotiate and draft what would become resolution 46/182.[70] The committee met for the first time in October 1991.[71] Its deliberations were informed by the Secretary-General's October 1991 report 'on the review of the capacity, experience, and coordination arrangements in the United Nations system for humanitarian

[62] UN Charter (n 3) art 62(1).

[63] Eliasson interview (n 54).

[64] ECOSOC, 'Resolutions and Decisions of the Economic and Social Council', Second Regular Session of 1991, Geneva, 3–26 July 1991, Official Records, 1991, Supplement 1A, 1.

[65] Eliasson interview (n 54).

[66] ECOSOC, 'Report of the Economic and Social Council for the Year 1991', General Assembly, Official Records, 46th Session, Supp no 3 (A/46/3/Rev.1) Annex IV, 'Response of the United Nations to Emergencies: Summary Prepared by the Chairman of the Third (Programme and Coordination) Committee'.

[67] ibid.

[68] Eliasson interview (n 54).

[69] UNGA, 'Report of the Secretary-General on the Review of the Capacity, Experience, and Coordination Arrangements in the United Nations System for Humanitarian Assistance' (17 October 1991) A/46/560 (Humanitarian Assistance S-G Report).

[70] Eliasson interview (n 54).

[71] ibid.

assistance'.[72] The report noted that, as the UN had 'increasingly been called upon to play the crucial role of framing the international response' to emergencies, the 'issue that arises is how the response can be made more coherent, timely, effective, commensurate with need and assured of cohesive leadership'.[73] The Secretary-General went on to identify two essential conditions for such a response: sufficient and readily available resources, and effective coordination.[74] To satisfy these conditions, he made five sets of recommendations, relating to early warning, prevention, preparedness and stand-by capacity, consolidated appeals, and strengthened coordination and leadership.[75] The Secretary-General thus based several of his recommendations on the ECOSOC Third Committee deliberations and added his own recommendations about early warning, consolidated appeals, and leadership.

The final draft of resolution 46/182 was supplied by Sweden[76] and adopted by the General Assembly on 19 December 1991 without a vote—a procedure that reflects strong consensus. The sections in the resolution's operative Annex—guiding principles; prevention; preparedness; stand-by capacity; consolidated appeals; coordination, cooperation and leadership; and continuum from relief to rehabilitation and development—largely follow the recommendations contained in the Secretary-General's October 1991 report, which the resolution notes 'with satisfaction'.[77] Zwitter characterizes resolution 46/182 as 'in its nature a decision that adopts the [Secretary-General's] report and requests' him 'to implement it'.[78] This characterization, however, understates the significance of the General Assembly's drafting process. According to Eliasson, contemporaneous media accounts, and a subsequent account authored by individuals who had been present,[79] the negotiations in the drafting committee were both 'intense'[80] and 'difficult',[81] culminating in overnight talks on 17–18 December 1991.

Resolution 46/182 was adopted to strengthen 'the coordination of emergency humanitarian assistance of the' UN system.[82] Its Annex begins with a section on 'Guiding Principles'. This section introduces three key principles that govern humanitarian assistance to this day. In view of these contributions, resolution 46/182 has been called humanitarianism's 'magna carta'[83] and its 'blueprint'.[84] The first principle is that

[72] Humanitarian Assistance S-G Report (n 69).
[73] ibid, paras 1–2.
[74] ibid, para 4.
[75] ibid.
[76] UNGA, 'Strengthening of the Coordination of the Humanitarian Emergency Assistance of the United Nations' (17 December 1991) A/46/L.55; UNGA, 'Strengthening of the Coordination of the Humanitarian Emergency Assistance of the United Nations' (18 December 1991) A/46/L.55/Corr.1.
[77] Res 46/182 (n 50) preambular para 5.
[78] Zwitter (n 24) 55.
[79] Tsui and Myint-U (n 28) 1; Scheffer (n 52) 314.
[80] Eliasson interview (n 54).
[81] Paul Lewis, 'UN to Centralize its Relief Efforts' *The New York Times* (New York, 18 December 1991) A19.
[82] Res 46/182 (n 50) para 1.
[83] Michael O'Flaherty, 'The Human Rights Field Operation in Partnership for Humanitarian Relief and Reconstruction' in Michael O'Flaherty (ed), *The Human Rights Field Operation: Law, Theory and Practice* (Ashgate 2007) 160.
[84] Dug Cubie, *The International Legal Protection of Persons in Humanitarian Crises: Exploring the Acquis Humanitaire* (Hart 2017) 15.

'humanitarian assistance *should* be provided with the consent of the affected country and *in principle* on the basis of an appeal by the affected country'.[85] Eliasson described the language of 'should' as a major victory in the negotiation of resolution 46/182.[86] The principle recognizes the sovereignty and territorial integrity of the affected state, while at the same time leaving

> the door ajar for exceptional circumstances that may demand intervention in the absence of consent. [. . .] Further, the principle refers to the consent of the 'country', not of the 'government'. The distinction can be of considerable significance when the territory where the humanitarian relief is required is controlled by rebels, or by no discernible authority. It is equally significant that 'in principle' the affected country should have appealed for humanitarian assistance; this allows for circumstances in which the appeal cannot be ascertained but the need for aid is overwhelming.[87]

Scheffer further explains that the precise wording cited above 'was the subject of intense negotiations until the early hours of December 17, 1991', with the final language reflecting a 'careful and subtle balance [. . .] between sovereignty and the imperative requirements of international emergency assistance'.[88] The General Assembly's recognition of the need to strike this balance was prescient, as borne out by events over two decades later in Syria.[89] The balance is reflected in the current law on humanitarian access in armed conflict,[90] and the emerging peacetime framework.[91]

The second key principle introduced by resolution 46/182 is that 'humanitarian assistance must be provided in accordance with the principles of humanity, neutrality and impartiality'.[92] These principles in the UN context were addressed in detail in Chapter 2.[93] Finally, the resolution recognizes that each 'state has the responsibility first and foremost to take care of the victims of natural disasters and other emergencies occurring on its territory'.[94] As shown in Chapter 1,[95] this primary responsibility is the starting point for the law on humanitarian assistance in both armed conflict and in peacetime. As a result, 'the affected State has the primary role in the initiation, organization, coordination, and implementation of humanitarian assistance within its territory'.[96]

Resolution 46/182 also recognizes the 'central and unique role' of the UN 'in providing leadership and coordinating the efforts of the international community to support' affected states, and notes that the organization 'should ensure the prompt and

85 Res 46/182 (n 50) Annex, para 3 (emphasis added).
86 Eliasson interview (n 54).
87 Scheffer (n 52) 314.
88 ibid.
89 See Section 4.4.2.
90 See Chapter 3, Section 4.3.
91 See Chapter 4, Section 2.2.
92 Res 46/182 (n 50) Annex, para 2.
93 See Chapter 2, Section 4.4.
94 Res 46/182 (n 50) Annex, para 4.
95 See Chapter 1, Section 2.
96 Res 46/182 (n 50) Annex, para 4.

smooth delivery of relief assistance in full respect of' the principles of humanity, neutrality, and impartiality.[97] The resolution created coordination and funding architecture to enable the UN to fulfil this role; it still exists, and is covered in the next section.

3. Coordination and funding architecture after 1991

Before turning to the coordination and funding architecture created by resolution 46/182, it is worth briefly outlining the third through sixth periods of UN engagement with humanitarian assistance. The third period began with the adoption of resolution 46/182 and the end of the Cold War in December 1991. As Eliasson, his colleagues, and many others had predicted, the demise of the bipolar world order brought about an increasing number of NIACs and, with them, intense human suffering and 'failed' or 'failing' states that threatened international peace and security. During the Cold War, states—particularly the superpowers—understood militarized disputes as the primary threat to international peace and security. However, with the end of the Cold War, 'failed' and 'failing' states came to be viewed as the pre-eminent security risk. For this reason, states became increasingly willing to work through the UN on peacebuilding: '[h]umanitarianism and security collapsed under peacebuilding'.[98] With this, the UN became significantly more involved in humanitarian assistance.[99]

The fourth period began around the turn of the millennium, when several trends—including the harm from post-Cold War civil wars, a new focus on shoring up fragile states to combat terrorism, and an emphasis in the West on 'joined up' governance—coalesced to produce increasingly structurally integrated UN missions in the field.[100] An integrated UN mission 'is one in which there is a shared vision among all United Nations actors, both military and civilian, as to the strategic objectives of the United Nations presence at country level'.[101] The decision to structurally integrate at the field level is 'driven by an assessment of whether or not it will add real value and improve the impact of' UN engagement.[102] Structurally integrated UN missions, particularly those involving peacekeeping operations, produced a range of concerns about adverse effects on humanitarian response, particularly the risk—actual or perceived—that integration could undermine the impartiality and neutrality of assistance.[103]

[97] ibid, Annex, para 12. On the omission of independence from this list of principles, see Chapter 2, Section 2.

[98] Barnett (n 8) 164. See also UN Secretary-General, 'An Agenda for Peace: Preventive Diplomacy, Peacemaking and Peace-keeping' (1992) ST/DPI/1247.

[99] Tsui and Myint-U (n 28) 4; Barnett (n 8) 169.

[100] Emily Paddon and Taylor Owen, 'Whither Humanitarian Space? The Costs of Integrated Peacebuilding in Afghanistan' in Benjamin Perrin (ed), *Modern Warfare: Armed Groups, Private Militaries, Humanitarian Organizations, and the Law* (UBC Press 2012) 269–71.

[101] Ben Klappe, 'Civil-Military Cooperation and Humanitarian Assistance' in Terry Gill and Dieter Fleck (eds), *The Handbook of the International Law of Military Operations* (2nd edn, OUP 2015) 534. See also UNSG, 'Note from the Secretary-General: Guidance on Integrated Missions' (9 February 2006) <https://unsdg.un.org/sites/default/files/Guidance-on-the-role-of-SRSG-and-DSRSG_RC_HC.pdf> accessed 22 May 2025.

[102] Klappe (n 101) 534.

[103] Espen Barth Eide, Anja Therese Kaspersen, and others, 'Report on Integrated Missions: Practical Perspectives and Recommendations—Independent Study for the Expanded UN ECHA Core Group' (2005) 28–33. See, generally, Erin Weir, 'Conflict and Compromise: UN Integrated Missions and the

The fifth period of UN engagement with humanitarian assistance was marked by member states' growing familiarity with the law governing such assistance and an increased willingness to address states' obligations in this regard. This period started with Secretary-General Ban's 2013 call for 'analysis and development' of the law on strategic consent to relief operations.[104] Major markers of this period included the Security Council's first-ever decision to impose relief (on Syria), discussed below;[105] member states' ongoing negotiation of a disaster response treaty;[106] and the General Assembly's request in 2024 for an ICJ advisory opinion on Israel's obligations in relation to the presence and activities of the UN, other international organizations, and third states in the Occupied Palestinian Territories.[107]

The second Trump presidency, which began in January 2025 and brought major cuts in US funding to the UN,[108] marked the beginning of the current—or sixth—period, characterized by the Secretary-General's ongoing UN80 reform initiative. The initiative, named to mark the eightieth anniversary of the UN Charter in October 2025, was announced by the Secretary-General in a non-public letter dated 11 March 2025. He went on to outline the details in a 12 May 2025 briefing to the General Assembly. While clearly a response to Trump administration cuts, UN80 is officially aimed at making the UN more effective and better able to deliver on the 2015 Sustainable Development Goals[109] and the Pact for the Future adopted by the General Assembly in 2024.[110] It consists of three 'workstreams': (i) the rapid identification of efficiencies and improvements that can be made to existing ways of working, particularly in the Secretariat; (ii) a review of how the UN implements the thousands of mandates bestowed upon it by member states;[111] and (iii) a UN system strategic review and realignment.[112] The Secretary-General established seven UN80 thematic 'clusters' to advance all three workstreams within each cluster. The 'Humanitarian' cluster is coordinated by the ERC (as defined below), WFP, UNICEF, UNHCR, and IOM[113]—though coordination by so many actors is unlikely to be

Humanitarian Imperative' (*Kofi Annan International Peacekeeping Training Centre*, 2006) <https://www.kaiptc.org/wp-content/uploads/2017/03/New%20folder/WeirE.-2006-Conflict-and-Compromise-UN-Integrated-Missions-and-Humanitarian-Imperative.pdf> accessed 22 May 2025. This issue is addressed in Section 5.3 below.

104 UNSC, 'Report of the Secretary-General on the Protection of Civilians in Armed Conflict' (2013) S/2013/689, para 58 (Protection of Civilians in Armed Conflict S-G Report). See Chapter 3, Section 4.2.
105 See Section 4.4.2.
106 See Chapter 4, Section 2.3.2.4.
107 UNGA Res 79/232 (19 December 2024) A/RES/79/232 (Res 79/232).
108 Farnaz Fassihi, 'UN Orders Agencies to Find Budget Cuts, including via Staff Relocations from NY' (*The New York Times*, 29 April 2025) <https://www.nytimes.com/2025/04/29/world/un-budget-cuts-trump.html> accessed 30 April 2025.
109 UNGA Res 70/1 (21 October 2015) A/RES/70/1.
110 UNGA Res 79/1 (22 September 2024) A/RES/79/1 (Res 79/1).
111 See UN, 'UN80 Initiative Workstream 2: Report of the Mandate Implementation Review' (31 July 2025) <https://www.un.org/un80-initiative/sites/default/files/2025-08/UN_MIR_2025_0853.pdf> accessed 24 August 2025.
112 UN Secretary-General, 'Secretary-General, Briefing on UN80 Initiative, Lays out System-Wide Reform Plans to Make United Nations More Effective, Nimble, Fit for Today's Challenges' (12 May 2025) SG/SM/22644 <https://digitallibrary.un.org/record/4081972> accessed 5 June 2025.
113 ibid.

effective. The ERC termed this cluster's work the 'Humanitarian Reset'; it is addressed below.[114]

3.1. The Under-Secretary-General for Humanitarian Affairs and Emergency Relief Coordinator and the Office for the Coordination of Humanitarian Affairs

Resolution 46/182 created the position of Emergency Relief Coordinator, a 'high-level official [. . .] designated by the Secretary-General'.[115] Secretary-General Boutros-Ghali added the Under-Secretary-General designation,[116] such that the position is termed UN Under-Secretary-General for Humanitarian Affairs and Emergency Relief Coordinator (ERC). The Under-Secretary-General rank is equivalent to that of the heads of operational UN humanitarian bodies such as UNICEF.[117] Eliasson was the first ERC, serving from 1992 until 1994. The ERC was intended to consolidate functions previously fulfilled by *ad hoc* representatives of the Secretary-General and the head of UNDRO.[118] Working 'under the aegis of the General Assembly' and at the 'direction of the Secretary-General', the ERC was mandated to: receive requests from UN member states for humanitarian assistance; coordinate and facilitate UN humanitarian assistance; organize joint needs assessments and prepare consolidated appeals to be issued by the Secretary-General; facilitate humanitarian access by obtaining the consent of states concerned; manage the CERF and chair the IASC (both of which are discussed below); and prepare annual reports of the Secretary-General related to humanitarian assistance.[119]

In April 1992, shortly after resolution 46/182 created the position of ERC, the DHA was established within the UN Secretariat to support the new high-level official.[120] While under resolution 46/182 the ERC's office was to be 'based on a strengthened' UNDRO,[121] in practice UNDRO was folded into the new DHA.[122] DHA established its Field Coordination Support Section in 1996 to 'develop, prepare and maintain standby capacity for rapid deployment to sudden-onset emergencies',[123] in order to support the affected state and the country-level UN Resident Coordinator.[124]

According to Weiss, both the ERC and DHA suffered significant shortcomings. Among them, the ERC had difficulty coordinating operational UN humanitarian

[114] See Section 3.5.
[115] Res 46/182 (n 50) Annex, para 34.
[116] Thomas G. Weiss, 'Civilian-Military Interactions and Ongoing UN Reforms: DHA's Past and OCHA's Remaining Challenges' (1998) 5 International Peacekeeping 49, 55.
[117] Tsui and Myint-U (n 28) 10.
[118] Res 46/182 (n 50) Annex, para 34.
[119] ibid, para 35.
[120] UNGA, 'Report of the Secretary-General—Renewing the United Nations: A Programme for Reform' (14 July 1997) A/51/950 (Annan Report) para 184.
[121] Res 46/182 (n 50) Annex, para 36.
[122] Weiss (n 51) 10.
[123] UN, 'Protection of Persons in the Event of Disasters: Memorandum by the Secretariat' (11 December 2007) A/CN.4/590, para 179.
[124] See Section 3.4.

bodies with heads of the same rank and control of 'vastly superior human and financial resources'.[125] Regarding DHA, he noted that it had 'insufficient qualified staff, resources, and authority [. . .] to become what was necessary' for effective coordination.[126]

These and other issues were addressed in 1997 in the context of Secretary-General Annan's broader UN reform agenda. One proposal—ultimately abandoned due to opposition from the heads of operational bodies such as UNICEF and WFP—emerged to incorporate DHA into UNHCR.[127] Instead, Annan ultimately proposed refocusing the ERC's mandate on three core functions: policy development; Security Council advocacy; and coordination.[128] To support this narrower mandate, DHA would be replaced by an office that would support these functions,[129] with its main operational commitments on land mines and Iraq reassigned within the UN Secretariat.[130] The General Assembly accepted Annan's proposals.[131] The changes were fully operationalized in 1999, when DHA was terminated and the ERC's new secretariat was established as OCHA.[132]

OCHA is headquartered in New York and Geneva, with additional regional, field, and liaison offices worldwide.[133] It is headed by the ERC.[134] The ERC is assisted by the Assistant-Secretary-General for Humanitarian Affairs and Deputy ERC (Deputy ERC),[135] who focuses on policy and management.[136] Both the ERC and Deputy ERC have offices within OCHA, which provide OCHA's executive management.[137] Much of OCHA's global-level coordination work is executed through the IASC, for which OCHA serves as secretariat; the IASC is addressed separately in the next section. The Geneva-based Response Support Branch—successor to DHA's Field Coordination Support Section—is OCHA's main internal coordination body. Its Emergency Response Section is a key coordination node, providing personnel surge capacity, serving as the secretariat for the International Search and Rescue Advisory Group (INSARAG), and managing the UN Disaster Assessment and Coordination (UNDAC) system. INSARAG is an international network of emergency management officials and practitioners.[138] Several INSARAG innovations, such as its Guidelines[139]

[125] Weiss (n 51) 12.
[126] ibid.
[127] Crisp (n 26) 590.
[128] Annan Report (n 120) para 186.
[129] ibid, para 188.
[130] ibid, para 187.
[131] UNGA Res 52/12 (14 November 1997) A/RES/52/12.
[132] UN Secretariat, 'Secretary-General's Bulletin: Organization of the Office for the Coordination of Humanitarian Affairs' (22 June 1999) ST/SGB/1999/8 (S-G Bulletin 8) s 2.
[133] Higgins and others (n 7) 714.
[134] S-G Bulletin 8 (n 132) s 2.3.
[135] ibid, s 5.
[136] Higgins and others (n 7) 714.
[137] ibid.
[138] On urban search and rescue more generally, see Kirsten Nakjavani Bookmiller, 'The International Law of 96 Hours: Urban Search and Rescue Teams and the Current State of International Disaster Response Law' in David D. Caron, Michael J. Kelly, and Anastasia Telesetsky (eds), *The International Law of Disaster Relief* (CUP 2014).
[139] INSARAG, Guidelines 2020 (INSARAG 2020) <https://insarag.org/methodology/insarag-guidelines/> accessed 4 February 2025.

and the UNDAC system, have strengthened disaster response, particularly in relation to search and rescue.[140] UNDAC teams are deployed rapidly to sudden-onset disasters to assist UN entities and the affected state with coordination during the first phase of an emergency response.[141] UNDAC coordination encompasses various components, including staff, methodology, mobilization, and equipment.[142]

OCHA also operates a civil-military coordination service (CMCS). It is the UN's focal point for civil-military coordination in contexts where military actors provide support to humanitarian operations.[143] CMCS conducts four key activities: supporting field-level operations; building capacity to ensure expertise in the field; outreach and advocacy; and guiding the development of civil-military coordination policy.[144] In connection with this policy role, CMCS is the custodian of UN guidelines on civil-military coordination in humanitarian contexts, including the Guidelines on the Use of Foreign Military and Civil Defence Assets in Disaster Relief and the Guidelines on the Use of Military and Civil Defence Assets to Support United Nations Humanitarian Activities in Complex Emergencies (MCDA Guidelines).[145]

3.2. The Inter-Agency Standing Committee and the cluster approach

The IASC was created by resolution 46/182.[146] It is an inter-agency forum for humanitarian coordination, policy development, priority setting, and resource mobilization.[147] The IASC is chaired by the ERC and includes 'all operational organizations',[148] where 'operational' is defined as UN humanitarian bodies that provide 'protection or material aid' or deploy staff 'to assist affected populations with immediate needs'.[149] Today, the IASC is comprised of the FAO, IOM,[150] the Office of the High Commissioner for Human Rights (OHCHR), OCHA, the UN Development Programme (UNDP), UNICEF, UNHCR, the UN Human Settlements Programme (UN-HABITAT), the UN Population Fund (UNFPA), UN Women, WFP, and the

140 Bookmiller (n 138) 111–12.

141 OCHA, 'United Nations Disaster Assessment and Coordination Field Handbook' (7th edn, United Nations 2018).

142 Giovanni De Siervo, 'Actors, Activities, and Coordination in Emergencies' in Andrea de Guttry, Marco Gestri, and Gabriella Venturini (eds), *International Disaster Response Law* (Springer 2012) 504.

143 See Chapter 7, Section 3.2.

144 <https://www.dialoguing.org/about/about-ocha-cmcs> accessed 9 June 2025.

145 OCHA, 'Oslo Guidelines on the Use of Foreign Military and Civil Defence Assets in Disaster Relief' (2007) <https://www.unocha.org/publications/report/world/oslo-guidelines-guidelines-use-foreign-military-and-civil-defence-assets-disaster-relief-revision-11-november-2007-enzh> accessed 28 May 2025; OCHA, 'Guidelines on the Use of Military and Civil Defence Assets to Support United Nations Humanitarian Activities in Complex Emergencies' (revision 1, 2005) <https://www.unocha.org/publications/report/world/guidelines-use-military-and-civil-defence-assets-support-united-nations-humanitarian> accessed 9 June 2025 (MCDA Guidelines). See Chapter 7, Section 3.3.

146 Res 46/182 (n 50) Annex, para 38.

147 IASC <https://interagencystandingcommittee.org/the-inter-agency-standing-committee> accessed 11 February 2025.

148 Res 46/182 (n 50) Annex, para 38.

149 IASC, IASC Membership <https://interagencystandingcommittee.org/iasc-about/iasc-membership> accessed 11 February 2025 (IASC Membership).

150 IOM became a UN related organization in 2016 (UNGA Res 70/296 (25 July 2016) A/RES/70/296).

World Health Organization (WHO).[151] Resolution 46/182 gave the International Committee of the Red Cross (ICRC) and the International Federation of Red Cross and Red Crescent Societies (IFRC) 'a standing invitation' to the IASC;[152] similar invitations have since been extended to the UN Special Rapporteur on the Human Rights of Internally Displaced Persons (IDPs) and the World Bank.[153] Relevant NGOs 'can be invited to participate on an ad hoc basis';[154] the NGO consortia International Council of Voluntary Agencies, InterAction, and the Steering Committee for Humanitarian Response now enjoy permanent invitations.[155]

The IASC has employed several approaches to coordination, including a lead agency approach[156] and a collaborative approach.[157] Its current 'cluster approach' emerged in 2005 from ERC Jan Egeland's Humanitarian Response Review, which launched in 2004 in response to shortcomings of the UN's work with IDPs, particularly in Darfur.[158] The Review concluded in 2005 with three main outcomes: the creation of an expanded and more flexible CERF;[159] strengthening of the Humanitarian Coordinators system;[160] and the introduction of the cluster approach.[161]

The cluster approach is a coordination mechanism used in humanitarian response. It organizes IASC members into clearly defined, sector-specific groups under designated leadership, known as clusters. By clarifying roles, the cluster approach aims to improve humanitarian response at the global and national levels. Globally, it aims to ensure leadership and accountability.[162] Nationally, it promotes more strategic and effective emergency response.[163] There are 11 clusters: camp coordination and management (led by IOM in disasters and UNHCR in armed conflict); early recovery (UNDP); education (Save the Children and UNICEF); emergency telecommunications (WFP); food security (FAO and WFP); health (WHO); logistics (WFP); nutrition (UNICEF); protection (UNHCR); shelter (IFRC in disasters and UNHCR in armed conflict); and water, sanitation, and hygiene (WASH; UNICEF).[164] Cluster leads also serve as the aid provider of last resort.[165] Clusters are activated at the country level by the IASC when 'there is a sharp deterioration or significant change in

151 IASC Membership (n 149).
152 Res 46/182 (n 50) Annex, para 38.
153 IASC Membership (n 149).
154 Res 46/182 (n 50) Annex, para 38.
155 IASC Membership (n 149).
156 Guy Goodwin-Gill and Jane McAdam, *The Refugee in International Law* (4th edn, OUP 2021) 504.
157 Crisp (n 26) 592.
158 ibid.
159 See Section 3.3.
160 See Section 3.4.
161 Crisp (n 26) 592; see UN, 'Humanitarian Response Review: Commissioned by the United Nations Emergency Relief Coordinator and Under-Secretary-General for Humanitarian Affairs' (UN 2005) <https://interagencystandingcommittee.org/sites/default/files/migrated/2014-12/Humanitarian%20Response%20Review%202005.pdf> accessed 11 February 2025.
162 Higgins and others (n 7) 715.
163 ibid, 715–16. For a critique of the cluster approach, see J Benton Heath, 'Managing the "Republic of NGOs": Accountability and Legitimation Problems Facing the UN Cluster System' (2014) 47 Vanderbilt Journal of Transnational Law 239.
164 <https://www.unocha.org/we-coordinate> accessed 11 February 2025. For more on the cluster approach, see De Siervo (n 142) 500–04.
165 Higgins and others (n 7) 716.

the humanitarian situation, leading to gaps in the humanitarian response or humanitarian coordination'.[166]

Further to its policy development role, the IASC has published a range of policy documents. These include the Operational Guidelines on the Protection of Persons in Situations of Natural Disasters[167] and the Non-Binding Guidelines on the Use of Armed Escorts for Humanitarian Convoys (Armed Escort Guidelines).[168]

3.3. The Central Emergency Response Fund

By pooling funds and giving one entity the authority to disburse them, donors reduce the influence of non-need-based factors in humanitarian funding decisions.[169] Resolution 46/182 created a pooled fund known as the Central Emergency Revolving Fund (the Revolving Fund). The Revolving Fund was 'a cash-flow mechanism to ensure the rapid and coordinated response of the organizations of the [UN] system'.[170] The Revolving Fund advanced resources to operational UN bodies 'on the understanding that they would reimburse' it from 'voluntary contributions received in response to consolidated appeals'.[171] The Revolving Fund suffered several shortcomings, notably the requirement that any funds withdrawn be reimbursed within six months.[172] The General Assembly decided in 2005 to upgrade the Revolving Fund by adding a grant facility 'to ensure a more predictable and timely response to humanitarian emergencies', while at the same time renaming it the CERF.[173]

The CERF receives voluntary contributions, primarily from UN member states. Humanitarian actors can apply for CERF funds to finance emergency responses, with grants approved in as little as 48 hours.[174] CERF funds can also be applied to underfunded crises.[175] The CERF is managed by the ERC on behalf of the Secretary-General.[176] The CERF primarily funds UN agencies, funds, and programmes.[177] It does not finance OCHA, which is funded by the regular UN budget and voluntary contributions.[178]

The funding of UN humanitarian operations through voluntary contributions rather than from member states' regular UN budget assessments contributes to a

166 ibid.

167 (*The Brookings-Bern Project on Internal Displacement*, 2011) <https://www.unhcr.org/media/iasc-operational-guidelines-protection-persons-situations-natural-disasters-2011> accessed 11 February 2025.

168 (*IASC*, 2013) <https://www.refworld.org/policy/legalguidance/iasc/2013/en/22033> accessed 11 February 2025.

169 Miriam Bradley, *The Politics and Everyday Practice of International Humanitarianism* (OUP 2023) 328.

170 Res 46/182 (n 50) Annex, para 23.

171 ibid, paras 24–25.

172 UN Secretary-General, 'Improvement of the Central Emergency Revolving Fund: Report of the Secretary-General' (20 October 2005) A/60/432, para 5.

173 UNGA Res 60/124 (15 December 2005) A/RES/60/124, para 15.

174 Bradley (n 169) 329.

175 ibid.

176 <https://cerf.un.org/about-us/who-we-are> accessed 17 February 2025.

177 Higgins and others (n 7) 717–18.

178 ibid, 715.

significant and persistent humanitarian financing gap. UN Secretary-General Ban Ki-moon addressed humanitarian underfunding in 2015 by convening a nine-person group of experts, known as the High-Level Panel on Humanitarian Financing. The Panel's report was published in 2016 to coincide with the World Humanitarian Summit, which is discussed in Section 4.1. The report made three central recommendations: address the root causes of humanitarian need by preventing conflict and reducing the risk of disasters, by directing development assistance primarily to situations of fragility; deepen the humanitarian financing base by turning to untapped resources such as social impact bonds and Islamic social finance; and improve efficiency through a 'Grand Bargain' between major donors and humanitarian actors.[179]

Despite these recommendations, humanitarian financing remains a major issue. As of 30 June 2025, OCHA's Global Humanitarian Overview 2025—which provides an annual assessment of global humanitarian needs and outlines response plans for individual emergencies—was short by about US$33 billion, with 43 individual country appeals on average only 13.5 per cent funded.[180] This figure was approximately one-third lower than the funding recorded at the same point in 2024.[181] The humanitarian financing gap will likely continue to widen, due in large part to a major review of US funding to the UN ordered by President Trump.[182] The UN may respond to this funding crisis with major structural reforms,[183] which at the time of writing remained under consideration as part of the UN80 reform initiative. The 'Humanitarian Reset' dimension of UN80 is discussed in Section 3.5.

3.4. State-level coordination and funding

The UN Humanitarian Coordinator is responsible for in-country coordination of a UN humanitarian response, with assistance from OCHA.[184] This individual is appointed by the ERC, who will either appoint a Humanitarian Coordinator or call on the existing UN Resident Coordinator to also serve as Humanitarian Coordinator. The Resident Coordinator is the highest UN official in a country, except when the Secretary-General has appointed a Special Representative, which occurs in countries with large multidisciplinary UN field operations.[185] The Resident Coordinator position is often filled by the UNDP Resident Representative.[186] Where a Humanitarian

[179] High-Level Panel on Humanitarian Financing, 'Report to the Secretary-General—Too Important to Fail: Addressing the Humanitarian Financing Gap' (January 2016) <https://reliefweb.int/report/world/high-level-panel-humanitarian-financing-report-secretary-general-too-important-fail> accessed 17 February 2025. The Grand Bargain is discussed in Section 4.1.

[180] OCHA, 'Global Humanitarian Overview 2025: Snapshot as of 30 June 2025' (2025) <https://www.unocha.org/publications/report/world/global-humanitarian-overview-2025-may-june-update-snapshot-30-june-2025> accessed 16 July 2025 (GHO 2025) 2.

[181] ibid.

[182] Fassihi (n 108).

[183] Emma Farge and John Shiffman, 'Exclusive: UN Eyes Big Overhaul Amid Funding Crisis, Internal Memo Shows' (*Reuters*, 2 May 2025) <https://www.reuters.com/world/un-eyes-major-overhaul-amid-funding-crisis-internal-memo-shows-2025-05-01/> accessed 2 May 2025.

[184] Res 46/182 (n 50) Annex, para 39; Higgins and others (n 7) 720.

[185] MCDA Guidelines (n 145) para 8.

[186] De Siervo (n 142) 499.

Coordinator has been appointed, a Humanitarian Country Team will also be established and led by the Humanitarian Coordinator. A Humanitarian Country Team can also be appointed without a Humanitarian Coordinator if there is a crisis or if a situation of chronic need deteriorates sharply.[187] The Humanitarian Country Team is a strategic coordination body, while cluster leads, discussed above,[188] coordinate operational response within their sector.[189] If an emergency affects more than one country, the ERC may appoint a regional Humanitarian Coordinator.[190]

State-level funding comes from country-based pooled funds, which are created by the ERC and locally managed by OCHA via the Humanitarian Coordinator.[191] UN operational entities,[192] as well as IOM, Movement components, and national and international NGOs can draw on the pooled fund.[193] Disbursements from country-based pooled funds are made according to the country-level Humanitarian Response Plan.[194]

3.5. The 'Humanitarian Reset'

The humanitarian coordination and funding architecture in place since 1991 appears set to change significantly in the context of the 'Humanitarian Reset' component of the Secretary-General's UN80 reform initiative.[195] On 11 March 2025, the same day UN80 was announced, the ERC wrote to all IASC principals regarding the need to 'reimagine' humanitarian response in light of a 'profound crisis of legitimacy, morale, and funding'.[196] The letter identified three 'strategic priorities': (i) 'the best possible crisis response with the resources we have'; (ii) 'urgent work to reform and reimagine how we work'; and (iii) a shift in 'power to our humanitarian leaders in country, and the people we serve'.[197] The ERC went on to state that he was taking ten immediate actions to advance these priorities: providing as much funding as possible to local and national actors; asking Humanitarian Coordinators to simplify country-level coordination structures; tasking the Emergency Directors' Group—an IASC body comprised of the emergency directors of all IASC members—to create a prioritization

[187] Higgins and others (n 7) 720.
[188] See Section 3.2.
[189] IASC, 'Standard Terms of Reference for Humanitarian Country Teams' (February 2017) <https://interagencystandingcommittee.org/sites/default/files/migrated/2019-02/hct_tors.pdf> accessed 7 April 2025, 1.
[190] MCDA Guidelines (n 145) para 8.
[191] Higgins and others (n 7) 721.
[192] See Section 5.2.
[193] Higgins and others (n 7) 721.
[194] Bradley (n 169) 330.
[195] Slim has usefully situated the Reset in the context of previous transformations of the humanitarian sector. See Hugo Slim, 'Humanitarian Resets Past and Present—Where Have We Come From and Where Shall We Go?' (*LSE Blogs*, 28 August 2025) <https://blogs.lse.ac.uk/activism-influence-change/2025/08/28/humanitarian-resets-past-and-present-where-have-we-come-from-and-where-shall-we-go/> accessed 30 August 2025.
[196] Tom Fletcher, 'The Humanitarian Reset' (*OCHA*, 11 March 2025) <https://www.unocha.org/publications/report/world/humanitarian-reset-erc-letter-iasc-principals-11-march-2025> accessed 5 June 2025.
[197] ibid.

plan for how to save as many lives as possible with the limited resources available; integrating existing humanitarian reform initiatives; asking OCHA to 'ramp up' advocacy communications to 'demonstrate the value of what we do'; tasking a WFP official to work on reducing inefficiency, duplication, and bureaucracy at country level; calling on IASC principals to 'be ruthless in eliminating turf wars'; proposing pooled financing for common services and certain aspects of operations, such as needs assessments; simplifying the cluster system; and making the IASC 'more focused and effective'.[198] In a follow-up statement three months later, the ERC characterized this 'ten-point plan' as aimed at moving towards a humanitarian response system 'that is locally led and globally supported' and driven not 'by the money we can raise' but by the 'greatest need'.[199]

The follow-up statement also outlined key elements of the Reset's second phase, framed in four categories: define, deliver, devolve, and defend. Under 'define', it promised a 'hyper-prioritized' Global Humanitarian Overview, focusing on just 114 million people, compared to the current 300 million people identified as in need.[200] 'Deliver' commitments included shared services, such as needs assessment, by default; increased cash assistance; new financing sources; a simplified IASC; 'ruthlessly simplified' planning and appeals; and greater emphasis on transitioning out of humanitarian action. Elements under 'devolve' included 'context-specific' coordination; more funding for country-based pooled funds; streamlined clusters, with local cluster leadership where possible; and more funding for CERF, ideally US$1 billion per year. 'Defend' actions primarily centred on upholding humanitarian principles and international humanitarian law (IHL). The statement concluded by noting that the humanitarian sector's problem has historically not been a 'lack of ideas for reform', but rather a 'lack of execution'.[201] The Humanitarian Reset remains ongoing.

4. Norm-generating actors and bodies after 1991

While the basic architecture for the UN's coordination and funding of humanitarian assistance was created in 1991 with the adoption of resolution 46/182, the UN's role extends well beyond these functions. The Secretary-General, ECOSOC, the General Assembly, and the Security Council all exercise normative influence over humanitarian assistance. Their roles are addressed in this section.

4.1. The Secretary-General

Resolution 46/182 assigned the Secretary-General a leadership role in humanitarian response, to ensure 'rapid and coherent response to [. . .] natural disasters

[198] ibid.
[199] Tom Fletcher, 'Statement by Emergency Relief Coordinator Tom Fletcher: The Humanitarian Reset—Phase Two' (*OCHA*, 19 June 2025) <https://www.unocha.org/news/un-relief-chief-pushes-humanitarian-system-even-more-rooted-communities-we-serve> accessed 16 July 2025 (Reset Phase 2).
[200] GHO 2025 (n 180) 2.
[201] Reset Phase 2 (n 199).

and other emergencies'.[202] This leadership is primarily deployed through the ERC.[203] Additionally, as the UN's 'chief administrative officer',[204] the Secretary-General wields normative influence in relation to humanitarian assistance by shaping agendas, framing policy debates, and mobilizing state commitments. The World Humanitarian Summit and its development of The Grand Bargain and the Secretary-General's reporting obligations to the UN's principal organs are key instances of this influence in relation to humanitarian assistance.[205] Additionally, the Secretary-General often calls for humanitarian access, as in Gaza,[206] or uses his office to facilitate access, as in Sudan.[207]

The World Humanitarian Summit took place in May 2016 in Istanbul, Türkiye. Secretary-General Ban called for the summit in 2012, in light of 'the growing number of people in crisis and the dramatic increase in funding requirements'.[208] Extensive consultations then took place over the next three years, culminating with the publication in 2015 of a synthesis report.[209] It identified a range of issues, to which Ban responded in his report for the World Humanitarian Summit. His report proposed five broad 'core responsibilities': political leadership for conflict prevention and resolution; enhanced compliance with IHL and international human rights law (IHRL); reaching everyone affected by armed conflict and disaster; ending humanitarian need; and political, institutional, and financial investments in 'humanity'.[210] An annex to the report, known as the Agenda for Humanity, proposed actions to advance each core responsibility. Shortly after the Summit, Ban reported on its outcomes, identifying five priority trends that emerged from the meeting: protecting civilians and minimizing human suffering; leaving no one behind; reducing humanitarian need through new ways of working; reducing the risk of disasters

[202] Res 46/182 (n 50) Annex, para 33.
[203] ibid, para 34.
[204] UN Charter (n 3) art 97.
[205] It would be impossible for reasons of space to address all the Secretary-General's initiatives in relation to humanitarian assistance since 1945, or even since 1991. Additional initiatives were mentioned above—such as the creation of emergency offices for Africa and Ethiopia in the 1980s and the High-Level Panel on Humanitarian Financing—and elsewhere in this book—such as Secretary-General Ban's call for analysis and development of the law on strategic consent to emergency relief operations (see Chapter 3, Section 4.2). For a broader account of one Secretary-General and humanitarian assistance, see Martin Barber, *Blinded by Humanity: Inside the UN's Humanitarian Operations* (IB Tauris & Co Ltd 2015) ch 6, which covers Secretary-General Annan.
[206] For example, in March 2025 Secretary-General António Guterres appealed for 'unimpeded humanitarian assistance to be reestablished' in Gaza (Farhan Haq, 'Statement Attributable to the Spokesperson for the Secretary-General—on Gaza' (*UN*, 18 March 2025) <https://www.un.org/sg/en/content/sg/statement/2025-03-18/statement-attributable-the-spokesperson-for-the-secretary-general-%E2%80%93-gaza> accessed 22 April 2025).
[207] 'Sudan's Military Accepts UN Proposal of a Weeklong Ceasefire in El Fasher for Aid Distribution' (*AP*, 28 June 2025) <https://apnews.com/article/sudan-war-un-aid-rsf-el-fasher-6ccfe84779a2a2ab8b634563e26b2099> accessed 29 June 2025.
[208] 'One Humanity: Shared Responsibility—Report of the Secretary-General for the World Humanitarian Summit' (2 February 2016) A/70/709, para 8 (World Humanitarian Summit S-G Report).
[209] World Humanitarian Summit secretariat, 'Restoring Humanity: Synthesis of the Consultation Process for the World Humanitarian Summit' (2015) <https://reliefweb.int/report/world/restoring-humanity-global-voices-calling-action-synthesis-consultation-process-world> accessed 25 February 2025.
[210] World Humanitarian Summit S-G Report (n 208) 6–45.

and climate adaptation; and increasing the resource base, including by increasing efficiency.[211]

While the World Humanitarian Summit failed to advance any significant reforms, its normative legacy lies in the 'Grand Bargain'. As mentioned above, the Grand Bargain originated in the report of the High-Level Panel on Humanitarian Financing. It is a set of commitments between major donors and humanitarian organizations aimed at improving the effectiveness of humanitarian action by overhauling funding (e.g. reducing earmarking and encouraging multi-year funding, cash-based programming, and joint needs assessments).[212]

The Secretary-General has an important reporting and documentation function derived from his role as the UN's chief administrative officer. The Secretary-General prepares the agenda and documents for all meetings of the UN's principal organs—including ECOSOC, the General Assembly, and the Security Council—and prepares reports and technical studies at the request of these organs or on the Secretary-General's own initiative.[213] For example, the Security Council has invited the Secretary-General to report on humanitarian access in general,[214] on 'the risk of conflict-induced famine and widespread food insecurity in armed conflict',[215] and on the unintended humanitarian consequences of Security Council sanctions.[216] The General Assembly recently requested the Secretary-General to provide it with a report on the safety and security of humanitarian personnel and the protection of UN personnel.[217] The Secretary-General's reports can be influential. For example, according to one account, the Security Council's ongoing thematic focus on the protection of civilians in armed conflict, which is discussed below,[218] originated in Secretary-General Annan's 1998 report to the Security Council on armed conflict in Africa.[219]

The Secretary-General also has a more general standing reporting function under resolution 46/182, which requires the Secretary-General to report annually to the General Assembly, through ECOSOC, on 'the coordination of humanitarian emergency assistance'.[220] The Secretary-General thus issues a report every May titled 'Strengthening of the Coordination of Emergency Humanitarian Assistance of the

211 'Outcome of the World Humanitarian Summit: Report of the Secretary-General' (23 August 2016) A/71/353.

212 Bradley (n 169) 331. While it was initially conceptualized as a deal between the five biggest donor states and the six largest UN humanitarian bodies, as of November 2023 (the most recent date for which information is available), the Grand Bargain had 68 signatories, including 25 states, 12 UN agencies, 27 NGOs, and two Movement components. The Grand Bargain has been reviewed twice since the World Humanitarian Summit, most recently in June 2023 (IASC, 'About the Grand Bargain' <https://interagencystandingcommittee.org/about-the-grand-bargain> accessed 25 February 2025).

213 Higgins and others (n 7) 530–33.

214 See, for example, UNSC Res 1296 (19 April 2000) S/RES/1296, para 8; UNSC Res 1894 (11 November 2009) S/RES/1894, para 17; UNSC Res 2417 (24 May 2018) S/RES/2417 (Res 2417) para 4.

215 Res 2417 (n 214) para 12. See Section 4.4.1.

216 See Section 4.4.3.

217 UNGA Res 78/118 (13 December 2023) A/RES/78/118 (Res 78/118). The Secretary-General responded with: UN Secretary-General, 'Safety and Security of Humanitarian Personnel and Protection of United Nations Personnel: Report of the Secretary-General' (12 July 2024) A/79/149. See Section 5.4.

218 See Section 4.4.1.

219 Emily Paddon Rhoads and Jennifer M Welsh, 'Close Cousins in Protection: the Evolution of Two Norms' (2019) 95 International Affairs 597, 600.

220 Res 46/182 (n 50) Annex, para 35(i).

United Nations'. This report, which is prepared by the ERC,[221] tends to follow a set format. In recent years, it has provided overviews of trends in humanitarian assistance; new or ongoing humanitarian emergencies; key humanitarian response challenges; and operational and coordination developments. The report also includes a set of recommendations. The report goes first to ECOSOC and then to the General Assembly, which use it to develop their annual resolutions related to humanitarian assistance, which are discussed in the sections below.

4.2. The Economic and Social Council

As one of the principal organs of the UN, ECOSOC provides a specialized forum for the discussion and debate of sustainable development issues. Indeed, the General Assembly has described ECOSOC as the 'principal organ for coordination, policy review, policy dialogue and recommendations on issues of economic and social development'.[222] Composed of 54 member states,[223] ECOSOC's broad mandate covers making or initiating 'studies and reports with respect to international economic, social, cultural, educational, health, and related matters'.[224] Further, ECOSOC may make 'recommendations with respect to any such matters', and with respect to human rights, to the General Assembly, member states, and UN specialized agencies.[225] ECOSOC holds one substantive and one organizational session per year.

ECOSOC's humanitarian engagement is centred on its annual humanitarian affairs segment, held each June as part of its substantive session. This segment, which follows a designated theme—in 2025, 'Renewing global solidarity for humanity: saving lives, reducing suffering and mobilizing solutions for humanitarian action'[226]—provides a space for states, NGOs, and UN entities to discuss emerging humanitarian issues. The segment's primary outcome is a negotiated resolution, typically titled 'Strengthening of the coordination of emergency humanitarian assistance of the United Nations',[227] which reflects a set of shared commitments.

The humanitarian affairs segment is a product of incremental reform. Secretary-General Annan established it within his 1997 reforms, to enable ECOSOC to 'give guidance on overall humanitarian issues and coordination',[228] in order to improve 'the management and coherence' of the UN system's humanitarian activities.[229] ECOSOC's mandate in relation to humanitarian affairs was further strengthened following the 2005 World Summit, which recommended that ECOSOC promote 'global dialogue and partnership on global policies and trends in the [. . .] humanitarian' field

221 ibid.
222 UNGA Res 75/290 (28 June 2021) A/RES/75/290, para 2.
223 UN Charter (n 3) art 61(1).
224 ibid, art 62.
225 ibid.
226 ECOSOC, 'Theme of the Humanitarian Affairs Segment of the 2025 Session of the Economic and Social Council' E/2025/L.4 (10 April 2025).
227 See, for example, ECOSOC, Res 2023/16 (23 June 2023); ECOSOC, Res 2024/8 (27 June 2024).
228 Annan Report (n 120) para 193.
229 UN Secretary-General, 'Strengthening the Coordination of Emergency Humanitarian Assistance of the United Nations' (23 June 2005) A/60/87-E/2005/78, para 41.

and support and 'complement international efforts aimed at addressing humanitarian emergencies'.[230]

4.3. The General Assembly

The General Assembly is the UN's main deliberative body. It is composed of all UN member states, each of which has one vote.[231] The General Assembly can discuss any matter within the scope of the UN Charter and make recommendations to member states or the Security Council.[232] It exercises normative influence in relation to humanitarian assistance through its resolutions, which can set agendas and forge consensus. The General Assembly's resolutions are drafted in six committees. Most resolutions relating to humanitarian assistance emanate from the Social, Humanitarian, and Cultural Committee (Third Committee); UNRWA is addressed in the Special Political and Decolonization Committee (Fourth Committee).[233]

The General Assembly meets annually in a regular session that begins in September. This session contains a standing humanitarian affairs agenda item,[234] typically titled 'Strengthening of the coordination of humanitarian and disaster relief assistance of the United Nations, including special economic assistance'.[235] Several resolutions are adopted annually under this agenda item; they signal priorities and sustain norms over time. Since resolution 46/182 in 1991, the General Assembly has adopted an annual omnibus resolution titled 'Strengthening of the coordination of emergency humanitarian assistance of the United Nations'.[236] In 1997, the General Assembly began adopting a biennial resolution on humanitarian personnel, titled 'Safety and security of humanitarian personnel and Protection of United Nations personnel'.[237] More recently, as the risks for humanitarian personnel have increased, the General Assembly has adopted this resolution every year.[238] Since 2004,[239] the General Assembly has adopted an annual resolution on 'International cooperation on humanitarian assistance in the field of natural disasters, from relief to development'.[240] The General Assembly also adopts annual resolutions that address, among other

[230] UNGA Res 60/1 '2005 World Summit Outcome' (24 October 2005) A/RES/60/1, para 155. See also UNGA Res 61/16 (9 January 2007) A/RES/61/16, paras 12–14.

[231] UN Charter (n 3) arts 9(1) and 18(1).

[232] ibid, art 10.

[233] Higgins and others (n 7) 180.

[234] On the procedure in this regard, see Higgins and others (n 7) 37–44.

[235] UNGA, 'Agenda of the Seventy-ninth Session of the General Assembly' (13 September 2024) A/79/251, para 72.

[236] See, for example, UNGA Res 78/119 (13 December 2023) A/RES/78/119; UNGA Res 79/140 (12 December 2024) A/RES/79/140. Early on, the resolution was titled 'Strengthening of the coordination of humanitarian emergency assistance of the United Nations'; see, for example, Res 46/182 (n 50) and UNGA Res 48/57 (14 December 1993).

[237] UNGA Res 52/167 (18 February 1998) A/RES/52/167 (adopted 16 December 1997). See Section 5.4.

[238] See, for example, UNGA Res 79/138 (12 December 2024) A/RES/79/138; Res 78/118 (n 217). The protection of UN humanitarian personnel is discussed at Section 5.4.

[239] UNGA Res 59/141 (25 February 2005) A/RES/59/141 (adopted 15 December 2004).

[240] See, for example, UNGA Res 79/139 (12 December 2024) A/RES/79/139; UNGA Res 78/120 (13 December 2023) A/RES/78/120.

things, humanitarian assistance for Palestinians[241] and for people forcibly displaced in Africa.[242]

In addition to recurring annual resolutions, the General Assembly adopts other resolutions in response to current events and emerging priorities, signalling its responsiveness to crises and evolving realities. These often relate to humanitarian access, such as in Gaza,[243] Kosovo,[244] Syria,[245] and Ukraine.[246] Other General Assembly resolutions relate to specific events or thematic priorities, such as the 2010 earthquake in Haiti,[247] the implementation of the Convention on the Rights of Persons with Disabilities in situations of risk and humanitarian emergencies,[248] and the impact of counterterrorism measures on humanitarian action.[249] More recently, in its Pact for the Future, the General Assembly committed to ensuring 'that people affected by humanitarian emergencies receive the support they need'.[250] This included specific commitments in relation to prevention and mitigation; forced and protracted displacement; hunger, food insecurity, and famine; and financial and other forms of support.[251]

Resolutions are not the General Assembly's only normative development tool; it also exercises considerable influence through the entities it creates. The General Assembly can 'initiate studies and make recommendations for [. . .] the progressive development of international law and its codification'.[252] It has delegated this function to the International Law Commission, which in 2016 adopted Draft Articles on the Protection of Persons in the Event of Disasters (Draft Articles);[253] the Assembly is now the forum for the negotiation of an international disaster response law treaty based on the Draft Articles.[254] The General Assembly can also make recommendations to member states or the Security Council regarding matters 'relating to the powers and functions of any' UN organs.[255] As shown above, with resolution 46/182 the General Assembly created the current humanitarian coordination and funding architecture within the Secretariat. Additionally, in 1996, it called on the Secretary-General to appoint a Special Representative 'on the impact of armed conflict on children'.[256] The Special Representative was appointed and still exists, and since 2005 has worked with

[241] See, for example, UNGA Res 79/141 (12 December 2024) A/RES/79/141; UNGA Res 78/121 (13 December 2023) A/RES/78/121.

[242] See, for example, UNGA Res 78/185 (22 December 2023) A/RES/78/185; UNGA Res 77/199 (3 January 2023) A/RES/77/199.

[243] UNGA Res ES-10/21 (30 October 2023) A/RES/ES-10/21, paras 2–4; UNGA Res ES-10/22 (12 December 2023) A/RES/ES-10/22, para 3; UNGA Res ES-10/27 (13 June 2025) A/RES/ES-10/27, paras 6 and 9.

[244] UNGA Res 53/164 (25 February 1999) A/RES/53/164, paras 10 and 17.

[245] UNGA Res 66/253 (7 August 2012) A/RES/66/253, para 12.

[246] UNGA Res ES-11/2 (24 March 2022) A/RES/ES-11/2, para 7.

[247] UNGA Res 64/250 (30 April 2010) A/RES/64/250.

[248] UNGA Res 78/195 (22 December 2023) A/RES/78/195.

[249] See, for example, UNGA Res 72/284 (26 June 2018) para 7. See Section 4.4.3.

[250] Res 79/1 (n 110) Action 15.

[251] ibid, para 36.

[252] UN Charter (n 3) art 13(1).

[253] See Chapter 4, Section 2.3.2.

[254] See Chapter 4, Section 2.3.2.4.

[255] UN Charter (n 3) art 10.

[256] UNGA Res 51/77 (12 December 1996) A/RES/51/77, para 35.

the Monitoring and Reporting Mechanism on Grave Violations Against Children in Situations of Armed Conflict established by the Security Council.[257] Additionally, the General Assembly can create subsidiary organs.[258] It has created operational bodies with mandates that include humanitarian assistance, such as UNHCR, UNICEF, WFP, and UNRWA; these are addressed below.[259]

4.4. The Security Council

The UN Security Council is mandated to maintain international peace and security.[260] It consists of five permanent members and ten rotating members,[261] each of which has one vote.[262] The permanent members—China, France, Russia, the United Kingdom, and the US—enjoy an effective veto over all non-procedural matters.[263] When the Security Council intends a resolution to be binding—evidenced by, for example, its use of obligatory language—the resolution binds all UN member states, regardless of whether it was adopted under Chapter VII of the UN Charter.[264] Binding resolutions are termed 'decisions'. The Council can adopt resolutions or decisions, for example, to highlight and call for the cessation of violations of international law; create subsidiary organs,[265] such as committees, working groups, and tribunals; refer a matter to the International Criminal Court;[266] levy sanctions;[267] impose a relief action;[268] or authorize the use of force.[269] The Security Council's normative influence in relation to humanitarian assistance lies in how it has expanded its understanding of threats to international peace and security to include humanitarian issues, embedded them within its thematic agendas, and issued decisions that have impacted state behaviour and operational practice.

A distinctive feature of the post-Cold War period has been an expansion of what the Security Council deems a threat to international peace and security to include humanitarian crises. According to Weiss, no Security Council resolution mentioned the humanitarian dimension of an armed conflict until the 1967 Arab-Israeli War.[270] Such

[257] See Section 4.4.1.
[258] UN Charter (n 3) arts 7(2) and 22.
[259] See Section 5.2.
[260] UN Charter (n 3) art 24(1).
[261] ibid, art 23(1).
[262] ibid, art 27(1).
[263] ibid, art 27(3).
[264] ibid, art 25; *Legal Consequences for States of the Continued Presence of South Africa in Namibia (South West Africa) notwithstanding Security Council Resolution 276* (Advisory Opinion) [1971] ICJ Rep 16, paras 113–14; Rosalyn Higgins, 'The Advisory Opinion on Namibia: Which UN Resolutions are Binding under Article 25 of the Charter?' (1972) 21 International & Comparative Law Quarterly 270. For a more recent discussion of this issue in the context of humanitarian assistance, see Andreas Zimmermann, 'Humanitarian Assistance and the Security Council' (2017) 50 Israel Law Review 3, 15–17.
[265] UN Charter (n 3) art 29.
[266] Rome Statute of the International Criminal Court (adopted 17 July 1998, entered into force 1 July 2002) 2187 UNTS 3, art 13(b).
[267] UN Charter (n 3) arts 39 and 41.
[268] See Section 4.4.2.
[269] UN Charter (n 3) art 42.
[270] Thomas G Weiss, 'Humanitarian Action' in Jacob Katz Cogan, Ian Hurd, and Ian Johnstone (eds), *The Oxford Handbook of International Organizations* (OUP 2016) 301.

mentions markedly increased in the early 1990s. For example, resolution 688, passed in 1991, characterized the forced displacement of Kurds from Iraq as a threat to 'international peace and security in the region'.[271] The following year, resolution 792 broke 'records in making eighteen references to "humanitarian" in authorizing the US-led action in Somalia'.[272] The Security Council explicitly acknowledged the importance of humanitarian issues in a statement issued in 1992, in which its President noted that 'non-military sources of instability in the economic, social, humanitarian and ecological fields have become threats to peace and security' and urged UN member states, 'working through the appropriate bodies [. . .] to give the highest priority to the solution of these matters'.[273]

4.4.1. Thematic agenda on the protection of civilians in armed conflict

In 1999, the Security Council began to focus on the humanitarian dimensions of armed conflict in a sustained way when, in the wake of the failures of peacekeeping operations to protect civilians in Bosnia and Herzegovina (1992–1995) and Rwanda (1994),[274] it launched a thematic agenda on the protection of civilians in armed conflict. This agenda includes, but is broader than, humanitarian assistance. While this book focuses on humanitarian assistance and protection is largely beyond its scope, post-1999 Security Council humanitarian assistance initiatives form part of the Council's thematic agenda on the protection of civilians in armed conflict, and so must be understood in this context.

The Security Council's first open debate on the protection of civilians in armed conflict was held in February 1999, under Canada's presidency.[275] Barber recalls that the 'meeting attracted so many member states and international organizations to speak that it had to be continued for a full second day'.[276] In the Presidential Statement that emerged from the debate, the Council called on the Secretary-General 'to submit a report containing concrete recommendations' on how it 'could improve the physical and legal protection of civilians in situations of armed conflict'.[277] This led to the Secretary-General's first report on the protection of civilians in armed conflict,[278] which is published regularly to this day.[279] The initial Secretary-General report informed the Security Council's first resolution on the protection of civilians in armed conflict, which was drafted by Canada[280] and adopted in 1999.[281] A few short weeks later, the Council, for the first time, decided to establish a peacekeeping operation—in Sierra Leone—with a mandate 'to afford protection to civilians under imminent

[271] UNSC Res 688 (5 April 1991) S/RES/688 (Res 688) preambular para 4.
[272] Weiss (n 270) 301.
[273] UNSC Presidential Statement (31 January 1992) S/23500, 3.
[274] Bruno Stagno Ugarte, 'Security Council Diplomacy on the Protection of Civilians: A Convoluted History' in Haidi Willmot and others (eds), *Protection of Civilians* (OUP 2016) 294–99.
[275] UNSC Presidential Statement 6 (12 February 1999) S/PRST/1999/6 (UNSC Presidential Statement).
[276] Barber (n 205) 130.
[277] UNSC Presidential Statement (n 275) 3.
[278] (8 September 1999) S/1999/957.
[279] UN Secretary-General, 'Protection of Civilians in Armed Conflict: Report of the Secretary-General' (15 May 2025) S/2025/271 (S-G PoC Report).
[280] Ugarte (n 274) 298.
[281] UNSC Res 1265 (17 September 1999) S/RES/1265.

threat of physical violence'.[282] This 'embryonic language' remains the template for all UN peacekeeping operations with a Chapter VII mandate to use force to protect civilians.[283] Since around 2005, nearly all UN peacekeeping operations have been given such a mandate.[284]

The Security Council has never explicitly defined the scope of its protection of civilians agenda.[285] However, several key sub-themes have emerged over time: enhancing IHL compliance; preventing and responding to forced displacement; protecting women, in particular from conflict-related sexual violence; ensuring humanitarian access; protecting children in armed conflict;[286] and, most recently, addressing conflict-induced hunger.[287] The last three sub-themes are particularly relevant to humanitarian assistance. The balance of this section covers the children in armed conflict and hunger sub-themes. Security Council humanitarian access initiatives are then addressed in a dedicated section, followed by an additional section on the Security Council's approach to the unintended consequences of counterterrorism measures on humanitarian access.

The protection of children in armed conflict emerged as a clear sub-theme at the very outset of the Security Council's work on the protection of civilians.[288] In 2004, the Council requested that the Secretary-General develop 'a systematic and comprehensive monitoring and reporting mechanism' on 'the recruitment and use of child soldiers in violation of applicable international law and on other violations and abuses committed against children affected by armed conflict'.[289] The following year, the Security Council called on Secretary-General Annan to implement the proposed mechanism and created the Security Council Working Group on Children and Armed Conflict (WGCAC), composed of all 15 Council members.[290] The resulting mechanism—the Monitoring and Reporting Mechanism on Grave Violations Against Children in Situations of Armed Conflict—has been in place since 2005. It provides for the systematic gathering of information on six serious violations of international law against children, including humanitarian access denials.[291] Information collected

[282] UNSC Res 1270 (22 October 1999) S/RES/1270, para 14.

[283] Ugarte (n 274) 299.

[284] See Section 5.3.

[285] Ralph Mamiya, 'A History and Conceptual Development of the Protection of Civilians' in Haidi Willmot and others (eds), *Protection of Civilians* (OUP 2016) 77.

[286] Leonie Arendt, 'Building a Culture of Protection: 20 Years of Security Council Engagement on the Protection of Civilians' (OCHA Occasional Policy Paper 2019) 5. The Security Council's work on the protection of civilians in armed conflict is summarized in OCHA's 'Aide Memoire', which is organized by theme: <https://poc-aide-memoire.unocha.org> accessed 25 March 2024.

[287] Res 2417 (n 214).

[288] UNSC Res 1261 (30 August 1999) S/RES/1261. See, generally, Shamala Kandiah Thompson, 'Children and Armed Conflict' in Jared Genser and Bruno Stagno Ugarte (eds), *The United Nations Security Council in the Age of Human Rights* (CUP 2014); Francesca Capone, 'A Critical Overview of the United Nations Architecture on Children and Armed Conflict: What Role for Sanctions' (2017) 27 Italian Yearbook of International Law 115; Katrina Lee-Koo, 'The Intolerable Impact of Armed Conflict on Children: The United Nations Security Council and the Protection of Children in Armed Conflict' (2018) 10 Global Responsibility to Protect 57.

[289] UNSC Res 1539 (22 April 2004) S/RES/1539, para 2.

[290] UNSC Res 1612 (26 July 2005) S/RES/1612, paras 2–3 and 8.

[291] Nathalie Weizmann, 'Ensuring Respect for IHL as it Relates to Humanitarian Activities' in Eve Massingham and Annabel McConnachie (eds), *Ensuring Respect for International Humanitarian Law* (Routledge 2020) 208.

by the Monitoring and Reporting Mechanism is published annually in the Report of the Secretary-General on Children and Armed Conflict.[292] This Report is reviewed by the WGCAC, which can recommend responses to the Security Council.[293] In addition, the Security Council adopts regular resolutions on children in armed conflict, which often strongly condemn humanitarian access denials.[294]

Food insecurity is a significant problem during armed conflict. It can arise when hostilities disrupt food production, distribution, or how civilians typically obtain food. Food insecurity can also arise from the deliberate use of starvation of civilians as a weapon of war,[295] which is prohibited by IHL.[296] Regardless of the cause, humanitarian assistance can play a major role in alleviating conflict-induced hunger.

The Security Council unanimously adopted its first thematic resolution on conflict-related hunger—resolution 2417—in 2018.[297] It had previously avoided the issue for two main reasons. First, some member states, including permanent members Russia, China, and the US, were reluctant to stray beyond the Council's core mandate for international peace and security in specific situations.[298] Second, there was concern that hunger was primarily a development issue, and therefore outside the Council's mandate.[299] There was also some concern that 'thematic issues could be employed (including through humanitarian assistance) as tools to interfere in the internal affairs of states'.[300] This resistance was overcome in 2018, largely because over the previous two decades, the Council had increasingly engaged with thematic issues—not least the protection of civilians in armed conflict—and because the problem of conflict-induced hunger had become significantly worse.[301]

The process that led to the resolution 2417 began with Secretary-General Guterres's 2017 call for member states to respond to the threat of famine linked to armed conflicts in Nigeria, Somalia, South Sudan, and Yemen.[302] This was followed later that year by an Arria formula meeting[303] and a Security Council Presidential Statement relating to the four situations Guterres had highlighted.[304] The Presidential Statement declared

[292] See, for example, UNGA, 'Children and Armed Conflict: Report of the Secretary-General' (3 June 2024) A/78/842-S/2024/384.
[293] Weizmann (n 291) 209.
[294] See, for example, UNSC Res 2764 (20 December 2024) S/RES/2764, para 1.
[295] Joanna Macrae and Anthony Zwi, 'Food as an Instrument of War in Contemporary African Famines: A Review of the Evidence' (1992) 16 Disasters 299; Mark W. Charlton, 'Famine and the Food Weapon: Implications for the Global Food Aid Regime' (1997) 17 Journal of Conflict Studies 28.
[296] Protocol Additional to the Geneva Conventions of 12 August 1949, and relating to the Protection of Victims of International Armed Conflicts (adopted 8 June 1977, entered into force 7 December 1978) 1125 UNTS 3 (API) art 54; Protocol Additional to the Geneva Conventions of 12 August 1949, and relating to the Protection of Victims of Non-International Armed Conflicts (adopted 8 June 1977, entered into force 7 December 1978) 1125 UNTS 609 (APII) art 14. See Chapter 3, Section 7.1.1.
[297] Res 2417 (n 214).
[298] Salvatore Zappalà, 'Conflict Related Hunger, "Starvation Crimes" and UN Security Council Resolution 2417 (2018)' (2019) 17 Journal of International Criminal Justice 881, 885–86.
[299] ibid, 886.
[300] ibid, 887.
[301] ibid, 887.
[302] ibid, 882.
[303] Arria formula meetings are 'informal, confidential gatherings which enable Security Council members to have a frank and private exchange of views, within a flexible procedural framework, with persons whom the inviting member or members of the Council [. . .] believe it would be beneficial to hear and/or to whom they may wish to convey a message' (UNSC, *Working Methods Handbook* (2012) 13).
[304] UNSC Presidential Statement 14 (2017) S/PRST/2017/14.

that parties to these conflicts had 'failed to ensure unfettered and sustained access for deliveries of vital food assistance as well as other forms of humanitarian aid' and, accordingly, called on them 'to allow the safe, timely and unhindered access for humanitarian assistance to all areas and to facilitate access for essential imports of food, fuel and medical supplies into each country, and their distribution throughout'.[305] It further urged 'all parties to protect civilian infrastructure which is critical to the delivery of humanitarian aid in the affected countries'[306] and called on them to 'urgently take steps that would enable a more effective humanitarian response'.[307]

Resolution 2417 devotes significant attention to the role of humanitarian assistance in combating hunger caused by armed conflict. It underlines the importance of humanitarian access in terms of both strategic consent by affected and transit states and the obligation to allow and facilitate passage,[308] and it strongly condemns violations of these obligations.[309] The resolution demands respect for obligations relating to the protection of humanitarian medical personnel[310] and humanitarian personnel more generally.[311] It also addresses the conditions in which relief is provided, urging 'all parties to protect civilian infrastructure which is critical to the delivery of humanitarian aid'[312] and recalling 'its intention to mandate' UN 'peacekeeping and other relevant missions, where appropriate, to assist in creating conditions conducive to safe, timely and unimpeded humanitarian assistance'.[313] On accountability, resolution 2417 recalls the Security Council's ability to sanction individuals who, or entities that, obstruct humanitarian assistance,[314] and it urges states to investigate and, where appropriate, take action under domestic and international law to address the starvation of civilians as a method of warfare, including the unlawful impeding of relief.[315]

4.4.2. Humanitarian access

The Security Council has addressed humanitarian access since the early 1990s, which predates its agenda on the protection of civilians in armed conflict. Since this time, it has both found that access denials can threaten international peace and security,[316] including in the hunger resolution discussed above,[317] and it has addressed humanitarian access as one dimension of a broader threat to international peace and security.[318] The Security Council's approach to practical access challenges has taken five principal forms: (i) non-binding resolutions calling for access; (ii) binding decisions demanding access without any authorization of force; (iii) binding decisions backed by an authorization to use force to ensure humanitarian access; (iv) the imposition of

[305] ibid, para 7.
[306] ibid.
[307] ibid, para 8.
[308] Res 2417 (n 214) preambular para 16 and para 4.
[309] ibid, para 6.
[310] ibid, preambular para 18. See Chapter 6, Section 3.3.1.
[311] ibid, preambular paras 19 and 1.
[312] ibid, para 7.
[313] ibid, preambular para 17. See Section 5.3.
[314] ibid, para 9.
[315] ibid, para 10. See Chapter 3, Section 7.1.1.
[316] UNSC Res 1296 (19 April 2000) S/RES/1296, para 8.
[317] Res 2417 (n 214) para 4.
[318] See, for example, UNSC Res 794 (3 December 1992) S/RES/794, preambular para 4.

relief actions; and (v) the use of targeted sanctions.[319] Each of these five approaches is addressed in turn below. In addition to them, the Security Council often mandates the peacekeeping operations it creates to facilitate the delivery of humanitarian assistance. However, peacekeeping is addressed separately below,[320] as such mandates are not usually these operations' primary purpose.

The first and most common form of Security Council engagement on humanitarian access is through resolutions that call on, but do not demand, conflict parties to grant humanitarian access. Such calls appear in both thematic resolutions[321] and those addressing specific situations, such as Afghanistan,[322] Mali,[323] and Sudan.[324] In both cases, the language used recognizes states' authority to consent to, or refuse, humanitarian assistance. However, the Council has recently shown an increased willingness to suggest specific measures to facilitate access.[325]

A second form of engagement involves the Security Council demanding humanitarian access without authorizing the use of force to ensure compliance. This was the case in, for example, the Central African Republic (CAR),[326] Gaza,[327] and Sudan.[328] Zimmermann notes that similar calls were issued in relation to Afghanistan, Angola, Armenia/Azerbaijan, the Democratic Republic of the Congo (DRC), Gaza, Georgia, Kosovo, Rwanda, and Somalia.[329]

In a third form of engagement, the Security Council has authorized the use of force, either by a coalition of member states or a UN peace operation, to create security conditions to allow for the delivery of humanitarian assistance and, in certain cases, also to deliver humanitarian assistance and create and defend protected zones for civilians. This has occurred only three times, all during the 1990s: in Iraq, Bosnia and Herzegovina, and Somalia.

In the Iraq case, force was not expressly authorized. Towards the end of the first Gulf War in early 1991, the Kurds of northern Iraq began a rebellion, which Iraq moved to

[319] This typology of Security Council action draws on Emanuela-Chiara Gillard, 'Cross-Border Relief Operations: A Legal Perspective' (2014) OCHA Policy Series <https://www.unocha.org/sites/unocha/files/dms/Documents/Legal%20Perspective%20Cross-border%20relief%20operations.pdf> accessed 18 March 2024, 41.

[320] See Section 5.3.

[321] See, for example, UNSC Res 1502 (26 August 2003) S/RES/1502, para 4; UNSC Res 1894 (11 November 2009) S/RES/1894, para 14; UNSC Res 2175 (29 August 2014) S/RES/2175, para 3; Res 2417 (n 214) para 4; UNSC Res 2475 (20 June 2019) S/RES/2475, para 3.

[322] UNSC Res 1974 (22 March 2011) S/RES/1974, para 18; UNSC Res 2041 (22 March 2012) S/RES/2041, para 29.

[323] UNSC Res 2295 (29 June 2016) S/RES/2295, para 37.

[324] UNSC Res 2724 (8 March 2024) S/RES/2724, para 2; UNSC Res 2736 (13 June 2024) S/RES/2736, para 3.

[325] Emanuela-Chiara Gillard, 'The United Nations Security Council and Humanitarian Operations in Syria: A Legal Analysis' (*Diakonia International Humanitarian Law Centre*, 2022) <https://www.diakonia.se/ihl/news/the-united-nations-security-council-and-humanitarian-operations-in-syria-a-legal-analysis-2/> accessed 1 June 2023, 11.

[326] See, for example, UNSC Res 2134 (28 January 2014) S/RES/2134, para 26.

[327] UNSC Res 1860 (8 January 2009) S/RES/1860, para 2; UNSC Res 2712 (15 November 2023) S/RES/2712, paras 2, 4, and 5; UNSC Res 2720 (22 December 2023) S/RES/2720, para 3.

[328] See, for example, UNSC Res 2113 (30 July 2013) S/RES/2113, para 16; UNSC Res 2179 (14 October 2014) S/RES/2179, para 20; UNSC Res 2296 (29 June 2016) S/RES/2296, para 22.

[329] Zimmermann (n 264) 5. On earlier Security Council practice, see BG Ramcharan, 'The Security Council and Humanitarian Emergencies' (1991) 9 Netherlands Quarterly of Human Rights 19.

suppress, killing about 13,000 Kurds and forcing about 1.8 million to flee.[330] In April 1991, the Security Council issued resolution 688 insisting, *inter alia*, 'that Iraq allow immediate access by international humanitarian organizations to all those in need of assistance in all parts of Iraq and make available all necessary facilities for their operations'.[331] While resolution 688 recognized that Iraq's repression of its Kurdish population threatened international peace and security,[332] it did not clearly authorize the use of force, nor was it expressly adopted under Chapter VII. Nevertheless, France, the United Kingdom, and the US referred to resolution 688 to justify establishing a no-fly zone over Iraq in April 1991 without Iraqi consent. The coalition dropped supplies, took measures to protect displaced people, and created a 'safe zone' in northern Iraq to facilitate civilians' return to their homes.[333] Gillard questions whether Iraq's consent was even relevant, pointing out that the territory in question was removed from Iraq's control during the Gulf War (August 1990–February 1991), so the situation in northern Iraq was more akin to occupation.[334] In any case, by May 1991, Iraq had consented to the operation.[335]

The protection of humanitarian assistance 'became the de facto raison d'être of the UN mission' in Bosnia.[336] The Security Council became involved in Yugoslavia in February 1992 when it created the UN Protection Force (UNPROFOR),[337] which was subsequently extended to cover Bosnia and Herzegovina.[338] The Security Council issued a series of resolutions relating to humanitarian assistance to Bosnia, beginning in May 1992 with resolution 752, which called on 'all parties and others concerned to ensure that conditions are established for the effective and unhindered delivery of humanitarian assistance'.[339] The Security Council deployed mandatory language two weeks later, demanding in a decision adopted under Chapter VII 'that all parties and others concerned create immediately the necessary conditions for unimpeded delivery of humanitarian supplies to' the Bosnian capital of Sarajevo and other locations in Bosnia.[340] Acting again under Chapter VII, in mid-August, the Security Council issued a decision devoted entirely to humanitarian access, in which it noted that it was '[d]eeply disturbed by' the situation prevailing in Sarajevo, where humanitarian relief operations were being impeded by Serb forces. It called on all states 'to take nationally or through regional agencies or arrangements all measures' to facilitate the delivery of humanitarian assistance.[341] In response to this call, several states made

[330] Mary Ellen O'Connell, 'Humanitarian Assistance in Non-International Armed Conflict: the Fourth Wave of Rights, Duties and Remedies' (2001) 31 Israel Yearbook on Human Rights 183, 200.

[331] Res 688 (n 271) para 3.

[332] ibid, para 1.

[333] Christine Gray, *International Law and the Use of Force* (4th edn, OUP 2018) 362; Emanuela-Chiara Gillard, '"Safe Areas": The International Legal Framework' (2017) 99 International Review of the Red Cross 1075, 1090.

[334] Gillard (n 319) 43.

[335] O'Connell (n 330) 201.

[336] John Hillen, *Blue Helmets: The Strategy of UN Military Operations* (Brassey's 1998) 172. On the humanitarian crisis during the Bosnian war, see Bradley (n 169) 59–72.

[337] UNSC Res 743 (21 February 1992) para 2.

[338] UNSC Res 758 (8 June 1992).

[339] (15 May 1992) para 8.

[340] UNSC Res 757 (30 May 1992) para 17.

[341] UNSC Res 770 (13 August 1992) S/RES/770, preambular para 7 and para 2.

additional military personnel available to UNPROFOR and its size and mandate were enlarged to include the delivery of humanitarian relief.[342] With little improvement, in October 1992, the Security Council banned military flights from Bosnian airspace as 'an essential element for the safety of the delivery of humanitarian assistance'.[343] In April 1993, the Security Council created a 'safe area' in Srebrenica;[344] the following month additional safe areas were created in Sarajevo and other 'threatened areas'.[345] UNPROFOR was in June authorized to use force to defend these areas and to respond to any deliberate obstruction of the freedom of movement of humanitarian convoys.[346] However, Gillard points out that no additional troops were allocated for these tasks; this, along with a failure to demilitarize safe areas, contributed to the 1995 Srebrenica massacre.[347]

The Security Council issued the first in a series of resolutions relating to humanitarian assistance to Somalia in January 1992. The resolution called on all parties to facilitate the delivery of humanitarian assistance by the UN.[348] This and subsequent similar resolutions went unheeded by the de facto authorities,[349] who continued to impede relief operations. In December 1992, the Security Council adopted a Chapter VII decision authorizing member states to establish an operation that would 'use all necessary means to establish as soon as possible a secure environment for humanitarian relief operations in Somalia'.[350] Three months later, the size of the operation and its mandate were expanded to include, *inter alia*, the direct provision of humanitarian assistance.[351] The second UN Operation in Somalia (UNOSOM II) was deployed in May 1993.[352] On 5 June 1993, twenty-four of the operation's soldiers were killed and a further fifty-six were injured in a clash with Somali warlord Mohamed Farah Aidid. The Security Council responded by reaffirming that the operation was authorized 'to take all necessary measures against all those responsible for the armed attacks [. . .] including to secure the investigation of their actions and their arrest and detention for prosecution, trial and punishment'.[353] After the attack, 'the humanitarian mission quickly degenerated' and 'rapidly transformed into special operations manhunts'.[354] Then, in October 1993, two US Black Hawk helicopters were shot down by Aidid's forces, killing eighteen US soldiers; more than a thousand Somalis died in the ensuing battle to rescue the surviving American troops.[355] US President Bill Clinton

[342] UNSC Res 776 (14 September 1992) S/RES/776, preambular para 4 and para 2.

[343] UNSC Res 781 (9 October 1992) S/RES/781, preambular para 8 and para 1.

[344] UNSC Res 819 (16 April 1993) para 1.

[345] UNSC Res 824 (6 May 1993) para 3.

[346] UNSC Res 836 (4 June 1993) S/RES/836, paras 5 and 9.

[347] Gillard (n 333) 1091; see also Karin Landgren, 'Safety Zones and International Protection: A Dark Grey Area' (1995) 7 International Journal of Refugee Law 442, 445–47.

[348] UNSC Res 733 (23 January 1992) para 7.

[349] UNSC Res 746 (17 March 1992); UNSC Res 751 (24 April 1992); UNSC Res 767 (27 July 1992) S/RES/767; UNSC Res 775 (28 August 1992) S/RES/775.

[350] UNSC Res 794 (3 December 1992) S/RES/794, para 10.

[351] UNSC Res 814 (26 March 1993) S/RES/814, paras 4(a) and 5.

[352] Conor Foley, *UN Peacekeeping Operations and the Protection of Civilians* (CUP 2018) 85.

[353] UNSC Res 837 (6 June 1993) S/RES/837, para 5.

[354] Human Rights Watch, cited in Foley (n 352) 86.

[355] Foley (n 352) 87.

announced three days later that all US forces would withdraw from UNOSOM II by March 1994;[356] the operation was terminated in March 1995.[357]

The fourth form of Security Council engagement on humanitarian access is the imposition of a relief operation on a state withholding its consent to the same. This has only occurred once, in Syria from 2014. The current armed conflict in Syria began in 2011 as part of the broader Arab Spring phenomenon. Throughout the conflict, the Assad government politicized humanitarian assistance, using aid to 'reward its allies and punish its adversaries'.[358] The Security Council's response became increasingly interventionist over the course of about a year beginning in October 2013, when it adopted a Presidential Statement that addressed conflict parties' obligations in 'unprecedented detail'.[359] The Statement noted that more than 100,000 people had already been killed in the conflict and urged the Syrian government to implement a series of measures to address the most significant impediments to relief operations, including a specific suggestion of cross-border operations.[360] When the Statement proved ineffective, the Council adopted resolution 2139 in February 2014, which included several binding demands relating to humanitarian access.[361] Of particular note was paragraph 6, the legal effect of which was to *require* Syria and relevant transit states to consent to relief operations.[362]

With this demand unheeded, the Security Council in July 2014 adopted resolution 2165, taking the unprecedented step of authorizing relief operations in Syria without the government's consent.[363] The resolution imposed cross-border operations into rebel-held north-west Syria from four points in Iraq, Jordan, and Türkiye,[364] under a monitoring mechanism overseen by the Secretary-General,[365] and also authorized operations, including cross-line operations, throughout the country.[366] The cross-border arrangement was regularly re-authorized until the end of 2019, when Russia—at Syria's behest—and China began using their vetoes to progressively shrink the scope of the relief operation enabled by resolution 2165. By July 2020, only one crossing point remained: Bab al-Hawa on the Turkish border.[367] The cross-border operation continued via Bab al-Hawa until February 2023, when an earthquake struck

[356] ibid.
[357] UNSC Res 954 (4 November 1994) S/RES/954.
[358] Natasha Hall, 'Rescuing Aid in Syria' (*Centre for Strategic & International Studies*, 2022) <https://www.csis.org/analysis/rescuing-aid-syria> accessed 6 June 2023, VI.
[359] Gillard (n 325) 11.
[360] Statement by the President of the Security Council (2 October 2013) S/PRST/2013/15, 3.
[361] UNSC Res 2139 (22 February 2014) S/RES/2139, paras 4–7.
[362] Paragraph 6 of Resolution 2139 (n 361) demanded 'that all parties, in particular the Syrian authorities, promptly allow rapid, safe and unhindered humanitarian access for [... UN] humanitarian agencies and their implementing partners, including across conflict lines and across borders, in order to ensure that humanitarian assistance reaches people in need through the most direct routes'.
[363] There is debate as to whether the resolution was legally necessary; see Chapter 3, Section 4.3.2, and Rebecca Barber, 'Does International Law Permit the Provision of Humanitarian Assistance Without Host State Consent? Territorial Integrity, Necessity and the Determinative Function of the General Assembly' in Terry D. Gill and others (eds), *Yearbook of International Humanitarian Law 2020*, vol 23 (Springer 2022).
[364] UNSC Res 2165 (14 July 2014) S/RES/2165, para 2
[365] ibid, para 3.
[366] ibid, para 6.
[367] UNSC Res 2533 (11 July 2020) S/RES/2533, para 2.

Türkiye and north-west Syria and severely damaged the crossing. When resolution 2165 came up for re-authorization in July 2023, disagreements between Russia and other Council member states prevented its renewal, bringing the cross-border operation to an end.[368]

The fifth and final type of engagement is the Security Council's characterization of '[o]bstructing the delivery of humanitarian assistance [. . .] or access to, or distributions of, humanitarian assistance' as a ground for the imposition of sanctions.[369] These may include asset freezes and other financial sanctions, arms embargoes, travel bans, and restrictions on the sale of certain items. As of April 2025, seven Security Council sanctions regimes—CAR, DRC, Haiti, Mali, Somalia, South Sudan, and Yemen—included this ground,[370] and sanctions had been imposed in five of them (CAR, DRC, Mali, Somalia, and South Sudan).[371] For example, in the now-expired Mali sanctions regime, established by Security Council resolution 2374,[372] an armed group member was sanctioned because he was 'manipulating humanitarian aid to fulfil his personal interests and the political interests of' his group 'by exercising terror, threatening NGOs and controlling their operations, all of which results in obstruction and hindrance of aid'.[373] However, such sanctions are not always welcomed by humanitarians negotiating access, who caution that including humanitarian operations within sanctions regimes 'could jeopardise their ability to engage with the designated groups and undermine' perceptions of their neutrality.[374]

While the Security Council has, as outlined above, often taken steps to facilitate humanitarian access, permanent Council members have also used their veto to block access, beyond just the Syria case discussed above. In 2016, for example, China and Russia vetoed a proposed week-long ceasefire that would have allowed humanitarian assistance into Aleppo, Syria.[375] More recently, in 2024, the US vetoed a resolution

[368] Security Council Report, 'In Hindsight: The Demise of the Syria Cross-Border Aid Mechanism' (31 July 2023) <https://www.securitycouncilreport.org/monthly-forecast/2023-08/in-hindsight-the-demise-of-the-syria-cross-border-aid-mechanism.php> accessed 28 March 2025.

[369] This language, drawn from resolution 2399 ((30 January 2018) S/RES/2399, para 21(f)), is the boilerplate language typically used by the Security Council. See also Res 2417 (n 214) para 9.

[370] CAR: UNSC Res 2399 (30 January 2018) S/RES/2399, para 21(f); DRC: UNSC Res 2293 (23 June 2016) S/RES/2293, para 7(f); Haiti: UNSC Res 2653 (21 October 2022) S/RES/2653, para 16(g); Mali: UNSC Res 2374 (5 September 2017) S/RES/2374, para 8(e) (regime expired in 2023); Somalia: UNSC Res 1844 (20 November 2008) S/RES/1844, para 8(c); South Sudan: UNSC Res 2206 (3 March 2015) S/RES/2206, para 7(f); Yemen: UNSC Res 2216 (14 April 2015) S/RES/2216, para 19. See, generally, Benjamin Spatz, Oliver Windridge, and Catriona Murdoch, 'Sanctions as a Mechanism for Accountability for Starvation Crimes' in Bridget Conley and others (eds), *Accountability for Mass Starvation: Testing the Limits of the Law* (OUP 2022).

[371] UK Foreign, Commonwealth & Development Office and Ministry of Defence, 'Conflict, Hunger and International Humanitarian Law: A Practitioner's Legal Handbook' (2025) <https://www.gov.uk/government/publications/conflict-hunger-and-international-humanitarian-law-a-practitioners-legal-handbook> accessed 23 May 2025, 103–04.

[372] (5 September 2017) S/RES/2374, para 9.

[373] UNSC Mali Sanctions Committee (10 July 2019) MLI.004, cited in Weizmann (n 291) 210.

[374] Dapo Akande and Emanuela-Chiara Gillard, 'Promoting Compliance with the Rules Regulating Humanitarian Relief Operations in Armed Conflict: Some Challenges' (2017) 50 Israel Law Review 119, 134.

[375] Jennifer Trahan, *Existing Legal Limits to Security Council Veto Power in the Face of Atrocity Crimes* (CUP 2020) 287–88.

concerning a humanitarian ceasefire in Gaza,[376] and Russia vetoed a resolution calling for the delivery of humanitarian assistance in Sudan.[377]

4.4.3. Counterterrorism

While the Security Council has used sanctions in response to humanitarian access obstructions, when imposed in the counterterrorism context, sanctions, as well as states' criminal counterterrorism measures, can themselves impede the delivery of aid. Awareness of the human cost of sanctions emerged following the comprehensive sanctions imposed on Iraq following its 1990 invasion of Kuwait.[378] In 1999, the Security Council imposed its first 'smart' (targeted) sanctions.[379] Nevertheless, the sanctions and other counterterror measures imposed after the terrorist attacks of 11 September 2001 (9/11) posed major challenges for humanitarian actors. This led to important literature on the interface between counterterrorism and humanitarian action.[380] This section draws on it to explain the problem and how the Security Council has responded.

The international community's counterterrorism efforts, particularly since 9/11, have focused on suppressing terrorist financing. This has been pursued in two main ways. First, designated terrorist groups are sanctioned,[381] either by the UN Security Council or through autonomous measures adopted by regional organizations, such

[376] Edith Lederer, 'The US Vetoes an Arab-Backed UN Resolution Demanding an Immediate Humanitarian Ceasefire in Gaza' (*AP*, 20 February 2024) <https://apnews.com/article/un-israel-palestinians-gaza-ceasefire-resolution-vote-350c86ef261bf1a00a2515cf22764de5> accessed 22 April 2025.

[377] Daphne Psaledakis and David Brunnstrom, 'Russia Vetoes UN Security Council Action on Sudan War' (*Reuters*, 18 November 2024) <https://www.reuters.com/world/russia-vetoes-un-security-council-action-sudan-war-2024-11-18/> accessed 22 April 2025.

[378] See Matthew Craven, 'Humanitarianism and the Quest for Smarter Sanctions' (2002) 13 European Journal of International Law 43.

[379] UNSC Res 1267 (15 October 1999) S/RES/1267.

[380] See the 2021 issue of the International Review of the Red Cross titled 'Counterterrorism, Sanctions and War', especially Tristan Ferraro, 'International Humanitarian Law, Principled Humanitarian Action, Counterterrorism and Sanctions: Some Perspectives on Selected Issues' (2021) 103 International Review of the Red Cross 109 and Nathalie Weizmann, 'Respecting International Humanitarian Law and Safeguarding Humanitarian Action in Counterterrorism Measures: United Nations Security Council Resolutions 2462 and 2482 Point the Way' (2021) 103 International Review of the Red Cross 325. See also Naz Modirzadeh, Dustin A. Lewis, and Claude Bruderlein, 'Humanitarian Engagement under Counter-Terrorism: A Conflict of Norms and the Emerging Policy Landscape' (2011) 93 International Review of the Red Cross 623; Emanuela-Chiara Gillard, 'Recommendations for Reducing Tensions in the Interplay Between Sanctions, Counterterrorism Measures and Humanitarian Action' (*Chatham House*, 2017) <https://www.chathamhouse.org/sites/default/files/publications/research/CHHJ5596_NSAG_iv_research_paper_1708_WEB.pdf> accessed 31 March 2025; Jessica S. Burniske and Naz K. Modirzadeh, *Pilot Empirical Survey Study on the Impact of Counterterrorism Measures on Humanitarian Action* (*Counterterrorism and Humanitarian Engagement Project*, 2017); David McKeever, 'International Humanitarian Law and Counter-terrorism: Fundamental Values, Conflicting Obligations' (2020) 69 International & Comparative Law Quarterly 43; Emanuela-Chiara Gillard and Nathalie Weizmann, 'Humanitarian Relief in Situations of Armed Conflict' in Robin Geiß and Nils Melzer (eds), *The Oxford Handbook of the International Law of Global Security* (OUP 2021); Emanuela-Chiara Gillard, 'IHL and the Humanitarian Impact of Counterterrorism Measures and Sanctions' (*Chatham House*, 2021) <https://www.chathamhouse.org/2021/09/ihl-and-humanitarian-impact-counterterrorism-measures-and-sanctions> accessed 31 March 2025 (Gillard 2021); Sue E. Eckert, 'Counterterrorism, Sanctions and Financial Access Challenges: Course Corrections to Safeguard Humanitarian Action' (2021) 103 International Review of the Red Cross 415.

[381] Gillard and Weizmann (n 380) 519.

as the European Union, or individual states. These sanctions, commonly referred to as 'financial sanctions', freeze assets and prohibit the provision of funds and other resources to designated terrorist groups.[382] Second, the international community has criminalized activities that provide direct or indirect material support to designated terrorist groups. The International Convention for the Suppression of the Financing of Terrorism (Terrorist Financing Convention) requires states to criminalize the provision or collection of 'funds with the intention that they should be used or in the knowledge that they are to be used, in full or in part, in order to carry out' a terrorist act.[383] Similarly, starting with resolution 1373,[384] which was adopted in the weeks following 9/11, the Security Council has adopted a series of decisions requiring that states prohibit individuals and entities from making any funds, financial assets, economic resources, or financial or other services available, directly or indirectly, for the benefit of persons who commit, attempt to commit, facilitate, or participate in terrorist acts.[385] Security Council sanctions regimes designate terrorist groups, while under the Terrorist Financing Convention and the 1373 series of decisions, states make their own terrorist designations. Groups that have been designated as terrorist entities include Al Shabaab in Somalia, Al-Qaeda in the Arabian Peninsula in Yemen, Boko Haram in Nigeria, ISIS in Syria, and Hamas in Gaza.[386]

Both financial sanctions and criminal measures can obstruct humanitarian work in areas where designated groups operate or control territory. Humanitarian organizations risk violating financial sanctions, criminal measures, or both, if, for example, they make incidental payments to such groups (e.g. by paying a tax or a toll), provide medical care to a member of a designated group[387] in line with medical ethics and IHL,[388] or if assistance is diverted en route to its destination. This risk has led some humanitarian organizations to scale back their operations, and has made it more difficult for them to operate in accordance with the core humanitarian principles, particularly the principle of impartiality.[389] Financial sanctions and criminal measures also raise problems because banks must comply with them.[390] This has led to 'de-risking', meaning that banks refuse to serve humanitarian organizations that operate in places where designated groups are present.[391] Akande and Gillard note that the 'impact of

[382] ibid, 519–20.
[383] (Adopted 9 December 1999, entered into force 10 April 2002) 2178 UNTS 197, art 2.
[384] UNSC Res 1373 (28 September 2001) S/RES/1373.
[385] See, for example, UNSC Res 2178 (24 September 2014) S/RES/2178; UNSC Res 2462 (28 March 2019) S/RES/2462 (Res 2462); UNSC Res 2482 (19 July 2019) S/RES/2482 (Res 2482). For an overview of this series of decisions, see Weizmann (n 380) 328–30 and Gillard 2021 (n 380) 12–27.
[386] Gillard and Weizmann (n 380) 521.
[387] ibid.
[388] Geneva Convention for the Amelioration of the Condition of the Wounded and Sick in Armed Forces in the Field (adopted 12 August 1949, entered into force 21 October 1950) 75 UNTS 31, art 12; Geneva Convention for the Amelioration of the Condition of Wounded, Sick and Shipwrecked Members of Armed Forces at Sea (adopted 12 August 1949, entered into force 21 October 1950) 75 UNTS 85, art 12; API (n 296) art 10; APII (n 296) art 7. See Chapter 3, Section 5.1.
[389] See Chapter 2, Section 4.
[390] Gillard and Weizmann (n 380).
[391] Weizmann (n 380) 339.

banking-sector restrictions is so significant that some humanitarian actors have noted that banks are effectively dictating where they can operate'.[392] Finally, donor states have specified in humanitarian funding agreements that funds cannot be used in ways that benefit designated groups.[393]

Initially, the Security Council's responses to these challenges were ad hoc and rare. It decided with resolution 1916 in 2010 that the financial sanctions it had imposed on Al Shabaab 'shall not apply to the payment of funds, other financial assets or economic resources necessary to ensure the timely delivery of urgently needed humanitarian assistance in Somalia, by the' UN, 'its specialized agencies or programmes, humanitarian organizations having observer status with the United Nations General Assembly that provide humanitarian assistance, or their implementing partners'.[394] Over ten years later in 2021, following the Taliban's return to power in Afghanistan, the Council adopted its second humanitarian carve out.[395] Financial sanctions imposed on Haiti in 2022 also included a humanitarian carve out.[396] The Security Council adopted a case-by-case approach to exempting humanitarian assistance from the sanctions it imposed on North Korea in 2017.[397]

Early indications of a more systemic approach to the counterterrorism-humanitarian interface appeared in 2019, when the Security Council adopted two resolutions, 2462 on the financing of terrorism and 2482 on the links between terrorism and organized crime, that both mentioned states' international legal obligations, including under IHL.[398] Major change, though, did not arrive until 2022, when under Irish leadership the Council adopted its landmark Chapter VII resolution 2664.

Resolution 2664's preamble notes 'the importance of assessing potential humanitarian impacts prior to a Council decision to establish a sanctions regime'.[399] Further, it recalls that states must ensure that measures to implement sanctions comply with their obligations under international law, including IHL, and notes IHL rules regarding respect for and protection of humanitarian personnel and consignments and on 'the non-punishment of any person for carrying out medical activities compatible with medical ethics'.[400] Additionally, the preamble emphasizes that counterterrorism measures 'are not intended to have adverse humanitarian consequences for civilian populations' or for 'humanitarian activities or those carrying them out' and expresses the Security Council's 'readiness to review, adjust and terminate' its sanctions regimes 'to minimize unintended adverse humanitarian effects'.[401]

[392] Dapo Akande and Emanuela-Chiara Gillard, 'Conflict-induced Food Insecurity and the War Crime of Starvation of Civilians as a Method of Warfare: The Underlying Rules of International Humanitarian Law' (2019) 17 Journal of International Criminal Justice 753, 776.

[393] Weizmann (n 380) 337–39; Gillard 2021 (n 380) 45–53.

[394] (19 March 2010) S/RES/1916, para 5.

[395] UNSC Res 2615 (22 December 2021) S/RES/2615, para 1.

[396] UNSC Res 2653 (21 October 2022) S/RES/2653, para 10.

[397] UNSC Res 2397 (22 December 2017) S/RES/2397, para 25. See Eckert (n 380) 428–31.

[398] Res 2462 (n 385) paras 5–6; Res 2482 (n 385) para 16. For analysis of these resolutions, see Weizmann (n 380) 342–48.

[399] UNSC Res 2664 (9 December 2022) S/RES/2664 (Res 2664) preambular para 5.

[400] ibid, preambular para 7.

[401] ibid, preambular paras 8–9.

Resolution 2664's key operative paragraphs decide that 'the provision, processing or payment of funds, other financial assets, or economic resources, or the provision of goods and services necessary to ensure the timely delivery of humanitarian assistance' by a wide range of humanitarian actors 'are permitted and are not a violation of' existing or future financial sanctions imposed by the Security Council or its sanctions committees.[402] The Security Council went on to invoke this humanitarian exception in its ISIL (Da'esh) and Al-Qaeda sanctions regime.[403]

Resolution 2664's scope is limited: it applies only to Security Council sanctions, not to autonomous regimes imposed by regional organizations or individual states. Nor does resolution 2664 explicitly cover criminal measures adopted by states pursuant to the Terrorist Financing Convention or the 1373 series of decisions. Resolution 2664 does, however, urge states 'when designing and applying measures to counter the financing of terrorism, to take into account the potential effect of those measures on exclusively humanitarian activities'.[404] The decision thus sends a clear signal that humanitarian exemptions should be factored into how member states implement counterterrorism measures, including under the Terrorist Financing Convention and the 1373 series of decisions. Kapoor and others even argue that resolution 2664's paragraph on conflicts, which provides that the humanitarian exception supersedes previous conflicting Security Council resolutions,[405] means that states 'arguably need to evaluate what aspects of their implementation of resolution 1373 (2001) et seq.—and any other potentially relevant Security Council resolutions—may be implicated by resolution 2664'.[406] They further argue that where there is a conflict between a state's 'interpretations of and corresponding measures implementing previous Security Council resolutions and its interpretations of and corresponding measures implementing resolution 2664', the state 'needs to take action to bring the former into alignment with the latter'.[407]

Resolution 2664 includes several implementation mechanisms. It requests the ERC to brief every Security Council sanctions committee within the resolution's mandate annually on 'the delivery of humanitarian assistance' and directs sanctions committees to 'assist Member States in properly understanding and fully implementing' resolution 2664 and to monitor its implementation.[408] It also requested that the Secretary-General, within nine months, issue a report 'on unintended adverse humanitarian consequences of Security Council sanctions measures'.[409]

[402] ibid, paras 1 and 4.

[403] UNSC Res 2761 (6 December 2024) S/RES/2761, para 1.

[404] Res 2664 (n 399) preambular para 6.

[405] ibid, para 4.

[406] Radhika Kapoor, Dustin Lewis, and Naz Modirzadeh, 'An Interpretive Note for UN Member States on Security Council Resolution 2664 (2022)' (*Harvard Law School Program on International Law and Armed Conflict*, March 2023) <https://hls.harvard.edu/wp-content/uploads/2023/09/HLS-PILAC-Res.-2664-Interpretive-Note.pdf> accessed 2 April 2025, 45.

[407] ibid.

[408] Res 2664 (n 399) paras 5–6.

[409] ibid, para 7. The report is: UN Secretary-General, 'Implementation of Security Council Resolution 2664 (2022): Report of the Secretary-General' (8 September 2023) S/2023/658.

5. Operational entities

Several operational UN entities play major humanitarian assistance roles: UNHCR, UNICEF, WFP, and UNRWA. The mandate, governance, and practical humanitarian assistance work of each is briefly outlined below. The other UN entities and UN system components with IASC membership (OHCHR, UNDP, UNFPA, UN-HABITAT, UN Women, FAO, IOM, and WHO) are not addressed because they play a relatively smaller role in relation to humanitarian assistance. Indeed, Forsythe terms UNHCR, UNICEF, and WFP the 'big three', noting that as of late 2022, they had together received about 40 per cent of all global humanitarian funding for the year.[410] This section also addresses UN peacekeeping operations and SPMs. Since the UN and its personnel—including almost all the staff of the entities discussed in this section—enjoy privileges and immunities that facilitate humanitarian work, these are addressed first.

5.1. Privileges and immunities

Privileges and immunities are a legal tool that allow the UN and its personnel to operate independently and effectively, including in politically sensitive or high-risk humanitarian environments. Rooted in the principle of functionality[411]—that an international organization must be able to carry out the mandate conferred upon it by states—they protect the UN from interference by states and facilitate the rapid, impartial provision of humanitarian assistance.[412] The UN's property, assets, and officials, and experts on mission for the UN,[413] enjoy privileges and immunities pursuant to article 105 of the UN Charter and the Convention on the Privileges and Immunities of the United Nations (the General Convention).[414] Privileges and immunities may also derive from headquarters and host country agreements.

Privileges and immunities derived from the General Convention that facilitate the UN's provision of humanitarian assistance include the organization's legal personality;[415] its immunity from every form of legal process;[416] the inviolability of UN premises and the immunity of its property and assets from search and seizure;[417] its freedom from financial controls and regulations;[418] its exemptions from import

[410] David P Forsythe, *The Contemporary International Committee of the Red Cross: Challenges, Changes, Controversies* (CUP 2024) 28.

[411] *Obligations of Israel in Relation to the Presence and Activities of the United Nations, Other International Organizations and Third States in and in Relation to the Occupied Palestinian Territory* (Advisory Opinion) 2025 <https://www.icj-cij.org/sites/default/files/case-related/196/196-20251022-adv-01-00-en.pdf> accessed 31 October 2025 (*Israel Obligations AO*) para 183.

[412] See ibid, paras 188–215.

[413] The ICJ addressed the meaning of this term in *Applicability of Article VI, Section 22, of the Convention on the Privileges and Immunities of the United Nations* (Advisory Opinion) [1989] ICJ Rep 177 (*Muzila*).

[414] (Adopted 13 February 1946, entered into force 17 September 1946) 1 UNTS 15.

[415] ibid, art I, s 1.

[416] ibid, art II, s 2.

[417] ibid, art II, s 3.

[418] ibid, art II, s 5.

restrictions, taxes, and customs duties;[419] and its entitlement to most-favoured-nation treatment in relation to communications.[420]

The General Convention left it to the Secretary-General to specify the categories of UN official who would enjoy protection.[421] He specified, and the General Assembly agreed, that 'officials' within the meaning of the General Convention consists of 'all members of the staff of the United Nations, with the exception of those who are recruited locally and are assigned to hourly rates'.[422] UN peacekeepers' privileges and immunities derive from agreements between the parties involved, known as status of forces agreements.[423] UN officials enjoy functional immunity from legal process,[424] while senior UN officials enjoy diplomatic immunity.[425] The Secretary-General may waive an official's immunity if it 'would impede the course of justice'.[426] UN officials also enjoy immunity from immigration restrictions and alien registration.[427] They must be allowed to travel on a UN-issued laissez-passer[428] and the visa applications of laissez-passer holders must 'be dealt with as speedily as possible'.[429] In view of these privileges, the UN maintains that its personnel 'travelling to fulfil their functions [. . .] should be granted freedom of movement by all Member States'.[430] The foregoing privileges and immunities apply equally during peacetime and armed conflict,[431] and may not be 'qualified or overridden by any demands of military expediency or security'.[432]

5.2. General Assembly semi-autonomous subsidiary organs

Other than OCHA and peacekeeping operations, all operational UN bodies with major humanitarian assistance roles are subsidiary to the General Assembly.[433] The General Assembly's many subsidiary organs are not classified in any consistent way.[434] Those relevant to humanitarian assistance and covered here all fall into the category Higgins and others term 'semi-autonomous subsidiary organs'.[435] This category has also been termed, notably by the UN itself, 'funds and programmes'.[436] Organs in this category 'possess a considerable amount of autonomy from the principal organs that

419 ibid, art II, s 7.
420 ibid, art II, s 9.
421 ibid, art V, s 17.
422 UNGA Res 76 (I) (7 December 1946) para 1.
423 Higgins and others (n 7) 607.
424 General Convention (n 414) art V, s 18(a).
425 ibid, art V, s 19.
426 ibid, art V, s 20.
427 ibid, art V, s 18(d).
428 ibid, art VII, s 24.
429 ibid, art VII, s 25.
430 'The Practice of the United Nations, the Specialized Agencies and the International Atomic Energy Agency Concerning their Status, Privileges and Immunities: Study Prepared by the Secretariat' (1967) II Yearbook of the International Law Commission, A/CN.4/L.118, para 364.
431 *Israel Obligations AO* (n 411) para 196.
432 UN Juridical Yearbook 2003, part 2, ch IV, 522.
433 See UN Charter (n 3) arts 7(2) and 22.
434 Higgins and others (n 7) 157.
435 ibid, 188.
436 <https://www.un.org/en/delegate/page/un-system-chart> accessed 8 April 2025.

created them and from the UN more broadly', notably in terms of the 'nature of their work, their distinct organizational structure (including, frequently, an executive head and staff), the fact that they function on a continuing basis, the fact that they are generally financed outside the regular [UN] budget, and the fact that, in carrying out their mandate, these subsidiary organs have the authority to make final decisions within their terms of reference'.[437] Higgins and others go on to explain that as a result of this autonomy, these organs 'have much in common with UN specialized agencies'; however, unlike specialized agencies, they do not enjoy international legal personality.[438]

5.2.1. The Office of the United Nations High Commissioner for Refugees

The General Assembly created UNHCR in 1950 in response to the displacement caused by World War II.[439] UNHCR's original mandate was to provide refugees—as defined in the organization's Statute and,[440] subsequently, the Convention relating to the Status of Refugees (Refugee Convention) and its Protocol relating to the Status of Refugees[441]—with international protection and to seek 'permanent solutions' to their plight through voluntary repatriation or 'assimilation within new national communities'.[442] Initially created for a three-year term,[443] UNHCR's mandate was extended several times before, in 2004, being renewed 'until the refugee problem is solved'.[444]

The scope of UNHCR's work has expanded considerably over time. Its humanitarian assistance role grew during the 1980s as it shifted away from protection work towards providing assistance to refugees in camps,[445] often through NGO 'implementing partners'.[446] This humanitarian assistance role expanded further during the 1990s, especially in the second half of the decade, when UNHCR began to work increasingly with IDPs.[447] While the organization has always been able to 'engage in such additional activities [. . .] as the General Assembly may determine',[448] in 1998 the General Assembly formally extended UNHCR's mandate to include 'providing humanitarian assistance and protection' to IDPs further to 'specific requests from the Secretary-General or the competent organs of the' UN.[449] This provided a

437 Higgins and others (n 7) 188–89 (internal quotations and citations omitted).

438 ibid, 190.

439 UNGA Res 428 (V) (14 December 1950) A/RES/428(V).

440 ibid, Annex (UNHCR Statute) para 6.

441 (Adopted 28 July 1951, entered into force 22 April 1954) 189 UNTS 137 (Refugee Convention) art 1A(2); Protocol relating to the Status of Refugees (adopted 31 January 1967, entered into force 4 October 1967) 606 UNTS 267, art I(2). These provisions together define a refugee as any person who 'owing to a well-founded fear of being persecuted for reasons of race, religion, nationality, membership of a particular social group or political opinion, is outside the country of his nationality and is unable or, owing to such fear, is unwilling to avail himself of the protection of that country; or who, not having a nationality and being outside the country of his former habitual residence as a result of such events, is unable or, owing to such fear, is unwilling to return to it'.

442 UNHCR Statute (n 440) para 1.

443 ibid, para 5.

444 UNGA Res 58/153 (24 February 2004) A/RES/58/153, para 9.

445 Alexander Betts, Gil Loescher, and James Milner, *UNHCR: The Politics and Practice of Refugee Protection* (2nd edn, Routledge 2012) 3.

446 Forsythe (n 410) 28.

447 Betts and others (n 445) 3.

448 UNHCR Statute (n 440) para 9.

449 UNGA Res 53/125 (12 February 1999) A/RES/53/125, para 16.

clear basis for UNHCR's IDP work, though not a general or exclusive IDP mandate.[450] UNHCR's shift away from protection to the provision of humanitarian assistance has been criticized. Aleinikoff and Zamore argue that the organization has moved from a focus on 'rights, asylum, and permanent resettlement in the West, to safety and short term assistance in the region of origin'.[451] By the second decade of the new millennium, UNHCR's work had grown further to also include stateless people, migrants, and people affected by disasters.[452] The coordination roles assigned to UNHCR reflect this broad scope of work. As mentioned above, it is the IASC cluster lead for camp coordination and management, shelter in situations of armed conflict, and protection.[453] It also plays a normative role further to 'its duty of supervising the application of' the Refugee Convention.[454]

UNHCR's authority derives from the General Assembly, which can set policy directives for the agency and requires it to report annually through ECOSOC.[455] The agency's principal governance and advisory body, the Executive Committee (ExCom), is established under UNHCR's Statute, which empowered ECOSOC to create 'an advisory committee on refugees' comprised of member states.[456] ECOSOC established this committee in 1951, and—at the General Assembly's request—reconstituted it in 1958. ExCom may advise the High Commissioner on any aspect of their work in the field of international protection[457] and approve the use of funds as well as proposed programmes and projects.[458]

5.2.2. The United Nations Children's Fund

UNICEF was created by the General Assembly in 1946, further to a recommendation from ECOSOC, originally as an emergency fund for the benefit of children in countries liberated from Axis powers or receiving UNRRA assistance and for 'child health purposes generally'.[459] Today, UNICEF is mandated to 'advocate for the protection of children's rights, to help meet their basic needs and to expand their opportunities to reach their full potential', in accordance with the Convention on the Rights of the Child.[460] This includes the provision of humanitarian assistance in both armed conflict and peacetime. UNICEF's approach to humanitarian action is outlined in its 2020 'Core Commitments for Children in Humanitarian Action', which sets out the organization's overarching commitments in relation to preparedness, coordination, supply and logistics, humanitarian access, protection from sexual exploitation

[450] Walter Kälin, *Internal Displacement and the Law* (OUP 2023) 211.

[451] Alexander Aleinikoff and Leah Zamore, *The Arc of Protection: Reforming the International Refugee Regime* (Stanford University Press 2019) 23.

[452] Betts and others (n 445) 3.

[453] See Section 3.2.

[454] Refugee Convention (n 441) art 35.

[455] ECOSOC may also provide policy guidance to UNHCR (UNHCR Statute (n 440) para 3).

[456] UNHCR Statute (n 440) para 4.

[457] UNGA Res 1166 (XII) (26 November 1957) para 5(b).

[458] ECOSOC Res 672 (XXV) (30 April 1958) para 2(c).

[459] UNGA Res 57 (I) (11 December 1946) A/RES/57(I), para 1.

[460] Executive Board of the United Nations Children's Fund, 'Report on the First, Second, and Third Regular Sessions and Annual Session of 1996' (1996) E/ICEF/1996/12/Rev.1 <https://www.unicef.org/executiveboard/media/1286/file/1996-12-Rev1-Board_report_annex-Compendium_of_decisions_1996-EN-ODS.pdf> accessed 18 August 2025, 122.

and abuse, and accountability, as well as sectoral commitments in areas including health and nutrition.[461] UNICEF's Office of Emergency Programmes is responsible for emergency preparedness, information gathering and dissemination, and coordination during emergency relief operations.[462] UNICEF is the IASC cluster lead for nutrition and WASH, and the co-lead (with Save the Children) for education in emergencies. Like UNHCR, UNICEF also has a normative role, derived from its mandate to promote the effective implementation of the Convention on the Rights of the Child.[463] UNICEF is governed by an executive board 'responsible for providing inter-governmental support to and supervision of' the organization's activities, 'in accordance with the overall policy guidance of the General Assembly' and ECOSOC.[464] The Executive Board approves UNICEF's programmes[465] and its financial plans and budgets.[466]

5.2.3. The World Food Programme

WFP was created by the General Assembly in 1961 as a joint UN and FAO initiative to facilitate 'the best possible use of food surpluses for the economic development of the less developed countries'.[467] Initially conceived as an 'experimental' three-year initiative,[468] WFP was extended in 1965 'for as long as multilateral food aid is found feasible and desirable'.[469] WFP has a broad mandate consisting of responding to food crises, improving nutrition, and reducing populations' vulnerability to food insecurity.[470] It now undertakes the latter in part through the Integrated Food Security Phase Classification initiative (IPC),[471] as a member of its High Level Executive Committee, its Global Steering Committee, and its Technical Advisory Group.[472] WFP's practical work consists primarily of providing and delivering food aid in armed conflict and peacetime emergencies.[473] It has particular expertise addressing the challenges of inadequate infrastructure and transportation, reaching individuals in remote locations, and setting up communications infrastructure.[474] Accordingly, WFP is the IASC cluster lead for logistics and emergency telecommunications, as well as the co-lead (with FAO) for food security. WFP also manages the UN Humanitarian Air Service,

[461] <https://www.unicef.org/emergencies/core-commitments-children> accessed 15 April 2025, 24–29 and 36–67.

[462] Peter Walker and Daniel Maxwell, *Shaping the Humanitarian World* (Routledge 2008) 103.

[463] (Adopted 20 November 1989, entered into force 2 September 1990) 1577 UNTS 3, art 45.

[464] UNGA Res 48/162 (14 January 1994) A/RES/48/162, Annex (Res 48/162) para 21.

[465] ibid, para 22(e).

[466] ibid, para 22(f).

[467] UNGA Res 1714 (XVI) (19 December 1961) A/RES/1714(XVI), preambular para 2.

[468] ibid.

[469] UNGA Res 2095 (XX) (20 December 1965) para 1.

[470] Walker and Maxwell (n 462) 102.

[471] The IPC is a multi-stakeholder global initiative that operates a classification system, comprised of five levels (minimal, stressed, crisis, emergency, catastrophe/famine), to 'determine the severity and extent of acute and chronic food insecurity and acute malnutrition situations within countries, according to internationally recognised standards' (<https://www.ipcinfo.org/ipcinfo-website/ipc-overview-and-classification-system/en/> accessed 29 May 2025).

[472] IPC, 'IPC Partnership and Governance' <https://www.ipcinfo.org/ipcinfo-website/ipc-global-partnership-and-programme/partnership/en/> accessed 23 May 2025.

[473] Walker and Maxwell (n 462) 102.

[474] ibid.

which provides air transportation for humanitarian personnel and light cargo to and from crisis-affected areas, particularly when normal transport links have broken down due to armed conflict or disaster. WFP is governed by an executive board composed of UN and FAO member states,[475] which is subject to policy guidance from the General Assembly and ECOSOC,[476] as well as from certain FAO bodies.

5.2.4. The United Nations Relief and Works Agency for Palestine Refugees in the Near East

UNRWA is the institutional component of the 'distinctive institutional and normative regime applicable to Palestinian refugees'.[477] During the 1948–1949 Arab-Israeli war, the General Assembly established the United Nations Conciliation Commission for Palestine (UNCCP) to reach 'final settlement of all questions outstanding between' the conflict parties, including the Palestinian refugee issue.[478] The same resolution also affirmed that 'refugees wishing to return to their homes and live at peace with their neighbours should be permitted to do so at the earliest practicable date'.[479] However, UNCCP was 'powerless in the face of Israel's refusal to allow' Palestinians to return.[480] In 1949, the General Assembly recognized that 'continued assistance for the relief of the Palestine refugees is necessary to prevent conditions of starvation and distress among them and to further conditions of peace and stability'.[481] Accordingly, it created UNRWA to conduct 'direct relief and works programmes' and 'to consult with the interested Near Eastern Governments concerning measures to be taken by them preparatory to the time when international assistance for relief and works projects is no longer available'.[482]

UNRWA's mandate was designed to complement that of UNCCP, which would continue its conciliation efforts, so UNRWA was not given any durable solutions role. However, UNCCP terminated its repatriation, resettlement, and compensation work in 1952, without having solved these problems.[483] This created what has become known as the UNRWA 'protection gap'.[484] UNHCR does not fill this gap because when it was created in 1950, Palestinian refugees were excluded from its mandate.[485] This exclusion was affirmed in the Refugee Convention when it was adopted the following year.[486]

475 UNGA Res 50/8 (1 November 1995) A/RES/50/8, para 1.
476 Res 48/162 (n 464) para 30.
477 Ardi Imseis, *The United Nations and the Question of Palestine: Rule by Law and the Structure of International Legal Subalternity* (CUP 2023) 137. On UNRWA, see also Benjamin Schiff, *Refugees Unto the Third Generation: UN Aid to Palestinians* (Syracuse University Press 1995); Francesca Albanese and Lex Takkenberg, *Palestinian Refugees in International Law* (2nd edn, OUP 2020) ch II; Anne Irfan, *Refuge and Resistance: Palestinians and the International Refugee System* (Columbia University Press 2023).
478 UNGA Res 194 (III) (11 December 1948) para 5.
479 ibid, para 11.
480 Imseis (n 477) 138.
481 UNGA Res 302 (IV) (8 December 1949) A/RES/302(IV) (Res 302), para 5.
482 ibid, para 7.
483 Imseis (n 477) 138.
484 Michael Kagan, 'Is there Really a Protection Gap? UNRWA's Role Vis-à-Vis Palestinian Refugees' (2010) 28 Refugee Survey Quarterly 511.
485 UNHCR Statute (n 440) para 7(c).
486 Refugee Convention (n 441) art 1D.

As it is the only UN entity with a general mandate to assist Palestinian refugees, the General Assembly has renewed UNRWA's temporary mandate every three years since the organization was created in 1949.[487] During the 1967 Six-Day War, Israel occupied Gaza and the West Bank (including East Jerusalem). Following this, the General Assembly expanded UNRWA's mandate to include individuals displaced by the 1967 armed conflict[488] and Israel concluded an agreement with UNRWA. The agreement provided that 'UNRWA would continue its assistance to Palestine refugees, with full co-operation of Israeli authorities, in the West Bank and Gaza Strip areas' and that Israel would facilitate this.[489] UNRWA now provides well over five million Palestinian refugees[490] in Gaza, the West Bank (including East Jerusalem), Jordan, Lebanon, and Syria with education, health care, relief, and social services.[491] Its staff does this work at considerable personal risk. As of July 2025, over 320 UNRWA staff had been killed since hostilities between Israel and Hamas escalated following the attacks of 7 October 2023.[492] Given its very specific mandate, UNRWA is not part of the humanitarian coordination system outlined in Section 3.2 above. Its operational head is known as the Commissioner General; this official is supported by an Advisory Commission composed of UN member states.[493] UNRWA is governed directly by the General Assembly.[494]

In October 2024, following Israeli allegations that UNRWA staff were involved in the 7 October 2023 attacks,[495] the Israeli Knesset (parliament) passed two laws regarding UNRWA. One law banned UNRWA from conducting any activities inside Israel, defined to include East Jerusalem, Gaza, and the West Bank. The other designated UNRWA as a terrorist group, effectively prohibiting state interaction with the organization.[496] The General Assembly responded by issuing a resolution in support of UNRWA and 'deploring' the new laws.[497] Both Israeli laws took effect on 30 January 2025, forcing international UNRWA staff based in East Jerusalem to leave Israel; the organization continues to operate in Gaza and the West Bank, though at significantly reduced capacity.[498]

[487] Most recently in UNGA Res 77/123 (12 December 2022) A/RES/77/123, para 6.

[488] UNGA Res 2252 (4 July 1967) A/RES/ES-V/2252, para 6.

[489] Cited in *Israel Obligations AO* (n 411) para 50.

[490] UNRWA defines a 'Palestinian refugee' as any person 'whose normal place of residence was Palestine during the period 1 June 1946 and 15 May 1948, and who lost both home and means of livelihood as a result of the 1948 conflict' (Imseis (n 477) 164–65).

[491] Imseis (n 477) 139.

[492] UNRWA, 'Situation Report #179 on the Humanitarian Crisis in the Gaza Strip and the West Bank, including East Jerusalem' (11 July 2025) <https://www.unrwa.org/resources/reports/unrwa-situation-report-179-situation-gaza-strip-and-west-bank-including-east-jerusalem>. See Section 5.4.

[493] Res 302 (n 481) para 8.

[494] ibid, para 9(a).

[495] See Independent Review Group on UNRWA, 'Final Report for the United Nations Secretary-General: Independent Review of Mechanisms and Procedures to Ensure Adherence by UNRWA to the Humanitarian Principle of Neutrality' (20 April 2024) <https://www.un.org/unispal/document/report-independent-review-group-on-unrwa-22april2024/> accessed 2 May 2024.

[496] Andrew Roth, 'Israeli Parliament Votes to Ban UNRWA from Israel Within 90 Days' (*The Guardian*, 28 October 2024) <https://www.theguardian.com/world/2024/oct/28/israeli-lawmakers-pass-bill-that-could-halt-unwra-relief-work-in-gaza> accessed 28 April 2025.

[497] UNGA Res ES-10/25 (16 December 2024) A/RES/ES-10/25, para 2.

[498] Peter Beaumont and Sam Jones, 'International UNRWA Staff Leave as Israel's Ban on Activity Takes Effect' *The Guardian* (30 January 2025) <https://www.theguardian.com/world/2025/jan/30/unrwa-staff-forced-to-leave-israel-after-ban-comes-into-effect> accessed 28 April 2025.

The Israeli laws against UNRWA contributed to a Norwegian initiative in the General Assembly, which culminated in December 2024 with a request for an ICJ advisory opinion on Israel's obligations in relation to the presence and activities of the UN, other international organizations, and third states in the Occupied Palestinian Territories.[499] In October 2025, the ICJ opined that Israel 'has an obligation to co-operate in good faith with' the UN 'by providing every assistance in any action' the UN, including UNRWA, takes in accordance with its Charter.[500]

5.3. United Nations peacekeeping operations and special political missions

This section surveys the role of UN peacekeeping operations and SPMs in relation to humanitarian assistance.[501] UN peacekeeping can provoke considerable confusion, as it has no clear legal basis in the UN Charter and has evolved significantly since it was first used in 1948.[502] For this reason, the section begins with an explanation of UN peacekeeping.

There is no one definition of UN peacekeeping. It has been defined as a UN authorized and led force, 'consisting of civilian and/or military personnel contributed by states or seconded by the UN Secretariat, physically present in a country or countries with a view to facilitating the maintenance of peace, most commonly after a conflict has ceased'.[503] Such operations may be created by the General Assembly or the Security Council;[504] however, in practice, all UN peacekeeping operations since 1962 have been established by the Security Council.[505] Peacekeeping operations under UN command and control are managed and supported by the Department of Peace Operations (DPO) within the UN Secretariat and staffed by military and/or police personnel contributed by UN member states, as well as by civilian UN officials.

In their early years, UN peacekeeping operations were based on three core principles: impartiality, in the sense of not taking the side of any conflict party; non-use of force, other than in self-defence; and host state consent. Peacekeeping operations adhering to these principles are sometimes termed 'traditional', 'first-generation', or

[499] The question posed to the ICJ is '[w]hat are the obligations of Israel, as an occupying Power and as a member of the United Nations, in relation to the presence and activities of the United Nations, including its agencies and bodies, other international organizations and third States, in and in relation to the Occupied Palestinian Territory, including to ensure and facilitate the unhindered provision of urgently needed supplies essential to the survival of the Palestinian civilian population as well as of basic services and humanitarian and development assistance, for the benefit of the Palestinian civilian population, and in support of the Palestinian people's right to self-determination?' (Res 79/232 (n 107) para 10).

[500] *Israel Obligations AO* (n 411) para 223.

[501] Not all peace operations come under UN command and control; state commanded operations can also play a role in relation to humanitarian assistance. They are addressed in Chapter 7, Section 3.2.

[502] The first UN peacekeeping operation was the UN Truce Supervision Organization, which was established by the Security Council in 1948 to monitor the ceasefire in the Arab–Israeli War (UNSC Res 50 (29 May 1948) para 6).

[503] Higgins and others (n 7) 1030.

[504] *Certain Expenses of the United Nations (Article 17, paragraph 2, of the Charter)* (Advisory Opinion) [1962] ICJ Rep 1962 151, 163.

[505] Higgins and others (n 7) 1030.

'classic' peacekeeping. However, as mentioned above in the discussion of the Security Council's thematic agenda on the protection of civilians,[506] since 1999 UN peacekeeping operations have been authorized under Chapter VII of the UN Charter to use force to protect civilians; such peacekeeping operations are often termed 'robust'. The Security Council's creation of robust peacekeeping operations increased considerably after the 2000 publication of the Brahimi Report, a major study of UN peacekeeping commissioned by Secretary-General Annan, which found that peacekeepers must be 'capable of defending themselves, other mission components and the mission's mandate'.[507] The majority of twenty-first century UN peacekeeping operations have been robust.[508]

Another change emerged after the Cold War, when the Security Council significantly enlarged the range of functions it assigned to peacekeeping operations, particularly those in situations of NIAC. New functions included 'responsibilities relating to the establishment of a lasting peace (including, for example, facilitating peace agreements), or ensuring that conditions of peace prevailed through a variety of political and social endeavours (including, for example, monitoring elections, promoting human rights, or aiding in the reintegration of combatants)'.[509] Peacekeeping operations with these broader functions became known as multidimensional peacekeeping operations.

The facilitation of humanitarian assistance is among the functions that have been assigned to multidimensional peacekeeping operations. Operations with such a mandate include UNPROFOR and UNOSOM II, discussed above,[510] as well as the peacekeeping operations established for Abyei (UNISFA),[511] CAR (MINUSCA),[512] Darfur (UNAMID),[513] DRC (MONUSCO),[514] Haiti (MINUSTAH),[515] Lebanon (UNIFIL),[516] Mali (MINUSMA),[517] Rwanda (UNAMIR II),[518] and South Sudan (UNMISS).[519] Mandated tasks relating to the facilitation of humanitarian assistance

[506] See Section 4.4.1.

[507] Panel on United Nations Peace Operations, 'Report of the Panel on United Nations Peace Operations' (21 August 2000) A/55/305-S/2000/809, para 55.

[508] Higgins and others (n 7) 1036. Paddon Rhoads and Welsh note that even robust peacekeeping operations are often unable to protect civilians in practice due to reticence to use force stemming from insufficient operational capacity and unclear civilian protection mandates ((n 219) 613–14).

[509] ibid.

[510] See Section 4.4.2.

[511] UNSC Res 1990 (27 June 2011) S/RES/1990, para 2(d).

[512] UNSC Res 2149 (10 April 2014) S/RES/2149 (Res 2149) para 30(c); UNSC Res 2448 (13 December 2018) S/RES/2448, para 39(c). This was the last new UN peacekeeping operation established by the Security Council; MINUSCA, as well as MINUSMA, MINUSTAH, and MONUSCO, are 'stabilization' missions. There is no single definition of the concept of stabilization; de Coning notes that 'the essential difference between peacekeeping and stabilization seems to be that in peacekeeping the aim is to arrive at and maintain a ceasefire and/or implement a peace agreement among the parties to a conflict, whilst in stabilization, the theory of change is to achieve peace by managing or removing an aggressor' (cited in Higgins and others (n 7) 1067).

[513] UNSC Res 2429 (13 July 2018) S/RES/2429, paras 7(ii) and 11(i).

[514] UNSC Res 2463 (29 March 2019) S/RES/2463, paras 29(i) and 37.

[515] UNSC Res 1542 (30 April 2004) S/RES/1542, para 9.

[516] UNSC Res 2433 (30 August 2018) S/RES/2433, para 19.

[517] UNSC Res 2423 (28 June 2018) S/RES/2423, para 38(f).

[518] UNSC Res 918 (17 May 1994) S/RES/918, para 3(b).

[519] UNSC Res 2459 (15 March 2019) S/RES/2459, paras 7(a)(ii) and 7(b)(i) (Res 2459). In December 2013, civilians in South Sudan began spontaneously seeking shelter in and around UNMISS bases, creating

include creating conditions for the safe, timely, and unhindered civilian-led delivery of humanitarian assistance; ensuring the safety, security, and freedom of movement of humanitarian personnel; and strengthening collaboration and coordination between peacekeepers and humanitarian actors.[520] MINUSMA, for example, was mandated in 'support of the Malian authorities, to contribute to the creation of a secure environment for the safe, civilian-led delivery of humanitarian assistance, in accordance with humanitarian principles'.[521] MINUSCA was mandated to 'contribute, including through effective civil-military coordination and in close coordination with humanitarian actors, to the creation of a secure environment for the immediate, full, safe and unhindered, civilian-led delivery of humanitarian assistance, in accordance with United Nations guiding humanitarian principles and relevant provisions of international law'.[522]

This specification in the foregoing examples that humanitarian assistance should be delivered by civilians reflects the concern, introduced in Section 3 above, that military involvement in delivery could compromise the core humanitarian principles. A UN peacekeeping force deployed to a situation of armed conflict with a robust mandate may need to become actively engaged in the conflict to discharge its mandate, for example, to protect civilians. IHL is applicable to UN forces 'when in situations of armed conflict they are actively engaged therein as combatants, to the extent and for the duration of their engagement'.[523] If peacekeepers at times become actively engaged in the armed conflict, it will at those times be impossible for them to act in accordance with neutrality and independence, and perceptions of their neutrality and impartiality will at all times be compromised. Indeed, DPO policy recognizes that humanitarian actors rely on the humanitarian principles 'to discharge their mandates effectively and safely and it is therefore necessary to maintain a clear distinction between their role and that of political and military actors, including peacekeeping operations'.[524] This is why UN peacekeeping operations are typically mandated to facilitate the delivery of humanitarian assistance, rather than to deliver it directly. However, as discussed in Section 4.4.2 above, in two exceptional cases, UNOSOM II and UNPROFOR were mandated by the Security Council to directly deliver humanitarian assistance.

In practice, when a UN peacekeeping operation is given a facilitation mandate, it typically involves providing humanitarian actors with logistical support, such as transportation; security support, such as armed escorts for humanitarian convoys;[525]

what became known as 'protection of civilian sites'. Civilians at these sites sought assistance from UNMISS; however, the direct provision of humanitarian assistance was beyond the scope of the mission's mandate. For more on protection of civilians sites in South Sudan, see Gillard (n 333) 1093–96.

[520] Arendt (n 286) 44.

[521] Res 2459 (n 519) para 7.

[522] Res 2149 (n 512) para 30(c).

[523] UN Secretary-General, 'Secretary-General's Bulletin: Observance by United Nations Forces of International Humanitarian Law' (6 August 1999) ST/SGB/1999/13, para 1.1.

[524] DPO, 'Policy: The Protection of Civilians in United Nations Peacekeeping' (1 May 2023) Ref. 2023.05, para 28.

[525] See Armed Escort Guidelines (n 168) 93. These guidelines provide that humanitarian convoys should not in general be protected by armed or military escorts, though armed escorts may be used in certain exceptional circumstances. See, generally, Jamie Williamson, 'The Use of Armed Security Escorts: A Challenge to Independent and Neutral Humanitarian Action' in Benjamin Perrin (ed), *Modern Warfare* (UBC Press

and information.[526] Relevant guidance can be found in the MCDA Guidelines,[527] as well as in UN (especially IASC) policy documents.[528]

An SPM is a type of UN field presence created by the General Assembly or the Security Council to support peace and security using political and diplomatic means, rather than military force. SPMs do not include military or police contingents; rather, they are comprised of civilians, including leadership by a Special Representative or Special Envoy of the Secretary-General. They tend to be created to support peace processes, preventive diplomacy, conflict mediation, political transition, or institution-building. SPMs are managed by the Department of Political and Peacebuilding Affairs within the UN Secretariat. Like peacekeeping operations, SPMs are also sometimes given a mandate in relation to humanitarian assistance. For example, the UN Support Mission in Libya was mandated to provide 'support, on request, for the provision of essential services, and delivery of humanitarian assistance in accordance with humanitarian principles'.[529] The UN Assistance Mission in Afghanistan and the UN Assistance Mission for Iraq (UNAMI) were also mandated to coordinate and facilitate the delivery of humanitarian assistance.[530]

UNAMI provides a tragic illustration of the risks UN personnel take to do their work. On 19 August 2003, a suicide truck bomb exploded outside the Canal Hotel in Baghdad, which was serving as UNAMI's headquarters. The attack killed 22 UN staff, including the Secretary-General's Special Representative (and former ERC) Sérgio Vieira de Mello, as well as visitors to the hotel. Over 150 staff and visitors were injured.[531] As a result, the UN pulled most of its international staff from Iraq. 19 August is now commemorated every year by the UN as World Humanitarian Day, 'in order to contribute to increasing public awareness about humanitarian assistance activities worldwide and the importance of international cooperation in this regard, as well as to honour all humanitarian and United Nations and associated personnel who have lost their lives in the cause of duty'.[532] The next section addresses the protection of UN operations and personnel.

2012) and Annabel Bassil, 'Armed Escorts to Humanitarian Convoys: An Unexplored Framework Under International Humanitarian Law' (2020) 102 International Review of the Red Cross 559.

[526] Bradley (n 169) 364.

[527] MCDA Guidelines (n 145). As these Guidelines also relate to state military and civil defence assets deployed in support of UN humanitarian activities, they are discussed in Chapter 7 on state humanitarian actors (see Section 3.3.2).

[528] See, for example, IASC, 'Civil-Military Relationship in Complex Emergencies: An IASC Reference Paper' (28 June 2004) <https://interagencystandingcommittee.org/focal-points/iasc-reference-paper-civil-military-relationship-complex-emergencies-2004> accessed 22 May 2025; IASC, 'Civil-Military Guidelines & Reference for Complex Emergencies' (2008) <https://interagencystandingcommittee.org/other/documents-public/civil-military-guidelines-and-references-complex-emergencies> accessed 22 May 2025; DPO, 'Policy: Civil-Military Coordination in UN Integrated Peacekeeping Missions' (1 January 2022) Ref. 2022.01.

[529] UNSC Res 2434 (2018) S/RES/2434, para 2(ii).

[530] Afghanistan: UNSC Res 2405 (8 March 2018) S/RES/2405, para 7(c); Iraq: UNSC Res 2421 (14 June 2018) S/RES/2421, para 2(c)(i).

[531] 'Report of the Independent Panel on the Safety and Security of UN Personnel in Iraq' (20 October 2003) <https://digitallibrary.un.org/record/529406?ln = en&v = pdf> accessed 30 June 2025, 1.

[532] UNGA Res 63/139 (11 December 2008) A/RES/63/139, para 26.

5.4. The protection of United Nations operations and personnel

Humanitarian personnel increasingly perform their work at considerable personal risk. 2024 was the deadliest year on record for humanitarians:[533] according to the Aid Worker Security Database, there were 402 major attacks on aid workers, up from 194 in 2014.[534] Similar information is provided in the Secretary-General's annual report to the General Assembly on the safety and security of humanitarian personnel and the protection of UN personnel. The most recent report indicates that in 2023, 1,915 UN civilian personnel were affected by safety and security incidents, there were 491 attacks on UN premises and vehicles, and 310 critical security incidents affected personnel of UN implementing partners.[535] The UN Secretariat includes a department dedicated to staff security, the Department of Safety and Security.

The General Assembly has recognized the risks of attacks on aid workers in annual resolutions since 1997. Initially, its first resolutions covered UN[536] and other humanitarian personnel separately;[537] however, since 1999, a single annual resolution has covered all humanitarian personnel.[538] The Security Council also adopts regular resolutions on the protection of UN personnel, associated personnel, and humanitarian personnel in conflict zones.[539] Its most recent resolution in this regard, led by Switzerland, highlighted the emerging threat of disinformation campaigns aimed at undermining humanitarian work, and mandated the Secretary-General to provide the Council with recommendations on how to prevent attacks against humanitarian personnel and combat impunity.[540] Following broad consultations, Secretary-General Guterres responded in a November 2024 letter to the President of the Security Council, outlining six recommendations aimed at 'enhancing the prevention of and response to incidents affecting humanitarian personnel and [. . . UN] and associated personnel, including national and locally recruited personnel, premises and assets'. The main recommendations were to: (i) respect international law, including IHL, IHRL, the Convention on the Safety of United Nations and Associated Personnel (UN Safety Convention, discussed below), the General Convention, and the seven UN road safety conventions; (ii) uphold principled humanitarian action and facilitate humanitarian access; (iii) maintain consistent standards; (iv) support personnel who have suffered attacks; (v) embed safety and security considerations in Security Council mandates; and (vi) ensure effective investigations and accountability.[541]

[533] S-G PoC Report (n 279) para 35.

[534] <https://www.aidworkersecurity.org> accessed 1 May 2025. This database defines 'major attacks' as airstrikes, assaults, attacks with explosives, shooting, and kidnapping.

[535] UNGA, 'Safety and Security of Humanitarian Personnel and Protection of United Nations Personnel: Report of the Secretary-General' (12 July 2024) A/79/149, 24–27. Note that security incidents affecting UNRWA personnel are reported separately (see page 28 of the report).

[536] UNGA Res 52/126 (12 December 1997) A/RES/52/126.

[537] UNGA Res 52/167 (16 December 1997) A/RES/52/167.

[538] See, for example, UNGA Res 70/104 (28 December 2015) A/RES/70/104; Res 78/118 (n 217).

[539] See, for example, UNSC Res 1502 (26 August 2003) S/RES/1502; UNSC Res 2175 (29 August 2014) S/RES/2175; UNSC Res 2286 (3 May 2016) S/RES/2286.

[540] UNSC Res 2730 (24 May 2024) S/RES/2730, paras 12 and 16.

[541] UN Secretary-General, 'Letter dated 22 November 2024 from the Secretary-General addressed to the President of the Security Council' (25 November 2024) S/2024/852.

International law affords humanitarian personnel, including UN staff, a range of protections. Primary responsibility for the security and protection of humanitarian personnel lies with the host state or, in occupied territory, with the occupying power.[542] The privileges and immunities described above provide a measure of protection.[543] As discussed elsewhere in this book, all humanitarian personnel, including UN personnel, are protected by IHL during armed conflict,[544] and those who attack them can be held accountable under international criminal law.[545] In disaster situations, humanitarian and UN personnel are protected by some international disaster response law treaties.[546] Additionally, certain transnational criminal law treaties, such as the International Convention Against the Taking of Hostages[547] and the International Convention for the Protection of All Persons from Enforced Disappearance,[548] aim to suppress and punish crimes that pose a particular risk to humanitarians.

UN officials enjoy additional, dedicated protections. The UN can bring a claim against a state responsible for injury to one of its officials,[549] and its officials are protected under the UN Safety Convention. The UN Safety Convention was adopted by the General Assembly in 1995,[550] in response to increasing attacks against UN peacekeepers and civilian personnel deployed with peacekeeping operations.[551] It provides that UN Personnel (as defined below) and associated personnel,[552] their equipment, and their premises 'shall not be made the object of attack or of any action that prevents them from discharging their mandate'.[553] Further, the Convention requires states parties to 'take all appropriate measures to ensure the safety and security of' UN and associated personnel,[554] and it provides that if any UN or Associated Personnel are captured or detained in the course of their work, 'they shall not be subjected to interrogation and they shall be promptly released and returned' to the UN or other appropriate authorities.[555] At the same time, states parties must prevent[556] and criminalize: (i) the murder, kidnapping, or any other attack on the person or liberty of any UN or associated personnel and (ii) the violent attack of their official premises, private accommodation, or transportation if the attack is likely to endanger their person or liberty.[557] The Convention also requires states to criminalize threats and attempts

[542] Convention (IV) respecting the Laws and Customs of War on Land (adopted 18 October 1907, entered into force 26 January 1910) Annex (Regulations) (Hague Regulations) art 43.

[543] See Section 5.1.

[544] See Chapter 3, Section 4.4.4.

[545] See Chapter 3, Section 7.1.1.

[546] See the list of relevant treaty provisions in Chapter 6, Section 3.3.

[547] (Adopted 17 December 1979, entered into force 3 June 1983) 1316 UNTS 205.

[548] (Adopted 20 December 2006, entered into force 23 December 2010) 2716 UNTS 3.

[549] *Reparation for Injuries Suffered in the Service of the United Nations* (Advisory Opinion) [1949] ICJ Rep 174.

[550] UNGA Res 49/59 (17 February 1995) A/RES/49/59.

[551] Evan T Bloom, 'Protecting Peacekeepers: The Convention on the Safety of United Nations and Associated Personnel' (1995) 89 American Journal of International Law 621, 621. For further analysis of the UN Safety Convention, see also Antoine Bouvier, 'Convention on the Safety of United Nations and Associated Personnel: Presentation and Analysis' (1995) 35 International Review of the Red Cross 638.

[552] Associated Personnel are addressed in Chapter 6, Section 3.3.

[553] (Adopted 9 December 1994, entered into force 15 January 1999) 2051 UNTS 363, art 7(1).

[554] ibid, art 7(2).

[555] ibid, art 8.

[556] ibid, art 11.

[557] ibid, art 9(1).

to commit the above-mentioned acts and acting as an accomplice in or organizing or ordering their commission.[558] Each state party must establish its jurisdiction over such offences committed within its jurisdiction or when the alleged offender is one of its nationals,[559] and either extradite or prosecute the alleged offender.[560]

For the purposes of the UN Safety Convention, 'UN Personnel' comprises individuals deployed on UN peacekeeping operations, UN officials (staff), and experts on mission for the UN.[561] When it was adopted in 1995, the UN Safety Convention only applied to UN Personnel deployed on UN peacekeeping operations or where the Security Council or General Assembly had made a declaration of 'exceptional risk to the safety of the personnel' involved.[562] Thus, absent an exceptional risk declaration, UN personnel delivering humanitarian assistance outside a UN peacekeeping operation were not covered by the Convention. The 2005 Optional Protocol to the UN Safety Convention (2005 Optional Protocol) expanded its scope to cover UN personnel delivering 'emergency humanitarian assistance' and 'humanitarian, political or development assistance in peacebuilding'.[563] However, the 2005 Optional Protocol does not apply to any permanent UN office, such as its headquarters.[564] Furthermore, it includes an opt-out clause allowing that a 'host state may make a declaration to the Secretary-General' of the UN 'that it shall not apply the provisions of' the Protocol with respect to an operation that 'is conducted for the sole purpose of responding to a natural disaster'.[565] Both the original requirement of an exceptional risk declaration and the Protocol's natural disaster opt-out clause arose from states' concerns about sovereignty and non-intervention. They were included on the view that in relatively less risky situations, 'the laws of the receiving (host) State should provide adequate protection to personnel and, accordingly, there was no need for additional protection under international law'.[566]

The 1973 Convention on the Prevention and Punishment of Crimes against Internationally Protected Persons, including Diplomatic Agents (IPP Convention) takes a similar approach to the UN Safety Convention in the sense of establishing an *aut dedere aut judicare* regime for crimes within its scope.[567] However, it only applies to international organization officials 'entitled pursuant to international law to special protection from any attack on his person, freedom or dignity'.[568] The IPP Convention thus covers senior UN officials with diplomatic status, but not the regular UN officials who would comprise most of the staff on a humanitarian operation.

[558] ibid.
[559] ibid, art 10.
[560] ibid, arts 14–15.
[561] ibid, art 1(a). On the meaning of 'experts on mission', see *Muzila* (n 413).
[562] ibid, art 1(c).
[563] Optional Protocol to the Convention on the Safety of United Nations and Associated Personnel (adopted 8 December 2005, entered into force 19 August 2010) 2689 UNTS 59, art II(1). Note, however, that this Protocol has only 33 states parties, while the UN Safety Convention has 95.
[564] ibid, art II(2).
[565] ibid, art II(3).
[566] UN, 'Protection of Persons in the Event of Disasters: Memorandum by the Secretariat' (11 December 2007) A/CN.4/590, para 206.
[567] (Adopted 14 December 1973, entered into force 20 February 1977) 1035 UNTS 167.
[568] ibid, art 1(b).

6. Conclusion

This chapter has examined the UN's role in humanitarian assistance, tracing its evolution from a generalized humanitarian mandate in the UN Charter to a multifaceted set of functions: coordination and funding, normative, and operational. It explained the post-Cold War emergence of the UN's humanitarian coordination and funding architecture, including the roles of the ERC, OCHA, the IASC, the CERF, and state-level structures. It addressed the UN's role in developing norms and practice relating to humanitarian assistance, particularly through initiatives of the Secretary-General, and through ECOSOC, the General Assembly, and the Security Council. Finally, the chapter covered the UN's operational role, through semi-autonomous subsidiary organs of the General Assembly as well as peacekeeping operations and SPMs.

The chapter has demonstrated that since the end of the Cold War, the UN has played an increasingly important role in humanitarian assistance. Its unparalleled convening power generates law, policy, operational frameworks, and funding, and it provides assistance directly through its operational bodies. While the resolutions and initiatives that emanate from ECOSOC, the General Assembly, and the Security Council are generated by member states—and thus inherently political—the core humanitarian principles seem to serve as a north star of sorts, keeping the UN's normative initiatives largely in line with them. Over time, however, the UN has encountered a range of challenges, such as humanitarian financing shortfalls and the unintended consequences of its sanctions regimes. While it has recently made significant progress on the latter, US funding cuts have exacerbated the former. It remains to be seen whether the Humanitarian Reset will provide a solution. Whatever its outcome, the Reset's effects will be felt beyond the UN, as it is set to reshape coordination and funding mechanisms that also involve non-state actors. The next chapter turns to those actors.

6
Non-state Actors

1. Introduction

The International Red Cross and Red Crescent Movement (the Movement) and non-governmental organizations (NGOs) are critical humanitarian actors. The Movement consists of a set of distinct but related organizations formed under Swiss law or, in the case of National Red Cross and Red Crescent Societies (National Societies), under the municipal law of the state where the National Society operates. These organizations, known as the Movement's 'components', are the International Committee of the Red Cross (ICRC), the International Federation of Red Cross and Red Crescent Societies (IFRC), and the 191 National Societies,[1] such as the Australian Red Cross and the Egyptian Red Crescent.

There is no universal definition of an NGO. Indeed, according to Boyle and Chinkin, NGOs 'are primarily defined through what they are not'.[2] A humanitarian NGO is defined here as a legal entity formed on private initiative to undertake humanitarian activities in accordance with the core humanitarian principles or a similar set of principles.[3] Many humanitarian NGOs also do development work. There are both local and national NGOs, on the one hand, and international NGOs, on the other. Local and national NGOs are formed and operate in only one state, whereas international NGOs operate in more than one state. The critical role of local and national NGOs was recognized by The Grand Bargain,[4] in which signatories committed to providing at least 25 percent of humanitarian funding to local and national actors by 2020.[5] While this pledge was not fully realized,[6] the 'localization agenda' now forms a key part of the United Nations' (UN) ongoing Humanitarian Reset reform initiative.[7]

The components of the Movement are sometimes referred to as NGOs.[8] However, this fails to capture their *sui generis* character. The ICRC in particular has been characterized as an international organization, though not of the usual intergovernmental

[1] <https://www.ifrc.org/national-societies-directory> accessed 14 July 2025.

[2] Alan Boyle and Christine Chinkin, *The Making of International Law* (OUP 2007) 52.

[3] As explained in Chapter 2 (Section 2), some humanitarian NGOs use slightly different sets of principles.

[4] See Chapter 5, Section 4.1.

[5] The Grand Bargain (2016) <https://interagencystandingcommittee.org/sites/default/files/migrated/2017-02/grand_bargain_final_22_may_final-2_0.pdf> accessed 27 June 2025, 5.

[6] Humanitarian Policy Group, 'The Grand Bargain in 2021: An Independent Review' (June 2022) <https://media.odi.org/documents/Grand_Bargain_2022_ogGQS0m.pdf> accessed 28 July 2025, 60–64.

[7] See Chapter 5, Section 3.5.

[8] See, for example, Peter MacAlister-Smith, 'Humanitarian Action by Non-Governmental Organizations: National and International Law Perspectives' (1987) 18 Bulletin of Peace Proposals 119, 123.

Humanitarian Assistance in International Law. Marina Sharpe, Oxford University Press.
DOI: 10.1093/9780198994695.003.0009

type.[9] The Movement components' unique status flows from the roles accorded to the ICRC and National Societies under international humanitarian law (IHL)[10] and from the conferral by states of each component's mandate.[11] It is reflected in the UN General Assembly observer status enjoyed by the ICRC[12] and the IFRC,[13] and in the many bilateral status agreements between the ICRC or IFRC and states,[14] which confer privileges, immunities, and facilities similar to those enjoyed by the UN.

The Movement and NGOs are thus addressed separately. The Movement is addressed first because of its central role 'in disseminating the organizational model of the international relief NGO'.[15] Section 2 explains the Movement's history, structure, and basic governance, and outlines the mandates of each of the ICRC, the IFRC, and National Societies, with a focus on their humanitarian assistance activities. Section 2 then covers the privileges, immunities, and facilities enjoyed by certain Movement components and the protection of Movement personnel. Section 3 addresses NGOs, including their relationship with, and facilities and protection under, international law. The latter section includes a focus on how health care is protected in armed conflict, to clarify the protections that medical NGOs do, and do not, enjoy under IHL. Section 4 addresses the Movement and NGOs' role in setting quality and accountability standards for humanitarian action. Section 5 concludes.

2. The International Red Cross and Red Crescent Movement

The Movement's origins can be traced to the 1859 Battle of Solferino.[16] As mentioned in Chapter 2,[17] Swiss businessman Henri Dunant was in Castiglione when he happened upon the Battle's bloody aftermath. His experience of voluntarily caring for wounded soldiers gave rise to two ideas, which he laid out in his influential 1862 book *A Memory of Solferino*: the formation of 'relief societies for the purpose of having care given to the wounded in wartime' by volunteers, and the formulation of 'some international principle, sanctioned by a Convention' that would constitute the legal basis for such societies.[18] An associate of Dunant's, Geneva lawyer Gustave Moynier, put

[9] Els Debuf, 'Tools to do the Job: The ICRC's Legal Status, Privileges and Immunities' (2016) 97 International Review of the Red Cross 319, 321–25.

[10] The relevant provisions are listed below (for the ICRC, see note 42; for National Societies, see note 70).

[11] See Section 2.

[12] UNGA Res 45/6 (16 October 1990) A/RES/45/6, para 1. See, generally, Christian Koenig, 'Observer Status for the International Committee of the Red Cross at the United Nations—A Legal Viewpoint' (1991) 31 International Review of the Red Cross 37.

[13] UNGA Res 49/2 (19 October 1994) A/RES/49/2, para 1.

[14] See Section 2.3.

[15] Shai Dromi, *Above the Fray: The Red Cross and the Making of the Humanitarian NGO Sector* (University of Chicago Press 2020) 7.

[16] This history outlined here is based on François Bugnion, 'Birth of an Idea: The Founding of the International Committee of the Red Cross and of the International Red Cross and Red Crescent Movement: from Solferino to the Original Geneva Convention (1859–1864)' (2012) 94 International Review of the Red Cross 1299. On the history of the Movement and the ICRC, see also Caroline Moorehead, *Dunant's Dream: War, Switzerland and the History of the Red Cross* (HarperCollins 1998); Daniel Palmieri, 'An Institution Standing the Test of Time? A Review of 150 Years of the History of the International Committee of the Red Cross' (2012) 94 International Review of the Red Cross 1273; Dromi (n 15).

[17] See Chapter 2, Section 3.1.

[18] Henri Dunant, *A Memory of Solferino* (American Red Cross translation, 1939) 85 and 93.

these proposals to the Geneva Society for Public Welfare, an existing charity Moynier chaired. In February 1863, the Society struck a committee—composed of Dunant, Moynier, Louis Appia, Guillaume-Henri Dufour, and Théodore Maunoir—to write up Dunant's ideas for submission to an international conference set to take place in Berlin. The convening of this committee marks the founding of the ICRC, though it was known initially as the Permanent International Committee for the Relief of Wounded Soldiers (International Committee); it adopted the name ICRC in 1875. The International Committee developed Dunant's ideas, deciding that to work safely and effectively, the volunteers, as well as military medical personnel, would need to be recognizable by way of a distinctive sign, the red cross, and shielded from combat.

When the Berlin conference was cancelled, the International Committee decided to convene its own event in Geneva. The Geneva International Conference to Study Ways of Overcoming the Inadequacy of Army Medical Services in the Field (1863 Geneva Conference) took place in October 1863. It adopted ten resolutions, which served as the statutory foundations of the Movement—then known as the International Red Cross—until the creation of the League of Red Cross Societies (now known as the IFRC) in 1919 necessitated more formal statutes, which were ultimately adopted in 1928.

Following the 1863 Geneva Conference, the International Committee set about arranging a diplomatic conference to transform the ten resolutions into a treaty. The diplomatic conference was convened by Switzerland in August 1864. Delegates from sixteen states gathered in Geneva to discuss a draft convention prepared by the International Committee. They ultimately adopted the very first Geneva Convention (1864 Geneva Convention);[19] its key provisions were summarized in Chapter 2.[20] As the first treaty adopted in peacetime to protect the victims of future armed conflicts and as the starting point from which subsequent Geneva conventions were iterated (in 1906, 1929, and 1949), the 1864 Geneva Convention represents the foundation of contemporary IHL.

As mentioned in the introduction above, the Movement has three components: the ICRC, the IFRC, and National Societies. Its overall mission is laid out in the 2006 Statutes of the International Red Cross and Red Crescent Movement (Movement Statutes)—the modern version of the statutes adopted in 1928—as 'to prevent and alleviate human suffering wherever it may be found, to protect life and health and ensure respect for the human being, in particular in times of armed conflict and other emergencies, to work for the prevention of disease and for the promotion of health and social welfare, to encourage voluntary service and a constant readiness to give help by the members of the Movement, and a universal sense of solidarity towards all those in need of its protection and assistance'.[21] The Movement Statutes also articulate the seven fundamental principles—humanity, impartiality, neutrality, independence, voluntary service, unity, and universality (Fundamental Principles)—that guide the

[19] Convention for the Amelioration of the Conditions of the Wounded in Armies in the Field (adopted 22 August 1864, entered into force 22 June 1865).

[20] See Chapter 2, Section 3.1.

[21] Statutes of the International Red Cross and Red Crescent Movement (1986, as amended in 1995 and 2006) <https://www.icrc.org/en/doc/assets/files/other/statutes-en-a5.pdf> accessed 24 February 2022 (Movement Statutes) preambular para 1.

Movement,[22] and which states undertake in the Movement Statutes to respect.[23] The Fundamental Principles were discussed in Chapter 2.[24]

The Movement is governed by three entities, known as the 'statutory bodies': the International Conference of the Red Cross and Red Crescent (International Conference), the Standing Commission of the Red Cross and Red Crescent (Standing Commission), and the Council of Delegates of the International Red Cross and Red Crescent Movement (Council of Delegates). The International Conference, which was convened for the first time in Paris in 1867,[25] is the Movement's 'supreme deliberative body'.[26] It brings Movement components and states parties to the Geneva Conventions together once every four years to 'examine and decide upon humanitarian matters of common interest'.[27] The functions of the International Conference include electing members of the Standing Commission (discussed below); adopting resolutions; assigning mandates to the ICRC and the IFRC; and adopting, amending, and interpreting the Movement Statutes.[28] The latter function has an important legal effect: because the International Conference includes all states parties to the Geneva Conventions, Movement components are entitled to insist upon the recognition by states of their powers under the Movement Statutes.[29] In other words, because states conferred each Movement component's mandate, they are obligated to cooperate with Movement components in the exercise of those mandates. The Standing Commission is the 'trustee' of the International Conference between conferences.[30] It consists of nine members drawn from the Movement components,[31] who do logistical and procedural work to prepare the International Conference.[32] The Council of Delegates is a meeting of 'representatives of all the components of the Movement', who 'meet to discuss matters which concern the Movement as a whole'.[33] It meets prior to the opening of each International Conference, and can also meet between Conferences.[34]

The Movement Statutes lay out the role of each Movement component and provide that the ICRC and the IFRC can also 'conclude with each other any agreements required to harmonize the conduct of their respective activities'.[35] In 1997, the Council of Delegates adopted an agreement, known as the Seville Agreement, to clarify operational roles and coordination arrangements within the Movement;[36] the Seville Agreement was supplemented in 2005 and replaced in 2022 by the Movement

[22] ibid, preambular para 2.
[23] ibid, art 2(4).
[24] See Chapter 2, Section 4.2.
[25] François Bugnion, 'Red Cross Law' (1995) 35 International Review of the Red Cross 491, 494.
[26] Movement Statutes (n 21) art 8.
[27] ibid, arts 8–9 and 11.
[28] ibid, art 10.
[29] Bugnion (n 25) 502.
[30] Movement Statutes (n 21) art 16.
[31] ibid, art 17.
[32] ibid, art 18.
[33] ibid, art 12.
[34] ibid, art 15(1).
[35] ibid, art 7(3).
[36] Agreement on the Organization of the International Activities of the Components of the International Red Cross and Red Crescent Movement (26 November 1997) <https://www.ifrc.org/document/seville-agreement> accessed 10 July 2025.

Coordination for Collective Impact Agreement, known as the Seville Agreement 2.0.[37] Seville 2.0 determines Movement coordination in large-scale or prolonged emergencies that require a collective Movement response.[38] In such situations, the local National Society is 'entrusted with the role of "convenor"'; in situations of international and non-international armed conflict and internal strife, the ICRC is co-convenor, while in disasters, postconflict situations, and forced displacement, the IFRC serves as co-convenor.[39] No Movement component is part of the Inter-Agency Standing Committee cluster system.[40]

2.1. The International Committee of the Red Cross

The ICRC's role is laid down in identical provisions of the ICRC Statutes, which were first adopted in 1915, and the Movement Statutes.[41] It is mandated to: disseminate the Fundamental Principles; recognize National Societies; 'undertake the tasks incumbent upon it under the Geneva Conventions';[42] endeavour to ensure the protection of and assistance to military and civilian victims of armed conflict or internal strife;[43] ensure the operation of the Central Tracing Agency, which works to reunite people separated in war; contribute to training medical personnel and preparing medical equipment for armed conflict; and carry out mandates entrusted to it by the International Conference.[44] Additionally, the ICRC may, in line with the GCs,[45] 'take any humanitarian initiative which comes within its role as a specifically neutral and

[37] (20 October 2022) <https://www.ifrc.org/document/seville-agreement-2> accessed 10 July 2025.

[38] ibid, art 5.4.

[39] ibid, art 5.1.

[40] See Chapter 5, Section 3.2.

[41] On the ICRC generally, see David P Forsythe, *The Humanitarians: The International Committee of the Red Cross* (CUP 2005); David P Forsythe and Ann Barbara Rieffer-Flanagan, *The International Committee of the Red Cross: A Neutral Humanitarian Actor* (Routledge 2016); John F Hutchinson, *Champions of Charity: War and the Rise of the Red Cross* (Routledge 2018); David P Forsythe, *The Contemporary International Committee of the Red Cross: Challenges, Changes, Controversies* (CUP 2024).

[42] Geneva Convention for the Amelioration of the Condition of the Wounded and Sick in Armed Forces in the Field (adopted 12 August 1949, entered into force 21 October 1950) 75 UNTS 31 (GCI) arts 3, 9, 10, 11, and 23; Geneva Convention for the Amelioration of the Condition of Wounded, Sick and Shipwrecked Members of Armed Forces at Sea (adopted 12 August 1949, entered into force 21 October 1950) 75 UNTS 85 (GCII) arts 3, 9, 10, and 11; Geneva Convention Relative to the Treatment of Prisoners of War (adopted 12 August 1949, entered into force 21 October 1950) 75 UNTS 135 (GCIII) arts 3, 9, 10, 11, 56, 72, 73, 75, 79, 81, 123, 125, and 126; Geneva Convention Relative to the Protection of Civilian Persons in Time of War (adopted 12 August 1949, entered into force 21 October 1950) 75 UNTS 287 (GCIV) arts 3, 10, 11, 12, 14, 30, 59, 61, 76, 96, 102, 104, 108, 109, 111, 140, 142, and 143; Protocol Additional to the Geneva Conventions of 12 August 1949, and relating to the Protection of Victims of International Armed Conflicts (adopted 8 June 1977, entered into force 7 December 1978) 1125 UNTS 3 (API) arts 5, 6, 33, 78, 81, 97, and 98. Additionally, several GC and API provisions refer to the functions of the Protecting Power (see Chapter 3, Section 3), which are in practice often fulfilled by the ICRC.

[43] For a critical account of the utility and limits of the ICRC's humanitarian assistance mandate, see Rotem Giladi, 'The Utility and Limits of Legal Mandate: Humanitarian Assistance, the International Committee of the Red Cross, and Mandate Ambiguity' in Andrej Zwitter and others (eds), *Humanitarian Action: Global, Regional and Domestic Legal Responses* (CUP 2015).

[44] Statutes of the International Committee of the Red Cross (adopted 21 December 2017, entered into force 1 January 2018) <https://www.icrc.org/en/document/statutes-international-committee-red-cross-0> accessed 10 July 2025 (ICRC Statutes) art 4(1); Movement Statutes (n 21) art 5(2).

[45] Geneva Conventions (n 42) articles 9/9/9/10.

independent institution and intermediary, and may consider any question requiring examination by such an institution'.[46]

Regarding IHL, the ICRC is mandated to work for its faithful application, understanding, and dissemination; take cognizance of complaints of alleged breaches; and 'prepare any development thereof'.[47] Due to these roles and its history, the ICRC is sometimes referred to as IHL's 'guardian', though this term does not appear in the Movement Statutes, the ICRC Statutes, or the GCs or their APs. According to former ICRC President Jakob Kellenberger, the ICRC discharges its IHL mandate primarily by providing 'expertise, support, and authoritative guidance in at least three areas: better compliance with existing IHL rules; clarification of key legal concepts that may be necessary as a consequence of developments in the character of armed conflicts', and the development of treaty-based IHL.[48] The ICRC has recently provided critical IHL guidance through at least three major publications: on customary IHL;[49] on the notion of direct participation in hostilities;[50] and in its updated commentaries on the Geneva Conventions.[51]

The foregoing broad mandate can be summarized as ensuring the protection of and assistance to victims of armed conflict and violence not amounting to armed conflict, promoting the faithful application of IHL, and serving as a neutral intermediary between parties to armed conflicts. The first of these roles is particularly relevant here. Kellenberger explains that the ICRC focuses its humanitarian assistance activities in four areas: health services; water and habitat; economic security; and physical rehabilitation.[52] The personnel who do this work in the field are referred to within the ICRC as 'delegates'.[53] Key features of ICRC programming are the extent of its access to persons in need of assistance, the fact that the ICRC directly implements activities in the majority of its operations (it does not use implementing partners), the multidisciplinary nature of ICRC responses, and its rapid deployment capacity.[54]

The ICRC's humanitarian assistance work is guided by its 2004 Assistance Policy.[55] According to this policy, the ICRC provides humanitarian assistance to meet '[u]nmet essential needs' in situations of acute and chronic crisis, as well as in postcrisis situations.[56] It prioritizes taking action in situations where it can add value, in particular

[46] ICRC Statutes (n 44) art 4(2); Movement Statutes (n 21) art 5(3).

[47] ICRC Statutes (n 44) art 4(1); Movement Statutes (n 21) art 5(2).

[48] Jakob Kellenberger, 'The Role of the International Committee of the Red Cross' in Andrew Clapham and Paola Gaeta (eds), *The Oxford Handbook of International Law in Armed Conflict* (OUP 2014) 22. See also Robin Geib, Andreas Zimmermann, and Stefanie Haumer (eds), *Humanizing the Laws of War: The Red Cross and the Development of International Humanitarian Law* (CUP 2018).

[49] Jean-Marie Henckaerts and Louise Doswald-Beck, *Customary International Humanitarian Law*, vol I (CUP 2005).

[50] ICRC, *Interpretive Guidance on the Notion of Direct Participation in Hostilities under International Humanitarian Law* (ICRC 2009).

[51] <https://www.icrc.org/en/law-and-policy/geneva-conventions-and-their-commentaries> accessed 10 July 2025. All updated commentaries have been published except the updated commentary on GCIV.

[52] Kellenberger (n 48) 20.

[53] See Brigitte Troyon and Daniel Palmieri, 'The ICRC Delegate: An Exceptional Humanitarian Player?' (2007) 89 International Review of the Red Cross 97.

[54] Kellenberger (n 48) 21.

[55] ICRC, 'ICRC Assistance Policy' (2004) 86 International Review of the Red Cross 677 (ICRC Assistance Policy).

[56] ibid, 678 and 685.

where its status as a neutral and independent organization and intermediary can facilitate humanitarian access; its integrated approach to assistance and protection can promote respect for individual rights; its presence and knowledge of a situation provide particular legitimacy; or it can mobilize the resources necessary to provide essential assistance.[57] ICRC humanitarian assistance takes five forms—persuasion, mobilization, support, direct provision, and, in exceptional cases, denunciation[58]—and is provided in line with several 'strategies'[59] and following clear operational directives.[60] When the ICRC provides assistance directly to an affected population, it avoids relieving the authorities of their responsibilities in this regard; rather, it continues to urge them to 'fully meet their obligations'.[61] The ICRC provides humanitarian assistance in line with five 'guiding principles': taking the affected group's needs into account; providing effective and high-quality assistance; respecting the Fundamental Principles, the 'do no harm' principle, and the Code of Conduct for the International Red Cross and Red Crescent Movement and Non-Governmental Organizations in Disaster Relief (Code of Conduct);[62] in compliance with its responsibilities under the Movement Statutes and the Seville Agreement 2.0; and in partnership with 'humanitarian actors whose working methods and policies are compatible' with the ICRC's 'principles and work'.[63]

2.2. National Red Cross and Red Crescent Societies and the International Federation of Red Cross and Red Crescent Societies

National Societies originate in the 1863 Geneva Conference, which resolved that '[e]ach country shall have a Committee whose duty it shall be, in time of war and if the need arises, to assist the Army Medical Services by every means in its power'.[64] Six years later, the second International Conference in 1869 affirmed National Societies' broader role in providing relief 'in case of public calamity which, like war, demands immediate and organized assistance';[65] this was necessary in part to ensure a role for National Societies even in peacetime. National Societies' modern role is broadly to serve as auxiliaries to the public authorities 'in their humanitarian tasks, according to

[57] ibid, 679.
[58] ibid, 679–80.
[59] Based on a needs assessment; using an integrated approach; combining different modes of action; coordinated, shared, and in partnership with other humanitarian actors; and in an adaptive and innovative manner (ibid, 681–85).
[60] Involving the affected group in programme planning and management; conducting an integrated needs assessment and background analysis; following the ICRC's 'Planning for Results' framework; implementation with the necessary skills, capacities, or partnership agreements in place; clear entry and exit strategies; with ongoing monitoring, review, and evaluation (ibid, 691–93).
[61] ibid, 680.
[62] IFRC and ICRC, 'The Code of Conduct for the International Red Cross and Red Crescent Movement and Non-Governmental Organizations (NGOs) in Disaster Relief' (1994) <https://www.icrc.org/en/doc/assets/files/publications/icrc-002-1067.pdf> accessed 30 June 2025. See Chapter 2, Section 2.
[63] ICRC Assistance Policy (n 55) 680–81.
[64] Article 1, cited in Bugnion (n 16) 1319.
[65] Cited in David Fisher, 'The Law of International Disaster Response: Overview and Ramifications for Military Actors' (2008) 38 Israel Yearbook on Human Rights 115, 117.

the needs of the people'.[66] To this end, when there is no emergency, National Societies 'cooperate with the public authorities in the prevention of disease, the promotion of health and the mitigation of human suffering' through programming in the fields of 'education, health and social welfare',[67] and they disseminate IHL and the 'principles and ideals of the Movement'.[68] During armed conflict, National Societies organize with the authorities 'emergency relief operations and other services',[69] as contemplated by the GCs and their APs.[70] They also assist victims of 'natural disasters and other emergencies'.[71] National Societies also have an international role in armed conflict and disasters: they may provide 'services and personnel' and 'material, financial and moral support' in emergencies in other countries, through the local National Society, the ICRC, or the IFRC.[72] For example, personnel from a National Society may be seconded to another Movement component to assist in an armed conflict or disaster abroad.[73]

In 1919, National Societies' role was reinforced by the Covenant of the League of Nations, in which states agreed 'to encourage and promote the establishment and co-operation of duly authorized voluntary national Red Cross organisations having as purposes the improvement of health, the prevention of disease and the mitigation of suffering throughout the world',[74] and by the creation of the League of Red Cross Societies, now known as the IFRC. The object of the IFRC 'is to inspire, encourage, facilitate and promote at all times all forms of humanitarian activities by the National Societies'.[75] To achieve this, the IFRC in practice provides National Societies with a range of institutional supports.[76] It also carries out 'mandates entrusted to it by the International Conference'.[77] One such mandate was the IFRC's important disaster law work, which was discussed in Chapter 4.[78] Finally, the IFRC brings 'relief by all available means to all' persons affected by disaster;[79] it can also provide humanitarian assistance in armed conflict 'in accordance with the agreements concluded with other components of the Movement',[80] such as the Seville Agreement 2.0.

[66] Movement Statutes (n 21) art 3(1).

[67] ibid, art 3(2).

[68] ibid.

[69] ibid.

[70] GCI (n 42) art 26; GCIV (n 42) arts 25, 30, and 63; API (n 42) arts 6, 17, 33, and 81; Protocol Additional to the Geneva Conventions of 12 August 1949, and relating to the Protection of Victims of Non-International Armed Conflicts (adopted 8 June 1977, entered into force 7 December 1978) 1125 UNTS 609 (APII) art 18.

[71] Movement Statutes (n 21) art 3(2).

[72] ibid, art 3(3).

[73] For detailed analysis of the role of National Societies, see Christophe Lanord, 'The Legal Status of National Red Cross and Red Crescent Societies' (2000) 82 International Review of the Red Cross 1053.

[74] (Adopted 28 June 1919, entered into force 10 January 1920) 108 LNTS 188, art 25.

[75] Movement Statutes (n 21) art 6(3); IFRC Constitution (adopted 1987, amended 1991, 1999, 2007, 2015, 2017, 2019, and 2024) <https://www.ifrc.org/sites/default/files/2025-01/EN_Constitution2024_Adopted.pdf> accessed 14 July 2025 (IFRC Constitution) art 4.

[76] Movement Statutes (n 21) art 6(4); IFRC Constitution (n 75) art 5(1)(A).

[77] Movement Statutes (n 21) art 6(4)(l); IFRC Constitution (n 75) art 5(3).

[78] See Chapter 4, Section 2.3.1.

[79] Movement Statutes (n 21) art 6(4)(c); IFRC Constitution (n 75) art 5(B)(a). See generally Jean Pierre Revel, 'Role of the International Federation of Red Cross and Red Crescent Societies in Disaster Management' in Jan de Boer and Marcel Dubouloz (eds), *Handbook of Disaster Medicine* (CRC Press 2020).

[80] Movement Statutes (n 21) art 6(4)(i); IFRC Constitution (n 75) art 5(1)(B)(c).

When providing humanitarian assistance, the IFRC works 'through or in agreement with' the local National Society[81] and in accordance with the Principles and Rules for Red Cross and Red Crescent Humanitarian Assistance (Principles and Rules), which were first adopted by the XXIst International Conference in 1969,[82] and have since been updated several times, most recently in 2015. The Principles and Rules govern both the IFRC and National Societies.[83] They consist of ten principles, which are then elaborated and operationalized through a series of rules on coordination between and among National Societies and the IFRC. The rules recognize the dignity of persons affected by disasters and their entitlement to receive assistance, and commit National Societies and the IFRC to protect and advocate for, and provide appropriate, efficient, effective, and accountable humanitarian assistance to, people affected by disasters, with the consent of the affected state's National Society.[84] The rules also note that the IFRC and National Societies are 'each other's primary and preferred partners', but commit to coordinated partnerships with actors outside the Movement to increase operational reach, scale, and effectiveness.[85] For example, as mentioned in Chapter 4, the IFRC provides services aboard *SOS MEDITERRANEE*'s rescue ship *Ocean Viking*.[86] Finally, the rules note that the IFRC and National Societies provide humanitarian assistance that 'builds upon local capacities and complements local response mechanisms'.[87]

2.3. Privileges, immunities, and facilities and the protection of International Red Cross and Red Crescent Movement personnel

Chapter 5 covered how privileges and immunities accorded to the UN facilitate its humanitarian work.[88] The ICRC and IFRC enjoy similar privileges, immunities, and facilities, under the many bilateral status agreements concluded between the ICRC or IFRC, on the one hand, and the host state, on the other.[89] These agreements tend to provide the same privileges, immunities, and facilities as the Convention on the Privileges and Immunities of the United Nations[90] (the General Convention) and the

[81] Movement Statutes (n 21) art 6(5); IFRC Constitution (n 75) art 5(4).

[82] Dug Cubie, 'An Analysis of Soft Law Applicable to Humanitarian Action: Relative Normativity in Action?' (2011) 2 Journal of International Humanitarian Legal Studies 177, 194. The same International Conference also adopted the Declaration of Principles for International Humanitarian Relief to the Civilian Population in Disaster Situations (XXIst International Conference of the Red Cross and Red Crescent (6–13 September 1969) Resolution XXVI).

[83] Principles and Rules for Red Cross and Red Crescent Humanitarian Assistance (2013) <https://www.ifrc.org/document/principles-rules-humanitarian-assistance> accessed 14 July 2025 (Principles and Rules) 3.

[84] ibid, 4.

[85] ibid.

[86] See Chapter 4, Section 4.3.

[87] Principles and Rules (n 83) 4.

[88] See Chapter 5, Section 5.1.

[89] As of 2016, the ICRC had concluded 95 bilateral status agreements (Debuf (n 9) 327) and the IFRC had concluded over 80 (IFRC, 'Written Submission of the International Federation of Red Cross and Red Crescent Societies to the International Law Commission on the "Draft Articles on the Protection of Persons in the Event of Disasters"' (January 2016) <https://legal.un.org/ilc/sessions/68/pdfs/english/pop_ifrc.pdf> accessed 15 July 2025, 2).

[90] (Adopted 13 February 1946, entered into force 17 September 1946) 1 UNTS 15.

Vienna Convention on Diplomatic Relations.[91] In a small number of cases,[92] rather than concluding a status agreement with the ICRC, the host state has brought the ICRC within the scope of its domestic legislation according privileges and immunities to international organizations. As the relevant domestic legislation is typically General Convention implementing legislation, it reflects the privileges and immunities accorded under that treaty.[93] Thus whether under a bilateral status agreement or host state law, the ICRC and IFRC tend to enjoy the same privileges, immunities, and facilities as the UN.[94] These include, in relation to both the organization and its personnel, immunity from jurisdiction and the inviolability of premises, property, assets, documents, and data. Personnel specifically are entitled to personal inviolability and freedom of movement.[95]

Primary responsibility under international law for the security and protection of humanitarian personnel, including Movement personnel, lies with the affected state or, in occupied territory, with the occupying power.[96] Movement personnel deployed to respond to a humanitarian emergency in an affected state enjoy the protections owed by that state to all individuals on its territory or under its effective control under international human rights law (IHRL) and under national law. Additionally, the individual's state of nationality is entitled to provide them with consular assistance.[97] As discussed in Chapter 3, all humanitarian personnel in armed conflict, including of course Movement personnel, are protected by IHL,[98] and those who attack them can be held accountable under international criminal law (ICL).[99] Furthermore, certain transnational criminal law treaties, such as the International Convention Against the Taking of Hostages[100] and the International Convention for the Protection of All Persons from Enforced Disappearance,[101] aim to suppress and punish crimes that pose a particular risk to humanitarians, including Movement personnel.

Beyond these general protections, the privileges, immunities, and facilities outlined earlier in this section provide Movement personnel with an additional layer of protection. For example, personal inviolability can help protect Movement personnel from arbitrary detention by the host state.

[91] (Adopted 18 April 1961, entered into force 24 April 1964) 500 UNTS 95; UN, 'Protection of Persons in the Event of Disasters: Memorandum by the Secretariat' (11 December 2007) A/CN.4/590 (UN Secretariat Memo) para 154; Debuf (n 9) 331; Davorin Lapas, 'Diplomatic Privileges and Immunities for IGO-like Entities: A Step Towards a New Diplomatic Law' (2019) 16 International Organizations Law Review 378, 398–402.

[92] Eight in 2016 (Debuf (n 9) 331).

[93] Debuf (n 9) 331–32.

[94] ibid, 331; UN Secretariat Memo (n 91) para 154.

[95] Debuf (n 9) 339–40; UN Secretariat Memo (n 91) para 154. For a detailed list of the privileges, immunities, and facilities typically contained in the ICRC's bilateral status agreements, see Debuf (n 9) 335–36.

[96] Convention (IV) respecting the Laws and Customs of War on Land (1907) (adopted 18 October 1907, entered into force 26 January 1910) Annex (Regulations) (Hague Regulations) art 43.

[97] Vienna Convention on Consular Relations (adopted 24 April 1963, entered into force 19 March 1967) 596 UNTS 261, art 36.

[98] See Chapter 3, Section 4.4.4.

[99] See Chapter 3, Section 7.1.1.

[100] (Adopted 17 December 1979, entered into force 3 June 1983) 1316 UNTS 205.

[101] (Adopted 20 December 2006, entered into force 23 December 2010) 2716 UNTS 3.

As will be shown below,[102] some NGO personnel are protected by the Convention on the Safety of United Nations and Associated Personnel (UN Safety Convention).[103] However, as a result of their Fundamental Principle of independence, the ICRC and IFRC do not come within the scope of this treaty. Bouvier explains that when the UN Safety Convention was being negotiated, the ICRC indicated that it did not wish to be protected by it, because application of the treaty to the ICRC would imply a close association between the ICRC and the UN.[104]

Movement personnel are additionally protected by the fact that they are in certain circumstances permitted to don the distinctive red cross, red crescent, or (culturally neutral) red crystal emblem.[105] These emblems have two distinct uses: protective and indicative. When used protectively, they signal that the wearer is someone entitled to special protection under IHL. When used indicatively, they communicate that the wearer is a member of the Movement. Both uses are regulated by IHL. As a general rule, the emblems may not be employed, whether during armed conflict or in peacetime, 'except to indicate or to protect [...] medical units and establishments' and 'personnel and material protected by' IHL.[106] The ICRC is always permitted to use the emblems.[107] National Society personnel may don the emblems in armed conflict if they are serving as an auxiliary to the medical service of the state armed forces.[108] In times of peace, IFRC and National Society personnel may make indicative use of the emblems.[109] In its indicative use, the emblem must be 'comparatively small in size and may not be placed on armlets or on the roofs of buildings'.[110] Thus, IFRC and National Society personnel responding to a disaster or providing assistance at sea may don the emblems on these terms.

3. Non-governmental organizations

Many contemporary international NGOs were founded just before, during, or shortly after World War II.[111] Prior to World War II, few relief organizations were permanent;

[102] See Section 3.3.

[103] (Adopted 9 December 1994, entered into force 15 January 1999) 2051 UNTS 363.

[104] Antoine Bouvier, 'Convention on the Safety of United Nations and Associated Personnel: Presentation and Analysis' (1995) 35 International Review of the Red Cross 638, 655.

[105] Protocol Additional to the Geneva Conventions of 12 August 1949, and relating to the Adoption of an Additional Distinctive Emblem (adopted 8 December 2005, entered into force 17 January 2007) 2404 UNTS 261.

[106] GCI (n 42) art 44(1).

[107] ibid, art 44(3).

[108] ibid, art 40(1); API (n 42) art 18. Additionally, in NIACs covered by APII, 'already existing Red Cross groups or branches on the side opposing the Government and even improvised organizations which . . . come into existence only during the conflict' may use the distinctive emblem 'for pragmatic reasons, without recognizing as such a new Red Cross or Red Crescent Society' (Yves Sandoz, Christophe Swinarski, and Bruno Zimmermann (eds), *Commentary on the Additional Protocols of 8 June 1977 to the Geneva Conventions of 12 August 1949* (Martinus Nijhoff 1987) paras 4739–40 (internal citation omitted)); see also APII (n 70) art 12.

[109] GCI (n 42) art 44(2).

[110] ibid.

[111] Save the Children is a notable exception; it was founded in 1920 (Bruno Cabanes, *The Great War and the Origins of Humanitarianism 1918–1924* (CUP 2014) 248).

rather, they formed in response to an emergency and disbanded when it was over.[112] Even the ICRC was initially 'no more than an initiative committee, intended to promote [. . . certain] ideas, but set to be dissolved as soon as they had been given practical form'.[113] However, around the time of World War II, a new generation of NGOs arose to help war victims; nearly 200 were created between 1945 and 1949 alone.[114] Some subsequently expanded globally, and many still exist today.[115] For example, Oxfam was founded in 1942, Catholic Relief Services in 1943, CARE in 1945, and the Norwegian Refugee Council in 1946.[116] Of course, some international humanitarian NGOs have distinct origins. *Médecins Sans Frontières* (MSF), for example, was founded in 1971 by a group of French former ICRC physicians who objected to how the ICRC handled aspects of its work in the Biafra–Nigeria war.[117] *Médecins du Monde*, in turn, was formed in 1980 by former MSF doctors.[118] Islamic Relief was established in 1984 by a Birmingham-based medical student in response to the famine in East Africa.[119]

These international NGOs, as well as national and local NGOs, are major providers of humanitarian assistance. According to the UN Office for the Coordination of Humanitarian Affairs, about 20 per cent of global humanitarian funding in 2024 ultimately went to NGOs.[120] This is in part because many NGOs, particularly local and national NGOs, serve as UN implementing partners. The Office of the UN High Commissioner for Refugees, for example, has operational partnerships with over 900 NGOs, accounting for about 40 per cent of its annual expenditure.[121] Chapter 4 addressed their increasingly important role in maritime search and rescue.[122] However, despite their significant role in practice, NGOs face challenges in relation to the international legal framework for humanitarian assistance, particularly in peacetime, because they are not subjects of international law.

112 Thomas G Weiss, 'Humanitarian Action' in Jacob Katz Cogan, Ian Hurd, and Ian Johnstone (eds), *The Oxford Handbook of International Organizations* (OUP 2016) 308.

113 Bugnion (n 16) 1327.

114 Michael Barnett, *Empire of Humanity: A History of Humanitarianism* (Cornell University Press 2011) 112.

115 Weiss (n 112) 308.

116 It is beyond the scope of this chapter to describe the major international humanitarian NGOs. Barnett provides insightful overviews of CARE, Catholic Relief Services, World Vision International, and MSF (Barnett (n 114) 198–212). See also Daniel Maxwell and Kirsten Gelsdorf, *Understanding the Humanitarian World* (Routledge 2019) 99–100.

117 Marie-Luce Desgrandchamps, 'Revenir sur le mythe fondateur de Médecins sans frontières: les relations entre les médecins français et le CICR pendant la guerre du Biafra (1967–1970)' (2011) 2 *Relations internationales* 95.

118 <https://www.medecinsdumonde.org/en/our-history/> accessed 28 June 2025.

119 <https://islamic-relief.org/about-us/our-history/> accessed 28 June 2025.

120 Author's calculation, performed using data obtained from: <https://fts.unocha.org> accessed 8 August 2025.

121 <https://www.unhcr.org/about-unhcr/our-partners/non-governmental-organizations> accessed 28 June 2025.

122 See Chapter 4, Section 4.3.

3.1. Relationship with international law

A subject of international law is an entity with international rights and obligations and the capacity to maintain its rights by bringing international claims and to be responsible for its breaches by being subject to such claims.[123] NGOs do not possess these characteristics. This is illustrated by how the International Law Commission (ILC) addressed NGOs in its Draft Articles on the Protection of Persons in the Event of Disasters (Draft Articles). The ILC explained that the Draft Articles focus 'primarily on the activities of States and intergovernmental organizations [. . .] and other entities enjoying specific international legal competence in the provision of disaster relief assistance in the context of disasters', and that NGOs were 'included within the scope of the draft articles only in a secondary manner, either as direct beneficiaries of duties placed on States [. . .] or indirectly, as being subject to the domestic laws implementing the draft articles'.[124]

There is a long history of efforts to address NGOs' lack of international legal personality. In 1910, the *Institut de droit international* and the International Law Association began promoting a treaty to endow NGOs with international legal personality.[125] Two drafts were proposed, in 1923 and in 1950, but neither was successful because states were concerned about loss of control and NGOs about loss of autonomy.[126]

NGOs nevertheless play a role within the UN, as a result of article 71 of the organization's Charter. This provision allows the Economic and Social Council (ECOSOC) to 'make suitable arrangements for consultation with non-governmental organizations which are concerned with matters within' ECOSOC's competence.[127] Three distinct levels of NGO consultative status—general, special, and roster—determine the level of participation. NGOs must apply for consultative status through a procedure established by ECOSOC in 1996.[128] It makes consultative status contingent on the NGO having, *inter alia*, 'recognized standing within the particular field of its competence'; a headquarters and a democratically adopted constitution; and a representative governance structure with 'appropriate mechanisms of accountability' to members and 'transparent decision-making processes'.[129] Although article 71 refers only to ECOSOC, over time a consultative role for NGOs became established practice throughout the UN,[130] with ECOSOC serving as the 'gatekeeper'.[131] There is now 'widespread provision for national and international NGOs qualified in relevant fields to be accorded observer status at meetings of treaty parties, in law-making diplomatic

[123] James Crawford, *Brownlie's Principles of Public International Law* (9th edn, OUP 2019) 105.

[124] ILC, 'Report of the International Law Commission on the Work of its 68th Session' (2 May–10 June and 4 July–12 August 2016) A/71/10 (ILC Draft Articles) commentary to art 1, para 3.

[125] Steve Charnovitz, 'Nongovernmental Organizations and International Law' (2006) 100 American Journal of International Law 348, 356.

[126] ibid, 357.

[127] Charter of the United Nations (adopted 26 June 1945, entered into force 24 October 1945) 1 UNTS XVI, art 71.

[128] ECOSOC, 'Consultative Relationship between the United Nations and Non-Governmental Organizations', Res 1996/31 (25 July 1996).

[129] ibid, paras 9, 10, and 12.

[130] Charnovitz (n 125) 358.

[131] Boyle and Chinkin (n 2) 52.

conferences, global summits and other meetings held under UN auspices'.[132] NGOs have seized these opportunities. For example, they regularly participate in ECOSOC's annual humanitarian affairs segment, they are increasingly involved in the deliberations of the UN General Assembly and its committees,[133] and they were involved in the ILC's work on the Draft Articles.[134]

3.2. Facilities under international law

The impact of an NGO's lack of international legal personality on its work depends on whether it is operating in armed conflict or peacetime. As detailed in Chapter 3, IHL foresees that humanitarian assistance will be provided by non-state actors and places obligations on states to facilitate their work in certain circumstances.[135] While IHL does not refer to NGOs as such, they are nevertheless among the humanitarian actors it contemplates,[136] using terms such as 'impartial humanitarian body',[137] 'impartial humanitarian organization',[138] 'organizations whose object is to give [. . .] material relief',[139] and 'relief societies'.[140]

International NGOs face greater challenges in peacetime. As a creature of municipal law, an international NGO will not have a legal status outside the country where it was formed. Without legal personhood in its operational environment, an international NGO may face challenges in executing basic functions, such as leasing office space, sponsoring work visas for international staff, and importing supplies and equipment.[141] And because NGOs are not subjects of international law, there is no scope for bi- or multilateral treaties to address this issue in the way that they do for the UN[142] and states,[143] and even for the ICRC and IFRC.[144]

The UN General Assembly has spoken to this issue. In a resolution adopted in 1988, it stressed the 'important contribution made in providing humanitarian assistance' by NGOs 'working with strictly humanitarian motives', and called on states to facilitate

[132] ibid, 54.
[133] ibid, 77.
[134] Elena Evangelidis and Thérèse O'Donnell, 'NGOs and the International Law Commission Draft Articles on the Protection of Persons in the Event of Disasters: A Relationship of Mutual or Grudging Respect?' (2018) 1 Yearbook of International Disaster Law 116, 133.
[135] See Chapter 3, Sections 3–5.
[136] Jean Pictet and others, *Commentary: IV Geneva Convention Relative to the Protection of Civilian Persons in Time of War* (ICRC 1958) 321; Sandoz and others (n 108) para 4872; Kate Mackintosh, 'Beyond the Red Cross: The Protection of Independent Humanitarian Organizations and their Staff in International Humanitarian Law' (2007) 89 International Review of the Red Cross 113, 116; ICRC, *Commentary on the First Geneva Convention: Convention (I) for the Amelioration of the Condition of the Wounded and Sick in Armed Forces in the Field* (CUP 2016) paras 789 and 1156.
[137] GCIV (n 42) arts 3 and 61.
[138] ibid, arts 10 and 59.
[139] ibid, art 30(3).
[140] APII (n 70) art 18(1).
[141] See Stefano Silingardi, 'The Status of Emergency Workers' in Andrea Guttry, Marco Gestri, and Gabriella Venturini (eds), *International Disaster Response Law* (TMC Asser Press 2012) 567–74.
[142] See Chapter 5, Section 5.1.
[143] See Chapter 7, Section 3.
[144] See Section 2.3.

and support their work.[145] In its foundational resolution 46/182,[146] the General Assembly noted that NGOs 'working impartially and with strictly humanitarian motives should continue to make a significant contribution in supplementing national efforts', and accordingly called on states 'whose populations are in need of humanitarian assistance [. . .] to facilitate the work of these organizations'.[147]

While states may in practice facilitate the work of individual international NGOs, their international law response to these calls has been uneven. In 1986, the Council of Europe adopted a treaty to facilitate cross-border NGO operations by ensuring their legal recognition across member states.[148] The treaty thus facilitates international NGO operations in its twelve states parties,[149] though these are not states where humanitarian assistance is typically provided. Among international disaster response law (IDRL) treaties, only the Tampere Convention on the Provision of Telecommunications Resources for Disaster Mitigation and Relief Operations even mentions NGOs,[150] and it accords them facilities only implicitly.[151]

The Draft Articles have progressed this issue. The ILC acknowledged the role of NGOs in disaster response in its commentary on the Draft Articles, where it notes that NGOs 'may be well placed, because of their nature, location and expertise, to provide assistance in response to a particular disaster'.[152] International NGOs are thus included within the Draft Articles' defined term 'other assisting actor', which means 'a competent intergovernmental organization, or a relevant non-governmental organization or entity, providing assistance to an affected State with its consent'.[153] Draft article 15 on the facilitation of external assistance provides that the 'affected State shall take the necessary measures, within its national law, to facilitate the prompt and effective provision of external assistance, in particular regarding: (a) relief personnel, in fields such as privileges and immunities, visa and entry requirements, work permits, and freedom of movement; and (b) equipment and goods, in fields such as customs requirements and tariffs, taxation, transport, and the disposal thereof'. As 'relief personnel' includes personnel sent by an 'other assisting actor',[154] which in turn includes international NGOs, international NGO personnel are included within the scope of states' obligations under draft article 15. If states adopt an international disaster response treaty with a provision along the lines of draft article 15,[155] it will facilitate international NGOs' disaster relief work.

[145] UNGA Res 43/131 (8 December 1988) A/RES/43/131, paras 3–5.
[146] See Chapter 5, Section 2.2.
[147] UNGA, 'Strengthening of the Coordination of Humanitarian Emergency Assistance of the United Nations', Res 46/182 (19 December 1991) A/RES/46/182, Annex, paras 5–6.
[148] European Convention on the Recognition of the Legal Personality of International Non-Governmental Organisations (adopted 24 April 1986, entered into force 1 January 1991) ETS No 124.
[149] Austria, Belgium, Cyprus, France, Greece, Liechtenstein, North Macedonia, Netherlands, Portugal, Slovenia, Switzerland, and the United Kingdom.
[150] (Adopted 18 June 1998, entered into force 8 January 2005) 2296 UNTS 5, preambular para 19.
[151] ibid, arts 5 and 9.
[152] ILC Draft Articles (n 124) commentary to art 12, para 5.
[153] ibid, art 3(d). Note, the term 'other assisting actor' does not include local and national NGOs (ibid, commentary to art 3, para 21).
[154] ibid, art 3(f).
[155] See Chapter 4, Section 2.3.2.4.

3.3. The protection of non-governmental organization personnel

The general provisions that protect Movement personnel, which were outlined above,[156] also cover NGO personnel. NGO personnel may enjoy additional protection under the UN Safety Convention, which was introduced in Chapter 5.[157] The UN Safety Convention covers NGO personnel if they qualify as 'Associated Personnel' within the meaning of the Convention. The UN Safety Convention defines 'Associated Personnel' as persons assigned to 'carry out activities in support of the fulfilment of the mandate of a' UN operation by a government or an intergovernmental organization, the UN Secretary-General or a UN specialized agency, or a humanitarian NGO pursuant to an agreement between the NGO and the Secretary-General.[158] The latter suggests that personnel of a UN implementing partner NGO qualify as 'Associated Personnel' and are therefore protected under the Convention. In 2002, the General Assembly asked the UN Secretary-General to clarify this.[159] In response, the Secretary-General issued a model standard provision for inclusion in agreements between the UN and NGOs. The provision provides that individuals deployed by NGOs to work with the UN in states party to the UN Safety Convention are 'Associated Personnel' within the meaning of the Convention.[160] In addition to the UN Safety Convention's general protections, NGO personnel who qualify as Associated Personnel are also covered by any privileges and immunities the affected state grants the UN under the status agreement it is required to conclude with the UN under the UN Safety Convention.[161]

International NGOs may, however, be reluctant to collaborate with the UN, which they may perceive as inherently political and therefore a threat to their adherence to the humanitarian principles of neutrality and independence.[162] Indeed, as mentioned above, most UN implementing partners are local and national NGOs, not international NGOs. International NGO personnel are therefore typically protected not by the UN Safety Convention, but by specific treaty provisions, whose applicability depends on whether the context is one of armed conflict, where IHL applies, or peacetime. General protections under IHL, and ICL accountability for their violation, were

[156] See second paragraph of Section 2.3.
[157] See Chapter 5, Section 5.4.
[158] UN Safety Convention (n 103) art 1(b).
[159] UNGA Res 57/28 (3 February 2003) A/RES/57/28, para 6.
[160] UNGA, 'Report of the Secretary-General on the Scope of Legal Protection under the Convention on the Safety of United Nations and Associated Personnel' (28 July 2003) A/58/187. The model standard provision states: for 'the purposes of the Convention on the Safety of United Nations and Associated Personnel, persons deployed by [the humanitarian non-governmental organization or agency] under this Agreement shall be considered 'associated personnel' within the meaning of article 1 (b) (iii) of the Convention' (para 24).
[161] UN Safety Convention (n 103) art 4, which provides that the 'host State and the United Nations shall conclude as soon as possible an agreement on the status of the United Nations operation and all personnel engaged in the operation'. The situation is thus far simpler for NGO personnel who qualify as 'Associated Personnel' under the UN Safety Convention than Keller suggests in her article on applying derivative UN immunity to UN implementing partner NGOs, which does not consider the UN Safety Convention (Tori Keller, 'Applying Derivative United Nations Immunity to Humanitarian NGOs' (2023) 23 Chicago Journal of International Law 451).
[162] Mackintosh (n 136) 124.

addressed in Chapter 3;[163] additional IHL protections specific to health care are addressed below.

Regarding peacetime, several IDRL treaties provide that the affected state must ensure the protection of personnel, as well as equipment and materials, brought into its territory by an assisting party, without specifically including or excluding NGO personnel.[164] These provisions might therefore 'conceivably include representatives of non-governmental organizations where such organizations have been engaged as part of the relief effort'.[165] Additionally, Ulrich has argued that there is a norm of customary international law regarding the protection of relief personnel, including NGO personnel.[166] The Draft Articles advance international law in this area. They provide that the 'affected State shall take the appropriate measures to ensure the protection of relief personnel and of equipment and goods present in its territory, or in territory under its jurisdiction or control, for the purpose of providing external assistance'.[167] The reference to relief personnel includes international NGO personnel, but not personnel of local and national NGOs.[168]

Bilateral agreements between affected states and international NGOs that extend privileges, immunities, and facilities to international NGOs and their personnel, along the lines of the agreements between the ICRC or IFRC and states, could provide protection until the Draft Articles become binding treaty law and in states that do not join any such treaty. Seatzu has suggested that affected states should enter into agreements like status of forces agreements with NGOs, which would focus on 'the rights and needs of [NGO] humanitarian aid workers, above all the right to safety and security, the right to work and the right to free movement in and out of the host country'.[169] His suggestion relates to armed conflict—in which some of these issues are in fact already regulated under IHL—but such agreements could equally be adopted in peacetime. While there is nothing to prevent them from being concluded, in practice this rarely occurs.[170]

3.3.1. The protection of health care in armed conflict

Violence against health care, including medical relief operations, is a major issue in armed conflict,[171] and the problem is worsening. According to the Safeguarding

[163] See Chapter 3, Sections 4.4.4 and 7.1.

[164] Convention on Assistance in the Case of a Nuclear Accident or Radiological Emergency (adopted 26 September 1986, entered into force 26 February 1987) 1457 UNTS 133, art 3(b); Convention on the Transboundary Effects of Industrial Accidents (adopted 17 March 1992, entered into force 19 April 2000) 2105 UNTS 457, Annex X, para 2; Tampere Convention (n 150) art 5(3); Framework Convention on Civil Defence Assistance (adopted 22 May 2000, entered into force 23 September 2001) 2172 UNTS 213, art 4(a)(5).

[165] UN Secretariat Memo (n 91) 127.

[166] Lana Ulrich, 'The Customary International Law Obligation to Protect Foreign Disaster Relief Personnel and Their Equipment' (2014) 22 Willamette Journal of International Law and Dispute Resolution 343.

[167] ILC Draft Articles (n 124) art 16.

[168] ibid, commentary to art 16, para 12.

[169] Francesco Seatzu, 'Revitalizing the International Legal Protection of Humanitarian Aid Workers in Armed Conflict' (2017) 11 Revue des droits de l'homme 1, 8.

[170] UN Secretariat Memo (n 91) para 155.

[171] UNSC Res 2286 (3 May 2016) S/RES/2286, preambular para 10; 31st International Conference of the Red Cross and Red Crescent (28 November–1 December 2011) Resolution 5, 'Health Care in Danger: Respecting and Protecting Health Care', 31IC/11/R5; Elizabeth Rose Donnelly, 'Towards Greater

Health in Conflict Coalition, 2024 was the worst year on record for incidents of violence against or obstruction of health care, with 3,323 reported incidents of violence and 927 health workers killed.[172] Among health care workers in armed conflict—which include regular civilian medical professionals, military medics, and humanitarian medical personnel—NGO personnel are at particular risk, because they are not protected by IHL to the same extent as other health workers. When she was head of the Humanitarian Affairs Department at MSF's operational centre in Amsterdam, Mackintosh noted that the personnel of humanitarian NGOs 'have less protection, legally speaking, than most of them probably think'.[173] It is not surprising that this general observation was made by an MSF official, because it is nowhere truer than in relation to medical NGOs in armed conflict. It is widely known that health care enjoys special protection under IHL, but medical humanitarian NGOs in fact enjoy little protection beyond that accorded to NGOs more generally. It is worth detailing exactly how health care—including medical personnel, facilities, and transports—is protected under IHL, to clarify the protections that medical NGOs do and do not enjoy.[174] Medical personnel are addressed first, followed by health care facilities and transports.

IHL provides specific protection for medical personnel, but most humanitarian medical personnel do not fall within the ambit of this protection. Prior to the adoption of the APs, only military medical personnel,[175] the medical personnel of regular civilian hospitals,[176] and humanitarian medical personnel assigned to serve their own or another country's armed forces during IAC[177] received special protection under IHL. The APs extended this protection to '[c]ivilian medical personnel'.[178] However, API defines medical personnel, including civilian medical personnel, as personnel 'assigned' to medical tasks by a conflict party.[179] Three categories of medical personnel may be so assigned.[180] First, medical personnel of a conflict party. Second, medical personnel of National Societies and other duly recognized national voluntary aid societies,[181] provided the personnel in question have been authorized by a conflict

Legal Protection for Medical-Humanitarian NGOs in Situations of Armed Conflict' (2018) 3 Cambridge Law Review 144; Camille Michel, Kenneth Lavelle, and Thomas Nierle, 'Medical Care Under Fire: A Perspective From the International Medical Organization Médecins Sans Frontières' in Amy Kravitz (ed), *Oxford Handbook of Humanitarian Medicine* (OUP 2019); Philippe Calain, 'Attacks on Hospitals: An Alarming Problem for Military Medicine as Well as for Humanitarian Medicine' in Daniel Messelken and David Winkler (eds), *Health Care in Contexts of Risk, Uncertainty, and Hybridity* (Springer 2022).

[172] Safeguarding Health in Conflict, 'Epidemic of Violence: Violence Against Health Care in Conflict' (2024) <https://insecurityinsight.org/wp-content/uploads/2025/04/2024-SHCC-Annual-Report.pdf> accessed 2 July 2025, 7.

[173] Mackintosh (n 136) 129.

[174] For more detailed analysis of this issue, which also encompasses IHRL, see Johanna Michaels Kreisel, 'The "Benghazi Six" and International Medical Neutrality in Times of War and Peace' (2007) 1 Journal of Health Law & Policy 42.

[175] GCI (n 42) arts 24–25; GCII (n 42) art 36.

[176] GCIV (n 42) art 20.

[177] GCI (n 42) arts 26–27.

[178] API (n 42) art 15(1); APII (n 70) art 9(1).

[179] API (n 42) art 8(c); Sandoz and others (n 108) para 349; see also API (n 42) art 9(2).

[180] API (n 42) art 8(c)(i–iii).

[181] 'Duly recognized' means recognized in accordance with GCI (n 42) art 26 and GCII (n 42) art 24.

party.[182] Third, personnel made available to—and so working under the control of—a conflict party for humanitarian purposes by a neutral or third state, a recognized and authorized aid society of such a state, or an impartial humanitarian organization.[183] APII uses largely the same definition of medical personnel.[184] The customary rule, which applies in both IAC and NIAC, is essentially the same.[185] International humanitarian NGOs, however, will not typically agree to work under the control of a conflict party, because doing so compromises the humanitarian principles of neutrality and independence.[186] Thus, most NGO medical personnel do not qualify as 'medical personnel'; they are merely protected as civilians.[187]

NGO medical personnel who do not qualify as 'medical personnel' within the meaning of the APs are not, however, entirely without special protection. The APs provide several general protections for medical duties, which apply to all 'those performing medical activities or activities directly related thereto, whether or not they are considered to be medical personnel in the sense of' API.[188] These provide that no one will be punished for carrying out medical activities compatible with medical ethics, and protect persons from being forced to do work, or prevented from doing work, contrary to medical ethics or other rules for the benefit of the wounded and sick.[189] API also protects persons from revealing patient information if doing so would be harmful to the patient or their family.[190] The cognate protection in NIAC is weaker, as APII only protects medical confidentiality to the extent of national law.[191]

The GCs protect regular civilian hospitals in IAC.[192] Similar protection is implicit in NIAC under Common Article 3 as essential to ensuring that the wounded and sick are cared for.[193] The APs extended this protection to 'medical units',[194] which includes both regular civilian hospitals as well as other fixed or mobile medical facilities, such as blood transfusion centres, preventive medicine centres, and field hospitals and clinics.[195] However, the protection of hospitals and medical units in IAC depends on the medical unit belonging to, or having been recognized or authorized by, a conflict party.[196] The same IAC rules also apply to medical vehicles, such as ambulances.[197] The cognate customary rules are the same.[198] To preserve their independence and

182 Sandoz and others (n 108) para 358.
183 API (n 42) arts 8(c)(iii) and 9(2).
184 See Sandoz and others (n 108) paras 4661–67; Henckaerts and Doswald-Beck (n 49) 83.
185 Henckaerts and Doswald-Beck (n 49) rule 25.
186 Note, however, that some medical NGOs do not adhere strictly to the principle of neutrality. For example, Donnelly notes that *Médecins du Monde* has not infrequently taken a side in conflict (Donnelly (n 171) 149).
187 API (n 42) arts 48 and 51; APII (n 70) art 13.
188 Sandoz and others (n 108) para 649.
189 API (n 42) art 16; APII (n 70) art 10; see also Henckaerts and Doswald-Beck (n 49) rule 26.
190 API (n 42) art 16(3).
191 APII (n 70) art 10(3–4).
192 GCI (n 42) art 19(1); GCIV (n 42) art 18(1).
193 Henckaerts and Doswald-Beck (n 49) 93.
194 API (n 42) art 12(1); APII (n 70) art 11(1).
195 API (n 42) art 8(e). 'Medical units' is defined in API (article 8(e)), but not in APII. Henckaerts and Doswald-Beck explain that in 'the absence of a definition of medical units' in APII, the term 'may be understood as applying in the same sense in' NIAC as in IAC (Henckaerts and Doswald-Beck (n 49) 95).
196 GCIV (n 42) art 18(2–3); API (n 42) art 12(2).
197 GCIV (n 42) art 21; API (n 42) art 21.
198 Henckaerts and Doswald-Beck (n 49) rules 28 and 29.

neutrality, international NGOs will not typically work under the control of a conflict party. Medical units and vehicles not authorized by a conflict party in IAC are protected only as civilian objects.[199] Under APII, the special protection accorded to medical units and transports does not depend on conflict party recognition or authorization,[200] because states did not want to legitimize organized armed groups by giving them the power to recognize or authorize medical missions. Recall, however, that in practice APII applies only to a limited number of NIACs.[201]

As mentioned in Section 2.3 above, the protection of personnel and facilities is enhanced if they can don or display the distinctive red cross, red crescent, or red crystal emblem. Medical NGOs are not generally permitted to use the distinctive emblems.[202] However, this may be authorized on a case-by-case basis by the local National Society.[203] More often, a medical NGO will identify its personnel with its own logo, which may enhance protection if belligerents are familiar with it.[204]

4. Standard-setting

NGOs and the Movement have together made significant contributions to the professionalization of humanitarian assistance and humanitarian action more broadly by developing voluntary performance standards. The most significant[205] among these are the Code of Conduct,[206] which was discussed in Chapter 2,[207] and the Humanitarian Charter and Minimum Standards in Humanitarian Response (Sphere Handbook).[208] Both sets of standards apply in armed conflict as well as in peacetime.

Work on the Sphere Handbook began in 1997,[209] as a result of the scale and intensity of the humanitarian crisis—including in refugee camps in neighbouring Zaire—provoked by the 1994 genocide against the Tutsi in Rwanda.[210] A pilot version was

[199] API (n 42) arts 48 and 52.

[200] APII (n 70) art 11(1).

[201] See Chapter 3, Section 1.2.

[202] See Section 2.3 and Sandoz and others (n 108) para 2889.

[203] Emanuela-Chiara Gillard, 'Enhancing the Security of Civilians in Conflict: Notifications, Evacuations, Humanitarian Corridors, Suspensions of Hostilities and Other Humanitarian Arrangements' (*Chatham House*, 30 April 2024) <https://www.chathamhouse.org/2024/04/enhancing-security-civilians-conflict> accessed 12 July 2024, 9.

[204] See UNSC Res 2286 (3 May 2016) S/RES/2286, preambular para 7.

[205] Other voluntary standards are outlined in Peter Walker and Daniel Maxwell, *Shaping the Humanitarian World* (Routledge 2008) 129–34 and Catherine Gribbin and Ilario Maiolo, 'Legal Framework Applicable to Humanitarian Actors Responding to Disasters in Weak and Fragile States' in David D. Caron, Michael J. Kelly, and Anastasia Telesetsky (eds), *The International Law of Disaster Relief* (CUP 2014) 151–55.

[206] Code of Conduct (n 62).

[207] See Chapter 2, Section 3.2.

[208] Sphere, *The Sphere Handbook: Humanitarian Charter and Minimum Standards in Humanitarian Response* (Sphere Association 2018) <https://spherestandards.org/wp-content/uploads/Sphere-Handbook-2018-EN.pdf> (Sphere Handbook) accessed 30 June 2025.

[209] Evangelidis and O'Donnell (n 134) 129.

[210] Margie Buchanan-Smith, 'How the Sphere Project Came Into Being: A Case Study of Policy-Making in the Humanitarian Aid Sector and the Relative Influence of Research' (2003) ODI Working Paper 215 <https://odi.org/en/publications/how-the-sphere-project-came-into-being-a-case-study-of-policy-making-in-the-humanitarian-aid-sector-and-the-relative-influence-of-research/> accessed 27 July 2025.

published in 1998; the current fifth edition was published in 2018.[211] The Sphere Handbook consists of four interconnected sections: the Humanitarian Charter, protection principles, core humanitarian standards, and minimum standards.[212] The Humanitarian Charter is 'in part a statement of established legal rights and obligations' and 'in part a statement' of the NGO authors' 'shared belief[s]'.[213] It draws on IHL, IHRL, and international refugee law 'to assert that civilians affected by natural or human-made disasters or armed conflict have a right to life with dignity, and therefore a right to protection and assistance'.[214] The four protection principles that follow are aimed at operationalizing the Humanitarian Charter.[215] The bulk of the Sphere Handbook then consists of the core and minimum standards. While the core standards are framed as one 'Core Humanitarian Standard', they are in fact nine distinct 'commitments' that apply across all humanitarian sectors,[216] underpinned by one cross-cutting commitment to the core humanitarian principles.[217] Minimum standards are articulated for four sectors: water supply, sanitation, and hygiene promotion; food security and nutrition; shelter and settlement; and health. The minimum standards consist of specific quantitative or qualitative expectations, such as minimum shelter size, and include practical suggestions of how to meet the stated expectations. The Sphere Handbook represents 'the majority consensus of humanitarian workers in the sectors covered' and many states and UN operational entities require NGOs to commit to it as a condition of funding or partnership.[218]

5. Conclusion

This chapter has focused on non-state humanitarian actors, particularly the ICRC, IFRC, National Societies, and NGOs. It explained the origins and structure of the Movement and the mandates of each of its components, as well as the privileges, immunities, and facilities the ICRC and IFRC enjoy under bilateral status agreements, and how Movement personnel are protected under international law. It then addressed NGOs' relationship with, and facilities and protection under, international law, devoting particular attention to health care, given apparent misunderstanding of

[211] <https://spherestandards.org/handbook/editions/> accessed 30 June 2025.

[212] Sphere Handbook (n 208) 2.

[213] ibid, 28.

[214] Cubie (n 82) 202.

[215] 'Principle 1: Enhance people's safety, dignity and rights and avoid exposing them to further harm. Principle 2: Ensure people's access to impartial assistance, according to need and without discrimination. Principle 3: Assist people to recover from the physical and psychological effects of threatened or actual violence, coercion or deliberate deprivation. Principle 4: Help people to claim their rights' (Sphere Handbook (n 208) 34).

[216] Humanitarian response '1. [. . .] is appropriate and relevant; 2. [. . .] is effective and timely; 3. [. . .] strengthens local capacities and avoids negative effects; 4. [. . .] is based on communication, participation and feedback; 5. Complaints are welcomed and addressed; 6. Humanitarian response is coordinated and complementary; 7. Humanitarian actors continuously learn and improve; 8. Staff are supported to do their job effectively, and are treated fairly and equally; 9. Resources are managed and used responsibly for their intended purpose' (Sphere Handbook (n 208) 50).

[217] Sphere Handbook (n 208) 50.

[218] Cubie (n 82) 203.

how medical NGOs are protected by IHL. Finally, it addressed the Movement and NGOs' role in setting quality and accountability standards in humanitarian action.

This chapter has demonstrated that the Movement and NGOs occupy distinct yet complementary positions within the international humanitarian ecosystem. The *sui generis* nature of Movement components, rooted in IHL and buttressed by the privileges, immunities, and facilities accorded to the ICRC and IFRC under bilateral status agreements, stands in sharp contrast to the status of NGOs, which are creatures of municipal law. Yet both have profoundly shaped the practice and norms of humanitarian assistance. The Movement, and the ICRC in particular, is the progenitor of international humanitarian action. The Movement and NGOs have delivered extensive amounts of aid around the world and have driven the development of voluntary standards that reinforce quality and accountability. Together, the Movement and NGOs are indispensable in meeting humanitarian need in armed conflict and in peacetime, even as international law has thus far failed to provide NGOs with adequate facilities and their personnel with meaningful protection. However, they and the UN are not the only international humanitarian actors. States also play a role; they are addressed next.

7
States

1. Introduction

States play a significant role in relation to humanitarian assistance. They fund it and provide it in-kind, both bilaterally to crisis-affected states and through the United Nations (UN), the International Red Cross and Red Crescent Movement (the Movement), and non-governmental organizations (NGOs). They occasionally deploy civilian or military teams to provide direct assistance in emergencies abroad.[1] And international law clearly foresees state humanitarian action. Relevant treaty provisions are discussed throughout this chapter. Mackintosh points out that the 'whole thrust of the discussion of humanitarian assistance by the International Court of Justice in the Nicaragua case was to examine whether the intervention of the United States [(US)] in Nicaragua had been truly humanitarian in nature, clearly presupposing that it could be so'.[2] Additionally, the International Law Commission's Draft Articles on the Protection of Persons in the Event of Disasters (Draft Articles) contemplate that humanitarian assistance may be provided by an 'assisting State'.[3] This chapter thus considers states as humanitarian actors.

It does so in two main parts. Section 2 addresses states as donors and the standards to which they hold themselves in this regard. Section 3 then addresses direct state involvement in international humanitarian assistance. This covers civil defence engagement, including the international humanitarian law (IHL) regime on third state civil defence assistance in armed conflict, and military engagement. Section 3 also covers soft law guidance on the use of state civil defence and military assets in UN humanitarian activities in each of peacetime and complex emergencies (as defined below). Section 4 concludes, including a discussion, centred on the Gaza Humanitarian Foundation (GHF), of how states not only fund and deliver humanitarian assistance, but also sometimes act to undermine its provision.

Before proceeding, it is important to consider how states relate in practice to the core humanitarian principles of humanity, impartiality, neutrality, and independence. While they support UN, Movement, and NGO assistance in line with these principles, and may make policy or even legal commitments to upholding them,

[1] States are also humanitarian policymakers. Multilateral policymaking through the UN's Economic and Social Council, General Assembly, and Security Council was addressed in Chapter 5, Section 4. The humanitarian policymaking of individual states is beyond the scope of this book.

[2] Kate Mackintosh, 'Beyond the Red Cross: The Protection of Independent Humanitarian Organizations and their Staff in International Humanitarian Law' (2007) 89 International Review of the Red Cross 113, 125.

[3] ILC, 'Report of the International Law Commission on the Work of its 68th Session' (2 May–10 June and 4 July–12 August 2016) A/71/10, art 3(c).

Humanitarian Assistance in International Law. Marina Sharpe, Oxford University Press. © Marina Sharpe 2026.
DOI: 10.1093/9780198994695.003.0010

states do not consistently act in accordance with the principles, and are under no international legal obligation to do so.[4] Rather, their decisions about humanitarian issues are also shaped by electoral, policy, and strategic considerations,[5] as well as historical—often colonial—ties.[6] As former UN High Commissioner for Refugees Sadako Ogata once observed, the 'international response to humanitarian situations is largely determined by the degree of strategic interests held by the major states'.[7] This perception is echoed among NGOs, where there is a view 'that if relief is provided by a state, especially one with [. . .] strategic interests in an area, it cannot be truly humanitarian'.[8]

It is useful, however, to distinguish between state action at the strategic and operational levels. Strategic decisions—such as whether and how to provide assistance—are rarely made solely according to the principles. Operational delivery, however, can often, and generally should, follow the core humanitarian principles. In some circumstances, though, IHL requires assisting states to act under the control of a conflict party,[9] which precludes adherence to the principles of neutrality and independence. Additionally, it may be more difficult for military actors providing direct assistance to do so in accordance with the principles; the UN guidance covered in Section 3.3 addresses this by precluding the involvement of military forces with a combat mission in humanitarian assistance, and by insisting on the subsidiary role of all other military forces.[10]

[4] See Chapter 2, Section 4.5.1.

[5] Regarding humanitarian assistance funding in particular, see Helen Versluys, 'European Union Humanitarian Aid: Lifesaver or Political Tool?' in Jan Orbie (ed), *Europe's Global Role: External Policies of the European Union* (Routledge 2008); Günther Fink and Silvia Redaelli, 'Determinants of International Emergency Aid—Humanitarian Need Only?' (2011) 39 World Development 741; Travis Nelson, 'Determinants of Disaster Aid: Donor Interest or Recipient Need?' (2012) 24 Global Change, Peace & Security 109; Rob Kevlihan, Karl Derouen, and Glen Biglaiser, 'Is US Humanitarian Aid Based Primarily on Need or Self-Interest?' (2014) 58 International Studies Quarterly 839; Charlotte Dany, 'Politicization of Humanitarian Aid in the European Union' (2015) 20 European Foreign Affairs Review 419; Jonathan Whittall, 'Is Humanitarian Action Independent From Political Interests?' (2015) 12 International Journal on Human Rights 1; Neil Narang, 'Forgotten Conflicts: Need Versus Political Priority in the Allocation of Humanitarian Aid Across Conflict Areas' (2016) 42 International Interactions 189; Lina Gong, 'Humanitarian Diplomacy as an Instrument for China's Image-Building' (2021) 6 Asian Journal of Comparative Politics 238; Miriam Bradley, *The Politics and Everyday Practice of International Humanitarianism* (OUP 2023) 322.

[6] Thomas G Weiss, 'Humanitarian Action' in Jacob Katz Cogan, Ian Hurd, and Ian Johnstone (eds), *The Oxford Handbook of International Organizations* (OUP 2016) 316.

[7] Cited in David P Forsythe, *The Contemporary International Committee of the Red Cross: Challenges, Changes, Controversies* (CUP 2024) 33.

[8] Mackintosh (n 2) 125.

[9] See Section 3.1.1. Third state medical personnel must also operate under the control of a conflict party (Protocol Additional to the Geneva Conventions of 12 August 1949, and relating to the Protection of Victims of International Armed Conflicts (adopted 8 June 1977, entered into force 7 December 1978) 1125 UNTS 3 (API) arts 8(c)(iii) and 9(2)).

[10] OCHA, 'Oslo Guidelines on the Use of Foreign Military and Civil Defence Assets in Disaster Relief' (2007) <https://www.unocha.org/publications/report/world/oslo-guidelines-guidelines-use-foreign-military-and-civil-defence-assets-disaster-relief-revision-11-november-2007-enzh> accessed 28 May 2025 (Oslo Guidelines) paras 5 and 23; OCHA, 'Guidelines on the Use of Military and Civil Defence Assets to Support United Nations Humanitarian Activities in Complex Emergencies' (revision 1, 2005) <https://www.unocha.org/publications/report/world/guidelines-use-military-and-civil-defence-assets-support-united-nations-humanitarian> accessed 9 June 2025 (MCDA Guidelines) paras 7 and 25.

2. Funding

States provide significant funding for humanitarian assistance. This contributes to meeting their treaty obligations to realize rights extraterritorially, including through international assistance and cooperation.[11] The biggest donors are developed Western states and major emerging economies, which reflects the fact that the aforementioned obligation is 'particularly incumbent upon those states which are in a position to assist others'.[12]

These major donors are often grouped in two categories. The first is comprised of members of the Organisation for Economic Co-operation and Development's (OECD) Development Assistance Committee (DAC). This category includes Australia, Canada, many European Union (EU) member states, Norway, the United Kingdom (UK), and the US. Several countries in this category used to have dedicated government aid agencies, which provided both humanitarian and development assistance, primarily through the UN, Movement, and NGOs. Examples of such entities include AusAID (Australia), the Canadian International Development Agency (CIDA), the UK's Department for International Development (DfID), and the US Agency for International Development (USAID). However, most of these have now joined the relevant state's ministry of foreign affairs. AusAID joined the Australian Department of Foreign Affairs and Trade in 2013; also in 2013, CIDA merged with Canada's Department of Foreign Affairs, Trade and Development, which was in 2015 re-named Global Affairs Canada; and DfID joined the Foreign and Commonwealth Office in 2020 to form the Foreign, Commonwealth & Development Office. President Donald Trump abolished USAID in 2025. Some DAC donors, however, maintain dedicated agencies, such as Norway's Norad. Despite these structural shifts, DAC donors still provide significant humanitarian assistance funding,[13] primarily to the UN and international NGOs,[14] though the amounts pale in comparison to their defence budgets,[15] and, as mentioned in Chapter 5,[16] most UN humanitarian appeals are significantly underfunded.

The second category is comprised of donors that are not members of the OECD DAC, such as Brazil, China, India, Kuwait, Qatar, Saudi Arabia, Türkiye, and the United Arab Emirates (UAE).[17] These donors, often termed 'emerging donors', mainly

[11] Charter of the United Nations (adopted 26 June 1945, entered into force 24 October 1945) 1 UNTS XVI (UN Charter) arts 55 and 56; International Covenant on Economic, Social and Cultural Rights (adopted 16 December 1966, entered into force 3 January 1976) 993 UNTS 3, art 2(1).

[12] Committee on Economic, Social and Cultural Rights (CESCR), 'General Comment No. 3: The Nature of States Parties' Obligations (Art. 2, Para. 1, of the Covenant)' (1991) E/1991/23, para 14. See also CESCR, 'General Comment No. 14: The Right to the Highest Attainable Standard of Health (Art. 12)' (2000) E/C.12/2000/4, para 45.

[13] See the OECD Data Explorer (https://data-explorer.oecd.org), which provides data on members' official development assistance (ODA). Humanitarian assistance can be disaggregated from ODA; in OECD methodology, humanitarian assistance includes funds for emergency response, reconstruction relief and rehabilitation, and disaster prevention and preparedness.

[14] Bradley (n 5) 314.

[15] ibid.

[16] See Chapter 5, Sections 3.3 and 4.1.

[17] See, generally, Emma Mawdsley, '"Non-DAC" Humanitarian Actors' in Roger Mac Ginty and Jenny H Peterson (eds), *The Routledge Companion to Humanitarian Action* (Routledge 2015).

provide funding bilaterally or to national Red Cross or Red Crescent societies.[18] Their giving reflects their recent rapid economic growth, coupled with recognition that humanitarian funding is a way to demonstrate leadership internationally, regionally, and domestically.[19] Some non-DAC donors—notably the Gulf states mentioned above—provide more humanitarian assistance funding than several DAC donors.[20]

States also provide humanitarian assistance in kind, either within an established legal framework or *ad hoc* in response to need. The Food Assistance Convention is a salient example of the former.[21] The treaty, which replaced the earlier Food Aid Convention,[22] aims to 'save lives, reduce hunger, improve food security, and improve the nutritional status of the most vulnerable populations',[23] including in emergency situations,[24] through a system in which states parties commit to provide appropriate, timely, effective, efficient, and need-based food assistance,[25] in accordance with certain principles,[26] such as to not distort local economies.[27] Minimum annual commitments are lodged with the Convention secretariat, the International Grains Council, in monetary or volumetric terms.[28] States deliver on these commitments either by making financial contributions towards local food procurement or with in-kind donations of food or nutritional interventions to eligible countries.[29] The Convention also creates a Food Assistance Committee of all states parties, which serves as a forum to discuss matters such as how to mobilize assistance to 'specific emergency and crisis situations'.[30] The Committee's 21st session was held in London in June 2025. Members discussed 'current food emergencies' but did not provide information about which situations they addressed.[31]

As noted in the introduction, states do not consistently make their strategic humanitarian assistance decisions in line with the core humanitarian principles. Indeed, the Food Assistance Convention merely refers to the principles in its preamble;[32] states do not incur under the treaty any obligation to comply with them. With the Principles and Good Practice of Humanitarian Donorship (GHD Principles), states sought to address the concern that humanitarian assistance was not always

[18] Bradley (n 5) 315.

[19] Andrea Binder and Claudia Meier, 'Opportunity Knocks: Why Non-Western Donors Enter Humanitarianism and How to Make the Best of It' (2011) 93 International Review of the Red Cross 1135, 1140.

[20] Bradley (n 5) 315. See also Ghassan Elkahlout and Sansom Milton, 'The Evolution of the Gulf States as Humanitarian Donors' (2023) 45 Third World Quarterly 2246.

[21] For analysis of this Convention, see Annamaria La Chimia, 'Food Security and the Right to Food: Finding Balance in the 2012 Food Assistance Convention' (2016) 65 International & Comparative Law Quarterly 99.

[22] (Adopted 13 April 1999, entered into force 1 July 1999) 2073 UNTS 135.

[23] Food Assistance Convention (adopted 25 April 2012, entered into force 1 January 2013) 2884 UNTS 3 (Food Assistance Convention) art 1.

[24] ibid, preambular para 2.

[25] ibid, art 1(a–b).

[26] ibid, art 2.

[27] ibid, art 2(a)(v).

[28] ibid, arts 5 and 10.

[29] ibid, art 4.

[30] ibid, art 7(6).

[31] Food Assistance Committee, 'Press Release' (20 June 2025) <https://www.foodassistanceconvention.org/en/press/press.aspx> accessed 25 July 2025.

[32] Food Assistance Convention (n 23) preambular para 6.

distributed according to need.[33] The non-binding GHD Principles originated from a 2003 meeting convened by Sweden to discuss best practice in humanitarian donorship.[34] They are 'a framework to guide official humanitarian aid and a mechanism for encouraging greater donor accountability',[35] though accountability to whom is unclear. The GHD Principles note at the outset that humanitarian action 'should be guided by the humanitarian principles'.[36] The 'General Principles' section then continues in this vein, noting that donors should '[r]espect and promote the implementation of international humanitarian law, refugee law and human rights' and '[a]llocate humanitarian funding in proportion to needs and on the basis of needs assessments'.[37] Among the 'General Principles', donors also agree to '[s]upport and promote the central and unique role of the' UN 'in providing leadership and co-ordination of international humanitarian action, the special role of the International Committee of the Red Cross, and the vital role of' the UN, the Movement, and NGOs in 'implementing humanitarian action'.[38] The GHD Principles also include a section on 'Good Practices in Donor Financing, Management and Accountability'. In 2018, the GHD Principles were amended to include a principle encouraging donors to '[s]ystematically consider the use of cash transfers alongside other modalities according to context, in order to meet the humanitarian needs of people in the most effective and efficient manner'.[39] The GHD Principles have been influential. They were adopted by the OECD DAC in 2005 and are referred to in policy and treaties, such as the Food Assistance Convention.[40]

The same meeting that gave rise to the GHD Principles also produced the Good Humanitarian Donorship initiative, an informal forum and network that now consists of forty-three donors, including both DAC donors such as New Zealand and non-DAC donors such as Brazil.[41] It meets regularly to facilitate 'collective advancement of GHD principles and good practices' in order to 'encourage and stimulate principled donor behaviour and, by extension, improved humanitarian action'.[42]

3. Direct involvement

In addition to funding humanitarian assistance and providing it in-kind, states sometimes become directly involved in its provision, by deploying civil defence or military assets, including both equipment and personnel, to assist in an emergency—though the extent of this direct involvement pales in comparison to the funding described

[33] Bradley (n 5) 327.
[34] Principles and Good Practice of Humanitarian Donorship (2003, revised 2018) <https://www.ghdinitiative.org/ghd/gns/principles-good-practice-of-ghd/principles-good-practice-ghd.html> accessed 28 May 2025 (GHD Principles).
[35] ibid, preamble.
[36] ibid, para 2.
[37] ibid, paras 4 and 6.
[38] ibid, para 10.
[39] ibid, para 24.
[40] Food Assistance Convention (n 23) preambular para 7.
[41] <https://www.ghdinitiative.org/ghd/gns/about-us/our-members.html> accessed 28 May 2025.
[42] <https://www.ghdinitiative.org/ghd/gns/about-us/about-ghd.html> accessed 28 May 2025.

above.[43] While IHL explicitly contemplates the provision of humanitarian assistance by third states,[44] and stipulates that state assistance shall not be construed as interference in the armed conflict,[45] in practice states tend to avoid becoming directly involved in armed conflicts to which they are not party. Thus, when states deploy civil defence or military assets to a humanitarian operation, this is more often to peacetime disasters than to armed conflict or mixed situations. When a state does become involved in humanitarian operations in armed conflict or situations of violence not amounting to armed conflict, it is often because its military is already in theatre in a peacekeeping or other pre-existing capacity.

Third state military support to humanitarian operations in armed conflict must be distinguished from two other forms of military involvement in such assistance, which this book does not address. First, when a party to an armed conflict provides 'humanitarian' assistance to the local population for strategic reasons, such as to 'win hearts and minds' among the local population as part of a counterinsurgency operation.[46] Second, when a party to an armed conflict conducts a largely humanitarian operation in the context of, or in a context closely connected to, the conflict. For example, during the 1999 Kosovo crisis—which saw a coalition of states respond to Bosnia's ethnic cleansing of Kosovar Albanians by bombing Kosovo—the intervening states also set up refugee camps for Kosovar Albanians in neighbouring Macedonia.[47]

Any direct state involvement in humanitarian assistance, whether by civil defence or military actors, must be at the affected state's request or with its consent.[48] Some states and regional actors have set up dedicated bodies to receive such requests. For example, in 2001, the European Commission created the EU Civil Protection Mechanism (EUCPM).[49] Its Emergency Response Coordination Centre receives requests from disaster-affected states and EUCPM participating states then provide assistance, such as expert personnel and equipment.[50] European practice is generally to deploy civilian assets within Europe and military assets outside Europe.[51] In the Asia-Pacific, by contrast, military assets are primarily deployed within the region, and

[43] David Fisher, 'A Glass Half Full: The International Law Commission's Draft Articles and the Operational Challenges of International Disaster Response' (2020) 1 Yearbook of International Disaster Law 93, 98.

[44] See, for example, Geneva Convention Relative to the Protection of Civilian Persons in Time of War (adopted 12 August 1949, entered into force 21 October 1950) 75 UNTS 287, art 59(2). See also *Obligations of Israel in Relation to the Presence and Activities of the United Nations, Other International Organizations and Third States in and in Relation to the Occupied Palestinian Territory* (Advisory Opinion) 2025 <https://www.icj-cij.org/sites/default/files/case-related/196/196-20251022-adv-01-00-en.pdf> accessed 31 October 2025, para 95.

[45] API (n 9) arts 64(1) and 70(1).

[46] See, generally, Jamie Williamson, 'Using Humanitarian Aid to "Win Hearts and Minds": A Costly Failure?' (2011) 93 International Review of the Red Cross 1035.

[47] Sarah Kenyon Lischer, 'Military Intervention and the Humanitarian "Force Multiplier"' (2007) 13 Global Governance 99, 104.

[48] UN Charter (n 11) art 2(4). See Chapter 3, Section 4.3 and Chapter 4, Sections 2.2 and 2.3.2.1.

[49] Council Decision (EC) No 2001/792/EC of 23 October 2001 establishing a Community mechanism to facilitate reinforced cooperation in civil protection and assistance interventions, OJ L 297, 15/11/2001, 7–11.

[50] <https://civil-protection-humanitarian-aid.ec.europa.eu/what/civil-protection/eu-civil-protection-mechanism_en> accessed 4 June 2025.

[51] Gabrielle Simm, 'Disaster Militarism? Military Humanitarian Assistance and Disaster Relief' (2019) 22 Max Planck Yearbook of United Nations Law Online 347, 361.

rarely outside it.[52] Involvement may be direct in the sense of the 'face-to-face distribution of goods and services'; indirect in the sense of being 'at least one step removed from the population', for example transporting relief items or personnel; or it may come in the form of infrastructure support, such as road repair or power generation.[53]

Primary responsibility under international law for the security and protection of international humanitarian personnel, including state personnel (whether civilian or military), lies with the affected state. State personnel deployed to respond to a humanitarian emergency in another state enjoy the protections owed by the affected state to all individuals on its territory under international human rights law and national law. If no treaty governing the assistance to be provided exists, the affected and assisting states may conclude a bilateral agreement. As discussed in Chapter 3, all humanitarian personnel in armed conflict, including state personnel, are protected by IHL and those who attack them can be held accountable under international criminal law.[54]

Civil defence and military involvement are addressed in turn below. Soft law guidance around this involvement in UN humanitarian activities is addressed separately in a third section, because it depends on the context for which assistance is provided—either a peacetime disaster or a complex emergency—rather than on the nature of the actor providing it.

3.1. Civil defence involvement

The term of art for the non-military assets states deploy abroad is 'civil defence assets'. There is no single meaning of 'civil defence', and the concept can be confusing, for at least three reasons. First, states organize their national civil defence infrastructure in different ways. Some states have several distinct entities that respond to disasters and armed conflict, while others have one permanent civil defence organization (CDO).[55] Second, while civil defence bodies are usually state entities, some NGOs, such as the well-known White Helmets in Syria, refer to themselves in terms of civil defence.

Finally, 'civil defence' is not used consistently in non-legal or even legal sources. Among non-legal authors, the term has been used to refer to civilians' self-protection initiatives in wartime,[56] government initiatives to prepare civilians for a potential attack,[57] and to 'the ability of an entire society to withstand crisis',[58] among others. Legal usage is more consistent, but by no means uniform. Sandoz and others identify broad and narrow meanings of the term. In its broad sense, civil defence refers to 'all measures for national defence which are not of a military nature', whereas the narrow use

[52] Ibid.

[53] MCDA Guidelines (n 10) para 2.

[54] See Chapter 3, Sections 4.4.4 and 7.1.1.

[55] For example, the National Organization for Passive Defence in Iran and the Ministry of the Russian Federation for Civil Defence, Emergencies and Elimination of Consequences of Natural Disasters.

[56] David Alexander, 'From Civil Defence to Civil Protection—and Back Again' (2002) 11 Disaster Prevention and Management 209, 209.

[57] Andrew Burtch, *Give Me Shelter: The Failure of Canada's Cold War Civil Defence* (UBC Press 2012).

[58] Peter MacLeod, 'Canada Needs a New Civil Defence Corps' (*The Tyee*, 5 March 2025) <https://thetyee.ca/Opinion/2025/03/05/Canada-Needs-New-Civil-Defence-Corps/> accessed 30 May 2025.

of the term refers to a subset of such measures: those 'aimed at saving lives and limiting damage'.[59] The Framework Convention on Civil Defence Assistance (FCCDA) defines 'civil defence service' as 'a structure or any other state entity established with the aim of preventing disasters and mitigating the effects of such disasters on persons, on property and the environment'.[60] While the FCCDA goes on to define 'disaster' broadly as 'an exceptional situation in which life, property or the environment may be at risk',[61] the treaty and its depository, the International Civil Defence Organization (ICDO),[62] are both oriented towards peacetime disasters.

These various usages suggest that in the humanitarian assistance context, 'civil defence' can be defined as referring to all of the state's organized, non-military entities aimed at protecting the public and infrastructure from disasters and the consequences of armed conflict. Civil defence assets thus include equipment and personnel belonging to, for example, the state's fire service(s), its ambulance service(s), and its search-and-rescue service(s).

Recent examples of states sending civil defence assets to assist in a foreign crisis can be grouped by disaster type: wildfires; other disasters, principally earthquakes; and human-generated disasters.[63] For example, Canada has in recent years received firefighting assistance from Brazil,[64] South Africa,[65] South Korea,[66] and the US,[67] and its provinces have sent firefighters to the US (California).[68] The UK deployed at least sixty search-and-rescue experts to Morocco following a 2023 earthquake there.[69] Lebanon received search-and-rescue teams from Czechia, France, Greece, the Netherlands, Poland, Qatar, Russia, and Türkiye following the 2020 Beirut port explosion.[70]

[59] Yves Sandoz, Christophe Swinarski, and Bruno Zimmermann (eds), *Commentary on the Additional Protocols of 8 June 1977 to the Geneva Conventions of 12 August 1949* (Martinus Nijhoff 1987) 713.

[60] (Adopted 22 May 2000, entered into force 23 September 2001) 2172 UNTS 213, art 1(b).

[61] ibid, art 1(c).

[62] ibid, art 12.

[63] Of course, states also cooperate in maritime search and rescue; see Chapter 4, Section 4.2.

[64] Brazil Ministério das Relações Exteriores, 'Brazilian Humanitarian Mission to Fight Wildfires in Canada' (Press release, 20 July 2023) <https://www.gov.br/mre/en/contact-us/press-area/press-releases/brazil-sends-humanitarian-mission-to-fight-wildfires-in-canada> accessed 29 May 2025.

[65] Forestry, Fisheries and the Environment, 'South Africa Sends 200 Firefighters to Fight Wildfires in Canada' (Press release, 28 July 2024) <https://www.dffe.gov.za/mediareleases/wof_deployedtocanada#:~:text=South%20Africa%20sends%20200%20firefighters%20to%20fight%20wildland%20fires%20in%20Canada,-28%20July%202024&text=The%20Department%20of%20Forestry%2C%20Fisheries,wildfires%20in%20Alberta%20Province%2C%20Canada> accessed 29 May 2025.

[66] Jennifer Yoon, 'It's All the Same Forest, Say Korean Firefighters Battling Blazes in Northern Quebec' (*CBC*, 29 July 2023) <https://www.cbc.ca/news/canada/montreal/wildfires-quebec-south-korea-firefighter-1.6921380> accessed 29 May 2025.

[67] The White House, 'Statement from President Joe Biden on the Wildfires in Canada' (8 June 2023) <https://www.whitehouse.gov/briefing-room/statements-releases/2023/06/08/statement-from-president-joe-biden-on-the-wildfires-in-canada/#:~:text=Since%20May%2C%20more%20than%20600,here%20in%20the%20United%20States> accessed 23 December 2024.

[68] SOPFEU, 'Prêt de ressources: Le Québec enverra deux avions-citernes supplémentaires en Californie' (8 January 2025) <https://sopfeu.qc.ca/communiques/pret-de-ressources-le-quebec-enverra-deux-avions-citernes-supplementaires-en-californie/> accessed 19 January 2025.

[69] UK, 'UK Deploys Search and Rescue Teams to Morocco Following Earthquake' (9 September 2023) <https://www.gov.uk/government/news/uk-deploys-search-rescue-teams-to-morocco-following-earthquake> accessed 23 December 2024.

[70] Mazen El Sayed, 'Beirut Ammonium Nitrate Explosion: A Man-Made Disaster in the Times of the COVID-19 Pandemic' [2020] Disaster Medicine and Public Health Preparedness 1.

The legal framework for this assistance in peacetime is any applicable multilateral, regional, or bilateral treaty. The range of instruments in this regard was surveyed in Chapter 4, in the discussion of the patchwork of treaties that currently constitutes international disaster response law (IDRL).[71] While there is a treaty dedicated to civil defence cooperation—the FCCDA mentioned above—it has only been ratified by four states since its adoption in 2000.[72] If no relevant treaty exists, the legal framework of cooperation is negotiated bilaterally.

3.1.1. Third state civil defence in armed conflict

The IHL framework on civil defence, contained in API,[73] contemplates a situation where a state sends its civil defence assets to provide humanitarian assistance in an international armed conflict (IAC) to which it is not a party.[74] While this occurs only rarely in practice[75]—a known example being Denmark's deployment of its CDO to Bosnia in 1992[76]—the legal framework is nevertheless surveyed for completeness.

IHL defines civil defence in terms of its functions. It is 'the performance of some or all' listed 'humanitarian tasks intended to protect the civilian population against the dangers, and to help it to recover from the immediate effects of hostilities or disasters and also to provide the conditions necessary for its survival'.[77] The reference to 'disasters' in API's definition of civil defence means that a civil defence response to a natural or human-generated disaster in the territory of a conflict party would be covered by API.[78] The listed civil defence tasks include 'evacuation', shelter management, 'rescue', 'medical services', 'fire-fighting', and the 'provision of emergency accommodation and supplies'.[79] API goes on to define CDOs as 'those establishments and other units which are organized or authorized by the competent authorities of a Party to the conflict to perform' any of the listed tasks, provided the CDO is 'assigned and devoted exclusively to such tasks'.[80]

Article 64(1) of API foresees that civilian CDOs 'of neutral or other States not Parties to the conflict' might perform civil defence tasks in IAC, including situations of occupation, 'with the consent and under the control of' the conflict party in control of the territory where the civil defence assistance is provided. It should be noted that,

[71] See Chapter 4, Section 2.1.
[72] Jordan, Libya, Tunisia, and Ukraine.
[73] API (n 9) arts 61–67.
[74] IHL does not regulate civil defence in non-international armed conflict.
[75] Stéphane Jeannet, 'Civil Defence 1977–1997: From Law to Practice' (1998) 12 International Review of the Red Cross 715, 718.
[76] Flemming S. Nielsen, 'Civil Defence in International Humanitarian Relief Work, Seen in the Light of the Geneva Conventions' (1996) 9 Journal of Refugee Studies 421, 426–29.
[77] API (n 9) art 61(a).
[78] Sandoz and others (n 59) para 2349.
[79] API (n 9) art 61(a). The listed tasks in full are: '(i) warning; (ii) evacuation; (iii) management of shelters; (iv) management of blackout measures; (v) rescue; (vi) medical services, including first aid, and religious assistance; (vii) fire-fighting; (viii) detection and marking of danger areas; (ix) decontamination and similar protective measures; (x) provision of emergency accommodation and supplies; (xi) emergency assistance in the restoration and maintenance of order in distressed areas; (xii) emergency repair of indispensable public utilities; (xiii) emergency disposal of the dead; (xiv) assistance in the preservation of objects essential for survival; (xv) complementary activities necessary to carry out any of the tasks mentioned above, including, but not limited to, planning and organization'.
[80] ibid, art 61(b).

like the rules on emergency relief operations in occupied territory,[81] an occupying power 'may only exclude or restrict the activities of civilian' CDOs 'of neutral or other States not Parties to the conflict [. . .] if it can ensure the adequate performance of civil defence tasks from its own resources or those of the occupied territory'.[82] Additionally, an occupying power must provide the third state CDO with 'the facilities necessary for the performance of' its tasks.[83] Third state civil defence assistance must not 'be deemed to be an interference in the conflict'.[84] A conflict party benefitting from civil defence assistance from a third state must notify its adversary or adversaries about the assistance it is receiving.[85]

Provided the API article 64(1) consent and control requirements are met, a third state CDO enjoys the same protections as a CDO belonging to a conflict party. The third state CDO and its personnel 'shall be respected and protected'.[86] This supplements the protection all civilians enjoy under IHL.[87] Additionally, the CDO's buildings and materiel are immune from attack.[88] This similarly supplements the protection IHL affords to all civilian objects.[89] The third state CDO may signal this protection by displaying the international civil defence emblem, an equilateral blue triangle on an orange background, on its personnel, buildings, materiel, and any civilian shelters it manages.[90] Protection ceases if the third state CDO commits acts outside its proper task that are harmful to the enemy.[91]

API also encourages the conflict party receiving civil defence assistance and the third state providing it to 'facilitate international coordination of [. . .] civil defence actions', including through 'relevant international organizations'.[92] At the time of drafting, this reference to international organizations was to organizations that might be created in the future.[93] The ICDO already existed, but it was then—and remains—focused on promoting international civil defence cooperation in peacetime.[94]

3.2. Military involvement

Military forces, with their advanced communications, logistics, search and rescue, security, and transportation capabilities, can make a significant contribution to humanitarian operations in both peacetime and armed conflict. Military forces can become involved in humanitarian operations in several ways. A state may deploy its military to assist. For example, thirty-five states sent their militaries to participate in the 2004

81 See Chapter 3, Section 4.3.
82 API (n 9) art 64(3).
83 ibid, arts 64(1) and 63(1).
84 ibid, art 64(1).
85 ibid.
86 ibid, art 62(1).
87 ibid, art 51.
88 ibid, art 62(3).
89 ibid, art 52.
90 ibid, art 66.
91 ibid, art 65(1).
92 ibid, art 64(2).
93 Sandoz and others (n 59) para 2568.
94 ibid, para 2566.

Indian Ocean tsunami response,[95] and in July 2025 at least six states deployed their air forces to conduct airdrops of relief into Gaza.[96] A state may contribute troops to a UN peacekeeping operation which, as discussed in Chapter 5, may be mandated by the Security Council to facilitate humanitarian assistance.[97] State-led peacekeeping operations can also be given humanitarian assistance mandates. For example, the Multinational Security Support Mission for Haiti, which is under Kenyan command, has a mandate that includes supporting the Haitian National Police 'to help ensure unhindered and safe access to humanitarian aid for the population receiving assistance'.[98] Similarly, the multinational force for Liberia (ECOMIL), which was under Nigerian command, was mandated to 'secure the environment for the delivery of humanitarian assistance'.[99] A UN or state-led peacekeeping operation without a pre-existing humanitarian assistance mandate could also be authorized to respond to a sudden-onset disaster in theatre.

Militaries have been providing humanitarian assistance in disasters for decades. In 1985 and 1988, military aircraft from countries including Belgium, Canada, Germany, Poland, Sweden, and the UK airlifted food into Ethiopia;[100] Belgium also provided air support to Operation Lifeline Sudan.[101] Military teams from Australia, Belgium, Canada, France, Germany, Ireland, Israel, Japan, the Netherlands, New Zealand, and the US provided airlift capacity, engineering expertise, and water and sanitation in the refugee camps that were created in Goma, Democratic Republic of the Congo, during and immediately following the 1994 genocide against the Tutsi in Rwanda.[102] The widespread use of foreign military assets in disaster response began in 1998 with the response to Hurricane Mitch in Honduras and Nicaragua, which involved military forces from 12 states.[103] Since then, militaries have contributed to a range of disaster responses, including the 2003 earthquake in Bam, Iran; the 2005 earthquake in Pakistan-administered Kashmir; the 2010 earthquake in Haiti; the 2011 earthquake and tsunami in Japan;[104] Hurricane Katrina in the US in 2005;[105] the earthquake and tsunami in Sulawesi, Indonesia, in 2018;[106] and cyclone Idai in Mozambique in

[95] David Fisher, 'The Law of International Disaster Response: Overview and Ramifications for Military Actors' (2008) 38 Israel Yearbook on Human Rights 115, 141.

[96] Kristy Kirkup, 'Canada Among Six Countries that Airdropped Humanitarian Aid to Gaza' (*The Globe and Mail*, 4 August 2025) <https://www.theglobeandmail.com/politics/article-gaza-humanitarian-aid-airdrop-canada-israel-hamas-ceasefire/#:~:text=Canada%20was%20among%20six%20countries,for%20the%20residents%20of%20Gaza> accessed 4 August 2025.

[97] See Chapter 5, Section 5.3.

[98] UNSC Res 2699 (2 October 2023) S/RES/2699, para 2. See also UNSC Res 2751 (30 September 2024) S/RES/2751, which extended the mission's mandate until 2 October 2025.

[99] UNSC Res 1497 (1 August 2003) S/RES/1497, para 1.

[100] Meinrad Studer, 'The ICRC and Civil-Military Relations in Armed Conflict' (2001) 83 International Review of the Red Cross 367, 382.

[101] OECD DAC, 'Civilian and Military Means of Providing and Supporting Humanitarian Assistance During Conflict: A Comparative Analysis (Note by the Secretariat)' (5 September 1997) 6.

[102] ibid.

[103] Flavia Zorzi Giustiniani, *International Law in Disaster Scenarios* (Springer 2021) 187.

[104] Piero Calvi Parisetti, 'The Use of Civil and Military Defence Assets in Emergency Situations' in Andrea de Guttry, Marco Gestri, and Gabriella Venturini (eds), *International Disaster Response Law* (Springer 2012) 586.

[105] Fisher (n 95) 133.

[106] Australian Department of Foreign Affairs and Trade, 'Sulawesi Earthquake and Tsunami Response' <https://www.dfat.gov.au/crisis-hub/sulawesi-earthquake-and-tsunami-response> accessed 4 June 2025.

2019.[107] The militaries of states including Australia, Bangladesh, Canada, China, several European states, Indonesia, Japan, Malaysia, Singapore, South Korea, Taiwan, and Thailand all regularly provide disaster relief.[108] Some states have even formalized this role in domestic law or created dedicated military formations. Japan amended its international disaster response law in 1992 to carve out a role for its military,[109] and in 1996 Canada created the Disaster Assistance Response Team within the Canadian Armed Forces.[110] NATO created the Euro-Atlantic Disaster Response Coordination Centre in 1998; in 2005, it facilitated NATO's response to Hurricane Katrina and the earthquake in Pakistan-administered Kashmir.[111]

The Draft Articles clearly contemplate military involvement in disaster response. Article 3(f) defines 'relief personnel' as 'civilian or military personnel sent by an assisting State or other assisting actor for the purpose of providing disaster relief assistance'.[112] The commentary on this article notes that the reference to military personnel 'is intended as recognition of the important role played by military personnel, as a category of relief personnel, in the provision of disaster relief assistance'.[113] According to Simm, the military assets most often deployed to support humanitarian operations in disasters are, in order of frequency, air transport, medical support, and expert personnel.[114]

Third state military support for humanitarian assistance in armed conflict is rarer. During the Sri Lankan civil war, Indian military jets escorted cargo planes loaded with food and medical supplies into Sri Lankan airspace; the planes dropped twenty-five tons of relief in Jaffna.[115] More recently, throughout 2024 the Royal Jordanian Air Force dropped food and other relief items in Gaza,[116] sometimes in partnership with the US.[117] France and the UK also conducted air drops in Gaza in 2024.[118]

107 US Defense Security Cooperation Agency, 'CJTF-HOA Delivers Humanitarian Aid to Cyclone-Ravaged Mozambique' <https://www.dsca.mil/news-media/news-archive/cjtf-hoa-delivers-humanitarian-aid-cyclone-ravaged-mozambique> accessed 25 January 2025.

108 Simm (n 51) 348.

109 Fisher (n 95) 138.

110 See, generally, Aaida Mamuji, 'Canadian Military Involvement in Humanitarian Assistance: Progress and Prudence in Natural Disaster Response' (2012) 18 Canadian Foreign Policy Journal 208.

111 Fisher (n 95) 139.

112 Draft Articles (n 3).

113 ibid, commentary to art 3, para 27.

114 Simm (n 51) 349.

115 Paul Costa and Peter Evans, 'The Indian Supply Drop into Sri Lanka: Nonmilitary Humanitarian Aid and the Troubling Idea of Intervention' (1988) 3 Connecticut Journal of International Law 417, 425. Sri Lanka subsequently accused India of providing military support to Tamil rebels (Karsten Friis, 'Military and Humanitarian Actors' in Roger Mac Ginty and Jenny H Peterson (eds), *The Routledge Companion to Humanitarian Action* (Routledge 2015) 217). On airdrops generally, see Chapter 3, Section 4.1.

116 Suleiman Al-Khalidi, 'Jordan Airdrops Aid to Northern Gaza for First Time in Five Months, Official Source' (*Reuters*, 26 November 2024) <https://www.reuters.com/world/middle-east/jordan-airdrops-aid-northern-gaza-first-time-five-months-official-source-2024-11-26/> accessed 4 June 2025.

117 Joseph Clark, 'US, Jordanian Forces Deliver Humanitarian Aid to Civilians in Gaza' (*DOD News*, 2 March 2024) <https://www.defense.gov/News/News-Stories/Article/Article/3693302/us-jordanian-forces-deliver-humanitarian-aid-to-civilians-in-gaza/> accessed 4 June 2025. It later emerged that Jordan had profited from these operations (Middle East Eye, 'Exclusive: Jordan Profited up to $400,000 per Gaza Aid Airdrop, Sources Say' (8 May 2025) <https://www.middleeasteye.net/news/jordan-profited-gaza-aid-airdrop-sources> accessed 4 June 2025).

118 Amnesty International, 'Gaza: Airdrops and Sea Routes are no Alternative to Aid Delivery by Land' (13 March 2024) <https://www.amnesty.org/en/latest/news/2024/03/gaza-airdrops-and-sea-routes-are-no-alternative-to-aid-delivery-by-land/> accessed 4 June 2025 (Amnesty International).

Additionally, in May 2024, the US military built a pier on the Gaza coast to facilitate humanitarian access; it was dismantled two months later.[119] (The French, British, and American efforts were criticized in an open letter signed by twenty-five NGOs, which called on governments to prioritize a ceasefire and ground based delivery modalities as 'the only way to meet the unprecedented humanitarian needs in the enclave'.[120]) And, as mentioned above, Gaza airdrops resumed in July 2025, this time by Belgian, Canadian, Egyptian, Jordanian, and UAE military planes.[121]

When a third state sends its military to support humanitarian operations in an armed conflict to which it is not a party, its personnel are not combatants. Combatant status under IHL is limited to '[m]embers of the armed forces of a Party to the conflict'.[122]

Military participation in armed conflict and peacetime humanitarian operations raises a range of legal and operational issues that the assisting and the affected states must address. These include the facilities, privileges, and immunities visiting troops enjoy; the command relationship between the assisting forces and those of the affected state; and whether foreign forces should wear uniforms and carry arms.[123] Such issues are regulated by bilateral status of forces agreements concluded between the affected and assisting states.[124] Some issues are also addressed in regional treaties.[125]

3.3. Guidance on the use of state civil defence and military assets in United Nations humanitarian activities

The use of state civil defence and military assets in humanitarian operations raises several issues in both peacetime and armed conflict. It may compromise perception of humanitarian action as neutral and impartial, which can make humanitarian access more difficult. State actors may lack the 'cultural sensitivity' required for the effective provision of assistance.[126] State assets may cost more to deploy, be slow to arrive, or be inappropriate to the task at hand.[127] Assisting states may insist on force protection measures, which can reduce operational efficiency and intimidate local populations.[128]

119 ibid.

120 ibid.

121 Kirkup (n 96).

122 Geneva Convention Relative to the Treatment of Prisoners of War (adopted 12 August 1949, entered into force 21 October 1950) 75 UNTS 135, art 4(A)(1); API (n 9) art 43(2).

123 Fisher (n 95) 140; Simm (n 51) 351.

124 A model agreement is annexed to the Oslo Guidelines (n 10).

125 Agreement among the Governments of the Participating States of the Black Sea Economic Cooperation on Collaboration in Emergency Assistance and Emergency Response to Natural and Man-Made Disasters (adopted 15 April 1998) <https://www.bsec-organization.org/UploadedDocuments/StatutoryDocumentsAgreements/Emergencyagreement071116.pdf> accessed 13 June 2024; ASEAN Agreement on Disaster Emergency Management and Emergency Response (adopted 26 July 2005, entered into force 24 December 2009) <https://agreement.asean.org/media/download/20220330063139.pdf> accessed 13 June 2024.

126 UN, 'Protection of Persons in the Event of Disasters: Memorandum by the Secretariat' (11 December 2007) A/CN.4/590, para 190.

127 Parisetti (n 104) 598.

128 ibid.

These issues may be amplified in armed conflict, especially when the assisting actor is a military force. Additionally, humanitarians collaborating with military actors in armed conflict may make it more difficult for conflict parties to respect the principle of distinction, which may increase the risk of attack for humanitarians.[129] In light of these issues, organizations take a range of positions on whether to cooperate with military forces. Some, such as *Médecins Sans Frontières*[130] and the International Committee of the Red Cross,[131] follow internal guidance that precludes cooperation with military forces unless it is required in the circumstances. Other actors 'appear oblivious to the controversy and potential risks'.[132] Still others decide on a case-by-case basis.[133]

For the UN, there are two sets of guidelines aimed at formalizing the use of foreign civil defence and military assets in UN humanitarian activities and increasing their effectiveness. The Oslo Guidelines apply in peacetime[134] and the MCDA Guidelines in complex emergencies;[135] each is addressed in turn. The UN Office for the Coordination of Humanitarian Affairs (OCHA) also issues country-specific and operational level event-specific guidelines.[136]

3.3.1. Peacetime

The Oslo Guidelines were released at a conference held in Oslo in 1994, following a multi-stakeholder process involving states, NATO, UN entities, Movement components, NGOs, and universities.[137] They have since been revised twice, most recently in 2007.[138] The Guidelines aim to 'establish the basic framework for formalizing and improving the effectiveness and efficiency of the use of foreign military and civil defence assets in international disaster relief operations'.[139] The Oslo Guidelines apply in 'natural, technological and environmental emergencies in times of peace'; they do not apply in armed conflict.[140] They define military and civil defence assets (MCDA) as 'relief personnel, equipment, supplies and services provided by foreign military and

[129] For quantitative analyses of the effect of a military presence on humanitarians' security, see Kristian Hoelscher, Jason Miklian, and Mokleiv Håvard Nygård, 'Conflict, Peacekeeping, and Humanitarian Security: Understanding Violent Attacks Against Aid Workers' (2017) 24 International Peacekeeping 538; Emizet F Kisangani and David F Mitchell, 'The Impact of Integrated UN Missions on Humanitarian NGO Security: A Quantitative Analysis' (2021) 27 Global Governance 202.

[130] See, generally, Claire Magone, Michael Neuman, and Fabrice Weissman (eds), *Humanitarian Negotiations Revealed: The MSF Experience* (Hurst 2011).

[131] Studer (n 100) 380, 382–83.

[132] Simm (n 51) 364.

[133] ibid.

[134] There is also a set of regional guidelines applicable in peacetime: OCHA, 'Asia-Pacific Regional Guidelines for the Use of Foreign Military Assets in Natural Disaster Response Operations' (version 8.01, 2014) <https://disasterlaw.ifrc.org/sites/default/files/media/disaster_law/2021-03/Asia%20Pacific%20Guidelines_0.pdf> accessed 9 June 2025.

[135] Both sets of guidelines have been noted by the UN General Assembly; see, for example, UNGA Res 58/114 (5 February 2004) A/RES/58/114, para 9. Additionally, both sets of guidelines reflect issues highlighted in UN General Assembly resolutions on humanitarian-military relations in humanitarian assistance; for example, the General Assembly has emphasized the fundamentally civilian character of humanitarian assistance (UNGA Res 59/141 (25 February 2005) A/RES/59/141, para 11).

[136] Simm (n 51) 356.

[137] Oslo Guidelines (n 10) 1.

[138] ibid.

[139] ibid, para 9.

[140] ibid, para 10.

CDOs for international disaster relief assistance.[141] A CDO is defined as 'any organization that, under the control of a Government, performs the functions enumerated in' article 61(a) of API,[142] which was addressed above in Section 3.1.1.[143] UN operational humanitarian entities and the Inter-Agency Standing Committee have agreed to follow the Oslo Guidelines, whereas states and NGO implementing and operational partners are encouraged to follow them.[144]

The Oslo Guidelines govern the use of two forms of foreign MCDA. 'UN MCDA' are 'military and civil defence resources requested by the UN humanitarian agencies and deployed under UN control specifically to support humanitarian activities'.[145] 'Other Deployed Forces', by contrast, are 'all military and civil defence forces deployed in the region other than UN MCDA', including 'forces deployed by the Affected State and any foreign forces deployed under bilateral agreements or under the auspices of organizations other than the UN'.[146] 'Other Deployed Forces' do not include 'forces that may be perceived as belligerents or of units that find themselves actively engaged in combat in the affected country or region'. Indeed, as mentioned in the introduction, under the Oslo Guidelines forces with a combat mission may not support UN humanitarian operations.[147]

The Oslo Guidelines articulate the principles that guide the use of foreign MCDA in humanitarian operations and describe the tasks and responsibilities of key actors in situations where UN MCDA or Other Deployed Forces are used.[148] The core principle is that of last resort. Under the principle of last resort, foreign MCDA should only be used if four criteria are met: the MCDA offer a unique capability; the situation is urgent; the humanitarian operation remains under overall civilian control;[149] and the use of MCDA is limited in both time and scope.[150] Giustiniani explains that despite 'the apparent clarity of this principle, there has been wide disagreement over its interpretation and practical application within the humanitarian community'.[151]

Requests for MCDA to support the UN must be made by the UN Resident or Humanitarian Coordinator,[152] with the affected state's consent;[153] the affected state can decline the use of MCDA.[154] Military assets should insofar as possible not provide direct assistance.[155] Furthermore, UN MCDA in particular will '[u]nder no

[141] ibid, para 3.
[142] ibid.
[143] The list of functions enumerated in API article 61(a) is reproduced at note 79.
[144] Oslo Guidelines (n 10) para 16.
[145] ibid, para 11.
[146] ibid, para 4.
[147] ibid, para 23.
[148] The key actors are: affected state and transit states; the UN Humanitarian Coordinator or UN Resident Coordinator; UN operational humanitarian bodies; OCHA; and the assisting state and foreign military or civil defence commanders.
[149] Military assets as such may remain under military control (Oslo Guidelines (n 10) paras 32(iii) and 37).
[150] Oslo Guidelines (n 10) para 32; see also paras 72 and 80.
[151] Giustiniani (n 103) 190.
[152] See Chapter 5, Section 3.4.
[153] Oslo Guidelines (n 10) para 32(i); see also paras 68 and 77.
[154] ibid, para 51.
[155] ibid, para 32(iv); see also para 80.

circumstance' provide security for UN humanitarian operations,[156] in part because security is the affected state's responsibility.[157] If security is required to prevent personnel from being attacked while delivering humanitarian assistance, it may be provided by Other Deployed Forces or non-military actors, such as the affected state's police force or a private security company, pursuant to a set of guidelines distinct from the Oslo Guidelines. These guidelines provide that humanitarian convoys should not in general use armed or military escorts,[158] but in disasters 'resort to armed protection is indeed still the rule'.[159]

All foreign military and civil defence personnel deployed on humanitarian operations should wear their national uniform and should not be armed.[160] All UN MCDA should be clearly distinguished from security forces and any other forces deployed locally on other missions, such as UN peacekeeping operations.[161] This may be with the logo of the supported UN entity or using the internationally recognized civil defence emblem.[162] Military assets may bear white markings and the UN logo, whereas civil defence assets should bear the civil defence emblem.[163] Other Deployed Forces may not display the logo of the supported UN entity,[164] as Other Deployed Forces are not under UN command and control.

UN MCDA personnel deployed at OCHA's request are 'experts on mission',[165] within the meaning of the Convention on the Privileges and Immunities of the United Nations,[166] and thus enjoy its protection.[167] Additionally, UN MCDA shall 'have at least the same freedom of movement, immunities, privileges, and exemptions afforded to the UN humanitarian agencies when working in support of these activities'.[168] The affected state should facilitate the arrival and deployment of all foreign MCDA by ensuring overflight and landing permission; exemption from customs duties; waiver of commercial documentation and visa requirements; free access to affected areas; recognition of any foreign certificates; authorization to use transportation and communication facilities; and security.[169]

3.3.2. Complex emergencies

The MCDA Guidelines were humanitarians' response to the increased use of military forces in supporting humanitarian operations, the direct provision by militaries of humanitarian assistance in some contexts, and the prevailing drive, discussed in

[156] ibid, para 43.
[157] ibid, para 29.
[158] Non-Binding Guidelines on the Use of Armed Escorts for Humanitarian Convoys (IASC 2013) <https://www.refworld.org/policy/legalguidance/iasc/2013/en/22033> accessed 11 February 2025, 4.
[159] Giustiniani (n 103) 191.
[160] Oslo Guidelines (n 10) para 29; see also para 41.
[161] ibid, para 39.
[162] ibid, para 40. See Section 3.1.1.
[163] Oslo Guidelines (n 10) para 40.
[164] ibid, para 46.
[165] ibid, para 30.
[166] (Adopted 13 February 1946; entered into force 17 September 1946) 1 UNTS 15, art VI, s 22.
[167] See Chapter 5, Section 5.1.
[168] Oslo Guidelines (n 10) para 57.
[169] ibid, para 60.

Chapter 5,[170] towards the integration of humanitarian, political, and security objectives.[171] They were developed in 2003 by drafting and review committees consisting of states, NATO, UN entities, Movement components, NGOs, and regional bodies. Like the Oslo Guidelines, they apply in UN humanitarian activities.[172] Since the Oslo Guidelines already existed when the MCDA Guidelines were being developed, the latter are structured in much the same way as the former, employ many of the same definitions, and reflect many of the same principles. Because of the considerable overlap between the two, the coverage here is limited to those aspects of the MCDA Guidelines that are distinct from the Oslo Guidelines.

The key difference between the Oslo and MCDA Guidelines is that the latter apply in 'complex emergencies', whereas the Oslo Guidelines apply in peacetime. A complex emergency is 'a humanitarian crisis in a country, region, or society where there is a total or considerable breakdown of authority resulting from internal or external conflict and which requires an international response that goes beyond the mandate or capacity of any single agency and/or the ongoing UN country programme'.[173] This encompasses both mixed situations—defined in Chapter 4 as situations where a disaster and an armed conflict occur in the same place simultaneously[174]—and situations where the humanitarian crisis results from armed conflict, a postconflict situation, or some other societal breakdown, such as violence not amounting to armed conflict.[175]

As a result of the contexts in which the MCDA Guidelines apply, military actors are more likely to be present on the ground. The MCDA Guidelines' distinct features relate largely to this fact. First, they provide a more detailed definition of 'Other Deployed Forces'. Under the MCDA Guidelines, these are divided into four categories, based on their mission: peacetime missions, 'including training exercises in the region with no hostile intent'; UN commanded peacekeeping operations;[176] other peace operations, which are not under UN command and control; and combat missions.[177] This disaggregation by mission is necessary because the 'mission of a force is the primary factor that determines a military unit's availability and appropriateness to humanitarian tasks, as it impacts on whether or not it will be perceived by others as neutral and impartial'.[178] The MCDA Guidelines further provide that forces with a combat mission '*shall not* be used to support humanitarian activities'.[179]

Second, because of the likely proximity of capable military actors, the MCDA Guidelines stress the importance of *not* relying on them. They begin by outlining how using military resources in humanitarian operations can undermine humanitarian access and security:

170 See Chapter 5, Section 3.
171 Parisetti (n 104) 593.
172 MCDA Guidelines (n 10) para 12.
173 ibid, para 1.
174 See Chapter 4, Section 2.4.
175 See Chapter 4, Section 3.
176 See Chapter 5, Section 5.3.
177 MCDA Guidelines (n 10) para 5.
178 ibid.
179 ibid, para 25 (emphasis in original).

> UN humanitarian agencies and their implementing and operational partners [NGOs] rely upon States to guarantee their security and to respect the principle of full and unimpeded access to the affected population. When security cannot be assured by the host government (e.g. when areas are controlled by non state actors), and/or when there are difficulties accessing the affected people, the UN humanitarian agencies and their implementing and operational partners must rely upon their neutrality for security and use negotiation as the primary means of gaining access to the affected population. Therefore, the use of military and civil defence resources should under no circumstances undermine the perceived neutrality or impartiality of the humanitarian actors, nor jeopardize current or future access to affected populations.[180]

The MCDA Guidelines go on to outline when the use of MCDA is appropriate, noting that 'decision-makers must weigh the risk to relief workers and their ability to operate effectively at the moment, and in the future, against the immediacy of the needs of the affected population and the need for the use of military and civil defence assets'.[181] Overall guidance in this regard is provided by the UN Under-Secretary-General for Humanitarian Affairs and Emergency Relief Coordinator.[182] The MCDA Guidelines provide a list of ten questions to guide the decision, including whether the use of military and civil defence assets is the last resort option, whether the states offering them are party to the conflict, and how their use will end.[183] The MCDA Guidelines also note that the use of Other Deployed Forces in support of humanitarian operations is 'more problematic' than the use of UN MCDA, because international military forces' provision of support to humanitarian operations may be for ulterior motives, such as intelligence gathering.[184] The primary factors to consider in determining whether to use Other Deployed Forces, in particular, are the 'immediacy of need, [the] ability to fulfill needs with civilian assets, and the impact on the perceived neutrality and impartiality of the assistance effort'.[185]

4. Conclusion

This chapter has focused on states' contributions to humanitarian assistance. However, state action also sometimes undermines humanitarian assistance. For example, unilateral sanctions imposed by states to combat terrorism can complicate the delivery of humanitarian assistance,[186] and states have used their vetoes in the Security Council

[180] ibid, para 28; see also para 32.
[181] ibid, para 32.
[182] ibid, para 33.
[183] ibid.
[184] ibid, para 35.
[185] ibid, para 36.
[186] Security Council sanctions were addressed in Chapter 5, Section 4.4.3. On unilateral sanctions, particularly US sanctions, see Kate Mackintosh, '*Holder v. Humanitarian Law Project*: Implications for Humanitarian Action: A View from Médecins Sans Frontieres' (2011) 34 Suffolk Transnational Law Review 507; Justin Fraterman, 'Criminalizing Humanitarian Relief: Are US Material Support for Terrorism Laws Compatible with International Humanitarian Law?' (2014) 46 NYU Journal of International Law and Politics 399; Antonio Galli, 'The US Humanitarian Assistance Facilitation Act' (2014) 5 Journal of International Humanitarian Legal Studies 130.

to prevent or halt humanitarian assistance operations.[187] When states fight organized armed groups on their own territory in non-international armed conflict, they sometimes prevent relief from reaching their own citizens, as occurred in north-west Syria and Mosul (Iraq) in the 2010s and in Tigray (Ethiopia) in 2020–2022. The year 2025 brought two further significant instances of states acting against humanitarian assistance. First, as mentioned above, the Trump administration dismantled USAID, including most of its humanitarian programmes; remaining programmes are being transferred to the Department of State.[188] Public health scholars have calculated that these cuts could lead to fourteen million excess deaths by 2030.[189]

The second instance is the Gaza Humanitarian Foundation. Beginning on 2 March 2025, Israel besieged Gaza for the second time,[190] in clear violation of its duty as an occupying power[191] to allow relief into the enclave.[192] When conditions deteriorated as a result of the siege,[193] rather than allowing the OCHA-coordinated system to resume aid deliveries in line with its proposed plan,[194] Israel implemented a new, widely criticized[195] food assistance distribution system run under the banner of the Israeli-conceived[196] and partly US-funded GHF.[197] Under this system, food assistance is distributed from four sites in southern Gaza, which may be part of an evidently unlawful Israeli plan to forcibly displace Palestinians to a 'humanitarian city' in Rafah.[198]

[187] See Chapter 5, Section 4.4.2.

[188] Michelle Nichols, 'As US Restores Some Aid, Humanitarian Groups Ask: Where is the Money?' (*Reuters*, 7 March 2025) <https://www.reuters.com/business/healthcare-pharmaceuticals/us-restores-some-aid-humanitarian-groups-ask-where-is-money-2025-03-07/> accessed 17 June 2025.

[189] Danielle Medeiros Cavalcanti and others, 'Evaluating the Impact of Two Decades of USAID Interventions and Projecting the Effects of Defunding on Mortality up to 2030: A Retrospective Impact Evaluation and Forecasting Analysis' [2025] The Lancet <https://www.thelancet.com/journals/lancet/article/PIIS0140-6736(25)01186-9/fulltext> accessed 1 July 2025.

[190] See Tom Dannenbaum, 'Gaza and Israel's Renewed Policy of Deprivation' (*Just Security*, 21 March 2025) <https://www.justsecurity.org/109263/gaza-israel-renewed-policy-deprivation/> accessed 4 August 2025.

[191] *Legal Consequences Arising from the Policies and Practices of Israel in the Occupied Palestinian Territory, Including East Jerusalem* (Advisory Opinion) 2024 <https://www.icj-cij.org/sites/default/files/case-related/186/186-20240719-adv-01-00-en.pdf> accessed 1 August 2024, paras 86–94.

[192] Geneva Convention Relative to the Protection of Civilian Persons in Time of War (adopted 12 August 1949, entered into force 21 October 1950) 75 UNTS 287, art 59(1); UNGA Res ES-10/27 (13 June 2025) A/RES/ES-10/27, para 6, which '*Stresses* that an occupying Power is obliged under international law to ensure that humanitarian aid reaches all the population in need'. See Chapter 3, Section 2.

[193] Erika Solomon and Rawan Sheikh Ahmad, 'As Gaza Siege Grinds On, Gazan Children Go Hungry and Patients Die' *The New York Times* (New York, 4 May 2025) A1.

[194] OCHA, 'Briefing Note: UN-Coordinated Plan to Resume Humanitarian Aid Deliveries to Gaza' (16 May 2025) <https://www.ochaopt.org/content/briefing-note-un-coordinated-plan-resume-humanitarian-aid-deliveries-gaza> accessed 17 June 2025.

[195] European Union External Action, 'Joint Donor Statement on Humanitarian Aid to Gaza' (19 May 2025) <https://www.eeas.europa.eu/node/452674_fr> accessed 17 June 2025; Aaron Boxerman, 'UN Condemns Israel's New Aid Program in Gaza, After Chaotic Start' *The New York Times* (New York, 28 May 2025) A7.

[196] Patrick Kingsley, Ronen Bergman, and Natan Odenheimer, 'New Gaza Aid Plan, Bypassing UN and Billed as Neutral, Originated in Israel' *The New York Times* (New York, 25 May 2025) A6.

[197] Andrew Roth, 'US to Give $30M to Gaza Humanitarian Foundation Despite Violent and Chaotic Rollout of Food Distribution' (*The Guardian*, 24 June 2025) <https://www.theguardian.com/us-news/2025/jun/24/us-food-distribution-group-gaza> accessed 30 June 2025.

[198] Orna Ben-Naftali, Eyal Benvenisti, and others, 'Manifestly Illegal: Israeli International Law Scholars on the Stated Plan to "Concentrate" the Palestinian Population in South Gaza' (*Just Security*, 10 July 2025) <https://www.justsecurity.org/116904/israeli-international-law-scholars-gaza/> accessed 31 July 2025.

The sites' inner perimeters are secured by private US contractors, notably Safe Reach Solutions LLC, which also handles operations.[199] Outer perimeters are secured by the Israel Defense Forces (IDF), whose soldiers have reportedly been ordered to fire on civilians as a means of crowd control,[200] a manifest war crime. This is a highly anomalous example of state provision of humanitarian assistance because the state involved is not a third state but a conflict party, and it is not providing humanitarian assistance directly but rather through a private contractor.

Israel has claimed that the GHF system is necessary to prevent the diversion of assistance by Hamas.[201] However, the IDF 'never found proof that the Palestinian militant group had systematically stolen aid' from the UN.[202] On 19 May 2025, Israel allowed some humanitarian assistance to resume entering Gaza. According to the IDF, after this date half of the assistance distributed in Gaza was dispensed under the OCHA-coordinated system, and the other half by the GHF.[203] On 26 July 2025, following mounting pressure from states and humanitarian organizations,[204] the IDF said that it would implement humanitarian corridors and pauses to facilitate the movement of UN relief convoys, and airdrops resumed.[205]

The GHF does not operate in accordance with the core humanitarian principles. It appears to have been set up in response to Israeli priorities and concerns, such as about aid diversion, rather than to address human suffering (humanity). It assists individuals who can reach its distribution points, rather than according to need and without discrimination; additionally, some reports have indicated that assistance is only provided to individuals who have been screened (impartiality).[206] It was conceived by and receives operational support from a conflict party, so it is not neutral (neutrality). Finally, it does not operate autonomously from Israel's political and military objectives (independence). The GHF's operations are a tragic illustration of the importance of these principles to the safe and effective delivery of humanitarian assistance. As of 1 August 2025, nearly 1,400 Palestinians had been killed while seeking food assistance.[207] Additionally, the GHF distributes significantly less assistance than

[199] Rachel Abrams, 'How Seeking Food in Gaza Has Become So Deadly' (The Daily (podcast), *The New York Times*, 24 July 2025) accessed 24 July 2025.

[200] Nir Hasson, '"It's a Killing Field": IDF Soldiers Ordered to Shoot Deliberately at Unarmed Gazans Waiting for Humanitarian Aid' (*Haaretz*, 27 June 2025) <https://www.haaretz.com/israel-news/2025-06-27/ty-article-magazine/.premium/idf-soldiers-ordered-to-shoot-deliberately-at-unarmed-gazans-waiting-for-humanitarian-aid/00000197-ad8e-de01-a39f-ffbe33780000> accessed 29 June 2025.

[201] Tom Bateman, 'Searching for Answers About US-Backed Aid Agency in Gaza' (*BBC News*, 15 June 2025) <https://www.bbc.com/news/articles/c74ne108e4vo> (BBC) accessed 17 June 2025.

[202] Natan Odenheimer, 'Israeli Officials Rebut Netanyahu on Hamas Thefts' *The New York Times* (New York, 27 July 2025) A1.

[203] ibid.

[204] Global Affairs Canada, 'Joint Statement on behalf of 26 Partners on the Occupied Palestinian Territories' (21 July 2025) <https://www.canada.ca/en/global-affairs/news/2025/07/joint-statement-on-behalf-of-26-partners-on-the-occupied-palestinian-territories.html> accessed 22 July 2025 (Joint Statement); Matthew Mpoke Bigg, 'Aid Groups Blame Israel for Growing Hunger Crisis in Gaza' *The New York Times* (New York, 24 July 2025) A11.

[205] Patrick Kingsley, 'Amid Growing Fury Over Gaza, Israel Says it is Easing Aid Restrictions' (*The New York Times*, 26 July 2025) <https://www.nytimes.com/2025/07/26/world/middleeast/gaza-aid-restrictions-eased.html> accessed 28 July 2025.

[206] BBC (n 201).

[207] Kirkup (n 96).

the system it replaced,[208] and its very limited number of distribution points—four, compared to over 400 under the full OCHA system—require civilians to make long and perilous journeys to access food.[209] According to the Integrated Food Security Phase Classification initiative (IPC),[210] as of 22 August 2025, there is a famine unfolding in Gaza City.[211] On 27 August 2025, a joint statement issued by all members of the UN Security Council except the US called on Israel to allow the 'UN and humanitarian partners to operate safely and at scale' in Gaza and noted that the core humanitarian principles 'must be central to humanitarian action'.[212]

The GHF is, however, an anomalous example of state humanitarian action. States are often indispensable humanitarian actors. As donors, they fund the majority of international humanitarian assistance, whether bilaterally or through the UN, NGOs, and the Movement. As operational actors, they deploy civil defence and military assets to respond to disasters and, occasionally, to armed conflicts, situations of violence not amounting to armed conflict, and mixed situations in which they are not otherwise involved or involved in a peacekeeping role. Additionally, states provide humanitarian assistance at sea in line with their obligations under the legal framework outlined in Chapter 4,[213] although NGOs are playing an increasingly important role in this area.[214]

Yet state action at the strategic level is inherently shaped by political interests, domestic considerations, and historical factors. Even where states purport to operate in line with the core humanitarian principles, their engagement can create access and security challenges, particularly when military assets and situations of armed conflict are involved. The Oslo and MCDA Guidelines reflect an effort to mitigate these problems, by promoting subsidiarity and civilian control and by precluding combat forces from becoming involved in UN humanitarian activities.

[208] BBC (n 201).

[209] Rawan Sheikh and Adam Rasgon, 'The Lethal Risk of Seeking Food in Gaza' (*The New York Times*, 26 June 2025) <https://www.nytimes.com/2025/06/26/world/middleeast/gaza-aid-violence.html> accessed 27 June 2025.

[210] See Chapter 5, Section 5.2.3.

[211] IPC, 'Gaza Strip: Famine Confirmed in Gaza Governorate, Projected to Expand' (22 August 2025) <https://www.ipcinfo.org/fileadmin/user_upload/ipcinfo/docs/IPC_Gaza_Strip_Acute_Food_Insecurity_Malnutrition_July_Sept2025_Special_Snapshot.pdf> accessed 23 August 2025.

[212] Joint Statement Delivered by Ambassadors Persaud of Guyana and Drobic of Slovenia (27 August 2025) <https://www.gov.uk/government/speeches/we-express-our-profound-alarm-and-distress-at-the-ipc-data-on-gaza-that-unequivocally-confirms-famine-in-gaza-joint-statement-on-famine-in-gaza> accessed 27 August 2025.

[213] See Chapter 4,Sections 4.1–4.2.

[214] See Chapter 4, Section 4.3.

PART IV
CONCLUSIONS

8
Conclusion

1. Humanitarian Assistance in International Law

This book has delineated the international legal framework for humanitarian assistance according to its constitutive principles, governing rules, and implementing actors. This conclusion highlights its key contributions and identifies avenues for further research.

Humanitarian assistance was defined in Chapter 1 as essential goods and services provided in accordance with the principles of humanity, impartiality, neutrality, and independence—or a similar set of principles—to save lives, alleviate suffering, and uphold human dignity when the state is unable or unwilling to fulfil its primary responsibility in this regard. It thus began by highlighting a key characteristic of humanitarian assistance: its subsidiarity to the affected state's primary responsibility, as a function of sovereignty and under international human rights law (IHRL), to meet the basic needs of individuals on state territory or subject to the state's power or effective control.[1]

Part II of the book, comprised of Chapters 2–4, covered the core of the legal framework for humanitarian assistance. Chapter 2 analysed the humanitarian principles mentioned above through a legal-historical lens to shed light on their origins, and their legal character and normative content for each major category of humanitarian actor: the United Nations (UN), the International Red Cross and Red Crescent Movement (the Movement), non-governmental organizations (NGOs), and states. It demonstrated that while the humanitarian principles do not—as is often assumed—derive from international humanitarian law (IHL), there are nevertheless common understandings of them. And while there are ethical and operational reasons to follow the principles, they are also binding for most humanitarian actors.

While the core humanitarian principles, particularly neutrality and independence, facilitate humanitarian access, there are also legal rules in this regard, which often oblige states or conflict parties to provide humanitarian actors with access to individuals in need within their control. Chapter 3 covered these and other international legal rules applicable in situations of armed conflict. It began by drawing a distinction between the IHL rules that support the provision of preventive humanitarian assistance and those that ensure access when civilians are inadequately supplied, as the former legal framework has not received much attention over the past decade, when analysis has rightly focused on emergency relief operations.

[1] UNGA Res 46/182 (19 December 1991) A/RES/46/182 (Res 46/182) Annex, para 4. See additional sources cited in Chapter 1, Section 2.

Humanitarian Assistance in International Law. Marina Sharpe, Oxford University Press.
DOI: 10.1093/9780198994695.003.0012

Chapter 3 then addressed emergency relief operations, beginning with how they are conducted in practice, whether cross-border, cross-line, or using humanitarian corridors, airdrops, or protected zones. The chapter then covered the legal framework: IHL on emergency relief provides that when civilians are inadequately supplied and humanitarian actors offer to carry out relief operations that are impartial in character and conducted without adverse distinction, it is unlawful for the relevant conflict party to withhold consent to such actions. Next, conflict parties and any transit states must allow and facilitate the rapid and unimpeded passage of relief consignments, equipment, and personnel, subject to their right of control—within which they may address concerns relating to military necessity. Conflict parties must also respect and protect relief personnel.

Chapter 3 explained how understanding of the law governing the first (strategic consent) step of emergency relief operations advanced considerably over the past decade. This was due to a call from the UN Secretary-General for analysis and development of the law[2] and to the work of an expert group, led by Dapo Akande and Emanuela-Chiara Gillard, to deliver on his call,[3] as well as to publications spurred by access challenges, particularly in Syria.[4] Chapter 3 also aimed to contribute to the advance, by addressing two divergent interpretations of the law.

First, whether a conflict party has any latitude to withhold step one strategic consent when civilians within its control are inadequately supplied and impartial humanitarian actors have offered to conduct non-discriminatory relief actions. Akande and Gillard are of the view that it may, in certain limited circumstances.[5] The International Committee of the Red Cross (ICRC), by contrast, is of the view that the conflict party must consent to relief actions unless civilians are no longer in need or the humanitarian relief action proposed is not impartial in character or is not conducted without adverse distinction.[6] Chapter 3 aligned with the ICRC interpretation.

Second, whether conflict parties must allow relief to reach besieged civilians. Chapter 3 argued that the view that they need not is based in large part on analysis of siege as a matter of step one strategic consent, whereas it should usually be analysed within the frame of the step two obligation to allow and facilitate relief, because humanitarian actors will typically already be present in-country. Even in instances where relief operations are not already underway, in international armed conflict, strategic consent is a matter for the state where civilians in need are located; the besieging force's strategic consent is not required.

Chapter 3 also added to existing analyses by detailing the assistance entitlements of civilians deprived of their liberty and evacuated and displaced civilians. It concluded

[2] UNSC, 'Report of the Secretary-General on the Protection of Civilians in Armed Conflict' (2013) S/2013/689, para 58.

[3] Dapo Akande and Emanuela-Chiara Gillard, 'Oxford Guidance on the Law Relating to Humanitarian Relief Operations in Situations of Armed Conflict' (2016) <https://www.elac.ox.ac.uk/wp-content/uploads/2022/06/oxfordguidancepdfpdf.pdf> (Oxford Guidance) accessed 3 July 2025.

[4] Especially ICRC, 'ICRC Q&A and Lexicon on Humanitarian Access' (2014) 96 International Review of the Red Cross 359 (ICRC Lexicon).

[5] Dapo Akande and Emanuela-Chiara Gillard, 'Arbitrary Withholding of Consent to Humanitarian Relief Operations in Armed Conflict' (2016) 92 International Law Studies 483. See also Oxford Guidance (n 3).

[6] ICRC Lexicon (n 4).

by addressing the operational consequences of withheld strategic consent and individual accountability and international responsibility for the same, as well as for attacking humanitarian personnel or protected zones. The discussion of accountability and responsibility addressed the cases currently pending before the International Criminal Court (ICC) and the International Court of Justice (ICJ) regarding Israel's conduct in Gaza.

Chapter 4 covered humanitarian assistance in peacetime. It began by clarifying that peacetime humanitarian assistance is more accurately addressed as a matter of state obligation than as a matter of individual rights or the responsibility to protect. It then highlighted the major peacetime legal gap: international disaster response law (IDRL) remains comprised of an incomplete patchwork of sectoral, contextual, regional, sub-regional, and bilateral treaties. However, there have recently been major advances in this area, due to the work of the International Federation of Red Cross and Red Crescent Societies (IFRC) and the International Law Commission (ILC). In 2016, the ILC adopted Draft Articles on the Protection of Persons in the Event of Disasters (Draft Articles), with a recommendation that the UN General Assembly draw on them to elaborate a comprehensive IDRL treaty.[7] The UN General Assembly decided to elaborate and conclude a treaty before the end of 2027.[8]

Chapter 4 also discussed situations in which the distinction between armed conflict and peacetime is not clear-cut. In mixed situations—in which a disaster strikes during armed conflict or an armed conflict breaks out in a disaster zone—both IHL and IDRL apply, unless this produces a norm conflict. In such cases, IHL governs as the *lex specialis*. Efforts to elaborate a minimum legal framework for situations of violence not amounting to armed conflict, in which state derogations from IHRL may create a legal protection gap, are currently stalled. While there is no legal basis for humanitarian access in these circumstances because IHL does not apply, the ICRC is mandated, including by states,[9] to operate in situations of internal strife.[10] In conferring this mandate, states incurred an obligation to cooperate with the ICRC when the organization exercises it in situations of violence not amounting to armed conflict.

Monographs devoted in whole or in part to humanitarian assistance have not addressed its provision at sea.[11] Yet since the early 2010s, maritime migrants have increasingly been in need of humanitarian assistance—rescue and essential items, such as drinking water and life jackets—especially on the Mediterranean. Just as states have primary responsibility under IHRL to meet the basic needs of individuals on their territory or subject to their power or effective control, they are also obliged under the law of the sea to rescue individuals in distress at sea, whether the individuals are within the state's territorial sea or its designated search and rescue area, or encountered on

[7] ILC, 'Report of the International Law Commission on the Work of its 68th Session' (2 May–10 June and 4 July–12 August 2016) A/71/10, 13.

[8] UNGA Res 79/128 (12 December 2024) A/RES/79/128, para 4.

[9] See Chapter 6, Section 2.

[10] Statutes of the International Red Cross and Red Crescent Movement (1986, as amended in 1995 and 2006) <https://www.icrc.org/en/doc/assets/files/other/statutes-en-a5.pdf> accessed 24 February 2022 (Movement Statutes) art 5(2)(d).

[11] Emilie Kuijt, *Humanitarian Assistance and State Sovereignty in International Law: Towards a Comprehensive Framework* (Intersentia 2015); Dug Cubie, *The International Legal Protection of Persons in Humanitarian Crises: Exploring the Acquis Humanitaire* (Hart 2017).

the water. However, states are increasingly unwilling to fulfil these obligations in relation to migrants, and NGOs have stepped in to fill the gap. Chapter 4 concluded by explaining the governing law of the sea framework, NGOs' growing humanitarian assistance role within it, and how states have responded.

Part III, comprised of Chapters 5–7, covered humanitarian actors. Chapter 5 provided the literature's only comprehensive account of UN engagement with humanitarian assistance, including the coordination and funding architecture created by the General Assembly in 1991;[12] major norm-generating actors and bodies: the Secretary-General, Economic and Social Council, General Assembly, and Security Council—which can both impose access, as it did in Syria,[13] and inadvertently complicate it with counterterrorism sanctions; and operational entities, notably UNHCR, UNICEF, WFP, UNRWA,[14] peacekeeping operations, and special political missions. The chapter also covered how international law facilitates UN humanitarian operations via privileges and immunities and protects UN personnel under the Convention on the Safety of United Nations and Associated Personnel (UN Safety Convention).[15]

Chapter 6 was devoted to non-state humanitarian actors: the Movement and NGOs, with a focus on how international law facilitates their work and protects their personnel. NGOs face considerable disadvantages in this regard because they are not subjects of international law, though UN implementing partners are covered by the UN Safety Convention. With attacks on health care in armed conflict on the rise, medical humanitarian NGOs face particular risks. In light of the fact that the IHL health care framework is narrower than commonly thought, the chapter devoted specific attention to the protection of health care in armed conflict. It also addressed how the Movement and NGOs have together driven the development of voluntary performance and accountability standards in humanitarian action.

Finally, Chapter 7 covered states as humanitarian actors, drawing a distinction at the outset between their strategic decision-making and operational activities; the former are rarely if ever driven entirely by the humanitarian principles. The chapter covered the two main dimensions of state humanitarian action: funding and direct involvement. Direct engagement is via the contribution of civil defence or military assets to humanitarian response; the chapter covered how IHL addresses the former in armed conflict. It also addressed how the UN has responded to the many issues that arise when state assets are used in emergency response: with two sets of guidelines, applicable in UN humanitarian activities in each of peacetime and complex emergencies.

The foregoing has aimed to bolster understanding of humanitarian assistance as largely a matter of international legal obligation for states or conflict parties in control of individuals in need, across the full range of circumstances in which such need arises: armed conflict, violence not amounting to armed conflict, peacetime disasters, mixed situations, and at sea. State obligations both support humanitarian access and protect humanitarians. When civilians are in need in armed conflict, strategic consent

[12] Res 46/182 (n 1).

[13] UNSC Res 2165 (14 July 2014) S/RES/2165 (UNSC Res 2165) and subsequent related resolutions reauthorizing the cross-border aid mechanism.

[14] See list of acronyms and abbreviations.

[15] (Adopted 9 December 1994, entered into force 15 January 1999) 2051 UNTS 363.

to relief actions that are humanitarian and impartial in character and conducted without adverse distinction is required, and then conflict parties and any transit states must allow and facilitate the rapid and unimpeded passage of relief consignments, equipment, and personnel, subject to their right of control.[16] The foregoing rules also apply to relief actions for besieged civilians[17] and in mixed situations.[18] The UN Security Council has demonstrated, in the case of Syria, that it is willing to respond when these obligations are violated.[19] Under the emerging IDRL regime, while the 'provision of external assistance requires the consent of the affected State', such consent 'shall not be withheld arbitrarily'.[20] States must cooperate with the ICRC in situations of violence not amounting to armed conflict, in which they have mandated the organization to act.[21] And states have a clear duty to rescue individuals in distress at sea, pursuant to the customary and treaty-based duty to rescue and under search and rescue treaties.[22] All humanitarian personnel are protected by the affected state's IHRL obligations, and they enjoy additional specific protections that vary by context and personnel type. Humanitarian personnel in armed conflict are protected as civilians and as relief personnel;[23] medical personnel enjoy additional specific protections.[24] Personnel responding to a disaster are protected under the emerging IDRL regime.[25] UN personnel are protected by privileges and immunities,[26] and they and certain NGO personnel enjoy additional protections under the UN Safety Convention.[27] ICRC and IFRC personnel are similarly protected under bilateral status agreements.[28] The foregoing duties demonstrate that states have been willing to accept a range of obligations in relation to humanitarian assistance. However, they have been less willing to fully comply with them, as the situations in Gaza[29] and Sudan[30] and the rising number of attacks against humanitarian personnel attest.[31]

[16] Protocol Additional to the Geneva Conventions of 12 August 1949, and relating to the Protection of Victims of International Armed Conflicts (adopted 8 June 1977, entered into force 7 December 1978) 1125 UNTS 3 (API) art 70; Jean-Marie Henckaerts and Louise Doswald-Beck, *Customary International Humanitarian Law*, vol I (CUP 2005) rule 55. See Chapter 3, Section 4.

[17] API (n 16) art 70(2); Henckaerts and Doswald-Beck (n 16) rule 55. See Chapter 3, Section 6.2.1.

[18] Draft Articles (n 7) art 18(2). See Chapter 4, Section 2.4.

[19] UNSC Res 2165 (n 13). See Chapter 5, Section 4.4.2.

[20] Draft Articles (n 7) art 13. See Chapter 4, Section 2.3.2.1.

[21] Movement Statutes (n 10) art 5(2)(d). See Chapter 6, Section 2.

[22] See Chapter 4, Section 4.2.

[23] API (n 16) arts 48, 51, and 71; Henckaerts and Doswald-Beck (n 16) rule 31. See Chapter 3, Section 4.4.4.

[24] See Chapter 6, Section 3.3.1.

[25] Draft Articles (n 7) art 16. See Chapter 4, Section 2.3.2.3.

[26] Charter of the United Nations (adopted 26 June 1945, entered into force 24 October 1945) 1 UNTS XVI, art 105; Convention on the Privileges and Immunities of the United Nations (adopted 13 February 1946, entered into force 17 September 1946) 1 UNTS 15. See Chapter 5, Section 5.1.

[27] UN Safety Convention (n 15). See Chapter 5, Section 5.4 and Chapter 6, Section 3.3.

[28] See Chapter 6, Section 2.3.

[29] See Marina Sharpe, 'HumanUnder the formeritarian Access to Gaza' (*EJIL:Talk!*, 20 November 2023) <https://www.ejiltalk.org/humanitarian-access-to-gaza/> accessed 25 August 2025 and the news sources cited in Chapter 7, Section 4.

[30] Human Rights Council, 'Findings of the Investigations Conducted by the Independent International Fact-Finding Mission for the Sudan into Violations of International Human Rights Law and International Humanitarian Law, and Related Crimes, Committed in the Sudan in the Context of the Conflict that Erupted in mid-April 2023' (23 October 2024) A/HRC/57/CRP.6, paras 281–85.

[31] UN Secretary-General, 'Protection of Civilians in Armed Conflict: Report of the Secretary-General' (15 May 2025) S/2025/271, para 35.

There are many reasons why states do not always comply with their international legal obligations, most of which are beyond the scope of this book. However, one reason is squarely within its purview: poor public knowledge of the law governing humanitarian assistance. State understanding has increased dramatically over the last decade, due, as mentioned above, to work initiated by the UN Secretary-General, as well as to the work of the IFRC and the ILC.[32] However, the fact that humanitarian assistance is largely a matter of international legal obligation is not yet well known among the general public, as illustrated by television and social media pundits who opine that conflict parties have no obligations in relation to humanitarian assistance for enemy civilians—when in fact the law provides exactly the opposite.[33] Without strong democratic pressure to comply, it is easier for states to ignore their international legal obligations and to weaponize aid. IHL recognizes the importance of disseminating the law.[34] The law on humanitarian assistance should be disseminated more broadly, so it becomes widely known that humanitarian assistance is not merely a gift governed by good intentions, but rather a matter of international legal obligation. This book is a contribution to that effort.

2. Future research

Other scholars should build on it and continue to develop the doctrine on humanitarian assistance. Many issues remain ripe for academic investigation. Over the last decade, analysis has focused on the IHL framework on emergency relief operations; the rules on preventive assistance should also be highlighted. Humanitarian actors face major digital threats,[35] as well as opportunities, which scholars have only begun to explore.[36] Recent advances regarding the adverse impact of UN financial sanctions on humanitarian assistance[37] must be tracked and expanded into related areas, as other types of sanctions and autonomous regimes continue to impede humanitarian access.[38] Ongoing developments, such as the UN's 'Humanitarian Reset' and the IDRL

[32] See Chapter 4, Section 2.3.

[33] API (n 16) art 70(2).

[34] Geneva Convention for the Amelioration of the Condition of the Wounded and Sick in Armed Forces in the Field (adopted 12 August 1949, entered into force 21 October 1950) 75 UNTS 31, art 47; Geneva Convention for the Amelioration of the Condition of Wounded, Sick and Shipwrecked Members of Armed Forces at Sea (adopted 12 August 1949, entered into force 21 October 1950) 75 UNTS 85, art 48; Geneva Convention Relative to the Treatment of Prisoners of War (adopted 12 August 1949, entered into force 21 October 1950) 75 UNTS 135, art 127; Geneva Convention Relative to the Protection of Civilian Persons in Time of War (adopted 12 August 1949, entered into force 21 October 1950) 75 UNTS 287, art 144; API (n 16) art 83; Protocol Additional to the Geneva Conventions of 12 August 1949, and relating to the Protection of Victims of Non-International Armed Conflicts (adopted 8 June 1977, entered into force 7 December 1978) 1125 UNTS 609, art 19.

[35] ICRC, 'International Humanitarian Law and the Challenges of Contemporary Armed Conflicts' (2024) <https://www.icrc.org/en/report/2024-icrc-report-ihl-challenges> accessed 14 August 2024 (Challenges Report) s VI.2.

[36] See Fleur Johns, *#Help: Digital Humanitarianism and the Remaking of International Order* (OUP 2023).

[37] UNSC Res 2664 (9 December 2022) S/RES/2664. See Chapter 5, Section 4.4.3.

[38] Challenges Report (n 35) s VI.1.

treaty negotiation, must be followed and analysed. The impact of pending and recently concluded judicial proceedings—such as the Gallant and Netanyahu cases before the ICC, South Africa's genocide case against Israel at the ICJ, and the latter's advisory opinion on Israel's obligations regarding humanitarian actors—on humanitarian access in practice and on the law of humanitarian assistance should be addressed. The UN Office for the Coordination of Humanitarian Affairs has been woefully understudied; it is essential, particularly in the context of the Humanitarian Reset, to understand its role, contributions, and whether and how it might be improved. And just as this monograph was needed in relation to international law, there is scope for a book to address cognate issues on the regional and sub-regional planes, especially as the African Union works to operationalize its African Humanitarian Agency.

APPENDIX I

Select Provisions of the Geneva Conventions and their Additional Protocols

Common Article 3(1)(2) and 3(2)—Conflicts not of an international character

The wounded and sick shall be collected and cared for.

An impartial humanitarian body, such as the International Committee of the Red Cross, may offer its services to the Parties to the conflict.

GCIV art 10—Activities of the International Committee of the Red Cross

The provisions of the present Convention constitute no obstacle to the humanitarian activities which the International Committee of the Red Cross or any other impartial humanitarian organization may, subject to the consent of the Parties to the conflict concerned, undertake for the protection of civilian persons and for their relief.

GCIV art 23—Consignment of medical supplies, food and clothing

Each High Contracting Party shall allow the free passage of all consignments of medical and hospital stores and objects necessary for religious worship intended only for civilians of another High Contracting Party, even if the latter is its adversary. It shall likewise permit the free passage of all consignments of essential foodstuffs, clothing and tonics intended for children under fifteen, expectant mothers and maternity cases.

The obligation of a High Contracting Party to allow the free passage of the consignments indicated in the preceding paragraph is subject to the condition that this Party is satisfied that there are no serious reasons for fearing:

(a) that the consignments may be diverted from their destination,
(b) that the control may not be effective, or
(c) that a definite advantage may accrue to the military efforts or economy of the enemy through the substitution of the above-mentioned consignments for goods which would otherwise be provided or produced by the enemy or through the release of such material, services or facilities as would otherwise be required for the production of such goods.

The Power which allows the passage of the consignments indicated in the first paragraph of this Article may make permission conditional on the distribution to the persons benefited thereby being made under the local supervision of the Protecting Powers.

Such consignments shall be forwarded as rapidly as possible, and the Power which permits their free passage shall have the right to prescribe the technical arrangements under which such passage is allowed.

GCIV art 55—Food and medical supplies for the population

To the fullest extent of the means available to it, the Occupying Power has the duty of ensuring the food and medical supplies of the population; it should, in particular, bring in the necessary foodstuffs, medical stores and other articles if the resources of the occupied territory are inadequate.

The Occupying Power may not requisition foodstuffs, articles or medical supplies available in the occupied territory, except for use by the occupation forces and administration personnel, and then only if the requirements of the civilian population have been taken into account. Subject to the provisions of other international Conventions, the Occupying Power shall make arrangements to ensure that fair value is paid for any requisitioned goods.

The Protecting Power shall, at any time, be at liberty to verify the state of the food and medical supplies in occupied territories, except where temporary restrictions are made necessary by imperative military requirements.

GCIV art 59—Relief I. Collective relief

If the whole or part of the population of an occupied territory is inadequately supplied, the Occupying Power shall agree to relief schemes on behalf of the said population, and shall facilitate them by all the means at its disposal.

Such schemes, which may be undertaken either by States or by impartial humanitarian organizations such as the International Committee of the Red Cross, shall consist, in particular, of the provision of consignments of foodstuffs, medical supplies and clothing.

All Contracting Parties shall permit the free passage of these consignments and shall guarantee their protection.

A Power granting free passage to consignments on their way to territory occupied by an adverse Party to the conflict shall, however, have the right to search the consignments, to regulate their passage according to prescribed times and routes, and to be reasonably satisfied through the Protecting Power that these consignments are to be used for the relief of the needy population and are not to be used for the benefit of the Occupying Power.

GCIV art 60—Relief II. Responsibilities of the Occupying Power

Relief consignments shall in no way relieve the Occupying Power of any of its responsibilities under Articles 55, 56 and 59. The Occupying Power shall in no way whatsoever divert relief consignments from the purpose for which they are intended, except in cases of urgent necessity, in the interests of the population of the occupied territory and with the consent of the Protecting Power.

GCIV art 61—Relief III. Distribution

The distribution of the relief consignments referred to in the foregoing Articles shall be carried out with the cooperation and under the supervision of the Protecting Power. This duty may also be delegated, by agreement between the Occupying Power and the Protecting Power, to a neutral Power, to the International Committee of the Red Cross or to any other impartial humanitarian body.

Such consignments shall be exempt in occupied territory from all charges, taxes or customs duties unless these are necessary in the interests of the economy of the territory. The Occupying Power shall facilitate the rapid distribution of these consignments.

All Contracting Parties shall endeavour to permit the transit and transport, free of charge, of such relief consignments on their way to occupied territories.

API art 70—Relief actions

1. If the civilian population of any territory under the control of a Party to the conflict, other than occupied territory, is not adequately provided with the supplies mentioned in Article 69, relief actions which are humanitarian and impartial in character and conducted without any adverse distinction shall be undertaken, subject to the agreement of the Parties concerned in such relief actions. Offers of such relief shall not be regarded as interference in the armed conflict or as unfriendly acts. In the distribution of relief consignments, priority shall be given to those persons, such as children, expectant mothers, maternity cases and nursing mothers, who, under the Fourth Convention or under this Protocol, are to be accorded privileged treatment or special protection.
2. The Parties to the conflict and each High Contracting Party shall allow and facilitate rapid and unimpeded passage of all relief consignments, equipment and personnel provided in accordance with this Section, even if such assistance is destined for the civilian population of the adverse Party.
3. The Parties to the conflict and each High Contracting Party which allow the passage of relief consignments, equipment and personnel in accordance with paragraph 2:
   (a) shall have the right to prescribe the technical arrangements, including search, under which such passage is permitted;
   (b) may make such permission conditional on the distribution of this assistance being made under the local supervision of a Protecting Power;
   (c) shall, in no way whatsoever, divert relief consignments from the purpose for which they are intended nor delay their forwarding, except in cases of urgent necessity in the interest of the civilian population concerned.
4. The Parties to the conflict shall protect relief consignments and facilitate their rapid distribution.
5. The Parties to the conflict and each High Contracting Party concerned shall encourage and facilitate effective international co-ordination of the relief actions referred to in paragraph 1.

API art 71—Personnel participating in relief actions

1. Where necessary, relief personnel may form part of the assistance provided in any relief action, in particular for the transportation and distribution of relief consignments; the participation of such personnel shall be subject to the approval of the Party in whose territory they will carry out their duties.
2. Such personnel shall be respected and protected.
3. Each Party in receipt of relief consignments shall, to the fullest extent practicable, assist the relief personnel referred to in paragraph 1 in carrying out their relief mission. Only in case of imperative military necessity may the activities of the relief personnel be limited or their movements temporarily restricted.

4. Under no circumstances may relief personnel exceed the terms of their mission under this Protocol. In particular they shall take account of the security requirements of the Party in whose territory they are carrying out their duties. The mission of any of the personnel who do not respect these conditions may be terminated.

APII art 18—Relief societies and relief actions

1. Relief societies located in the territory of the High Contracting Party, such as Red Cross (Red Crescent, Red Lion and Sun) organizations, may offer their services for the performance of their traditional functions in relation to the victims of the armed conflict. The civilian population may, even on its own initiative, offer to collect and care for the wounded, sick and shipwrecked.
2. If the civilian population is suffering undue hardship owing to a lack of the supplies essential for its survival, such as foodstuffs and medical supplies, relief actions for the civilian population which are of an exclusively humanitarian and impartial nature and which are conducted without any adverse distinction shall be undertaken subject to the consent of the High Contracting Party concerned.

APPENDIX II

Select Rules of Customary International Humanitarian Law

These rules are drawn from the International Committee of the Red Cross study on customary international humanitarian law.[1] According to the study, the rules below apply in both international and non-international armed conflict.

Rule 31. Humanitarian relief personnel must be respected and protected.

Rule 32. Objects used for humanitarian relief operations must be respected and protected.

Rule 53. The use of starvation of the civilian population as a method of warfare is prohibited.

Rule 55. The parties to the conflict must allow and facilitate rapid and unimpeded passage of humanitarian relief for civilians in need, which is impartial in character and conducted without any adverse distinction, subject to their right of control.

Rule 56. The parties to the conflict must ensure the freedom of movement of authorized humanitarian relief personnel essential to the exercise of their functions. Only in cases of imperative military necessity may their movements be temporarily restricted.

[1] Jean-Marie Henckaerts and Louise Doswald-Beck, *Customary International Humanitarian Law*, vol I (CUP 2005).

Select Bibliography

Books

Aga Khan S, *Winning the Human Race? The Report of the Independent Commission on International Humanitarian Issues* (Zed Books 1988)

Albanese F and Takkenberg L, *Palestinian Refugees in International Law* (2nd edn, OUP 2020)

Aleinikoff A and Zamore L, *The Arc of Protection: Reforming the International Refugee Regime* (Stanford University Press 2019)

Aronsson-Storrier M and Breau S (eds), *Research Handbook on Disasters and International Law* (2nd edn, Edward Elgar 2024)

Bandopadhyay S, *All is Well: Catastrophe and the Making of the Normal State* (OUP 2022)

Barber M, *Blinded by Humanity: Inside the UN's Humanitarian Operations* (IB Tauris & Co Ltd 2015)

Barnett M, *Empire of Humanity: A History of Humanitarianism* (Cornell University Press 2011)

Barrat C, *Status of NGOs in International Humanitarian Law* (Brill 2014)

Beigbeder Y, *The Role and Status of International Humanitarian Volunteers and Organizations: The Right and Duty to Humanitarian Assistance* (Martinus Nijhoff 1991)

Bellal A and Casey-Maslen S, *The Additional Protocols to the Geneva Conventions in Context* (OUP 2022)

Betts A, Loescher G, and Milner J, *UNHCR: The Politics and Practice of Refugee Protection* (2nd edn, Routledge 2012)

Bothe M, Partsch K, and Solf W (eds), *New Rules for Victims of Armed Conflicts: Commentary on the Two 1977 Protocols Additional to the Geneva Conventions of 1949* (Martinus Nijhoff 1982)

Bothe M, Partsch K, and Solf W (eds), *New Rules for Victims of Armed Conflicts: Commentary on the Two 1977 Protocols Additional to the Geneva Conventions of 1949* (2nd edn, Martinus Nijhoff 2013)

Boyle A and Chinkin C, *The Making of International Law* (OUP 2007)

Bradley M, *The Politics and Everyday Practice of International Humanitarianism* (OUP 2023)

Burtch A, *Give Me Shelter: The Failure of Canada's Cold War Civil Defence* (UBC Press 2012)

Cabanes B, *The Great War and the Origins of Humanitarianism* 1918–1924 (CUP 2014)

Caron D, Kelly M, and Telesetsky A (eds), *The International Law of Disaster Relief* (CUP 2014)

Clapham A, Gaeta P, and Sassòli M (eds), *The 1949 Geneva Conventions: A Commentary* (OUP 2015)

Crawford E and Pert A, *International Humanitarian Law* (3rd edn, CUP 2024)

Crawford J, *Brownlie's Principles of Public International Law* (9th edn, OUP 2019)

Cubie D, *The International Legal Protection of Persons in Humanitarian Crises: Exploring the Acquis Humanitaire* (Hart 2017)

Donini A (ed), *The Golden Fleece: Manipulation and Independence in Humanitarian Action* (Kumarian Press 2012)

Dromi S, *Above the Fray: The Red Cross and the Making of the Humanitarian NGO Sector* (University of Chicago Press 2020)

Dunant H, *A Memory of Solferino* (American Red Cross tr, American Red Cross 1939)

Ferris E, *The Politics of Protection: The Limits of Humanitarian Action* (Brookings 2011)

Ferstman C, *International Organizations and the Fight for Accountability: The Remedies and Reparations Gap* (OUP 2017)

Foley C, *UN Peacekeeping Operations and the Protection of Civilians: Saving Succeeding Generations* (CUP 2018)

Forsythe D, *The Humanitarians: The International Committee of the Red Cross* (CUP 2005)

Forsythe D, *The Contemporary International Committee of the Red Cross: Challenges, Changes, Controversies* (CUP 2024)

Forsythe D and Rieffer-Flanagan A, *The International Committee of the Red Cross: A Neutral Humanitarian Actor* (Routledge 2016)
Geiß R, Zimmermann A, and Haumer S (eds), *Humanizing the Laws of War: The Red Cross and the Development of International Humanitarian Law* (CUP 2018)
Gill T and others, *Leuven Manual on the International Law Applicable to Peace Operations* (CUP 2017)
Ginty R and Peterson J (eds), *The Routledge Companion to Humanitarian Action* (Routledge 2015)
Giustiniani F, *International Law in Disaster Scenarios* (Springer 2021)
Glasman J, *Humanitarianism and the Quantification of Human Needs: Minimal Humanity* (Routledge 2019)
Goodwin-Gill G and McAdam J, *The Refugee in International Law* (4th edn, OUP 2021)
Gray C, *International Law and the Use of Force* (4th edn, OUP 2018)
Green L, *The Contemporary Law of Armed Conflict* (3rd edn, Manchester University Press 2008)
Hathaway J, *The Rights of Refugees Under International Law* (2nd edn, CUP 2021)
Haug H, *Humanity for All: The International Red Cross and Red Crescent Movement* (Haupt 1993)
Heffes E, *Detention by Non-State Armed Groups Under International Law* (CUP 2022)
Heintze H and Zwitter A (eds), *International Law and Humanitarian Assistance: A Crosscut Through Legal Issues Pertaining to Humanitarianism* (Springer 2011)
Henckaerts J-M and Doswald-Beck L, *Customary International Humanitarian Law*, vol I (CUP 2005)
Higgins R and others, *Oppenheim's International Law: United Nations* (OUP 2017)
Hill-Cawthorne L, *Detention in Non-International Armed Conflict* (OUP 2016)
Hillen J, *Blue Helmets: The Strategy of UN Military Operations* (Brassey's 1998)
Hutchinson J, *Champions of Charity: War and the Rise of the Red Cross* (Routledge 2018)
ICRC, *Interpretive Guidance on the Notion of Direct Participation in Hostilities under International Humanitarian Law* (ICRC 2009)
ICRC, *Commentary on the First Geneva Convention: Convention (I) for the Amelioration of the Condition of the Wounded and Sick in Armed Forces in the Field* (CUP 2016)
ICRC, *Professional Standards for Protection Work* (3rd edn, ICRC 2018)
Imseis A, *The United Nations and the Question of Palestine: Rule by Law and the Structure of International Legal Subalternity* (CUP 2023)
Irfan A, *Refuge and Resistance: Palestinians and the International Refugee System* (Columbia University Press 2023)
Jacques M, *Armed Conflict and Displacement* (CUP 2015)
Johns F, *#Help: Digital Humanitarianism and the Remaking of International Order* (OUP 2023)
Kaldor M, *New and Old Wars: Organized Violence in a Global Era* (3rd edn, Stanford University Press 2012)
Kälin W, *Internal Displacement and the Law* (OUP 2023)
Kalshoven F (ed), *Assisting the Victims of Armed Conflict and Other Disasters* (Martinus Nijhoff 1989)
Klabbers J, *An Introduction to International Organizations Law* (4th edn, CUP 2022)
Kuijt E, *Humanitarian Assistance and State Sovereignty in International Law: Towards a Comprehensive Framework* (Intersentia 2015)
MacAlister-Smith P, *International Humanitarian Assistance: Disaster Relief Actions in International Law and Organization* (Springer 1985)
Magone C, Neuman M, and Weissman F (eds), *Humanitarian Negotiations Revealed: The MSF Experience* (Hurst 2011)
Maxwell D and Gelsdorf K, *Understanding the Humanitarian World* (Routledge 2019)
Melzer N, *International Humanitarian Law: A Comprehensive Introduction* (ICRC 2019)
Milanović M, *Extraterritorial Application of Human Rights Treaties: Law, Principles, and Policy* (OUP 2011)
Minear L and Weiss T, *Humanitarian Action in Times of War: A Handbook for Practitioners* (Lynne Rienner Publishers 1993)
Moorehead C, *Dunant's Dream: War, Switzerland and the History of the Red Cross* (HarperCollins 1998)
Moreno-Lax V and Papastavridis E (eds), *'Boat Refugees' and Migrants at Sea: A Comprehensive Approach* (Brill Nijhoff 2016)

Ní Ghráinne B, *Internally Displaced Persons and International Refugee Law* (OUP 2022)
Ohlin J (ed), *Theoretical Boundaries of Armed Conflict and Human Rights* (CUP 2016)
Orbinski J, *An Imperfect Offering: Humanitarian Action in the Twenty-First Century* (Anchor 2009)
Papanicolopulu I, *International Law and the Protection of People at Sea* (OUP 2018)
Pictet J and others, *Commentary: IV Geneva Convention Relative to the Protection of Civilian Persons in Time of War* (ICRC 1958)
Program on Humanitarian Policy and Conflict Research at Harvard University, *Manual on International Law Applicable to Air and Missile Warfare* (CUP 2013)
Rossy K and Knapton S (eds), *Rehabilitation Among the Ruins: The United Nations Relief and Rehabilitation Administration* (Bloomsbury 2023)
Sandoz Y, Swinarski C, and Zimmermann B (eds), *Commentary on the Additional Protocols of 8 June 1977 to the Geneva Conventions of 12 August 1949* (Martinus Nijhoff 1987)
Sassòli M, *International Humanitarian Law: Rules, Controversies, and Solutions to Problems Arising in Warfare* (Edward Elgar 2019)
Sassòli M, Bouvier A, and Quintin A (eds), *How Does Law Protect in War? Cases, Documents and Teaching Materials on Contemporary Practice in International Humanitarian Law* (3rd edn, ICRC 2011)
Schiff B, *Refugees Unto the Third Generation: UN Aid to Palestinians* (Syracuse University Press 1995)
Sharpe M, *The Regional Law of Refugee Protection in Africa* (OUP 2018)
Shucksmith C, *The International Committee of the Red Cross and its Mandate to Protect and Assist: Law and Practice* (Hart 2017)
Slim H, *Humanitarian Ethics: A Guide to the Morality of Aid in War and Disaster* (OUP 2015)
Slim H, *Solferino 21: Warfare, Civilians and Humanitarians in the Twenty-First Century* (Hurst 2022)
Slim H, *Humanitarianism 2.0: New Ethics for the Climate Emergency* (Hurst 2024)
Swinarski C (ed), *Studies and Essays on International Humanitarian Law and Red Cross Principles in Honour of Jean Pictet* (Brill Nijhoff 1984)
Szurek S, Eudes M, and Ryfman P (eds), *Droit et pratique de l'action humanitaire* (LGDJ 2019)
Trahan J, *Existing Legal Limits to Security Council Veto Power in the Face of Atrocity Crimes* (CUP 2020)
Vanhullebusch M, *The Law of International Humanitarian Relief in Non-International Armed Conflicts* (Brill 2021)
Veerakatty V, *Arbitrary Withholding of Consent to Humanitarian Relief in Non-International Armed Conflict* (Brill 2024)
Verdirame G, *The UN and Human Rights: Who Guards the Guardians?* (CUP 2011)
Walker P and Maxwell D, *Shaping the Humanitarian World* (Routledge 2008)
Willmot H and others (eds), *Protection of Civilians* (OUP 2016)
Zwitter A and others (eds), *Humanitarian Action: Global, Regional and Domestic Legal Responses* (CUP 2015)

Articles, chapters, and papers

Akande D and Gillard E-C, 'Arbitrary Withholding of Consent to Humanitarian Relief Operations in Armed Conflict' (2016) 92 International Law Studies 483
Akande D and Gillard E-C, 'Oxford Guidance on the Law Relating to Humanitarian Relief Operations in Situations of Armed Conflict' (2016) OCHA <https://reliefweb.int/sites/reliefweb.int/files/resources/Oxford%20Guidance%20pdf.pdf> accessed 8 May 2023
Akande D and Gillard E-C, 'Humanitarian Actors' Engagement with Accountability Mechanisms in Situations of Armed Conflict: Workshop Report' (2017) 2016 Anuário Português de Direito Internacional 105
Akande D and Gillard E-C, 'Promoting Compliance with the Rules Regulating Humanitarian Relief Operations in Armed Conflict: Some Challenges' (2017) 50 Israel Law Review 119

Akande D and Gillard E-C, 'Conflict-induced Food Insecurity and the War Crime of Starvation of Civilians as a Method of Warfare: The Underlying Rules of International Humanitarian Law' (2019) 17 Journal of International Criminal Justice 753

Alexander D, 'The Study of Natural Disasters, 1977–1997: Some Reflections on a Changing Field of Knowledge' (1997) 21 Disasters 284

Alexander D, 'From Civil Defence to Civil Protection—and Back Again' (2002) 11 Disaster Prevention and Management 209

Alimonti G and Mariani L, 'Is the Number of Global Natural Disasters Increasing?' (2024) 23 Environmental Hazards 186

Allan C and O'Donnell T, 'An Offer You Cannot Refuse? Natural Disasters, the Politics of Aid Refusal and Potential Legal Implications' (2013) 5 Amsterdam Law Forum 36

Allen C, 'Civilian Starvation and Relief During Armed Conflict: The Modern Humanitarian Law' (1989) 19 Georgia Journal of International & Comparative Law 1

Arendt L, 'Building a Culture of Protection: 20 Years of Security Council Engagement on the Protection of Civilians' (OCHA Occasional Policy Paper 2019)

Aronsson-Storrier M and da Costa K, 'Regulating Disasters? The Role of International Law in Disaster Prevention and Management' (2017) 26 Disaster Prevention and Management 502

Barber R, 'Facilitating Humanitarian Assistance in International Humanitarian and Human Rights Law' (2009) 91 International Review of the Red Cross 371

Barber R, 'The Responsibility to Protect the Survivors of Natural Disaster: Cyclone Nargis, a Case Study' (2009) 14 Journal of Conflict & Security Law 3

Barber R, 'Does International Law Permit the Provision of Humanitarian Assistance Without Host State Consent? Territorial Integrity, Necessity and the Determinative Function of the General Assembly' in Gill T and others (eds), *Yearbook of International Humanitarian Law 2020*, vol 23 (Springer 2022)

Barber R, 'What Blocked the UN's Response to the Earthquakes in Northwest Syria? Reflections on a Humanitarian System Premised on Government Consent' (2023) 15 Journal of International Humanitarian Legal Studies 83

Barnes R, 'The International Law of the Sea and Migration Control' in Ryan B and Mitsilegas V (eds), *Extraterritorial Immigration Control: Legal Challenges* (Martinus Nijhoff 2010)

Bartels R, 'Denying Humanitarian Access as an International Crime in Times of Non-International Armed Conflict: The Challenges to Prosecute and Some Proposals for the Future' (2015) 48 Israel Law Review 281

Bartolini G, 'A Universal Treaty for Disasters? Remarks on the International Law Commission's Draft Articles on the Protection of Persons in the Event of Disasters' (2017) 99 International Review of the Red Cross 1103

Bassil A, 'Armed Escorts to Humanitarian Convoys: An Unexplored Framework Under International Humanitarian Law' (2020) 102 International Review of the Red Cross 559

Beauchamp S, '"Humanitarian Space" in Search of a New Home: (Limited) Guidance from International Law' in Perrin B (ed), *Modern Warfare* (UBC Press 2012)

Bettati M, 'Right of Humanitarian Intervention or the Right of Free Access to Victims?' (1992) 49 International Commission of Jurists Review 1

Bieńczyk-Missala A and Grzebyk P, 'Safety and Protection of Humanitarian Workers' in Gibbons P and Heintze H-J (eds), *The Humanitarian Challenge: 20 Years European Network on Humanitarian Action* (Springer 2015)

Binder A and Meier C, 'Opportunity Knocks: Why Non-Western Donors Enter Humanitarianism and How to Make the Best of It' (2011) 93 International Review of the Red Cross 1135

Bloom E, 'Protecting Peacekeepers: The Convention on the Safety of United Nations and Associated Personnel' (1995) 89 American Journal of International Law 621

Bookmiller K, 'The International Law of 96 Hours: Urban Search and Rescue Teams and the Current State of International Disaster Response Law' in Caron D, Kelly M, and Telesetsky A (eds), *The International Law of Disaster Relief* (CUP 2014)

Bookmiller K, 'Closing "The Yawning Gap"? International Disaster Response Law at Fifteen' in Breau S and Samuel K (eds), *Research Handbook on Disasters and International Law* (Edward Elgar Publishing 2016)

Boon K, 'The United Nations as Good Samaritan: Immunity and Responsibility' (2016) 16 Chicago Journal of International Law 341

Bothe M, 'Relief Actions' in Bernhardt R (ed), *Encyclopedia of Public International Law*, vol 1 (North-Holland 1982)

Bothe M, 'Relief Actions: The Position of the Recipient State' in Kalshoven F (ed), *Assisting the Victims of Armed Conflict and Other Disasters* (Martinus Nijhoff 1989)

Bothe M, 'Shedding Light on the Rules of Humanitarian Access: Reflections on the Occasion of the 40th Anniversary of the Protocols Additional to the Geneva Conventions' in Pocar F (ed), *The Additional Protocols 40 Years Later: New Conflicts, New Actors, New Perspectives* (FrancoAngeli 2018)

Bouchet-Saulnier F, 'Consent to Humanitarian Access: An Obligation Triggered by Territorial Control, Not States' Rights' (2014) 96 International Review of the Red Cross 207

Bouvier A, 'Convention on the Safety of United Nations and Associated Personnel: Presentation and Analysis' (1995) 35 International Review of the Red Cross 638

Breitegger A, 'The Legal Framework Applicable to Insecurity and Violence Affecting the Delivery of Health Care in Armed Conflicts and Other Emergencies' (2013) 95 International Review of the Red Cross 83

Breslawski J, 'The Shortcomings of International Humanitarian Law in Access Negotiations: New Strategies and Ways Forward' (2022) 24 International Studies Review 1

Bugnion F, 'Red Cross Law' (1995) 35 International Review of the Red Cross 491

Bugnion F, 'Birth of an Idea: The Founding of the International Committee of the Red Cross and of the International Red Cross and Red Crescent Movement: from Solferino to the Original Geneva Convention (1859–1864)' (2012) 94 International Review of the Red Cross 1299

Calain P, 'Attacks on Hospitals: An Alarming Problem for Military Medicine as Well as for Humanitarian Medicine' in Messelken D and Winkler D (eds), *Health Care in Contexts of Risk, Uncertainty, and Hybridity* (Springer 2022)

Canyon D and Burkle F, 'The 2016 World Humanitarian Summit Report Card: Both Failing Marks and Substantive Gains for an Increasingly Globalized Humanitarian Landscape' [2016] PLoS Currents Disasters

Capone F, 'A Critical Overview of the United Nations Architecture on Children and Armed Conflict: What Role for Sanctions' (2017) 27 Italian Yearbook of International Law 115

Charlton M, 'Famine and the Food Weapon: Implications for the Global Food Aid Regime' (1997) 17 Journal of Conflict Studies 28

Charnovitz S, 'Nongovernmental Organizations and International Law' (2006) 100 American Journal of International Law 348

Chetail V, 'The Contribution of the International Court of Justice to International Humanitarian Law' (2003) 85 International Review of the Red Cross 235

Chimia A, 'Food Security and the Right to Food: Finding Balance in the 2012 Food Assistance Convention' (2016) 65 International & Comparative Law Quarterly 99

Clement C, 'International Disaster Response Laws, Rules, and Principles: A Pragmatic Approach to Strengthening International Disaster Response Mechanisms' in Caron D, Kelly M, and Telesetsky A (eds), *The International Law of Disaster Relief* (CUP 2014)

Costa P and Evans P, 'The Indian Supply Drop into Sri Lanka: Nonmilitary Humanitarian Aid and the Troubling Idea of Intervention' (1988) 3 Connecticut Journal of International Law 417

Costello C and Foster M, 'Non-refoulement as Custom and *Jus Cogens*? Putting the Prohibition to the Test' (2016) 46 Netherlands Yearbook of International Law 2015 273

Coupland R, 'Humanity: What is it and How Does it Influence International Law?' (2001) 83 International Review of the Red Cross 969

Craven M, 'Humanitarianism and the Quest for Smarter Sanctions' (2002) 13 European Journal of International Law 43

Crawford E, 'Road to Nowhere? The Future for a Declaration on Fundamental Standards of Humanity' (2012) 3 Journal of International Humanitarian Legal Studies 43

Creta A, 'A (Human) Right to Humanitarian Assistance in Disaster Situations? Surveying Public International Law' in de Guttry A, Gestri M, and Venturini G (eds), *International Disaster Response Law* (Springer 2012)

Crisp J, 'Humanitarian Action and Coordination' in Weiss T and Daws S (eds), *The Oxford Handbook on the United Nations* (2nd edn, OUP 2018)
Cubie D, 'An Analysis of Soft Law Applicable to Humanitarian Action: Relative Normativity in Action?' (2011) 2 Journal of International Humanitarian Legal Studies 177
Cubie D, 'An Enchanted Tool? Humanitarian Assistance and the ILC Draft Articles on the Protection of Persons in the Event of Disasters' (2012) 4 Irish Yearbook of International Law 119
Cubie D, 'Complementarity Between Human Security and Legal Frameworks for Humanitarian Action' in Oberleitner G (ed), *Research Handbook on International Law and Human Security* (Edward Elgar 2022)
Cubie D and Hesselman M, 'Accountability for the Human Rights Implications of Natural Disasters: A Proposal for Systemic International Oversight' (2015) 33 Netherlands Quarterly of Human Rights 9
Cusumano E and Pattison J, 'The Non-Governmental Provision of Search and Rescue in the Mediterranean and the Abdication of State Responsibility' (2018) 31 Cambridge Review of International Affairs 53
Cusumano E and Villa M, 'From "Angels" to "Vice Smugglers": The Criminalization of Sea Rescue NGOs in Italy' (2021) 27 European Journal on Criminal Policy and Research 23
D'Alessandra F and Gillett M, 'The War Crime of Starvation in Non-International Armed Conflict' (2019) 17 Journal of International Criminal Justice 815
Dannenbaum T, 'Encirclement, Deprivation, and Humanity: Revising the San Remo Manual Provisions on Blockade' (2021) 97 International Law Studies 307
Dannenbaum T, 'Criminalizing Starvation in an Age of Mass Deprivation in War: Intent, Method, Form, and Consequence' (2022) 55 Vanderbilt Journal of Transnational Law 681
Dannenbaum T, 'Siege Starvation: A War Crime of Societal Torture' (2022) 22 Chicago Journal of International Law 368
Dany C, 'Politicization of Humanitarian Aid in the European Union' (2015) 20 European Foreign Affairs Review 419
Davey E, Borton J, and Foley M, 'A History of the Humanitarian System: Western Origins and Foundations' (2013) HPG Working Paper <https://odi.org/en/publications/a-history-of-the-humanitarian-system-western-origins-and-foundations/> accessed 14 March 2022
Debuf E, 'Tools to do the Job: The ICRC's Legal Status, Privileges and Immunities' (2016) 97 International Review of the Red Cross 319
de Guttry A, 'Surveying the Law' in de Guttry A, Gestri M, and Venturini G (eds), *International Disaster Response Law* (TMC Asser Press 2012)
De Siervo G, 'Actors, Activities, and Coordination in Emergencies' in de Guttry A, Gestri M, and Venturini G (eds), *International Disaster Response Law* (Springer 2012)
Desgrandchamps M-L, 'Revenir sur le mythe fondateur de Médecins sans frontières: les relations entre les médecins français et le CICR pendant la guerre du Biafra (1967–1970)' (2011) 2 Relations internationales 95
Dinstein Y, 'Siege Warfare and the Starvation of Civilians' in Delissen A and Tanja G (eds), *Humanitarian Law of Armed Conflict Challenges Ahead: Essays in Honour of Frits Kalshoven* (Martinus Nijhoff 1991)
Dinstein Y, 'The Right to Humanitarian Assistance' (2000) 53 Naval War College Review 77
Donini A, 'Between a Rock and a Hard Place: Integration or Independence of Humanitarian Action' (2011) 93 International Review of the Red Cross 152
Donnelly E, 'Towards Greater Legal Protection for Medical-Humanitarian NGOs in Situations of Armed Conflict' (2018) 3 Cambridge Law Review 144
Dörmann K and Ferraro T, 'Humanitarian Assistance' in Fleck D (ed), *The Handbook of International Humanitarian Law* (4th edn, OUP 2021)
Drew P, 'Can We Starve the Civilians? Exploring the Dichotomy Between the Traditional Law of Maritime Blockade and Humanitarian Initiatives' (2019) 95 International Law Studies 302
Droege C, 'The Interplay between International Humanitarian Law and International Human Rights Law in Situations of Armed Conflict' (2007) 40 Israel Law Review 310
DuBois M and Healy S, 'Imperfect Relief: Challenges to the Impartiality and Identity of Humanitarian Action' (2024) 106 International Review of the Red Cross 90

Dungel J, 'A Right to Humanitarian Assistance in Internal Armed Conflicts Respecting Sovereignty, Neutrality and Legitimacy: Practical Proposals to Practical Problems' [2004] Journal of Humanitarian Assistance

Durand A, '*Quelques remarques sur l'élaboration des principes de la Croix-Rouge chez Gustave Moynier*' in Swinarski C (ed), *Studies and Essays on International Humanitarian Law and Red Cross Principles in Honour of Jean Pictet* (Brill Nijhoff 1984)

Durham H and Wynn-Pope P, 'Protecting the "Helpers": Humanitarians and Health Care Workers During Times of Armed Conflict' in Schmitt M and Arimatsu L (eds), *Yearbook of International Humanitarian Law 2011*, vol 14 (TMC Asser Press 2012)

Eburn M, 'International Law and Disaster Response' (2010) 36 Monash University Law Review 162

Eckert S, 'Counterterrorism, Sanctions and Financial Access Challenges: Course Corrections to Safeguard Humanitarian Action' (2021) 103 International Review of the Red Cross 415

Elkahlout G and Milton S, 'The Evolution of the Gulf States as Humanitarian Donors' (2023) 45 Third World Quarterly 2246

Evangelidis E and O'Donnell T, 'NGOs and the International Law Commission Draft Articles on the Protection of Persons in the Event of Disasters: A Relationship of Mutual or Grudging Respect?' (2018) 1 Yearbook of International Disaster Law 116

Fast L, 'Unpacking the Principle of Humanity: Tensions and Implications' (2016) 97 International Review of the Red Cross 111

Ferraro R, 'Challenges to Implementation of Humanitarian Access Norms in the Sahel' (2021) 103 International Review of the Red Cross 859

Ferraro T, 'Relief Schemes and the Delivery of Humanitarian Activities in Situations of Armed Conflict: the ICRC's Perspective' in Pocar F (ed), *The Additional Protocols 40 Years Later: New Conflicts, New Actors, New Perspectives* (FrancoAngeli 2018)

Ferraro T, 'International Humanitarian Law, Principled Humanitarian Action, Counterterrorism and Sanctions: Some Perspectives on Selected Issues' (2021) 103 International Review of the Red Cross 109

Fidler D, 'Disaster Relief and Governance After the Indian Ocean Tsunami: What Role for International Law?' (2005) 6 Melbourne Journal of International Law 458

Fink G and Redaelli S, 'Determinants of International Emergency Aid—Humanitarian Need Only?' (2011) 39 World Development 741

Fisher D, 'Domestic Regulation of International Humanitarian Relief in Disasters and Armed Conflict: A Comparative Analysis' (2007) 89 International Review of the Red Cross 345

Fisher D, 'The Law of International Disaster Response: Overview and Ramifications for Military Actors' (2008) 38 Israel Yearbook on Human Rights 115

Fisher D, 'The Right to Humanitarian Assistance' (2010) 41 Studies in Transnational Legal Policy 47

Fisher D, 'The Future of International Disaster Response Law' (2012) 55 German Yearbook of International Law 87

Fisher D, 'A Glass Half Full: The International Law Commission's Draft Articles and the Operational Challenges of International Disaster Response' (2020) 1 Yearbook of International Disaster Law 93

Ford S, 'Is the Failure to Respond Appropriately to a Natural Disaster a Crime Against Humanity? The Responsibility to Protect and Individual Criminal Responsibility in the Aftermath of Cyclone Nargis' (2010) 38 Denver Journal of International Law and Policy 227

Forsythe D, 'On Contested Concepts: Humanitarianism, Human Rights, and the Notion of Neutrality' (2013) 12 Journal of Human Rights 59

Fraterman J, 'Criminalizing Humanitarian Relief: Are US Material Support for Terrorism Laws Compatible with International Humanitarian Law?' (2014) 46 NYU Journal of International Law and Politics 399

Friis K, 'Military and Humanitarian Actors' in Ginty R and Peterson J (eds), *The Routledge Companion to Humanitarian Action* (Routledge 2015)

Frowein J, 'United Nations' in Wolfrum R (ed), *Max Planck Encyclopedia of Public International Law* (OUP 2013)

Gaggioli G and Melzer N, 'Methods of Warfare' in Saul B and Akande D (eds), *The Oxford Guide to International Humanitarian Law* (OUP 2020)

Gal T, 'Territorial Control by Armed Groups and the Regulation of Access to Humanitarian Assistance' (2017) 50 Israel Law Review 25
Galli A, 'The US Humanitarian Assistance Facilitation Act' (2014) 5 Journal of International Humanitarian Legal Studies 130
Gavshon D, 'The Applicability of IHL in Mixed Situations of Disaster and Conflict' (2009) 14 Journal of Conflict & Security Law 243
Ghezelbash D and others, 'Securitization of Search and Rescue at Sea: The Response to Boat Migration in the Mediterranean and Offshore Australia' (2018) 67 International & Comparative Law Quarterly 315
Giladi R, 'The Utility and Limits of Legal Mandate: Humanitarian Assistance, the International Committee of the Red Cross, and Mandate Ambiguity' in Zwitter A and others (eds), *Humanitarian Action: Global, Regional and Domestic Legal Responses* (CUP 2015)
Gillard E-C, 'The Law Regulating Cross-Border Relief Operations' (2013) 95 International Review of the Red Cross 351
Gillard E-C, 'Cross-Border Relief Operations: A Legal Perspective' (2014) OCHA Policy Series <https://www.unocha.org/sites/unocha/files/dms/Documents/Legal%20Perspective%20Cross-border%20relief%20operations.pdf> accessed 18 March 2024
Gillard E-C, '"Safe Areas": The International Legal Framework' (2017) 99 International Review of the Red Cross 1075
Gillard E-C, 'Enhancing the Security of Civilians in Conflict: Notifications, Evacuations, Humanitarian Corridors, Suspensions of Hostilities and Other Humanitarian Arrangements' (*Chatham House*, 30 April 2024) <https://www.chathamhouse.org/2024/04/enhancing-security-civilians-conflict> accessed 12 July 2024
Gillard E-C and Weizmann N, 'Humanitarian Relief in Situations of Armed Conflict' in Geiß R and Melzer N (eds), *The Oxford Handbook of the International Law of Global Security* (OUP 2021)
Gombeer K, 'Human Rights Adrift? Enabling the Disembarkation of Migrants to a Place of Safety in the Mediterranean' in de Londras F and Mullally S (eds), *Irish Yearbook of International Law 2015*, vol 10 (Hart 2017)
Gombeer K and Fink M, 'Non-Governmental Organisations and Search and Rescue at Sea' (2018) 4 Maritime Safety and Security Law Journal 1
Gong L, 'Humanitarian Diplomacy as an Instrument for China's Image-Building' (2021) 6 Asian Journal of Comparative Politics 238
Gordon S and Donini A, 'Romancing Principles and Human Rights: Are Humanitarian Principles Salvageable?' (2016) 97 International Review of the Red Cross 77
Grace R, 'Humanitarian Negotiation with Parties to Armed Conflict: The Role of Laws and Principles in the Discourse' (2020) 11 Journal of International Humanitarian Legal Studies 68
Gribbin C and Maiolo I, 'Legal Framework Applicable to Humanitarian Actors Responding to Disasters in Weak and Fragile States' in Caron D and others (eds), *The International Law of Disaster Relief* (CUP 2014)
Haacke J, 'Myanmar, the Responsibility to Protect and the Need for Practical Assistance' (2009) 1 Global Responsibility to Protect 156
Hammond L, 'Neutrality and Impartiality' in Ginty R and Peterson J (eds), *The Routledge Companion to Humanitarian Action* (Routledge 2015)
Hardcastle R and Chua A, 'Victims of Natural Disasters: The Right to Receive Humanitarian Assistance' (1997) 1 The International Journal of Human Rights 37
Hardcastle R and Chua A, 'Humanitarian Assistance: Towards a Right of Access to Victims of Natural Disasters' (1998) 38 International Review of the Red Cross 589
Harroff-Tavel M, 'Neutrality and Impartiality: The Importance of these Principles for the International Red Cross and Red Crescent Movement and the Difficulties Involved in Applying Them' (1989) 29 International Review of the Red Cross 536
Hathaway J, 'The Human Rights Quagmire of "Human Trafficking"' (2008) 49 Virginia Journal of International Law 1
Heath J, 'Disasters, Relief, and Neglect: the Duty to Accept Humanitarian Assistance and the Work of the International Law Commission' (2011) 43 NYU Journal of International Law and Policy 419

Heath J, 'Managing the "Republic of NGOs": Accountability and Legitimation Problems Facing the UN Cluster System' (2014) 47 Vanderbilt Journal of Transnational Law 239
Heffes E, 'Armed Groups and the Protection of Health Care' (2019) 95 International Law Studies 226
Heffes E and Frenkel B, 'The International Responsibility of Non-State Armed Groups: In Search of the Applicable Rules' (2017) 8 Goettingen Journal of International Law 39
Heintschel von Heinegg W, 'Blockade' in Wolfrum R (ed), *Max Planck Encyclopedia of International Law* (OUP 2015)
Heintze H-J, 'Access to Victims and Humanitarian Assistance' in Heintze H-J and Thielbörger P (eds), *From Cold War to Cyber War: The Evolution of the International Law of Peace and Armed Conflict over the Last 25 Years* (Springer 2016)
Hesselman M, 'A Right to International (Humanitarian) Assistance in Times of Disaster: Fresh Perspectives from International Human Rights Law' in Giustiniani F and others (eds), *Routledge Handbook of Human Rights and Disaster* (Routledge 2018)
Higgins R, 'The Advisory Opinion on Namibia: Which UN Resolutions are Binding under Article 25 of the Charter?' (1972) 21 International & Comparative Law Quarterly 270
Hilhorst D, 'Dead Letter or Living Document? Ten Years of the Code of Conduct for Disaster Relief' (2005) 29 Disasters 351
Hoelscher K, Miklian J, and Håvard Nygård M, 'Conflict, Peacekeeping, and Humanitarian Security: Understanding Violent Attacks Against Aid Workers' (2017) 24 International Peacekeeping 538
Hoffman M, 'Towards an International Disaster Response Law' in Walker P and Walter J (eds), *World Disasters Report 2000* (IFRC 2000)
Hoffman M, 'What is the Scope of International Disaster Response Law?' in IFRC (ed) *International Disaster Response Laws, Principles and Practice: Reflections, Prospects and Challenges* (IFRC 2003)
Hoffmann S, 'Impartiality' in De Lauri A (ed), *Humanitarianism: Keywords* (Brill 2020)
Hutter S, 'Starvation in Armed Conflicts: An Analysis Based on the Right to Food' (2019) 17 Journal of International Criminal Justice 723
Hutter S, 'The Right to Food in Armed Conflict' in Conley B and others (eds), *Accountability for Mass Starvation: Testing the Limits of the Law* (OUP 2022)
Hyndman J, 'Preventive, Palliative or Punitive? Safe Spaces in Bosnia-Herzegovina, Somalia and Sri Lanka' (2003) 16 Journal of Refugee Studies 167
ICRC, 'ICRC Q&A and Lexicon on Humanitarian Access' (2014) 96 International Review of the Red Cross 359
International Institute of Humanitarian Law, 'Guiding Principles on the Right to Humanitarian Assistance' (1993) 33 International Review of the Red Cross 519
Jaeger G, 'On the History of the International Protection of Refugees' (2001) 83 International Review of the Red Cross 727
Jakovljević B, 'The Right to Humanitarian Assistance: Legal Aspects' (1987) 27 International Review of the Red Cross 469
Janner Torrens J, 'Migrant Search and Rescue Operations in the Mediterranean by Humanitarian Organizations: Migrant Smuggling or Humanitarian Assistance?' (2020) 8 Paix et Sécurité Internationales 381
Jawad M and others, 'Estimating Indirect Mortality Impacts of Armed Conflict in Civilian Populations: Panel Regression Analyses of 193 Countries, 1990–2017' (2020) 18 BMC Medicine 266
Jeannet S, 'Civil Defence 1977–1997: From Law to Practice' (1998) 12 International Review of the Red Cross 715
Jinks D, 'International Human Rights Law in Time of Armed Conflict' in Clapham A and Gaeta P (eds), *The Oxford Handbook of International Law in Armed Conflict* (OUP 2014)
Jordash W, Murdoch C, and Holmes J, 'Strategies for Prosecuting Mass Starvation' (2019) 17 Journal of International Criminal Justice 849
Kagan M, 'Is there Really a Protection Gap? UNRWA's Role Vis-à-Vis Palestinian Refugees' (2010) 28 Refugee Survey Quarterly 511
Kalshoven F, 'Impartiality and Neutrality in Humanitarian Law and Practice' (1989) 29 International Review of the Red Cross 523
Kellenberger J, 'The Role of the International Committee of the Red Cross' in Clapham A and Gaeta P (eds), *The Oxford Handbook of International Law in Armed Conflict* (OUP 2014)

Keller T, 'Applying Derivative United Nations Immunity to Humanitarian NGOs' (2023) 23 Chicago Journal of International Law 451
Kent R, 'The United Nations' Humanitarian Pillar: Re-Focusing the UN's Disaster and Emergency Roles and Responsibilities' (2004) 28 Disasters 216
Kevlihan R, Derouen K, and Biglaiser G, 'Is US Humanitarian Aid Based Primarily on Need or Self-Interest?' (2014) 58 International Studies Quarterly 839
Kisangani E and Mitchell D, 'The Impact of Integrated UN Missions on Humanitarian NGO Security: A Quantitative Analysis' (2021) 27 Global Governance 202
Klappe B, 'Civil-Military Cooperation and Humanitarian Assistance' in Gill T and Fleck D (eds), *The Handbook of the International Law of Military Operations* (2nd edn, OUP 2015)
Koenig C, 'Observer Status for the International Committee of the Red Cross at the United Nations—A Legal Viewpoint' (1991) 31 International Review of the Red Cross 37
Kovács G and Spens K, 'Humanitarian Logistics in Disaster Relief Operations' (2007) 37 International Journal of Physical Distribution & Logistics Management 99
Kraska J, 'Siege' in Wolfrum R (ed), *Max Planck Encyclopedia of International Law* (OUP 2009)
Kreisel J, 'The Benghazi Six and International Medical Neutrality in Times of War and Peace' (2007) 1 Health Law & Policy 42
Kyazze A, 'Walking the Walk: Evidence of Principles in Action from Red Cross and Red Crescent National Societies' (2016) 97 International Review of the Red Cross 211
Kyoichi S, 'The "Non-Political and Humanitarian" Clause in UNHCR's Statute' (1998) 17 Refugee Survey Quarterly 33
Labbé J, 'Les principes de l'action humanitaire' in Szurek S, Eudes M, and Ryfman P (eds), *Droit et pratique de l'action humanitaire* (LGDJ 2019)
Labbé J and Daudin P, 'Applying the Humanitarian Principles: Reflecting on the Experience of the International Committee of the Red Cross' (2016) 97 International Review of the Red Cross 183
Labonte M and Edgerton A, 'Towards a Typology of Humanitarian Access Denial' (2013) 34 Third World Quarterly 39
LaMunière C-H, 'Managing the UN's Emergency Operations in Africa: Lessons for Organizational Development' (1987) 7 Public Administration and Development 195
Landgren K, 'Safety Zones and International Protection: A Dark Grey Area' (1995) 7 International Journal of Refugee Law 442
Lanord C, 'The Legal Status of National Red Cross and Red Crescent Societies' (2000) 82 International Review of the Red Cross 1053
Lapas D, 'Diplomatic Privileges and Immunities for IGO-like Entities: A Step Towards a New Diplomatic Law' (2019) 16 International Organizations Law Review 378
Lattanzi F, 'Humanitarian Assistance' in Clapham A, Gaeta P, and Sassòli M (eds), *The 1949 Geneva Conventions: A Commentary* (OUP 2015)
Leader N, 'Proliferating Principles; Or How to Sup with the Devil without Getting Eaten' (1998) 22 Disasters 288
Lee-Koo K, 'The Intolerable Impact of Armed Conflict on Children: The United Nations Security Council and the Protection of Children in Armed Conflict' (2018) 10 Global Responsibility to Protect 57
L'Homme M, 'Humanitarian Corridors: Negotiated Exceptions at Risk of Manipulation' (2022) 4 Journal of Humanitarian Affairs 48
Lie J, 'The Humanitarian-Development Nexus: Humanitarian Principles, Practice, and Pragmatics' (2020) 5 Journal of International Humanitarian Action 1
Lischer S, 'Military Intervention and the Humanitarian "Force Multiplier"' (2007) 13 Global Governance 99
Luopajärvi K, 'Is There an Obligation on States to Accept International Humanitarian Assistance to Internally Displaced Persons under International Law?' (2003) 15 International Journal of Refugee Law 689
Mačák K, 'Principles of Neutrality and Impartiality of Humanitarian Action in the Aftermath of the 2011 Libyan Conflict' in Zwitter A and others (eds), *Humanitarian Action: Global, Regional and Domestic Legal Responses* (CUP 2015)

Mačák K, 'A Matter of Principle(s): The Legal Effect of Impartiality and Neutrality on States as Humanitarian Actors' (2016) 97 International Review of the Red Cross 157
MacAlister-Smith P, 'The International Relief Union: Reflections on Establishing an International Relief Union of July 12, 1927' (1986) 54 Legal History Review 363
MacAlister-Smith P, 'Humanitarian Action by Non-Governmental Organizations: National and International Law Perspectives' (1987) 18 Bulletin of Peace Proposals 119
MacAlister-Smith P, 'Protection of the Civilian Population and the Prohibition of Starvation as a Method of Warfare: Draft Texts on International Humanitarian Assistance' (1991) 31 International Review of the Red Cross 440
MacAlister-Smith P, 'The Right to Humanitarian Assistance in International Law' (1998) 66 Revue de droit international de sciences diplomatiques et politiques 211
Mackintosh K, 'The Principles of Humanitarian Action in International Humanitarian Law' (*ODI Humanitarian Policy Group*, 2000) <https://www.odi.org/sites/odi.org.uk/files/odi-assets/publications-opinion-files/305.pdf> accessed 12 June 2020
Mackintosh K, 'Beyond the Red Cross: The Protection of Independent Humanitarian Organizations and their Staff in International Humanitarian Law' (2007) 89 International Review of the Red Cross 113
Mackintosh K, 'Reclaiming Protection as a Humanitarian Goal: Fodder for the Faint-Hearted Aid-Worker' (2010) 1 Journal of International Humanitarian Legal Studies 382
Mackintosh K, '*Holder v. Humanitarian Law Project*: Implications for Humanitarian Action: A View from Médecins Sans Frontières' (2011) 34 Suffolk Transnational Law Review 507
Macleod R, 'The Evolution of the International Federation of Red Cross and Red Crescent Societies' Work in Disaster Law' in Aronsson-Storrier M and Breau S (eds), *Research Handbook on Disasters and International Law* (2nd edn, Edward Elgar 2024)
Macrae J and Zwi A, 'Food as an Instrument of War in Contemporary African Famines: A Review of the Evidence' (1992) 16 Disasters 299
Mamiya R, 'A History and Conceptual Development of the Protection of Civilians' in Willmot H and others (eds), *Protection of Civilians* (OUP 2016)
Mamuji A, 'Canadian Military Involvement in Humanitarian Assistance: Progress and Prudence in Natural Disaster Response' (2012) 18 Canadian Foreign Policy Journal 208
Massingham E and Thynne K, 'Humanitarian Relief Operations' in Akande D and Saul B (eds), *The Oxford Guide to International Humanitarian Law* (OUP 2020)
Mathew P, 'Australian Refugee Protectionin the Wake of the *Tampa*' (2002) 96 American Journal of International Law 661
Matyas D, 'Humanitarians and Their Law(s): An Expanded Inquiry' in Krieger H and others (eds), *Yearbook of International Humanitarian Law, Volume 26 (2023)* (TMC Asser Press 2025)
Mawdsley E, '"Non-DAC" Humanitarian Actors' in Ginty R and Peterson J (eds), *The Routledge Companion to Humanitarian Action* (Routledge 2015)
McKeever D, 'International Humanitarian Law and Counter-terrorism: Fundamental Values, Conflicting Obligations' (2020) 69 International & Comparative Law Quarterly 43
Mégret F, 'Activists on the High Seas: Reinventing International Law for the Mare Liberum?' (2021) 23 International Community Law Review 367
Meier-Ewert G, 'Humanitarian Assistance' in Volger H (ed), *A Concise Encyclopedia of the United Nations* (Brill 2010)
Meron T, 'On the Inadequate Reach of Humanitarian and Human Rights Law and the Need for a New Instrument' (1983) 89 American Journal of International Law 589
Meyer M, 'Humanitarian Action: A Delicate Balancing Act' (1987) 27 International Review of the Red Cross 485
Michel C, Lavelle K, and Nierle T, 'Medical Care Under Fire: A Perspective From the International Medical Organization Médecins Sans Frontières' in Kravitz A (ed), *Oxford Handbook of Humanitarian Medicine* (OUP 2019)
Milanović M, 'The Lost Origins of *Lex Specialis*: Rethinking the Relationship Between Human Rights and International Humanitarian Law' in Ohlin J (ed), *Theoretical Boundaries of Armed Conflict and Human Rights* (CUP 2016)

Minear L, 'The Theory and Practice of Neutrality: Some Thoughts on the Tensions' (1999) 81 International Review of the Red Cross 63
Mintz T, 'Substantive Technicalities: Understanding the Legal Framework of Humanitarian Assistance in Armed Conflicts through the Prescription of Technical Arrangements' (2019) 227 Military Law Review 275
Modirzadeh N, Lewis D, and Bruderlein C, 'Humanitarian Engagement under Counter-Terrorism: A Conflict of Norms and the Emerging Policy Landscape' (2011) 93 International Review of the Red Cross 623
Moreno-Lax V, 'The EU Humanitarian Border and the Securitization of Human Rights: the "Rescue-through-Interdiction/Rescue-without-Protection" Paradigm' (2018) 56 Journal of Common Market Studies 119
Moreno-Lax V, 'Towards a Thousand Little Morias: The EU (Non-)Rescue Scheme—Criminalizing Solidarity, Structuralising Defection' in Thym D (ed), *Reforming the Common European Asylum System: Opportunities, Pitfalls, and Downsides of the Commission Proposals for a New Pact on Migration and Asylum* (Nomos 2022)
Mussi F and Feith Tan N, 'Comparing Cooperation on Migration Control: Italy-Libya and Australia-Indonesia' in de Londras F and Mullally S (eds), *Irish Yearbook of International Law 2015*, vol 10 (Hart 2017)
Narang N, 'Forgotten Conflicts: Need Versus Political Priority in the Allocation of Humanitarian Aid Across Conflict Areas' (2016) 42 International Interactions 189
Nelson T, 'Determinants of Disaster Aid: Donor Interest or Recipient Need?' (2012) 24 Global Change, Peace & Security 109
Nielsen F, 'Civil Defence in International Humanitarian Relief Work, Seen in the Light of the Geneva Conventions' (1996) 9 Journal of Refugee Studies 421
Nishat N, 'The Right of Initiative of the ICRC and Other Impartial Humanitarian Bodies' in Clapham A, Gaeta P, and Sassòli M (eds), *The 1949 Geneva Conventions: A Commentary* (OUP 2015)
O'Connell M, 'Humanitarian Assistance in Non-International Armed Conflict: the Fourth Wave of Rights, Duties and Remedies' (2001) 31 Israel Yearbook on Human Rights 183
O'Flaherty M, 'The Human Rights Field Operation in Partnership for Humanitarian Relief and Reconstruction' in O'Flaherty M (ed), *The Human Rights Field Operation: Law, Theory and Practice* (Ashgate 2007)
Okimoto K, 'Humanitarian Activities Carried Out Across Borders in Times of Armed Conflict' in Gill T and others (eds), *Yearbook of International Humanitarian Law 2014*, vol 17 (Springer 2016)
Oswald B, 'The Creation and Control of Places of Protection during United Nations Peace Operations' (2001) 83 International Review of the Red Cross 1013
Pacholska M, '(Il)legality of Killing Peacekeepers: The Crime of Attacking Peacekeepers in the Jurisprudence of International Criminal Tribunals' (2015) 13 Journal of International Criminal Justice 43
Paddon E and Owen T, 'Whither Humanitarian Space? The Costs of Integrated Peacebuilding in Afghanistan' in Perrin B (ed), *Modern Warfare: Armed Groups, Private Militaries, Humanitarian Organizations, and the Law* (UBC Press 2012)
Palmieri D, 'An Institution Standing the Test of Time? A Review of 150 Years of the History of the International Committee of the Red Cross' (2012) 94 International Review of the Red Cross 1273
Papanicolopulu I, 'The Duty to Rescue at Sea, in Peacetime and in War: A General Overview' (2016) 98 International Review of the Red Cross 491
Parisetti P, 'The Use of Civil and Military Defence Assets in Emergency Situations' in de Guttry A, Gestri M, and Venturini G (eds), *International Disaster Response Law* (Springer 2012)
Paul S and Holland E, 'Principled Humanitarian Organizations and the Use of Force: Is There Space to Speak Out?' (2015) 1 DePaul International Human Rights Law Journal 1
Pejic J, 'The Right to Food in Situations of Armed Conflict: The Legal Framework' (2001) 83 International Review of the Red Cross 1097
Pictet J, 'Les principes de la Croix-Rouge (III)' (1955) 37 International Review of the Red Cross 633
Plattner D, 'Assistance to the Civilian Population: the Development and Present State of International Humanitarian Law' (1992) 32 International Review of the Red Cross 249

Ramcharan B, 'The Security Council and Humanitarian Emergencies' (1991) 9 Netherlands Quarterly of Human Rights 19
Revel J, 'Role of the International Federation of Red Cross and Red Crescent Societies in Disaster Management' in de Boer J and Dubouloz M (eds), *Handbook of Disaster Medicine* (CRC Press 2020)
Rhoads E and Sutton R, 'The (Self) Protection of Civilians in South Sudan: Popular and Community Justice Practices' (2020) 119 African Affairs 370
Rhoads E and Welsh J, 'Close Cousins in Protection: the Evolution of Two Norms' (2019) 95 International Affairs 597
Rodenhäuser T, 'The Legal Protection of Persons Living Under the Control of Non-State Armed Groups' (2020) 102 International Review of the Red Cross 991
Rodenhäuser T and Giacca G, 'The International Humanitarian Law Framework for Humanitarian Relief During Armed Conflicts and Complex Emergencies' in Breau S and Samuel K (eds), *Research Handbook on Disasters and International Law* (Edward Elgar 2016)
Rodenhäuser T and Mutasa S, 'The International Humanitarian Law Framework for Humanitarian Relief During Armed Conflicts and Complex Emergencies' in Aronsson-Storrier M and Breau S (eds), *Research Handbook on Disasters and International Law* (2nd edn, Edward Elgar 2024)
Roepstorff K, 'A Call for Critical Reflection on the Localisation Agenda in Humanitarian Action' (2019) 41 Third World Quarterly 284
Romeo F, 'Humanity' in Lauri A (ed), *Humanitarianism: Keywords* (Brill 2020)
Rottensteiner C, 'The Denial of Humanitarian Assistance as a Crime Under International Law' (1999) 81 International Review of the Red Cross 555
Russo F, 'Disasters Through the Lens of International Criminal Law' in de Guttry A, Gestri M, and Venturini G (eds), *International Disaster Response Law* (TMC Asser Press 2012)
Ryngaert C, 'Humanitarian Assistance and the Conundrum of Consent: A Legal Perspective' (2013) 5 Amsterdam Law Forum 5
Rysaback-Smith H, 'History and Principles of Humanitarian Action' (2015) 15 Turkish Journal of Emergency Medicine 5
Sandoz Y, '"*Droit*" or "*devoir d'ingérence*" and the Right to Assistance: the Issues Involved' (1992) 32 International Review of the Red Cross 215
Sandoz Y, 'The Establishment of Safety Zones for Persons Displaced within their Country of Origin' in Al-Nuaimi N and Meese R (eds), *International Legal Issues Arising under the United Nations Decade of International Law* (Martinus Nijhoff 1995)
Sandoz Y, 'Max Huber and the Red Cross' (2007) 18 European Journal of International Law 171
Sayed M, 'Beirut Ammonium Nitrate Explosion: A Man-Made Disaster in the Times of the COVID-19 Pandemic' (2020) Disaster Medicine and Public Health Preparedness 1
Scheffer D, 'The Expanding UN Role in Humanitarian Relief Operations' (1992) 86 American Society of International Law Proceedings 313
Schenkenberg van Mierop E, 'Coming Clean on Neutrality and Independence: The Need to Assess the Application of Humanitarian Principles' (2016) 97 International Review of the Red Cross 295
Schindler D, 'Humanitarian Assistance, Humanitarian Interference and International Law' in MacDonald R (ed), *Essays in Honour of Wang Tieya* (Martinus Nijhoff 1994)
Schmitt M, 'Charting the Legal Geography of Non-International Armed Conflict' (2014) 90 International Law Studies 1
Schwendimann F, 'The Legal Framework of Humanitarian Access in Armed Conflict' (2011) 93 International Review of the Red Cross 993
Seatzu F, 'Revitalizing the International Legal Protection of Humanitarian Aid Workers in Armed Conflict' (2017) 11 Revue des droits de l'homme 1
Sharpe M, 'It's All Relative: The Origins, Legal Character and Normative Content of the Humanitarian Principles' (2024) 106 International Review of the Red Cross 12
Silingardi S, 'The Status of Emergency Workers' in Guttry A, Gestri M, and Venturini G (eds), *International Disaster Response Law* (TMC Asser Press 2012)
Simm G, 'Disaster Militarism? Military Humanitarian Assistance and Disaster Relief' (2019) 22 Max Planck Yearbook of United Nations Law Online 347

Sivakumaran S, 'Arbitrary Withholding of Consent to Humanitarian Assistance in Situations of Disaster' (2015) 64 International & Comparative Law Quarterly 501

Sivakumaran S, 'Armed Conflict-Related Detention of Particularly Vulnerable Persons: Challenges and Possibilities' (2018) 94 International Law Studies 39

Sivakumaran S, 'Techniques in International Law-Making: Extrapolation, Analogy, Form and the Emergence of an International Law of Disaster Relief' (2018) 28 European Journal of International Law 1097

Slim H, 'Relief Agencies and Moral Standing in War: Principles of Humanity, Neutrality, Impartiality and Solidarity' (1997) 7 Development in Practice 342

Slim H, 'Wonderful Work: Globalizing the Ethics of Humanitarian Action' in Ginty R and Peterson J (eds), *The Routledge Companion to Humanitarian Action* (Routledge 2015)

Slim H and Gillard E-C, 'Ethical and Legal Perspectives on Cross-Border Humanitarian Operations' [2013] Humanitarian Practice Network 6

Smith A, 'Uncertainty, Alert and Distress: The Precarious Position of NGO Search and Rescue Operations in the Central Mediterranean' (2017) 5 Journal of International Law and International Relations 29

Sommario E, 'Limitation and Derogation Provisions in International Human Rights Law Treaties and Their Use in Disaster Settings' in Giustiniani F and others (eds), *Routledge Handbook of Human Rights and Disasters* (Routledge 2018)

Spatz B, Windridge O, and Murdoch C, 'Sanctions as a Mechanism for Accountability for Starvation Crimes' in Conley B and others (eds), *Accountability for Mass Starvation: Testing the Limits of the Law* (OUP 2022)

Spieker H, 'The Right to Give and Receive Humanitarian Assistance' in Heintze H-J and Zwitter A (eds), *International Law and Humanitarian Assistance: A Crosscut Through Legal Issues Pertaining to Humanitarianism* (Springer 2011)

Spieker H, 'Humanitarian Assistance, Access in Armed Conflict and Occupation' in Wolfrum R (ed), *Max Planck Encyclopedia of Public International Law* (OUP 2015)

Spieker H, 'The Legal Framework of Humanitarian Action' in Gibbons P and Heintze H (eds), *The Humanitarian Challenge: 20 Years European Network on Humanitarian Action* (Springer 2015)

Stoffels R, 'Legal Regulation of Humanitarian Assistance in Armed Conflict: Achievements and Gaps' (2004) 86 International Review of the Red Cross 515

Storey A, 'Non-Neutral Humanitarianism: NGOs and the Rwanda Crisis' (1997) 7 Development in Practice 384

Studer M, 'The ICRC and Civil-Military Relations in Armed Conflict' (2001) 83 International Review of the Red Cross 367

Sun C, 'Humanitarian Assistance by International Organisations: A Question of Compulsory Access to Victims' (1991) Singapore Journal of Legal Studies 320

Sutton R, 'Enacting the "Civilian Plus": International Humanitarian Actors and the Conceptualization of Distinction' (2020) 33 Leiden Journal of International Law 429

Sutton R and Gillard E-C, 'Beyond Compliance: International Humanitarian Law, Humanitarian Need and Civilian Harm in Armed Conflict' (*PeaceRep*, 2022) <https://peacerep.org/wp-content/uploads/2022/11/Beyond-Compliance-International-Humanitarian-Law-in-Armed-Conflict.pdf> accessed 12 October 2023.

Tazzioli M, 'Border Displacements: Challenging the Politics of Rescue between Mare Nostrum and Triton' (2016) 4 Migration Studies 1

Terry F, 'The International Committee of the Red Cross in Afghanistan: Reasserting the Neutrality of Humanitarian Action' (2011) 881 International Review of the Red Cross 175

Terry F, 'Violence Against Health Care: Insights from Afghanistan, Somalia, and the Democratic Republic of the Congo' (2013) 95 International Review of the Red Cross 23

Testa D, 'Safeguarding Human Life and Ensuring Respect for Fundamental Human Rights: A Consequential Approach to the Disembarkation of Persons Rescued at Sea' (2014) 28 Ocean Yearbook 555

Thompson A, 'Humanitarian Principles Put to the Test: Challenges to Humanitarian Action During Decolonization' (2015) 97 International Review of the Red Cross 45

Thompson S, 'Children and Armed Conflict' in Genser J and Ugarte B (eds), *The United Nations Security Council in the Age of Human Rights* (CUP 2014)
Tladi D, 'The International Law Commission's Draft Articles on the Protection of Persons in the Event of Disasters: Codification, Progressive Development or Creation of Law from Thin Air?' (2017) 16 Chinese Journal of International Law 425
Toebes B, 'Health and Humanitarian Assistance: Towards an Integrated Norm under International Law' (2013) 18 Tilburg Law Review 133
Tokunaga E, 'Evolution of International Disaster Response Law: Toward Codification and Progressive Development of the Law' in Caron D, Kelly M, and Telesetsky A (eds), *The International Law of Disaster Relief* (CUP 2014)
Toman J, 'Towards a Disaster Relief Law: Legal Aspects of Disaster Relief Operations' in Kalshoven F (ed), *Assisting the Victims of Armed Conflict and Other Disasters* (Martinus Nijhoff 1989)
Troyon B and Palmieri D, 'The ICRC Delegate: An Exceptional Humanitarian Player?' (2007) 89 International Review of the Red Cross 97
Tsui E and Myint-U T, 'The Institutional Response: Creating a Framework in Response to New Challenges' in OCHA, *The Humanitarian Decade: Challenges for Humanitarian Assistance in the last Decade and into the Future*, vol 2 (OCHA 2004)
Ugarte B, 'Security Council Diplomacy on the Protection of Civilians: A Convoluted History' in Willmot H and others (eds), *Protection of Civilians* (OUP 2016)
Ulrich L, 'The Customary International Law Obligation to Protect Foreign Disaster Relief Personnel and Their Equipment' (2014) 22 Willamette Journal of International Law and Dispute Resolution 343
van Aalst M, 'The Impacts of Climate Change on the Risk of Natural Disasters' (2006) 30 Disasters 5
van der Heijden I, 'Other Issues Relating to the Treatment of Civilians in Enemy Hands' in Clapham A, Gaeta P, and Sassòli M (eds), *The 1949 Geneva Conventions: A Commentary* (OUP 2015)
Vanhullebusch M, 'Do Non-State Armed Groups Have a Legal Right to Consent to Offers of International Humanitarian Relief?' (2020) 25 Journal of Conflict & Security Law 317
Ventura M, 'Prosecuting Starvation under International Criminal Law: Exploring the Legal Possibilities' (2019) 17 Journal of International Criminal Justice 781
Venturini G, 'Disasters and Armed Conflict' in de Guttry A, Gestri M, and Venturini G (eds), *International Disaster Response Law* (TMC Asser Press 2012)
Versluys H, 'European Union Humanitarian Aid: Lifesaver or Political Tool?' in Orbie J (ed), *Europe's Global Role: External Policies of the European Union* (Routledge 2008)
Victoria C and others, 'Maternal and Child Undernutrition: Consequences for Adult Health and Human Capital' (2008) 371 The Lancet 340
Vité S, 'Occupation' in Saul B and Akande D (eds), *The Oxford Guide to International Humanitarian Law* (OUP 2020)
Watts S, 'Humanitarian Logic and the Law of Siege: A Study of the Oxford Guidance on Relief Actions' (2019) 95 International Law Studies 1
Weiss T, 'Civilian-Military Interactions and Ongoing UN Reforms: DHA's Past and OCHA's Remaining Challenges' (1998) 5 International Peacekeeping 49
Weiss T, 'Humanitarian Shell Games: Whither UN Reform?' (1998) 29 Security Dialogue 9
Weiss T, 'Humanitarian Action' in Cogan J, Hurd I, and Johnstone I (eds), *The Oxford Handbook of International Organizations* (OUP 2016)
Weizmann N, 'Ensuring Respect for IHL as it Relates to Humanitarian Activities' in Massingham E and McConnachie A (eds), *Ensuring Respect for International Humanitarian Law* (Routledge 2020)
Weizmann N, 'Respecting International Humanitarian Law and Safeguarding Humanitarian Action in Counterterrorism Measures: United Nations Security Council Resolutions 2462 and 2482 Point the Way' (2021) 103 International Review of the Red Cross 325
Weller M, 'The Relativity of Humanitarian Neutrality and Impartiality' (1997) 91 American Society of International Law Proceedings 441
Welsh J and Zahar M, 'What Future for Peace Operations?' (2025) 38 Ethics & International Affairs 404

Whittall J, 'Is Humanitarian Action Independent From Political Interests?' (2015) 12 International Journal on Human Rights 1
Williams S and Simm G, 'Assistance to Disaster Victims in an Armed Conflict' in Giustiniani F and others (eds), *Routledge Handbook of Human Rights and Disasters* (Routledge 2018)
Williamson J, 'Using Humanitarian Aid to "Win Hearts and Minds": A Costly Failure?' (2011) 93 International Review of the Red Cross 1035
Williamson J, 'The Use of Armed Security Escorts: A Challenge to Independent and Neutral Humanitarian Action' in Perrin B (ed), *Modern Warfare* (UBC Press 2012)
Wynn-Pope P, Zegenhagen Y, and Kurnadi F, 'Legislating Against Humanitarian Principles: A Case Study on the Humanitarian Implications of Australian Counterterrorism Legislation' (2016) 97 International Review of the Red Cross 235
Zappalà S, 'Conflict Related Hunger, "Starvation Crimes" and UN Security Council Resolution 2417 (2018)' (2019) 17 Journal of International Criminal Justice 881
Zimmermann A, 'Humanitarian Assistance and the Security Council' (2017) 50 Israel Law Review 3
Zwitter A, 'United Nations' Legal Framework of Humanitarian Assistance' in Heintze H and Zwitter A (eds), *International Law and Humanitarian Assistance: A Crosscut Through Legal Issues Pertaining to Humanitarianism* (Springer 2011)

Index

For the benefit of digital users, indexed terms that span two pages (e.g., 52–53) may, on occasion, appear on only one of those pages.